Contents

*Addresses, phone numbers, opening hours and prices published in this guide
are accurate at press time. We apologize for any inconvenience resulting from
outdated information, and we welcome corrections and suggestions that may
assist us in preparing the next edition. Send us your comments:*

Michelin Travel Publications
Editorial Department
P.O. Box 19001
Greenville, SC 29602-9001

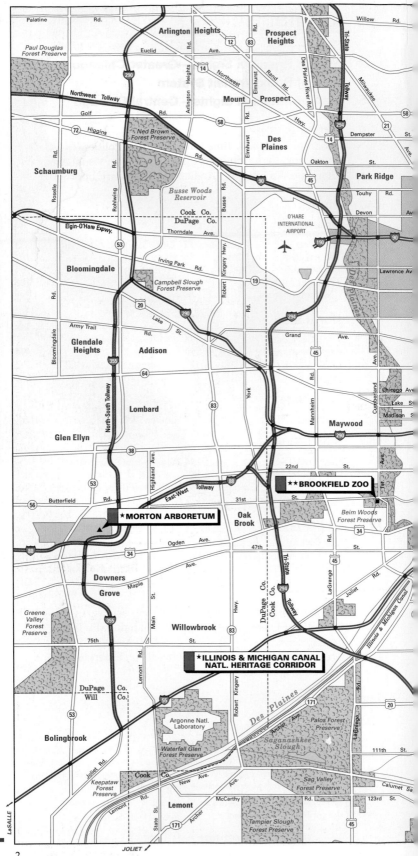

★★ BROOKFIELD ZOO

★ MORTON ARBORETUM

★ ILLINOIS & MICHIGAN CANAL
NATL. HERITAGE CORRIDOR

Principal Sights

GREATER CHICAGO

	Principal section in guide
★★★	Highly recommended
★★	Recommended
★	Interesting

Lake Michigan

★★NORTH SHORE

LAKEVIEW/WRIGLEYVILLE AND UPTOWN

MILWAUKEE AVE. CORRIDOR

★★★OAK PARK

NEAR WEST SIDE

LOWER WEST SIDE

BRIDGEPORT CANARYVILLE

NEAR SOUTH SIDE

★HYDE PARK KENWOOD

★★★THE MUSEUM OF SCIENCE AND INDUSTRY

★★THE UNIVERSITY OF CHICAGO

★PULLMAN

★INDIANA DUNES NATL. LAKESHORE

Central Chicago p. 5

3

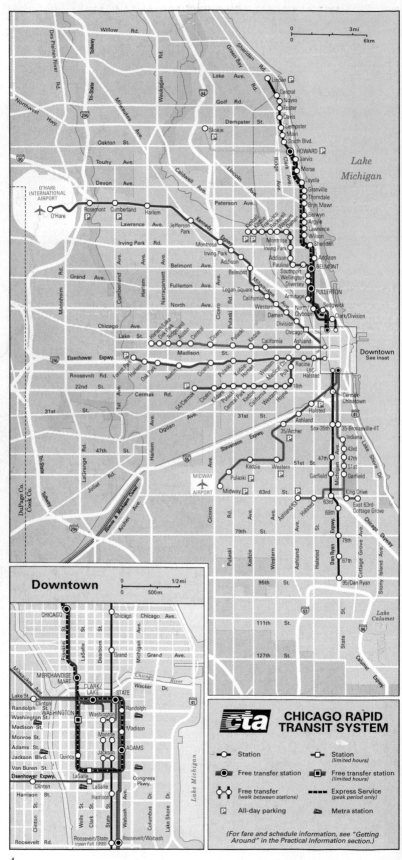

CHICAGO RAPID TRANSIT SYSTEM

Downtown

Symbol	Description	Symbol	Description
Station		Station *(limited hours)*	
Free transfer station		Free transfer station *(limited hours)*	
Free transfer *(walk between stations)*		Express Service *(peak period only)*	
All-day parking		Metra station	

(For fare and schedule information, see "Getting Around" in the Practical Information section.)

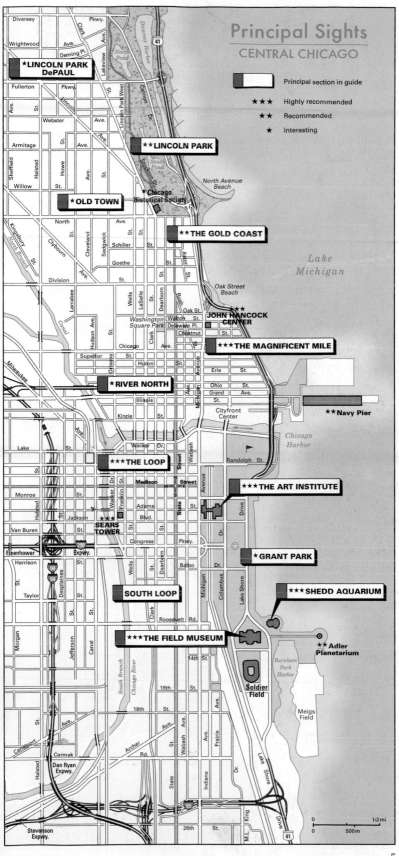

Principal Sights
CENTRAL CHICAGO

Principal section in guide

★★★ Highly recommended
★★ Recommended
★ Interesting

★LINCOLN PARK DePAUL

★★LINCOLN PARK

★OLD TOWN

★ Chicago Historical Society

★★THE GOLD COAST

North Avenue Beach

Lake Michigan

Oak Street Beach

★★★ JOHN HANCOCK CENTER

★★★THE MAGNIFICENT MILE

★RIVER NORTH

★★ Navy Pier

Chicago Harbor

★★★THE LOOP

★★★THE ART INSTITUTE

★★★ SEARS TOWER

★GRANT PARK

★★★ SHEDD AQUARIUM

SOUTH LOOP

★★★THE FIELD MUSEUM

★★ Adler Planetarium

Burnham Park Harbor

Soldier Field

Meigs Field

0   1/2mi
0   500m

Introduction to
Chicago

Geographical Notes

Located in Illinois, less than an hour's drive from Indiana to the southeast and Wisconsin to the north, Chicago occupies a strategic position on the southern end of Lake Michigan, at the point where America's heartland abuts the Great Lakes. Residences, commerce and industry crowding the shoreline all vie for visual and physical access to the vast body of water, the only Great Lake whose borders are entirely within the US. The lake has played a significant role in Chicago's phenomenal transformation into the commercial center of the country's agricultural midsection and primary hub of a national transportation network, funneling the Midwest's goods across the country and out to the world.

■ Quick Facts

Location:	Latitude 41° 50' N
	Longitude 87° 37' W
Area of city:	228sq mi/591sq km
Metro area:	4,653sq mi/12,051sq km
Altitude:	578ft/176m above sea level
Recreation:	574 parks, 31 beaches and 8 harbors totaling 6,756 acres
Lake Michigan:	fifth largest freshwater body in the world
Area of lake:	22,300sq mi/57,757sq km
Deepest point:	923ft/282m
Chicago shoreline:	29mi/47km
Water intake:	4,200mi/6,758km of water mains pump a billion gallons of water from the lake into the city daily

---

An Inauspicious Site... – Today's sprawling city lies on a plain flattened by glaciers and their meltwaters some 13,500 years ago. At that time, the site was located 60ft below the surface of glacial Lake Chicago (the ancestor of Lake Michigan). The weight of the ice and of the lake compacted a heavy layer of clay over the dolomite-limestone bedrock (Niagaran formation), which stretches across the Great Lakes area. The poor drainage of the soil above the clay created a very swampy, inhospitable site. Gradually, the glaciers retreated and, in places, the land rose, creating a subcontinental divide between the Great Lakes and the Mississippi River. The divide was defined by the Valparaiso Moraine—a glacial ridge that circles around the southern end of Lake Michigan about 8mi from the present shoreline—which contained the waters of Lake Chicago. The moraine was breached at the **Chicago Portage**, located at the southwestern edge of the modern city, and the lake's outflow carved the Des Plaines and Illinois River Valleys as the water drained toward the Mississippi River Valley. Originating in wetlands north and southwest of present-day Chicago, the Chicago River came into existence about 6,000 years ago; through the years, it remained a small, muddy channel which followed a meandering sandbar and emptied into Lake Michigan.

Around 4,000 years ago, the waters receded further and the earth rebounded, allowing the ridge to rise again and separate the Des Plaines and Illinois Rivers, which continued to flow toward the Mississippi River, from the Chicago River, which flowed lazily into Lake Michigan and the Great Lakes.

... Turns Opportune – The Potawatomi Indians populating the region in the 17C named the area around the present-day city *Checaugou*, referring to the garlic growing wild throughout the swamp. Not considered suitable for defense or settlement by Native Americans, the area was nevertheless chosen by trader **Jean Baptiste Point du Sable** *(p 10)*, who erected a homestead here in 1779. The Chicago Portage—one of the shortest and lowest points in the divide—provided a crucial link between the Great Lakes and the Mississippi River and would soon become the key to a major travel route through the midcontinent. Native Americans, traders and settlers portaged their canoes between the Des Plaines River and a low, wide, swampy fork of the Chicago River called "Mud Lake"; when the water was high, the portage even became navigable. Already in 1673, French explorer Louis Jolliet had proposed the construction of a canal to bridge the divide and effectively link the Atlantic Ocean to the Gulf of Mexico. The canal *(p 208)* would be realized almost two centuries later, spurring Chicago's prodigious growth.

The city's early history was characterized by the muddy soil on which the city rests. The quagmire not only thwarted road and building construction, but also contributed to the spread of disease in the population. In the 1850s, the city began installing sewers throughout the settlement. Since laying the lines underground proved nearly impossible, they were placed at street level and the streets and existing structures were raised or jacked up around them, sometimes by up to 12ft. Unfortunately, the sewers dumped both storm overflow and sewage into the Chicago River, which emptied into Lake Michigan, the source of the city's water supply. To keep the drinking water safe, engineers had to devise a way to reverse the flow of the river. A canal would not only provide a link from the Chicago River to the Des Plaines River, but—if deep enough—could also allow the river's waters to be diverted into it. Rather than continuing its natural course toward the lake, the river would empty into the canal. At the same time, locks would be needed to regulate the amount of lake water now draining into the unused section of the original river bed and into the canal.

■ A Feat of Engineering

The earliest designs for the Illinois & Michigan Canal *(p 208)* called for a channel 8ft deep and 60ft wide. Owing to financial constraints, the original canal bed was dug only to 6ft in depth; the proper water level was to be maintained by a pumping station and feeder canals. Although it was deepened to the planned 8ft in 1871, the canal remained too shallow to allow for the river's permanent reversal. Devastating epidemics—blamed on polluted drinking water—decimated the city in the 1880s, and the weary populace clamored for action. A Sanitary District was quickly created with a mission to dig a new, larger and more effective channel. The resulting Sanitary & Ship Canal was 25ft deep, 100ft wide and over 30mi long. Its construction entailed the removal of more earth than the Panama Canal, and when completed in 1900, it easily reversed the flow of the sluggish Chicago River. The Sanitary District also built the Calumet-Sag Channel and North Shore Channel in the early 20C to maintain water flow in the correct (wrong) direction. However, the combined storm and sewer system continued to back up after heavy rains, and the river would occasionally flow back into the lake. By the 1970s, the Sanitary District (now known as the Metropolitan Water Reclamation District of Greater Chicago) began construction of the Tunnel and Reservoir Project (TARP), or "deep tunnel," a giant underground reservoir 30ft in diameter and 300ft below the surface, that stores storm runoff until it can be treated. The deep tunnel will run 110mi through the metropolitan area when finally completed.

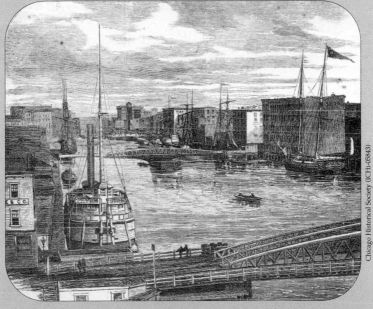

Illinois & Michigan Canal, 1859

Chicago Historical Society (ICHi-05843)

Time Line

EARLY HISTORY AND FIRST EXPLORERS

The swampy juncture of the sluggish Chicago River and Lake Michigan was valued by Native Americans and 17C French traders as a link between the Great Lakes and Mississippi River Valley settlements. After the US gained control of the area in the late 18C, the potential for a canal between Lake Michigan and the Illinois River led to the establishment of Fort Dearborn. The fledgling settlement at Chicago was a mélange of Native, French, Yankee and mixed-ancestry pioneers.

AD c.1000	Native Americans in Illinois begin to form larger, more permanent settlements and elaborate burial mounds under the influence of the Cahokia civilization near St. Louis.
c.1500	The prevalence of bison cause Illini tribes to adopt a more mobile lifestyle, traversing the Chicago Portage *(p 8)* between Lake Michigan and the Illinois River Valley.
c.1660	Iroquois tribes begin to raid Illini settlements in northeastern Illinois. By 1800, Potawatomi replace the Illini in the Chicago region.
1673	French explorer **Louis Jolliet** and missionary **Jacques Marquette** encounter the Grand Village of the Illinois *(p 214)* near Starved Rock and are directed through the Chicago Portage to Lake Michigan. A year later, Marquette winters at Chicago, dying the following spring in Michigan.
1779	African-American trader **Jean Baptiste Point du Sable** becomes the first permanent settler of Chicago, building a cabin and trading post on the north side of the Chicago River.
1803	The United States builds **Fort Dearborn** on the south side of the Chicago River.
1812	Frontier tensions spurred by war with England lead to a massacre by Potawatomi natives of 52 settlers fleeing Fort Dearborn.
1816	The Indian Boundary, securing a canal corridor from Chicago to the Illinois River, is established by treaty. Fort Dearborn is rebuilt after the War of 1812.
1830	The Illinois & Michigan Canal Commission hires surveyor James Thompson to plat two towns along the canal route, Chicago and Ottawa.
1832	Native tribes are expelled from Illinois following the suppression of an uprising led by **Chief Black Hawk**.
1833	About 400 residents incorporate the village of Chicago. The first balloon-frame *(p 32)* structure, St. Mary's Church, is built from presawn boards and nails.

INSTANT CITY

Canal construction turns Chicago from a frontier outpost to a boomtown, bringing waves of Yankee migrants, Irish canal workers and skilled Germans fleeing persecution after the failed 1848 revolutions in Europe. The city grows too fast for its own good, tardily adding sewers, parks and other basic amenities while culture languishes in the pursuit of fast money in real estate, lumber, agriculture, steel and livestock. Innovations like the grain elevator and refrigerated railroad car allow Chicago to become the conduit for the nation's cereal and meat products. The city mushrooms from less than 4,000 persons to over 300,000 in less than 35 years.

1836	Chicago is in the fever grip of land speculation as construction begins July 4 on the **Illinois & Michigan Canal** *(p 208)*.
1837	4,000 citizens incorporate the City of Chicago on March 4. The nationwide Panic of 1837 deflates local real estate speculation and eventually slows canal construction.
1847	The agricultural boom in the Illinois countryside, where the rich prairie soil is producing some of the nation's highest yields, leads **Cyrus Hall McCormick** to move his reaper factory from Cincinnati to Chicago. Within two years, he is expanding to fill 1,500 orders per year.
1848	A boatload of sugar and other goods traverses the newly opened Illinois & Michigan Canal en route from New Orleans to New York. Agricultural goods begin to flow east from Chicago, and the CHICAGO BOARD OF TRADE is created to regulate the grain trade. Chicago's first railroad, the Chicago and Galena Union, inaugurates service on a 10mi route.

1852	The city allows the Illinois Central Railroad to run tracks along the lakefront in exchange for building a breakwater to prevent erosion.
1855	**Lager Beer Riots**: immigrant Germans protest Mayor Levi Boone's temperance edicts, which prohibit the drinking of beer on Sunday as "un-American."
1856	**Chicago Historical Society** *(p 124)* created. US Senator Stephen A. Douglas founds the first University of Chicago in alliance with the Baptist church.
1860	**Abraham Lincoln** is nominated for President by the new Republican Party in Chicago's Wigwam hall, built for the occasion at Lake and Market (now Wacker Drive) Streets. Chicago is the center of the world's largest railroad network, totaling almost 3,000 miles of track.
1865	Civil War ends. The **Union Stock Yards** *(p 162)* are organized on Chicago's South Side to consolidate the city's slaughterhouses around a central railroad yard. Marshall Field and Levi Leiter form a dry-goods store that will become MARSHALL FIELD & CO.
1867	Chicago labor leaders begin the struggle for the 8-hour workday, choosing May 1 as the day to celebrate the contributions of labor to the American economy.
1869	Chicago's parks and boulevards system is created, setting aside over 1,600 acres of green space in the rapidly growing city. The three-part system is designed by Frederick Law Olmsted and Calvert Vaux (South Park), William Le Baron Jenney (West Parks), and Swain Nelson (Lincoln Park). The **Chicago Water Tower** *(p 83)* is constructed to regulate the pressure of water pumped into the city from Lake Michigan.

Chicago in Flames
View from Randolph Street Bridge

Chicago Historical Society (ICHi-02953)

THE FIRE

The devastation of the Chicago Fire appears catastrophic in the destruction of homes and businesses throughout the central area, but the city's enviable water and rail connections—and the majority of its industries—are unscorched, and rebuilding commences immediately. Chicago's phenomenal growth continues as the population triples in the decade after the Fire. The Fire also draws architects from across the country who develop the Chicago school *(p 33)*. By the 1880s, up to 10,000 immigrants arrive in the city each week, leading to health problems and overcrowding.

| 1871 | A "deep cut" of the Illinois & Michigan Canal attempts to reverse the Chicago River to limit pollution of drinking water taken from the lake. On October 8, the **Great Chicago Fire** starts in the barn behind Mrs. O'Leary's house at Jefferson and DeKoven Streets. For three days, the fire burns north and east, destroying the whole of downtown Chicago and much of the North Side. Only 300 die, but a third of the city's population of 300,000 is without shelter. |
| 1877 | The Great Railroad Strike affects Chicago as 30 workers are killed in the "Battle of the Viaduct" on Halsted Street. |

1879	The **Art Institute of Chicago** *(p 60)* is organized as the Chicago Academy of Design in leased office space. In 1885 the institute constructs its first edifice, designed by Burnham & Root, at Michigan Avenue and Van Buren Street (demolished).
1880	George Pullman hires architect Solon Beman to design the town and railroad-car factories of **Pullman** *(p 187)* near Lake Calumet.
1884	The first steel-framed building, the 10-story Home Insurance Company building, is erected in the Loop, designed by **William Le Baron Jenney** *(p 32)*.
1886	The **Haymarket Tragedy**: striking workers meet to hear the Mayor and other speakers at a May 4 meeting in Haymarket Square. As the meeting disperses, 170 police arrive and a bomb is thrown, killing seven policemen. Eight anarchist labor leaders are brought to trial in an event that garners worldwide attention and sympathy for workers, but Chicago civic leaders and newspapers condemn the anarchists. Four are eventually hanged and one commits suicide while three remain in jail.
1889	Social reformers Jane Addams and Ellen Gates Starr found **Hull-House** *(p 150)* on the Near West Side to aid the immigrant population, which outnumbers the US-born population of Chicago. The **Auditorium Building** *(p 43)* by Adler & Sullivan is completed.

WORLD'S FAIR, WORLD CITY

The city determines to prove that it is not an uncultured hog town by inviting the world to the largest party of the 19C, the World's Columbian Exposition of 1893 *(illustration p 6)*. The Fair's gleaming Neoclassical buildings celebrate the progress of the American Republic in sciences and arts, creating a seemingly perfect "White City." The success of the Fair engenders the "City Beautiful" movement nation wide. Chicago continues to feed the East and reap the West as an increasing populace migrates across the continent.

1891-92	Theodore Thomas founds the **Chicago Symphony Orchestra**. The **University of Chicago** *(p 166)* opens in Hyde Park thanks to the beneficence of oil magnate John D. Rockefeller. Local literary figures form the **Little Room** salon *(p 29)*.
1893	The **World's Columbian Exposition** *(p 181)* opens in Jackson Park, drawing 27 million visitors to the 650-acre "White City" over the course of the summer. The adjacent Midway features the first Ferris wheel and the racy "hootchie-kootchie" dancing of Little Egypt. The city's first elevated train brings visitors to the Fair from the Loop. Illinois Governor **John Peter Altgeld** pardons the three surviving Haymarket defendants, earning the enmity of business and anti-immigrant forces. The Field Columbian Museum, later the **Field Museum of Natural History** *(p 89)*, is founded.
1894	In the midst of a depression, the **Pullman Strike** *(p 188)* disrupts railroad traffic nation wide as workers suffer layoffs and wage cuts in George Pullman's controlled company town. President Grover Cleveland sends federal troops to break the strike under the aegis of protecting the US Mail. **Clarence Darrow** defends the strikers in a trial that leads to the end of the company town.
1897	The **Union Loop Elevated** railroad is completed, girdling the city's core with steel.
1900	The **Chicago Sanitary Canal** opens, permanently reversing the flow of the Chicago River. By 1914, it will replace the Illinois & Michigan Canal as the city's primary shipping route. The Chicago Stock Yards' hundred companies employ 30,000 persons.
1903	A fire at Chicago's Iroquois Theatre kills 596 persons.
1905	**Robert S. Abbott** founds the *Chicago Defender* to serve the city's growing African-American community.
1906	Upton Sinclair's **The Jungle** is published. His descriptions of the meat-packing industry lead to the reforms of the Pure Food and Drug Act.
1909	Daniel Burnham and Edward Bennett's **Plan of Chicago** is released, providing a classical template for the city's future development. Frank Lloyd Wright's **Robie House**, considered the quintessential Prairie-school building, is completed in Hyde Park.

1914-16	**Chicago Literary Renaissance**: a school of social realism in literature flourishes in Chicago. Margaret Anderson founds the *Little Review*; Edgar Lee Masters' *Spoon River Anthology* and Carl Sandburg's *Chicago Poems* are published. Theodore Dreiser and Sherwood Anderson release their early novels.
1919	A **race riot** leaves 40 dead and hundreds injured on the city's South Side. The Chicago White Sox lose the World Series, and a year later eight players are banned for conspiring with gamblers to "throw" the series.

Chicago Daily News/Chicago Historical Society (DN-097346)

Al Capone at Comiskey Park, 1931

PROGRESS AND PROHIBITION

Civic leaders work to transform downtown Chicago into a modern civic center with the creation of Wacker Drive, North Michigan Avenue and the museums of Grant Park. But the Roaring Twenties leave Chicago with a permanent scar as bootlegging gangs commit hundreds of murders in their attempts to control the illegal liquor business. **Al Capone** (1899-1947) becomes Chicago's most notorious figure, heading a large criminal syndicate that survives his imprisonment.

1922	The *Chicago Tribune* announces a worldwide competition to design its new skyscraper as Wacker Drive and North Michigan Avenue usher in modern development.
1924	There are approximately 20,000 illegal retail liquor outlets in Chicago. Bootlegger Dion O'Banion is killed in his North Side flower shop as Al Capone seeks to expand his empire.
1929	Seven members of the rival Bugs Moran gang are gunned down by Al Capone's men in the **St. Valentine's Day Massacre** on N. Clark Street. Capone is earning roughly $50 million a year bootlegging, and has become a media celebrity.
1931	Al Capone is sent to prison for tax evasion. He is released eight years later, his body and brain wracked by syphilis.
1933	Chicago Mayor **Anton Cermak** is killed by an assassin's bullet intended for President-elect Franklin Delano Roosevelt in Miami. The Mayor's office falls to **Ed Kelly**, who with Pat Nash founds the city's Democratic political machine *(p 19)*, dominant for the next 50 years.
1933-34	Chicago's **Century of Progress Exposition** draws millions to a new lakefront site inspired by the Burnham Plan. The fair focuses on the innovations of the modern era with exhibits like an all-glass house, a windowless Electrical Building and Buckminster Fuller's Dymaxion car. The **Museum of Science and Industry** *(p 182)* opens in Jackson Park. Public Enemy Number One **John Dillinger** is shot to death by federal agents outside the Biograph Theater *(p 126)* on N. Lincoln Avenue.
1937	Ten striking steelworkers and sympathizers are killed by police on Memorial Day as they march on the Republic Steel plant in South Chicago.

Time Line

MID-TO-LATE 20C

Chicago's population peaks in 1950, and the ensuing decades witness large-scale expressway and urban renewal projects that mark the triumph of the personal automobile. Chicago becomes the center of the nation's airline system at Midway and O'Hare airports. The social turbulence of the 1960s reaches one of its peaks at the Democratic National Convention in 1968. By the 1970s Chicago is in decline as its industrial base bleeds away and an increasing number of white middle-class residents move to the suburbs. The city's new ethnic mix elects the first African-American mayor in 1983 while its continuing role as a financial and commercial center spur new urban redevelopment efforts.

1942 | Enrico Fermi and a team of University of Chicago scientists create the first controlled, self-sustaining **nuclear reaction** (p 167) underneath the school's abandoned football stands.

1949 | Construction begins on 860-880 N. Lake Shore Drive by **Ludwig Mies van der Rohe** (p 35). Mies continues to design the ILLINOIS INSTITUTE OF TECHNOLOGY campus, where he has presided over the architecture program since 1939.

1955 | **Richard J. Daley** is elected Mayor of Chicago for the first of six times. He will die in office in 1976. O'Hare Airport opens on the northwestern fringe of the city.

1968 | **Rev. Dr. Martin Luther King, Jr.'s** assassination leads to widespread rioting on the South and West Sides. In August, demonstrators converge on the **Democratic National Convention**, provoking a violent response from police and US National Guard forces. Confrontations in Grant Park and Lincoln Park resound with the chant "The whole world is watching." While one commission calls it a "police riot," the **Chicago Seven** trial the following year holds radicals and student leaders responsible for the melees.

1971 | The Chicago Stock Yards close. MCCORMICK PLACE Convention Center, the largest in the world, opens on the south lakefront.

1974 | The **Sears Tower** (p 57) is topped off as the tallest building in the world.

1979 | A January blizzard dumps a record amount of snow and freezes the city for over a month. City Hall's unpreparedness and lackluster response to the snow leads to the ouster of Mayor Michael Bilandic by **Jane Byrne**, Chicago's first female mayor.

1983 | **Harold Washington** becomes Chicago's first African-American mayor. A city-council majority of 29 old-line white aldermen struggles for power during three years of bitter "council wars."

1987 | Mayor Washington dies seven months after his resounding re-election, leading to a traumatic 10-hour city-council session that elects **Eugene Sawyer** as mayor.

1988 | Lights for night baseball are installed at **Wrigley Field** (p 144).

CONTEMPORARY CHICAGO

A century after it first sought the world's approval, Chicago again seeks recognition as a world-class city. Still the fulcrum of American commerce, the city is redeveloping from within, transforming industrial land into middle-class neighborhoods, solidifying its role as a financial and convention center, and building its reputation as a tourist destination and cultural metropolis.

1989 | **Richard M. Daley**, son of Richard J. Daley, is elected mayor.

1991 | Michael Jordan and the **Chicago Bulls** (p 39) win the National Basketball Association championship for the first time, and proceed to triumph again in 1992 and 1993.

1992 | A company driving pilings into the Chicago River pierces a portion of the city's old freight-tunnel system, causing flooding in basements throughout the Loop and the evacuation of the entire Downtown in the middle of a business day.

1994 | The first soccer **World Cup** in the United States opens in Chicago with an elaborate ceremony and a 1-0 victory by Germany over Bolivia.

1995 | A summer heat wave kills more than 700 Chicagoans as the temperature reaches 106°F.

1996 | The Democratic National Convention returns to Chicago. The Petronas Towers in Kuala Lumpur, Malaysia, surpass the Sears Tower as tallest buildings in the world.

Economy

Chicago's economy has been shaped by its location at the nexus of the great inland waterways and at the heart of the nation's rich agricultural midsection. Throughout the 19C, as the central marketplace and entrepot for the bounty of Midwestern farms and fields, Chicago achieved its legendary status as "wheat stacker, hog butcher, and freight handler to the world." Still the most important railroad-freight hub in North America, the international center of futures trading and a major producer of food products, the Chicago metropolitan area cultivates roots in its economic past, while a booming service economy propels the city toward the 21C.

From Grain to Brain – The features that made Chicago a funnel for the foodstuffs of the Midwest—location and accessibility—also led to its growth as an industrial center of the Western world. The earliest industries were closely related to agriculture and husbandry: milling, tanning, woodworking and food processing. After the Civil War, the city began to expand its industrial base, as big steel, heavy manufacturing and meat packing came to dominate its economy. European immigrants flocked in by the thousands hoping for employment with a giant like United States Steel, International Harvester or the Union Stock Yards, or any of the hundreds of factories that lined the river and encircled the central business district. By 1960, manufacturing accounted for more than one-third of local jobs, but the stockyards closed forever in 1971, and the steel industry fell victim to recession. In recent years, as companies downsize and the manufacturing base dwindles further, the city has come to rely more and more on a service economy—from the largest accounting firms to the smallest shoeshine parlors—for its livelihood. Today, the service sector, including among others government, retail, transportation, hospitality, educational, legal and medical workers, claims 72 percent of the local work force. In fact, the area's largest single employer is the federal government. The annual value of Chicago's goods and services totals $150 billion.

■ Made in Chicago:

At the 1893 World's Columbian Exposition, Mayor Carter Harrison observed that Chicago "knows nothing that it fears to attempt, and thus far has found nothing that it cannot accomplish." Indeed the city's unofficial slogan—I Will—conveys the sense of purpose that built this list of local innovations:

Ferris wheel: George W. G. Ferris created a 264ft "bridge on an axle" for the Columbian Exposition. A modern rendition now dominates Navy Pier.

Skyscraper: William Le Baron Jenney designed the Home Insurance Building on LaSalle and Adams Streets around an iron-and-steel frame in 1884, thereby instituting the lineage of Chicago's 20C pride and joy, the Sears Tower.

Juvenile court system: Established in 1899, this division of the Circuit Court of Cook County was the brainchild of Julia Lathrop, an associate of pioneering social worker Jane Addams.

Lie detector: Leonarde Keeler, an employee of the Scientific Crime Detection Laboratory (the nation's first) at Northwestern University, devised the Keeler Polygraph. His invention earned him a part in the 1948 film *Call Northside 777.*

Successful heart surgery: Dr. Daniel Hale Williams, the first African-American member of the American College of Surgeons, saved James Cornish's life by tying off a severed artery and suturing the heart sac after a near deadly barroom brawl in 1893.

Blood bank and trauma center: Cook County Hospital opened the nation's first blood bank in 1937 and the first trauma center in 1966.

Drugstore lunch counter: Faced with a cold winter and falling ice cream sales, Myrtle Walgreen, wife of the drugstore's founder, began serving hot meals at their soda fountain counter around 1909.

Ice cream sundae: Around 1900, ice-cream-parlor owner Deacon Garwood circumvented temperance laws that forbade ice cream sodas on Sundays by dishing up a concoction of ice cream and syrup he called a sundae.

Ovaltine, Twinkies, Cracker Jack, Dove Bars: These popular sweets all originated in Chicago between 1893 and 1952.

Zipper: Called the "hookless fastener" when exhibited at the 1893 Columbian Exposition, the device would be dubbed "zipper" by the B.F. Goodrich Company, who used it on overshoes.

Roller skates: Levant M. Richardson made possible the modern roller skate when he invented the ball-bearing wheel in 1884.

Pinball: The automatic-game rage began in Chicago in 1930 with the ten-balls-for-a-nickel Whoopee Game.

City vs. Suburb – Another factor complicates regional economics: the relationship between the city proper, suburban Cook County and the collar counties, a symbiosis that is impossible to ignore. Many local employers have fled Downtown for less expensive, more hospitable locations outside the city limits, creating thriving economic corridors in surrounding communities like Schaumburg and Du Page County. As a result, of the 3.5 million people at work in the metropolitan area, less than half are employed in the city. Some analysts predict a slowing of the trend as the cost of downtown office space comes into line with suburban prices, and most agree that a balance between city and outskirts must be maintained for the economic good of the entire region.

Commercial Crossroads – As the freight hub of North America, Chicago supports a complex network of railroad, trucking, waterborne shipping and air-freight services. The nation's major inland port, Chicago is connected to the Atlantic Ocean via the St. Lawrence Seaway, which opened in 1959, and to the Gulf of Mexico via the Sanitary & Ship Canal and the Mississippi River. Even with the decline in the steel industry, iron ore remains the largest volume commodity to enter the port aboard deep-draft carriers, and grain is still exported by water around the world. Two commercial airports serve the city: **Midway**, the city's original air terminal on the Southwest Side; and **O'Hare International**, the world's busiest. O'Hare served 66.4 million passengers in 1994, including 6 million who passed through the airport's recently completed $618-million international terminal. O'Hare is also the nation's third largest air-freight depot, handling upwards of a million tons of cargo a year. As the national hub of passenger rail travel, downtown **Union Station** served in excess of 2 million riders in 1992. On a local scale, the buses, subways and elevated trains of the largely urban Chicago Transit Authority travel more than 400,000 miles daily. A consortium of suburban rail lines known as Metra operates over 425 miles of track in Illinois, with approximately 75 more miles that terminate in Kenosha, Wisconsin, and South Bend, Indiana. Altogether, this integrated system of rail, elevated, subway and bus lines ferries more than 500,000 commuters to work and back each day along with thousands of occasional riders.

Chicago Mercantile Exchange Trading Floor

Future Games – The **Chicago Board of Trade (CBOT)**, founded in 1848 and today the world's oldest and largest futures exchange, is a testament to Chicago's agrarian origins. Established to trade grain futures—bulk commodities bought and sold at a predetermined future time—in the days when 60 million bushels passed through the city each year, the CBOT now handles an array of commodities and financial futures. The **Chicago Mercantile Exchange (CME)**, historically the world's busiest market for perishable commodities such as pork bellies, now trades futures and options on agricultural commodities, interest rates, stock market indexes, gold and foreign currency futures through an international trading link established with

Singapore in 1984. In 1992, the exchange launched an electronic after-hours trading system to open up a truly global market. Generally, some 900,000 contracts trade daily at the CME; on one record-breaking day in 1994, 2.4 million changed hands. Together the CBOT and the CME make Chicago the world leader in futures trading. The **Chicago Stock Exchange**, which opened in 1882, is second in terms of dollar value of shares traded only to its New York counterpart. It trades exclusively in stocks at a rate of over 3.4 billion shares a year.

Corporate Superlatives – A survey of the highest income-earning public corporations in the Chicago metropolitan area reveals the wide range of concerns that make up the area's diversified economic base. Within the top ten alone are Sears Roebuck & Co., the world's largest retailer; the country's first and third biggest food producers (Kraft Foods, Inc. and Sara Lee Corp., respectively); Amoco Corp., a major oil company; electronics manufacturer Motorola, Inc.; Ameritech Corp., a communications service provider; and UAL Corp., parent of United Airlines. Over 80 foreign banks do business in the city. In addition, Chicago has ranked second to New York as a publishing center since the turn of the century, specializing largely in encyclopedias and educational materials. The area hosts the world's largest garbage disposal and recycling company, candy-manufacturing plant and gum maker. The most profitable drugstore chain—Walgreen Co.—and McDonald's Corp., the biggest seller of hamburgers, maintain headquarters outside of Chicago, along with Anatomical Chart Company, the nation's largest maker of artificial skeletons.

Conventions and Tourism – Chicago ranks as the undisputed convention capital of the US. In 1995, the city hosted 40,000 conventions, trade shows and corporate meetings, from the mammoth National Restaurant Show to such smaller, specialized events as the Powder and Bulk Solids Conference. This $3.5-billion-a-year industry brings more than four million visitors to the city annually. Estimates indicate that one convention alone can generate revenues as high as $66 million in six days, as delegates purchase goods and services during their stay. The Democratic National Convention to be hosted by Chicago in August 1996 is expected to yield $122 million. The centerpiece of Chicago's convention business is **McCormick Place**, the country's largest exhibition facility. When its $987-million expansion is completed in 1997, the 3-building complex will offer 2.2 million square feet of exhibit space. The city is becoming an increasingly popular destination for tourists as well, 26 million of whom visited in 1994. According to the US Travel and Tourism Administration, it ranks ninth among the top ten American travel destinations for overseas visitors. Attracted by Chicago's manageable scale and pleasing blend of museums, entertainment, dining and sporting events, international travelers now spend over one million dollars a year in the city. Combined, the convention and tourism industry supports 221,000 jobs.

Ivory Towers – Among Chicago's 96 colleges and universities can be counted the top graduate fine arts program in the nation at the School of the Art Institute of Chicago; the University of Chicago's law, medical, MBA, music and graduate programs, none of which ranks below eighth in the nation; and the well-respected Medill School of Journalism at Northwestern. The University of Illinois at Chicago has the largest enrollment with 25,000 students, followed by Northwestern (its main campus located in suburban Evanston) with 17,000.

We welcome corrections and suggestions that may assist us in preparing the next edition. Send us your comments:

Michelin Travel Publications
Editorial Department
P. O. Box 19001
Greenville, SC 29602-9001

Politics

Chicagoans who travel abroad are used to the reaction mention of their home city usually elicits. An enthusiastic "rat-a-tat-tat" prefaces any discussion of Chicago's art, music or culture, its quality of life or even the weather. The city's historic reputation for vice and corruption, epitomized by the machine-gun-toting gangsters of the 1920s, casts a long shadow over those other qualities that today make it a world-class metropolis.

This dual nature defines Chicago in all of its aspects, particularly politics. The city struts its gruff, wide-open, frontier reputation while successfully cultivating the trappings of class and sophistication. In city politics, the simultaneous tension and symbiosis between vice and virtue have created the inextricable tangle of good government and power politics that ultimately gave rise to the country's most enduring political Machine: a mighty Democratic Party dispensing influence and favors to keep the city running smoothly. Indeed, the successful among Chicago's 45 mayors have understood that the electorate's primary concern is with the efficient delivery of city services—from garbage pickup to safety on the streets.

Political Prelude – In 1837, Chicago's first mayor, **William Butler Ogden**, used his own wealth to finance city improvements and even bailed out the city on his personal credit when financial panic struck. As the city's population soared in two decades to over 93,000, the adolescent boomtown seethed with prostitution, gambling and crime.

Subsequent mayors—largely symbolic leaders with little real authority—turned a blind eye to the flourishing netherworld, but 6ft 6in **"Long John" Wentworth** burst into office in 1857 determined to purge the vice districts, perhaps the first effort at "reform" in Chicago. In a dramatic move, he and a posse literally pulled down the ramshackle brothels, saloons and gambling dens in a seedy patch by the river known as the Sands. Though demonstrative, his other attempts to eradicate such areas had little effect. Chicago's underworld had already taken sturdy root, and it would be for later mayors to discover the value of compromise.

The Smoke Clears – As Chicago reinvented itself in the aftermath of the Great Fire of 1871, the breach between wealth and poverty widened, enhancing the city's split personality. Growth continued unabated, dictating a personal kind of politics conducted in the neighborhoods. Vast inner-city immigrant populations represented powerful voting blocs, and ward bosses were quick to exchange jobs and other favors for their support. Nurtured by this ward-by-ward spoils system, the Machine began to incubate.

After the Fire, the Democratic Party gained momentum, propelled by the votes of the huge foreign-born population. With the election of **Carter Harrison, I** in 1879, a flamboyant Kentuckian with a sympathy for the working man and a live-and-let-live philosophy, Chicago had a modern mayor who understood his constituents' practical needs. His appeal crossed class and ethnic lines and his belief in personal liberties endeared him to the city's considerable underworld. He served four consecutive terms between 1879 and 1887, only to be assassinated in 1893 by a disgruntled office seeker on the heels of his proudest accomplishment: serving a fifth term as Chicago's "World's Fair Mayor" during the Columbian Exposition *(p 181)*. In spite of his tolerance of powerful gambling kingpin **Michael McDonald**, Harrison earned the devotion of the electorate as well as a reputation for honesty, even among his detractors. Meanwhile, "King Mike" presided over a wide-ranging empire—which included much of the county board, the police department, the Democratic Party and the Cook County sheriff, along with bunco artists and con men—from offices in the largest of his gambling emporiums, a lavish downtown establishment known as The Store. In years to come, Mike McDonald's most famous heir would be Al Capone.

From Saloon to City Hall – Harrison's tolerant administration—and the five intermittent terms served by his son, Carter Harrison, II, between 1897 and 1915—achieved a primitive balance between vice and virtue that later mayors would envy. Still, power resided in the wards and the saloons where the likes of Aldermen **"Bathhouse" John Coughlin** and **Michael "Hinky Dink" Kenna** held sway. Their rollicking First Ward included the infamous Levee *(p 154)*, the city's sprawling underbelly and home of the **Everleigh Club**, the most elite of 200 brothels in the district. Not satisfied with the take from protection money they earned in the Levee, the two staged annual 1st Ward balls to line the coffers of the ward organization. To these drunken brawls came prostitutes and politicians, policemen and aldermen, players in an absurd parody of city government.

■ **Coined in Chicago**
Along with colorful characters, Chicago's world of politics and crime has spawned some picturesque phraseology as well.

Underworld: Civic leaders of the 1850s elevated Chicago out of the marshland and resurfaced the "mudtropolis" with earth and stone. Crime lord Roger Plant and his gang of roughs took control of the resulting maze of tunnels, underground byways and caves which stretched from Wells Street to the South Branch of the Chicago River, creating the first "underworld" crime empire.

Smoke-filled room: Harry Daugherty, campaign manager for President Warren G. Harding in 1920, predicted that the Republican convention in Chicago would be decided by a small group of men sitting "around a table in a smoke-filled room."

"There's a sucker born every minute": Sometimes attributed to P. T. Barnum, local legend claims it the answer given by Mike McDonald, 1890s crime boss, to his partner who worried about attracting enough business to their many gaming tables.

Public enemies: Eye-catching title of the list—topped by Al Capone—of 28 gangsters given to the press by Col. Henry Barrett Chamberlain, operating director of the Chicago Crime Commission.

Mickey Finn: Owner of the Lone Star Saloon and Palm Garden in the late 1890s who concocted two knockout drinks to render patrons unconscious so that Mickey and his wife could rob them.

One-way ride: In the 1920s, gangster Hymie Weiss recognized that the secrecy and security of late-model cars offered the perfect venue for mobile murders. When hood Steve Wisniewski hijacked a beer truck, Weiss dispatched of him on the first one-way ride.

By the 1890s, aldermen were learning that more profit and long-term reward might be garnered in collusion with businessmen than on the streets of the Levee. Utilities wishing to lay cable and traction magnates seeking rights of way along city streets paid the aldermen thousands of dollars in "boodle" annually for favorable votes in council. In return, Chicago gained a modern transit system with electrified trains, and the burgeoning Machine rose from the saloons to City Hall.

In the meantime, the face of organized crime in Chicago was changing, developing into a vicious and insidious network supervised by the likes of Johnny Torrio, "Big Jim" Colosimo, Al Capone and their rivals. Whereas gambling had been the mainstay of the Victorian warlords, the gangsters of Prohibition made bootlegging their stock in trade and by 1920, the "Outfit" had a lock on the city that would last for decades. **Alphonse Capone** initiated the most infamous six years in Chicago's history when he succeeded Johnny Torrio as head of Chicago's syndicate in 1925. Capone eliminated his rivals in a bloody gang war that culminated in the 1929 St. Valentine's Day Massacre, when hitmen rubbed out several of gangster Bugs Moran's associates in a North Side garage. Between 1925 and 1931, 439 gangland slayings rocked Chicago, most of which were never solved. Indeed, bombastic mayor **William Hale "Big Bill" Thompson**, indebted to Capone for political and financial support, coddled the mob, and some Chicagoans even considered the ruthless Capone a folk hero. Although brought down by tenacious federal agent Eliot Ness for income tax evasion in 1931, Capone had established a dynasty that would last well beyond his death from syphilis in 1947.

The Modern Machine – Throughout the 1920s, "new-breed" Democrats had been working to create an organization with widespread influence over all of city government. Their quest to institutionalize the Machine coalesced under the leadership of **Anton J. Cermak**, who succeeded Thompson in 1931. Cermak built a revolutionary multiethnic coalition unified by a powerful party organization. He advocated reform, efficiency and economy and backed up his promises with the strength of that organization. Even though an assassin's bullet meant for President-elect Franklin Delano Roosevelt cut short his term in 1933, Anton J. Cermak had paved the way for the legendary Richard J. Daley.

In most cities, the Great Depression marked the end of urban self-sufficiency. Local organizations could no longer control money, policy and jobs because of the increasing presence of the federal government and unions. But the Chicago Machine gained momentum, expanding its base of support as far as Washington, DC, where leaders recognized the importance of a friendly Chicago mayor. At the same time, organized crime generated considerable income for the Machine through gambling and protection monies. The party courted and won the support of the city's increasing African-American population, only to stumble later over issues of open housing and desegregation.

The Machine hit its stride under **Richard J. Daley**, "Hizzoner da Mare," between 1955 and his death in 1976. A consummate administrator and career politician, Daley, like Cermak, believed in good government through party politics. He brought the rambunctious city council under control, consolidated the power of the mayor's office and extended his reach to state and nation. He engaged professionals to streamline the system. His "City that Works" did so because Daley understood how to exchange influence and favors to get things done. The stronger and more centralized his office, the greater his clout. By the late 1960s, however, chinks had begun to show in the armor. Daley grew more conservative, his organization less able to please and appease the city's increasingly disparate communities split by racial and political strife. Open housing marches, riots following the assassination of Dr. Martin Luther King, Jr., violence surrounding the 1968 Democratic National Convention, and the mayhem of the Days of Rage the following summer pushed the Machine to the limit. Still, Daley prevailed through a tumultuous time when other big-city mayors failed. He cultivated a reassuring civic stability that played well among a largely conservative electorate confused and somewhat threatened by rapidly changing times, and he delivered city services, thereby guaranteeing loyalty.

Richard J. Daley (r.) and President Prado of Peru, 1961

UPI/Bettman

The period following Daley's sudden death in 1976 could not have provided more of a contrast. Disputes over his successor set the tone as African-American politicians and their constituents—led by **Reverend Jesse Jackson**—clamored for recognition, and Poles, feeling too long estranged from city hall themselves, put forth their own candidates. Ultimately, mild-mannered Michael Bilandic, a Bridgeport alderman, came to office first as acting mayor and then by election in 1977. Although a competent mayor, he lacked Daley's ability to consolidate power, and the factions that had begun to form in the party gained strength.

It was a January blizzard in 1979 that sounded the death knell of the old Machine. Unable to liberate the city from its snowy grip, Mayor Bilandic succumbed to a challenge from the irrepressible, reform-minded **Jane Byrne**, Chicago's first woman mayor. With power leaking from the mayor's office, the next few years passed in a tumultuous free-for-all fueled by strikes and a difficult economy. When **Harold Washington**, the city's first African-American mayor, took office in 1983, the rhetoric turned shrill and racist, leading to a standoff between mayor and council that immobilized the city. Promising peacemaking efforts that marked Washington's second term were cut short by his untimely death in 1987.

The furor has quieted in the 1990s. **Richard M. Daley**, at first indebted to his father's legacy, has emerged as a no-nonsense mayor of moderation. He presides over a multicultural city council—one alderman for each of 50 wards—whose attentions have shifted from parochial infighting to the staggering concerns of all American cities: revenue generation, a growing underclass and gang violence, a deteriorating infrastructure and an economic challenge from the suburbs.

Population

Outranked in population size only by New York and Los Angeles, Chicago remains the bold and brash metropolis that Normal Mailer called "perhaps the last of the great American cities." In this polyglot city of nearly 3 million, the neighborhood is the common measure of all, a source of identity and pride and a lingering reflection of Chicago's incredible immigrant heritage. A patchwork of neighborhoods, some 175 in all, unfurls westward from the lakefront, from tiny Old Town Triangle on the North Side to the anchor communities of Rogers Park and Englewood. Some are the stuff of developers' dreams; others trace their outlines around historic ethnic enclaves.

The creators of this patchwork have been an eclectic lot since **Jean Baptiste Point du Sable**, a fur trader of French, Caribbean and African descent, built the earliest permanent dwelling on the banks of the river in 1779. At first a blended society of French, English and Indian settlers, the town developed a growing reputation for opportunities and accessibility, luring refugees from Europe by the 1830s. Fleeing famine, persecution and revolution, great waves of immigrants poured in between 1840 and 1924. By 1890, the foreign-born (largely German, Irish and Scandinavian) and their children accounted for 79 percent of a population of about 1.2 million. They transplanted their shtetls, villages and parishes to the shores of Lake Michigan, establishing neighborhoods that offered the familiarity of home. In a pattern that would repeat again and again, newcomers settled near Downtown and then dispersed outward—ultimately to the suburbs—as the next groups arrived.

Population from 1837 to 1992		
1837	4,066	Chicago incorporates as a city.
1848	20,243	**Chicago and Galena Union Railroad**, the city's first, begins operation.
1860	112,172	Chicago has become the center of the world's largest railroad network. The building of the railroads attracts many immigrants from the US and abroad.
1871	335,000	The **Chicago Fire** in October flattens much of the city, but the immediate push to rebuild sustains it through the financial panic of 1873.
1889	1,098,576	Chicago annexes 120 surrounding square miles by popular referenda, thereby boosting the population over the one million mark. The federal census of 1890 marks Chicago's official status as **"Second City,"** its population having surpassed that of Philadelphia.
1893	1,315,000	**World's Columbian Exposition** *(p 181)*.
1900	1,698,575	Chicago's population now includes more Poles, Swedes, Czechs, Dutch, Danes, Norwegians, Croatians, Slovaks, Lithuanians and Greeks than any other American city.
1914	2,437,526	Immigration from Europe slows with **World War I**. The migration of southern blacks, drawn in part by war-industry jobs, begins.
1920	2,701,705	African-American population reaches 109,000 and will continue to grow to a quarter million by 1929.
1924	2,939,605	The **Johnson-Reed Act** essentially ends foreign immigration through quotas.
1932	3,236,913	Chicago is hard hit by the **Great Depression**; more than 750,000 are unemployed. Migration and birthrate slow, and Chicago grows by only 20,000 between 1930 and 1940.
1950	3,620,962	A strong postwar economy along with the baby boom and the annexation of 41.1 additional square miles boosts Chicago's population to its peak.
1956	3,552,300	**O'Hare Airport** opens and soon becomes the world's busiest, maintaining Chicago's position as transportation hub. The urban population has begun to fall, however, and a corresponding increase throughout the metropolitan area indicates that the flight to the suburbs has begun.
1990	2,783,903	The population of the city proper falls below three million for the first time in 70 years. Los Angeles becomes the official "Second City."
1992	2,768,483	According to the 1992 census estimate, the city's population continues to decline.

This migratory ebb and flow has yielded a city that today is 39 percent African American, nearly 20 percent Hispanic and close to 4 percent Asian. Some 80 ethnic strains enrich the mix, from American Indians to Czechs, and Pacific Islanders to Assyrians.

The Irish – The first to arrive in large numbers, the Irish came to build the Illinois & Michigan Canal *(p 208)* in 1836 and to flee the potato famine of the 1840s. Many settled along the South Branch of the Chicago River in an area now called **Bridgeport** *(p 162)*, which in the 20C would produce four Chicago mayors of Irish descent, including **Richard J. Daley**. From humble beginnings as laborers, teamsters and domestic servants, Chicago's Irish rose to prominence in politics, the police department and the Catholic church.

Ukranian Independence Day Celebration

Germans – The failed revolution of 1848 drove Germans from their homeland by the thousands, and by 1860, they outnumbered other groups in Chicago. They moved north from Chicago Avenue, through **Old Town** *(p 120)* and Lakeview *(p 142)* and up along Lincoln Avenue, where **Lincoln Square** *(p 143)* remains a center of Teutonic society. Germans were as active in the labor movement as in the development of Chicago's culture, organizing trade unions and fraternal groups, singing and sporting clubs and even the Chicago Symphony Orchestra in 1891. In the shadow of anti-German sentiment during two world wars, German solidarity faded in favor of greater assimilation.

Scandinavians – Swedes, Norwegians and Danes streamed steadily into Chicago over the years, some to stay, others to seek out the rich farmland of the northern Midwest. Settling in shantytowns near the central city, they prospered in the construction trades, small businesses and later in the professions, eventually migrating north and northwest. **Humboldt Park** *(p 142)* was once a center of Norwegian and Danish life, and in Andersonville on the Far North Side, the Swedish influence lingers in shops and restaurants.

Jews – Jewish immigrants arrived in two great migrations. First came the generally affluent and secular German speakers from Central Europe, and beginning in the 1880s, mostly orthodox refugees fleeing pogroms in Eastern Europe flocked to the city's crowded **Near West Side** *(p 147)*. The urbane Germans assimilated easily, building retail and dry-goods businesses and adopting something of a paternalistic attitude toward their impoverished Russian and Polish counterparts abiding in the ghetto around Maxwell Street *(p 147)*. Out of that ghetto, however, came a profusion of actors and writers, jurists and businessmen. Many Jews today live on the city's Far North Side and in the northern suburbs.

The Poles – Chicago is home today to more than a million residents of Polish ancestry. They arrived in droves between 1870 and 1930, bringing a devotion to Catholicism that manifested itself in the building of elegant churches at the centers of their communities. Over the years, the Poles moved northwest along **Milwaukee Avenue** *(p 136)*, which remains in places a Polish commercial corridor, and today many concentrate in the Avondale neighborhood. Another wave of immigration followed the Solidarity movement in Poland in 1980.

Italians – Beginning in the 1880s, Italians flocked to Chicago. Hailing mostly from southern Italy, they sometimes transplanted entire villages to the New World. Newcomers were often at the mercy of unscrupulous padrones—labor agents—for railroad and construction work. As they settled in, however, many Italians opened small businesses, took up public service and went into stonecutting and masonry. **Little Italy** *(p 150)* on Chicago's Near West Side celebrated its heyday in the 1920s, and, though disrupted by urban renewal, remains a center of Italian culture today.

Greeks – Latecomers to Chicago, Greeks arrived after the turn of the century to settle in the Delta on the **Near West Side** *(p 147)*. Almost half of them were single men who came alone to earn a living and return to Greece. Still, by the late 1970s, Chicago had the largest Hellenic population outside of Greece. As restaurateurs the Greeks have been extremely successful; by 1919, they already owned one out of three Chicago eating establishments.

African Americans – Blacks had lived in Chicago since its first settler, and their numbers grew with the city's reputation for abolitionism. Not until the 1910s, however, did they arrive en masse in the Great Migration *(p 154)*, seeking jobs in an exodus from the increasing hardships of the rural South. The most populous "black belt" developed along the **Near South Side** *(p 154)*. At its heart, Bronzeville, "the Harlem of Chicago," pulsed with daily and nightly life, its lively restaurants, cabarets and theaters the incubators of the hot, new Chicago-style blues. Gradually, competition with whites for work and housing created conflict; at the same time, prejudice and racism stunted the progress of blacks attempting to escape the ghetto. The advent of public-housing in the 1940s relieved the worst of the slums, but institutionalized overcrowding in African-American neighborhoods, a situation that is only now being addressed with the transfer of public-housing authority to the federal government. On the other hand, a growing middle class, inheritors of the considerable legacy of Chicago's early African-American professionals and entrepreneurs, is dispersing throughout the city and suburbs, somewhat relieving the city's historic reputation for segregation.

Hispanics – Under the broad rubric "Hispanic" exists a tremendous divergence of experience. Mexican immigration began in earnest around 1916, as the railroads and steel mills recruited workers to make up for slackening European immigration in the face of World War I. Combined, the **Pilsen** *(p 152)* and Little Village neighborhoods are today home to the largest Mexican-American population in the region. Young Puerto Ricans, seeking a chance at prosperity on the mainland, are among the poorest Chicagoans, while Cubans, who first came in 1959 as political rather than economic refugees, have met with greater success. Central and South Americans are now increasing the numbers—and diversity—of Chicago's Hispanic community.

Asians – Located south of the Loop, **Chinatown** *(p 162)* is the city's oldest extant Asian neighborhood, established in 1912 by Chinese businessmen when the existing downtown enclave became overcrowded. By the 1920s, Filipinos and Japanese had also settled in the city. The greatest influx of Asian immigrants began in the 1960s and 70s, largely Southeast Asian refugees who established New Chinatown along **Argyle Street** *(p 143)* on the city's North Side. Farther north, along **Devon Avenue** *(p 146)*, Chicago's Asian Indians and Pakistanis have developed a bustling commercial corridor, and many of the city's Koreans have settled in Albany Park.

For more information on Chicago's fascinating neighborhoods,
see map and text on pp 222-223.

Performing Arts

It is the "lively arts" that give true expression to Chicago's character. Swaggering Chicago-style theater, the wail of the blues, the sardonic world of improvisational comedy and even television and movie producers all feed on the city's rough-cut persona.

Theater – In Chicago, virtually any theatrical taste can be indulged on a given evening. Some 120 professional theaters throughout the city present everything from sweeping Broadway musicals like *Show Boat* and *Phantom of the Opera* to the classics of Shakespeare and Tennessee Williams. *Shear Madness*, the city's longest-running performance, is a light comedy-mystery that has drawn huge crowds since 1982. But Chicago's native theatrical tradition has little to do with such crowd pleasing. The gritty edge of "off-Loop" theater, perhaps best exemplified by the work of local playwright **David Mamet** *(American Buffalo, Glengarry Glen Ross)* and the acting of John Malkovich and William L. Petersen, is in part the legacy of the Hull-House Players. Conceived by Jane Addams *(p 150)* as part of her social and community work at the turn of the century, the Players were reactivated in the revolutionary 1960s, introducing avant-garde theater to Chicago with plays by Edward Albee, Samuel Beckett, Athol Fugard and their contemporaries. Difficult subjects staged and acted with raw intensity, Hull-House productions prepared audiences to appreciate what would evolve into the visceral Chicago style. Small, innovative theaters with elemental names—Body Politic, Organic and Remains—flourished in the ensuing years, fueled by enthusiastic audiences, generous donors and an energetic crop of young performers, writers and directors. Today, as the Chicago style matures at theaters like Steppenwolf in an atmosphere of more restrained funding, scores of upstart, itinerant companies work to remain inventive and solvent, continuing to experiment with new, often outrageous approaches to stagecraft.

Dance – Although most of the performing arts have long found expression here, Chicago has been a slow starter when it comes to dance. In spite of the efforts of such dance greats as Ruth Page and Maria Tallchief Paschen, traditional ballet companies never gained a solid toehold in the city. While Ballet Chicago, established in 1987, is building a reputation for its interpretations of Balanchine and the classics, it is Hubbard Street Dance Chicago that has truly put the city on the terpsichorean map. Founded in 1977 by Lou Conte, the company pioneered a hybrid, thoroughly American style that incorporates the excitement and energy of jazz with the precision of ballet. In 1990, choreographer Twyla Tharp chose Hubbard Street as a repository for her small-scale works. Other notable Chicago dance ensembles include the Joseph Holmes Chicago Dance Theater, Gus Giordano Jazz Dance Chicago and Shirley Mordine and Company Dance Theater. A number of ethnic troupes interpret folk dances from everywhere from Africa to Ireland.

Hubbard Street Dance Chicago

Comedy – The twin muse of Chicago's dark dramatic style is the satirical, incredulous "improv" comedy that has shaped the national sense of humor since the television show *Saturday Night Live (SNL)* took to the air in 1975. Also vestiges of Hull-House, improvisational exercises were employed by recreational counselors there to help immigrants adjust to their new life. Modern progenitor of the style, the **Second City Theater** *(p 123)* was founded in Hyde Park in 1955 as the Compass Players and today thrives in Old Town. Scores of comedians started there, including Alan Alda, Elaine May, Ed Asner, Ann Meara, Joan Rivers and a galaxy of *SNL* stars led by John Belushi, Dan Aykroyd and Gilda Radner. Traditional comedy nightclubs throughout the city and suburbs—Zanies, Funny Firm, Comedy Womb—feature stand-up comics both known and new.

Cinema

Between 1897 and 1918, Chicago prospered as the capital of American filmmaking. William Selig built the world's first movie studio on the Near South Side in 1897, followed a decade later by George Spoor and Gilbert "Bronco Billy" Anderson's Essanay Motion Picture Company. Among them they produced thousands of pictures and employed hundreds of local vaudeville and entertainment professionals. Essanay signed a young Charlie Chaplin for $1,250 a week in 1915, and Selig Polyscope made more than 200 cowboy films featuring Tom Mix.

Eventually, California's better weather and new laws regarding motion picture rights ended the city's movie-making dominion. The lull lasted until 1976 when the city began an aggressive campaign to sell itself to location scouts. Since then, some 184 feature films have been made in the metropolitan area, their producers attracted by Chicago's fresh profile and cooperative atmosphere. Television has succumbed as well, although more in essence than actuality. Sitcoms and dramas, many filmed elsewhere, have nonetheless discovered that Chicago's working-class, no-nonsense ethos makes a good break from the well-worn stereotypes of New York and Los Angeles.

■ **Starring Chicago**

Underworld (1927)	**The Sting** (1973)
The Front Page (1931)	**The Fury** (1978)
Little Caesar (1931)	**The Blues Brothers** (1980)
Scarface (1932)	**My Bodyguard** (1980)
In Old Chicago (1937)	**Ordinary People** (1980)
His Girl Friday (1940)	**Risky Business** (1983)
Call Northside 777 (1948)	**Sixteen Candles** (1984)
Wabash Avenue (1950)	**Ferris Bueller's Day Off** (1986)
Native Son (1950, 1986)	**About Last Night** (1986)
Carrie (1952)	**The Color of Money** (1986)
The Man with the Golden Arm (1956)	**The Untouchables** (1987)
Al Capone (1959)	**Eight Men Out** (1988)
Compulsion (1959)	**Music Box** (1989)
A Raisin in the Sun (1961)	**Backdraft** (1991)
Robin and the Seven Hoods (1964)	**The Fugitive** (1993)
Gaily, Gaily (1969)	**Blink** (1994)
Medium Cool (1969)	**While You Were Sleeping** (1995)

Music

Chicago's development as an immigrant city has imbued it over the years with a rich musical heritage. But the most interesting phenomenon has been the power of the city to transform certain styles. The **blues**, for one, would never be the same once they came to Chicago. From the hollows, fields and churches of the rural South, migrants brought their music to the city in the 1910s. As artists like Big Bill Broonzy and Papa Charlie Jackson began to play together, a hybrid guitar-driven style based on urban themes emerged. In the 1940s, musicians experimented with amplification and by 1950, Chicago surfaced as the capital of the hard-driving electric blues, with Muddy Waters (McKinley Morganfield) as its king. Other greats like Willie Dixon, Howlin' Wolf and Sunnyland Slim spent their careers in Chicago, and today, veterans Buddy

Guy and Koko Taylor (the preeminent female blues artist) each own a local club. Every summer the public flocks by the thousands to the **Chicago Blues Festival** *(p 220)* to hear the world's best sing the blues.

Jazz came up from the South as well after the fall of New Orleans's Storyville vice district and in Chicago became an integrated art. During the 1920s, when jazzmen King Oliver and Louis Armstrong came to play the clubs in the Black Belt, young and restless white musicians like Gene Krupa, Bud Freeman and Jimmy McPartland embraced their style. The resulting hybrid Chicago-style jazz pulsed

Marc PoKempenner

Blues Musicians

with a hot tempo, explosive rhythm sections and elaborate instrumental interplay. Much fine jazz, from traditional to contemporary can be heard in clubs and cabarets around the city to this day, as well as at the **Chicago Jazz Festival** *(p 220)* each summer in Grant Park.

Chicago remains a center of innovation when it comes to contemporary music, particularly **rock**. On the heels of the meteoric rise of the Smashing Pumpkins, Liz Phair, Veruca Salt and Urge Overkill in the early 1990s, some industry prognosticators predicted that Chicago would rise to the top of the rock pile. With hundreds of venues, scores of recording studios, talented managers and enthusiastic audiences, the ascent seems likely. However, it remains to be seen whether a recognizable "Chicago-style" rock will coalesce from the diverse scene.

Classical Music – Chicago's considerable classical music heritage harkens back to early city elite who wished to convey a sophisticated image of Chicago by encouraging the development of "high culture." The first orchestra performed in 1850, and an opera house opened in 1865. Visiting artists and ensembles reinforced a taste for the classical, and by 1891 city boosters realized that a permanent orchestra would enhance Chicago's reputation. The **Chicago Symphony Orchestra (CSO)** was thus founded under the direction of Theodore Thomas of New York. Over the years, the CSO has grown in stature under the batons of such luminaries as Frederick Stock, Fritz Reiner, Sir Georg Solti and most recently, Daniel Barenboim.

Opera has always found a willing audience in Chicago, but the grand Italian style is expensive to produce, and at least six major companies have come and gone over the years. Finally in 1954, under the visionary leadership of Carol Fox, the **Lyric Opera** opened its first season with a performance of *Norma* featuring Maria Callas in her American debut. Current director Ardis Krainik's respect for the old and enthusiasm for the new—Philip Glass and Peter Sellars, for instance—have made the Lyric one of the world's most exciting opera companies. Small ensembles, choruses and ethnic companies abound in Chicago, and early music is particularly popular, especially when performed by Music of the Baroque, now the largest professional chorus and orchestra of its kind in the country.

Visual Arts

Chicago is today a city of great museums, ubiquitous public sculpture, active arts organizations, insightful critics, enthusiastic collectors and innovative artists, but a tension between its origins in industry and commerce and its early aspirations to gentility has played a major role in its uneasy artistic growth.

A Matter of Taste – The World's Columbian Exposition of 1893 did much to establish an artistic aesthetic that prevailed in the city for 40 years. The ART INSTITUTE of Chicago had been founded in 1879, and its president Charles L. Hutchinson believed strongly in the power of great art to uplift the human spirit and counter civic and commercial corruption. He also felt that a respected art museum would elevate Chicago's image. In the same vein, the hardworking industrial city hoped that the glittering Beaux-Arts World's Fair would appear sophisticated and genteel to the rest of the world, proving conclusively that though their money had been made in railroads and meat packing, Chicago's elite had also developed considerable taste. More than 10,000 art objects crowded the huge Palace of Fine Arts (p 182), most of them European works of conservative appeal. Volume and predictability, it seems, equaled culture.

Perhaps the best representative local artist of the day was sculptor **Lorado Taft**, whose works can be seen today in parks and cemeteries throughout the city. Employing a highly allegorical style, Taft believed, like his peers, in the ennobling power of art. His monumental *Fountain of the Great Lakes* (1913), outside the South Wing of the Art Institute, was the first public sculpture to be underwritten by the Ferguson Fund, established in 1905 (and still extant) by wealthy lumberman Benjamin Franklin Ferguson to decorate Chicago with European-style monuments. Even the School of the Art Institute, the Midwest's preeminent academy of the fine arts, trained students under the French academic plan, emphasizing the naturalistic rendering of the human form and the copying of classical art.

Among collectors, the impetus to acquire art was inspired largely by investment value and fashion, and focused on the works of European artists. The lavish collecting style of the Potter Palmers, eventually responsible for much of the Art Institute's famous French Impressionist collection, contrasted sharply with the more curatorial approach of later collectors like Arthur Jerome Eddy and Frederic Clay Bartlett, who championed the Modernist movements of the teens and twenties.

Turning Point – In 1913, the controversial **Armory Show** contested public taste by introducing Modernism into this milieu. The works of, among others, Gauguin, Picasso and Duchamp met with widespread chagrin, moving students at the School of the Art Institute to hang Matisse in effigy. Chicago's art world faced off: no-jury exhibitions challenged the conservative standards of the Art Institute and a new echelon of collectors promoted the avant-garde. A community of Modernists began to grow, among them painter **Rudolph Weisenborn** (*Chicago*, 1928), who may be best remembered for organizing several anti-establishment artists' groups. Highly diverse in style, Chicago's young artists shared instead a rejection of formal art training and, like abstract master Wassily Kandinsky (1866-1944), sought the inspiration of inner experience, a common thread in subsequent Chicago art. Finally, by 1933, the Century of Progress Exposition proudly proclaimed Chicago's embrace of the modern. The Art Institute exhibited 27 galleries of Modern art, signaling a mainstream acceptance of the movement.

From the American Scene to the Imagists – Some Chicago artists of the 1920s and 1930s combined elements of Modernism and Realism to depict the urban landscape around them, making the city a center of American scene painting. Inspired by the brief teaching stint of social realist George Bellows at the School of the Art Institute, painters like Emil Armin (*Towers*, 1931) and Ramon Shiva (*Chicago MCMXXIV*, 1924) rendered the city with an expressionistic edge and an honesty reminiscent of New York's Ash Can school. African-American painter **Archibald Motley, Jr.** (1891-1981) created lively scenes of life in Chicago's black neighborhoods (*Black Belt*, 1934). Linked to the larger Regionalist movement made popular by Art Institute students **Grant Wood**, John Steuart Curry and Thomas Benton, the Chicago scene painters shared a sense of place, recognizing Chicago's gritty urban landscape to be as legitimate a subject as the French countryside.

Members of the most recognizable Chicago "school" came to be known in the 1960s as **Imagists**. Precursors of the movement included **Ivan Albright** (*That Which I Should Have Done I Did Not Do*, 1931-41), whose disturbing canvases express a personal vision rather than an external reality, and artists June Leaf, H. C. Westermann and Leon Golub. Their work, dubbed "monster art" for its totemic, elemental style, drew inspiration from the Art Brut movement of the 1950s popularized by Jean Dubuffet (1901-1985). The Imagists, too, relied heavily on inner experience and personal imagery; their disparate work catalogues a fantastical world of organic abstraction with stronger ties to Surrealism than to the Abstract Expressionism of Jackson Pollock. Among the best known of the Imagists were the **Hairy Who**, a band of artists—including Gladys Nilsson, Art Green, Karl Wirsum, James Falconer and Suellen Rocca—whose group shows in the 1960s set off a flurry of outrageous exhibits that were part theater and part art. From the vibrant and ambiguous portraits of **Ed Paschke** (*Elcina*, 1973) to the darkly comic, misshapen figures of Jim Nutt (*Is This the Right Way*, 1979), the figurative fantasies of Imagism have influenced a generation of Chicago artists.

Adria by Ed Paschke, 1976

Museum of Contemporary Art

The Contemporary Scene – In recent years, Chicago has seen a burgeoning of interest in art and a commensurate increase in related activities. Since 1967, the MUSEUM OF CONTEMPORARY ART has made the artists of the avant-garde accessible to a broad and eager audience. That same year came the unveiling of the 50ft Picasso sculpture *(p 56)* in Daley Plaza, one of Chicago's first noncommemorative public artworks. Public sculpture has since proliferated, thanks in part to the Percent for Art Program enacted by the city in 1978, which mandates that one percent of the cost of every city project with public access be applied toward the purchase of art for the site. The million-dollar collection at the HAROLD WASHINGTON LIBRARY CENTER represents the largest project the program has undertaken.

A new generation of artists seeking inspiration beyond Imagism emerged in the late 1980s, fueling a phenomenal boom in the number and popularity of art galleries. At the same time, the WICKER PARK neighborhood grew into one of the country's most popular habitats for young artists. Art Chicago, the latest of several prestigious international art expositions held each spring at Navy Pier, ranks among the world's leading art marketplaces.

The Other Arts – Chicago occupies an undisputed place in the history of design and photography. European Modernist **Laszlo Moholy-Nagy** brought the principles of the German Bauhaus to the city in 1937, establishing a school that would evolve into the Institute of Design, a part of the ILLINOIS INSTITUTE OF TECHNOLOGY since 1949. The holistic curriculum reflected a well-integrated variety of disciplines from industrial and graphic design to architecture. As a center for the teaching of photography as art, the school boasts a fine roster of instructors over the years—Harry Callahan, Arthur Siegel and Aaron Siskind among them—as well as a long list of prominent graduates. Major collections of photography are located at the Art Institute and the MUSEUM OF CONTEMPORARY PHOTOGRAPHY.

" Chicago is the archetypal American city...
For visitors who are interested in a city that's really America,
this would be the one to visit."

Studs Terkel

Literature

The explosive growth that propelled Chicago from frontier outpost to major industrial center far surpassed any development in the arts—including literature—or in other refinements associated with civilization. The city throbbed with power, and when a literary culture did bloom in the late 19C, it was indelibly marked by the earthy, money-grubbing nature of the immigrant metropolis. Its tradition of social realism and street-level literature continues to present-day with columnist Mike Royko, interviewer Studs Terkel and poet Gwendolyn Brooks.

Literature in the Capitol of Capital – The writings emerging in Chicago during the mid-19C were indistinguishable from the mass of other moralistic or romantic works churned out by artists from London to New York to Los Angeles. Only after the 1893 Columbian Exposition focused world attention on this vibrant city did local writers emerge with a style to match the pace of Chicago life. During that frenetic decade, the city began to reduce its cultural shortcomings by erecting a new art institute (1893) and the first permanent library (1897), and by developing its musical and literary tastes. Still, the business of Chicago was business, and writers focused on the race to riches in novels like *The Cliff Dwellers* (1893) and *With the Procession* (1895) by Henry Blake Fuller, and *The Pit: A Story of Chicago* (1904) by Frank Norris. These early social realists, part of the **Little Room** salon, began exploring the contradictions of a society which, though modeled on democracy, favored the industrial elite over the working classes. This was the first literary school to look at both the front and the back, at the public and the private, and in so doing, discovered subject matter so rich that it remains fertile to this day.

Best known of these early novels is **Upton Sinclair's** *The Jungle* (1906), a stark, heartwrenching story meant to waken awareness of the plight of immigrant workers; instead, it fomented a reform of food laws following Sinclair's harrowing descriptions of life in the stockyards. Lamented the author: "I aimed at the public's heart, but by accident I hit it in the stomach." Probably the most important novel of the period was **Theodore Dreiser**'s *Sister Carrie*, written in 1900 but suppressed until 1912 due to the risqué nature of the story, which celebrates a heroine who parlays

---

Chicago *(Carl Sandburg, 1916)*

Hog Butcher for the World,
Tool Maker, Stacker of Wheat,
Player with Railroads and the Nation's Freight Handler;
Stormy, husky, brawling,
City of the Big Shoulders:

They tell me you are wicked and I believe them, for I have seen your
  painted women under the gas lamps luring the farm boys.
And they tell me you are crooked and I answer: Yes, it is true I have
  seen the gunman kill and go free to kill again.
And they tell me you are brutal and my reply is: On the faces of women
  and children I have seen the marks of wanton hunger.
And having answered so I turn once more to those who sneer at this
  my city, and I give them back the sneer and say to them:
Come and show me another city with lifted head singing so proud to
  be alive and coarse and strong and cunning.
Flinging magnetic curses amid the toil of piling job on job, here is a tall
  bold slugger set vivid against the little soft cities;
Fierce as a dog with tongue lapping for action, cunning as a savage
  pitted against the wilderness,
    Bareheaded,
    Shoveling,
    Wrecking,
    Planning,
    Building, breaking, rebuilding,
Under the smoke, dust all over his mouth, laughing with white teeth,
Under the terrible burden of destiny laughing as a young man laughs,
Laughing even as an ignorant fighter laughs who has never lost a battle,
Bragging and laughing that under his wrist is the pulse, and under his
  ribs the heart of the people,
    Laughing!
Laughing the stormy, husky, brawling laughter of Youth, half-naked,
  sweating, proud to be Hog Butcher, Tool Maker, Stacker of
Wheat, Player with Railroads and Freight Handler to the Nation.

her lost innocence into a successful career. It inspired the next generation of Chicago writers, who peered behind every street lamp and back alley in their search for the raw, rude stories of a fast-paced American city.

Many Chicago writers worked for the newspapers, and added a journalistic and often humorous strain to the Chicago tradition, as seen in Finley Peter Dunne's "Mr. Dooley" series and Ring Lardner's fictionalized sports stories. Some preferred fantasy to the starkness of urban life: Frank L. Baum and artist William Denslow completed the American classic *The Wizard of Oz* in 1900; and Edgar Rice Burroughs' 1912 *Tarzan* series was inspired by his visits to the Lincoln Park Zoo.

Carl Sandburg, c.1925

Chicago Literary Renaissance – In 1911 Harriet Monroe, whose "Columbian Ode" celebrated the 1893 World's Fair, founded *Poetry* magazine. The publication included the pioneering work of poets Marianne Moore and William Carlos Williams, and created a stir by publishing the modern, free verse works of T. S. Eliot and Carl Sandburg. Margaret Anderson's *Little Review* was born at the Fine Arts Building (*p 46*) in 1914. In it she serialized James Joyce's *Ulysses*, a novel that so scandalized conservative Midwesterners that the US Postal Service refused to handle the magazine; by 1917, both Anderson and her pathbreaking review had left town for New York. The year 1915 saw the publication of Edgar Lee Masters' *Spoon River Anthology*, a stark portrayal of the underside of small-town life. Sherwood Anderson continued the tradition of exposing rural America's hidden foibles in *Windy MacPherson's Son* (1916) and *Winesburg, Ohio* (1919), while Dreiser created more novels on the failings of the American Dream with *The Financier* (1912) and *The Titan* (1914). While a reporter for the

Milestones in Chicago Literary History

| 1872 — 1903 — 1912 — 1916 — 1935 |

1872
E.P. Roe, *Barriers Burned Away*

1880
The Dial founded

1893
Harriet Monroe, *Columbian Ode*

Henry Blake Fuller, *The Cliff Dwellers*

1895
Henry Blake Fuller, *With the Procession*

1900
Theodore Dreiser writes *Sister Carrie*. Frank L. Baum and William Denslow complete *The Wizard of Oz*

1903
Will Payne, *Mr. Salt*

1904
Robert Herrick, *The Common Lot*

Frank Norris, *The Pit: A Story of Chicago*

1906
Upton Sinclair, *The Jungle*

1909
Jane Addams, *Twenty Years at Hull-House*

1911
Harriet Monroe founds *Poetry* magazine

1912
Sister Carrie released

1914
Margaret Anderson founds *The Little Review*. Theodore Dreiser, *The Titan*

1915
Edgar Lee Masters, *Spoon River Anthology*. Willa Cather, *The Song of the Lark*. Sherwood Anderson, *Windy McPherson's Son*

1916
Carl Sandburg, *Chicago Poems*. Ring Lardner, *You Know Me Al*

1919
Sherwood Anderson, *Winesburg, Ohio*

1920
Floyd Dell, *The Moon-Calf*

1928
Ben Hecht and Charles MacArthur, *The Front Page*

1929-34
James T. Farrell writes *Studs Lonigan* trilogy

1935
Willa Cather, *Lucy Gayheart*

Chicago Daily News, **Carl Sandburg** published his *Chicago Poems* (1916) and later won a Pulitzer Prize for his biography of Abraham Lincoln. Sandburg's poem "Chicago" *(p 29)* remains the most frequently quoted description of the "City of the Big Shoulders."

The Daily News and the Depression – The Chicago literary renaissance ebbed in the 1920s, but the gutsy, lusty style of Chicago writing continued at the *Chicago Daily News*, where reporters Ben Hecht and Charles MacArthur penned *The Front Page* (1928), a hilarious send-up of journalistic moxie. Like many Chicago writers, the pair tasted success and soon moved to New York. The *Daily News* was also home to Eugene Field, the "children's poet" who rhymed the classics "Wynken, Blynken and Nod" and "Little Boy Blue."

The Depression set the tone for a return to social realism, and the Federal Writers' Project brought together the next generation of authors, including James T. Farrell, **Richard Wright**, **Nelson Algren**, **Gwendolyn Brooks**, Studs Terkel and Saul Bellow. Farrell recollected his rowdy Washington Park youth in the *Studs Lonigan* trilogy (1935), while Wright's epochal *Native Son* (1940), set on the South Side, launched a career that took him not only out of Chicago but out of the country whose racism he so eloquently exposed. The publication of Algren's first novel *Never Come Morning* (1942) was marred by the political reaction of Chicago's Polish community, who cringed at having its seamy underside exposed. Algren achieved greater success describing a war veteran hooked on morphine and poker in *The Man With the Golden Arm* (1949). Brooks—first black female Pulitzer Prize winner (1949)—published her first collection of poems, *A Street in Bronzeville*, in 1945, and remained in Chicago despite her fame. Today she is Poet Laureate of the State of Illinois.

The Last Few Decades – Oak Park native **Ernest Hemingway** was awarded the 1954 Nobel Prize for Literature for his magnificent *The Old Man and the Sea*. Lorraine Hansberry completed *A Raisin in the Sun* in 1959 before leaving for New York. Two writers emerged in the 1960s and 70s from the old Federal Writers' Project circle: **Saul Bellow** and **Studs Terkel**. Bellow released a series of novels that culminated in *Humboldt's Gift*, for which he received the 1976 Nobel Prize, while Terkel honed his skills as the nation's best interviewer with his television and radio programs and award-winning oral histories, including *Division Street America* (1967), *Working* (1974) and *The Good War* (1984). Newspaper columnist Mike Royko captured Mayor Richard J. Daley in *Boss* (1971), and works to carry on the tradition of Algren, Sandburg and Dreiser. Current literary figures include mystery writer Sara Paretsky, Larry Heineman *(Paco's Song)* and Sandra Cisneros *(The House on Mango Street)*.

1940

1940
Richard Wright,
Native Son

1942
Nelson Algren,
*Never Come
Morning*

1944
Saul Bellow,
Dangling Man

1945
Gwendolyn Brooks,
*A Street in
Bronzeville*

1949
Nelson Algren,
*The Man with the
Golden Arm*

Gwendolyn Brooks,
Annie Allen

1950

1951
Nelson Algren, *Chicago:
City on the Make*

1953
Hugh Hefner creates
Playboy magazine

1954
Saul Bellow,
*The Adventures of
Augie March.*
Nobel Prize to
Ernest Hemingway

1959
Lorraine Hansberry,
A Raisin in the Sun

1960
Gwendolyn Brooks,
The Bean Eaters

1960

1965

1965
Saul Bellow, *Herzog*

1967
Studs Terkel,
*Division Street
America*

1971
Mike Royko, *Boss:
Richard J. Daley of
Chicago*

1974
Studs Terkel,
Working

1975
Saul Bellow,
Humboldt's Gift

1975

1976
Nobel Prize to
Saul Bellow

1982

1982
Saul Bellow,
*The Dean's
December*

31

Architecture

For over a century, Chicago has been the capital of modern architecture. In the years following the Great Fire of 1871, architects came from all over the country to help rebuild the world's fastest-growing city and in the process created the skyscraper—America's great contribution to architecture. Chicago also nurtured the Prairie school architects who followed Frank Lloyd Wright in developing the clean horizontal lines of the modern American residence. The city remains a mecca for an international coterie of architects wishing to leave their mark on the famous skyline.

From Sticks to Steel – The earliest buildings date to the city's founding in the 1830s and exhibit the design features of the Greek Revival style *(p 36)* popular throughout Jacksonian America. In 1833 Chicago wrought its first architectural innovation with the development of the "**balloon frame**," so dubbed because it supposedly made house construction as easy as blowing up a balloon. Balloon framing involved the substitution of thin plates and studs, held together only by nails, for the ancient and expensive system of mortise and tenon joints. This method permitted the rapid construction of economical, lightweight buildings and was particularly suited to the Chicago area's relative lack of forest. Unfortunately, the preponderance of structures made of small timbers meant that the city was built of kindling, as it learned following the dry summer of 1871, when the Great Fire leveled the budding metropolis.

Frederick Wacker House, 1874

Wood-frame construction was banned after the Fire, but intact rail connections and industry ensured that the city would be rebuilt, and soon architects and engineers migrated en masse to Chicago. At first, the city resembled its pre-1871 self, as local architects John Mills Van Osdel and William Boyington rebuilt a downtown of 4- and 5-story Italianate buildings—often from pre-Fire plans. However, the Great Fire had proved that even cast-iron facades were vulnerable, and Chicago architects were called upon to develop better fire prevention techniques.

William Le Baron Jenney, trained at the Ecole Polytechnique and Ecole Centrale in Paris and a Civil War engineer, came to Chicago in 1870 to design the West Parks and Boulevards. Jenney advocated an iconoclastic "Western" style of architecture in contrast to the European models employed on the nation's East Coast and helped train Chicago school architects Louis Sullivan, William Holabird and Martin Roche. It was Jenney who developed the skeletal steel frame that allowed skyscrapers to be built. The steel members were sheathed in brick for fire prevention, and his 1884 Home Insurance Building (demolished 1929) was the first true skyscraper. In traditional masonry construction, the walls support the weight of the building. Jenney reversed this previously unquestioned principle of architecture. For the first time, the building supported the walls, which could be draped on the frame like a curtain. Since less space was needed for support, larger windows and hence more light and air could be admitted to upper-floor office spaces. This principle, called curtain-wall construction, made possible the development of modern high rises.

Other technical problems needed to be overcome to allow for buildings of more than 8 or 10 stories. First, the refinement of the elevator in the 1870s provided efficient vertical transportation. Secondly, Jenney and other Chicago architects developed a series of bracing techniques to reduce the effects of wind on tall buildings. A more difficult problem was posed by foundations sinking in Chicago's swampy, shifting soil. John Wellborn Root developed a floating foundation for the Montauk Block in 1882 that allowed building loads to spread out and grab hold in the infirm soil. Adler & Sullivan improved on the design with the development of the caisson foundation, still used today.

The Chicago School – These innovations, conceived and executed within the decade of the 1880s, gave birth to the Chicago school of architecture, recognized as the first significant new architecture since the Italian High Renaissance and characterized by the work of four prominent firms. William Le Baron Jenney's engineering innovations exceeded his talent for facade design in buildings like the 1891 MANHATTAN BUILDING, but he also helped usher in the department store with his Second Leiter Building of the same year. The partnership of **Daniel Burnham & John Wellborn Root** constructed the Montauk Block (demolished) in 1882, and followed with the ROOKERY in 1896, which used a partial steel frame, floating foundations, and featured an elegant terra-cotta facade and stunning light court. In 1891, the firm also designed the tallest office building utilizing traditional masonry construction, the 16-story MONADNOCK BUILDING. After Root's untimely death in 1891, Burnham's firm turned to more traditional styles. One notable exception was the RELIANCE BUILDING of 1895, designed by **Charles B. Atwood**. With its protruding bays, huge windows and narrow bands of

Reliance Building, 1895

white terra-cotta ornament, the building anticipated the glass skyscrapers of the 1980s. **Dankmar Adler & Louis Sullivan** combined the former's engineering and acoustical genius with the latter's unparalleled gift for ornament in the stunning AUDITORIUM BUILDING of 1899. This edifice owed some debt to the work of Bostonian H. H. Richardson, who had begun to reinterpret Romanesque architecture in a distinctly American vein. The firm's finest office structures were the Chicago Stock Exchange (1894-1972) and the Prudential Building (1894) in Buffalo, New York. Sullivan went on to design the CARSON, PIRIE, SCOTT & CO. department store in 1899, where his ornamental designs explode onto the street. The firm of **William Holabird & Martin Roche** combined the Chicago school innovations into a formula that was repeated in over 80 Loop buildings. Their PONTIAC BUILDING of 1891, MARQUETTE BUILDING of 1894 and CHICAGO BUILDING of 1905 stand as excellent examples of Chicago school skyscrapers.

An American Style – "Form Follows Function"

– While many of the new skyscrapers were cloaked with traditional ornament, a significant number abandoned historical precedent, notably the 1891 Monadnock Building where the only modulation was provided by protruding bay windows and a gentle flaring at the roof and base. Sullivan, more than any other architect, enunciated the new design philosophy with the phrase "Form follows function" and encouraged an approach to high-rise construction which expressed the steel frame beneath. The base should be distinct as the entrance of the building, according to Sullivan, who favored a semicircular arched entrance. The top of the building should be an overhanging cornice that terminates the composition. Between the base and the top, the office

Chicago Historical Society (ICHi-13745)

Louis Sullivan by Frank A. Werner, 1919

33

floors should be identical and create a vertical effect so that the building would be "every inch a proud and soaring thing." Holabird & Roche effectively utilized the style, which saw the grid of steel girders expressed on the exterior in brick or terra-cotta, while the bulk of the wall plane was filled with Chicago windows, composed of a large fixed pane flanked by smaller sliding sashes.

The World's Columbian Exposition *(p 181)*, under the direction of Daniel Burnham, adopted a Neoclassical style to celebrate the new American empire. Louis Sullivan's acclaimed Transportation Building, with its telescoping arched entrance, was the only building at the Fair to follow Chicago school precedents. He later lamented that the Exposition set American architecture back for 50 years.

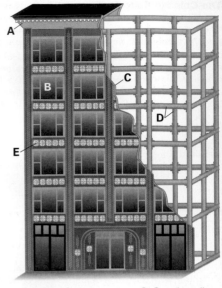

A Cornice
B Chicago-style window
C Curtain wall
D Steel frame
E Spandrel

The Prairie Style – As Sullivan was working on the pivotal Auditorium Building, he hired a young draftsman from Wisconsin, **Frank Lloyd Wright**, who left to form his own practice in 1893. In contrast to the soaring skyscrapers, Wright developed homes inspired by the flat Midwestern prairie, with overhanging eaves, horizontal lines and banded windows of stained glass. Wright also "broke the box" of traditional domestic architecture by allowing rooms to flow into one another, rather than organizing square rooms along long corridors. He eschewed attics and basements as unnecessary, and projected porches and rooflines in an attempt to meld building with landscape. His designs for UNITY TEMPLE and ROBIE HOUSE caused a worldwide stir when published in Germany in 1910. Contemporary George Washington Maher developed a more formal and symmetrical take on the horizontal Prairie style in a wealth of residential commissions at the turn of the century, while many other Prairie school architects learned their trade in Wright's OAK PARK office, including Walter Burley Griffin, Marion Mahoney Griffin, Francis Barry Byrne and John Van Bergen. Wright's practice became more eclectic in the 1920s after he left the Chicago area. Wright designed a "mile-high" skyscraper in his later years, but the horizontal lines of his early Chicago and Oak Park homes still define his role as America's most prominent architectural figure.

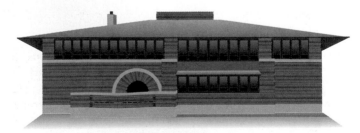

Arthur Heurtley House, 1902

Reaction and Revolution – By the 1910s, architectural styles in Chicago and America entered a conservative period, as new skyscrapers were clad in traditional styles, like the Renaissance-inspired PEOPLE'S GAS BUILDING of 1911 and the WRIGLEY BUILDING of 1921. In 1922, the *Chicago Tribune* held an international competition to design a new high rise for the newspaper, which drew 280 entries from around the world. While the winning design by Hood & Howells of New York had a Norman Gothic exterior, it was the second-place entry by Eliel Saarinen of Finland which garnered the approval of architectural critics for its modern verticality devoid of historical ornament. Saarinen's design also fit in with new zoning ordinances that called for stepped setbacks in high-rise construction. By 1928, Chicago boasted several Vertical style, or Art Deco skyscrapers, including 333 N. MICHIGAN AVENUE and the Palmolive Building *(p 85)* by Holabird & Root, the successor firm to Holabird & Roche, and the Daily News Building by Graham, Anderson, Probst & White, the successor firm to D.H. Burnham & Co.

International Style Comes to Chicago – The International style, which saw buildings as almost purely sculptural objects, originated in many ways with the Bauhaus of Germany in the 1920s and 30s. When the rize of Nazism precluded the modernistic innovations of the Bauhaus, one of its

leading lights, **Ludwig Mies van der Rohe**, emigrated to Chicago. As chairman of architecture at the ILLINOIS INSTITUTE OF TECHNOLOGY, Mies ushered in what came to be called the Second Chicago school. Following World War II, Mies designed new steel-and-concrete high rises in a completely stripped-down style where attached I beams provided the only ornament. Deceptively simple, the new architecture depended on a rigid calculation of proportion that allowed little room for error in design. Mies inspired a new generation of architects with designs like 860-880 N. LAKE SHORE DRIVE and the FEDERAL CENTER. Jacques Brownson of C.F. Murphy Assocs. contributed the 1965 RICHARD J. DALEY CENTER, perhaps the best Miesian building not designed by Mies.

Emerging as the premier firm in postwar Chicago, **Skidmore, Owings & Merrill** established an international practice in the design of modern high rises. The INLAND STEEL BUILDING of 1958 first expressed the possibilities of improved construction techniques with its column-free floors and double-glazed walls.

Ludwig Mies
van der Rohe, c.1961

Chicago Historical Society (HB-23200)

Engineer Fazlur Khan helped Skidmore create Chicago's modern landmarks, first with his innovative X-shaped cross bracing on the 1969 JOHN HANCOCK CENTER, and finally with the bundled-tube construction of the SEARS TOWER.

Post-Modern – The formula of the Skidmore firm held sway throughout the 1970s, as dark steel-and-glass office blocks filled Chicago's Loop. By 1980, the post-Modern movement had arrived, and in Chicago its standard-bearer was German-born Helmut Jahn, whose sculptural facades of mirrored glass seemed to echo the streamlined machine aesthetic of the Art Deco period. His Xerox Centre (now 55 WEST MONROE BUILDING) of 1980 led the way, followed by the daringly different JAMES R. THOMPSON CENTER of 1985 and United Airlines Terminal of 1990. Jahn is noted for his soaring interior atrium spaces. As the 1990s ushered in an era of real estate consolidation, Chicago also witnessed new buildings by architects from Japan, Spain, Italy and New York. Skidmore, Owings & Merrill joined the post-Modern fray with the 1989 NBC TOWER by Adrian Smith. A 1990 recession put a hold on plans for new skyscrapers in the Loop, including a proposed 125-story record-breaker designed by Cesar Pelli.

James R. Thompson Center, 1985

Architectural Glossary

Greek Revival (1820-1860) – Popular throughout America, the style adopts the pedimented, symmetrical order of Greek temples in a simplified vernacular form suitable for modest homes, grand mansions and larger public buildings. Classical columns in the Doric, Ionic and Corinthian order ornament the pedimented facade; roofs are often shallow, supported by a heavy cornice, and may include a cupola. The 1836 CLARKE HOUSE is a rare Chicago example.

Gothic Revival (1830-1870) – The picturesque, assymetrical forms of Gothic Revival facades often include towers, battlements and pointed-arch windows with leaded stained glass. Smaller homes have intricately decorated bargeboards at the eaves and steeply pitched roofs. The CHICAGO WATER TOWER is the city's most notable example.

Italianate (1840-1880) – This style defined much of 19C America through flat-roofed homes and storefronts with overhanging eaves and brackets. Long, narrow windows with rounded arches often include incised decoration at the lintels and sills. More elaborate homes in the style include rusticated corner quoins and a Classical cupola or tower modeled on Italian villas. The cast-iron front was usually Italianate, as seen in Chicago's PAGE BROTHERS BUILDING and Berghoff Restaurant (*p 52*). A good residential example is the NICKERSON HOUSE.

Second Empire (1860-1880) – Inspired by Baron Hausmann's redesign of Paris in the 1850s, this grandiose style is characterized by the short, steeply pitched mansard roof pierced by dormer windows. Generally symmetrical facades include quoined corners, projecting bays, windows flanked by pilasters, balustrades and an abundance of Classical decoration. Often mansard roofs were added to Italianate buildings in a close approximation of the style. Examples can be found in the JACKSON BOULEVARD and WICKER PARK Historic Districts of Chicago.

Romanesque Revival (1860-1900) – The round arches, deeply inset windows and door openings and rough stone finishes of the Romanesque style suggest medieval castles and inspired architects attempting to create permanence amid the rapidly changing landscape of late-19C America. The style was refined by Boston architect **H.H. Richardson**, who designed the JOHN JACOB GLESSNER HOUSE in 1886. Burnham & Root's ST. GABRIEL'S CHURCH is a fine example, as are the former Chicago Historical Society and the NEWBERRY LIBRARY by Henry Ives Cobb.

Queen Anne (1870-1900) – This style is the one most commonly identified as "Victorian" with its assymetrical composition, exuberant ornamentation and picturesque design marked by conical towers, projecting bays, elaborately decorated dormers and gables. Adapted to both large residences and city row houses, the style is found throughout Chicago's historic districts, especially OLD TOWN, PULLMAN and Wicker Park.

Chicago School (1880-1910) – The design of the world's first skyscrapers celebrated their engineering and purpose, summed up by Louis Sullivan's phrase "Form follows function." The steel-framed buildings express their construction in a grid-like facade of brick or terra-cotta, pierced by large areas of glass. A defined base, or entry level, is surmounted by a series of identical office floors with large "Chicago windows" characterized by a fixed single-pane window in the center flanked by smaller double-hung sliding sash windows. The roofline is capped by a cornice. The first 1880s skyscrapers borrowed elements of Romanesque, Italianate and Queen Anne architecture, but by 1894 most were adopting the new aesthetic of functionalism, eschewing historical ornament to create vertical sculptures made of piers, spandrels and windows. Four firms, **Adler & Sullivan, Burnham & Root,**

" Make no little plans; they have no magic to stir men's blood and probably themselves will not be realized. Make big plans; aim high in hope and work, remembering that a noble and logical diagram once recorded will never die, but long after we are gone will be a living thing, asserting itself with growing intensity. Remember that our sons and grandsons are going to do things that would stagger us. Let your watchword be 'order' and your beacon 'beauty.' "

The oft-repeated exhortation of Daniel Burnham

Holabird & Roche, and William Le Baron Jenney, are the standard-bearers of the Chicago school and are credited with establishing the Modern movement in the US. Chicago's ROOKERY and MONADNOCK BUILDING epitomize the early Chicago school, while the MARQUETTE and CHICAGO BUILDINGS demonstrate its maturity. The RELIANCE BUILDING of 1895 is agreed to be a worldwide landmark, prefiguring the present-day glass-and-steel skyscrapers.

Neoclassical or Beaux-Arts (1893-1920) – The success of the 1893 World's Columbian Exposition brought a revival of Roman imperial architecture—symbolizing the rise of the American Republic as a world power. Unlike the simpler Greek Revival, Neoclassical architecture revels in ornamentation and often features sumptuous interiors. Arched and arcaded windows, balustrades at every level, grand staircases, applied columns, decorative swags, garlands and even statuary embellish the edifices. A good residential example is 1500 N. Astor Street *(p 117)* in the GOLD COAST. Sometimes called Beaux-Arts for its association with Paris' Ecole des Beaux-Arts, the style was well-suited to public and cultural buildings, such as the 1893 ART INSTITUTE and 1897 CHICAGO CULTURAL CENTER.

Prairie Style (1895-1915) – Largely identified with Frank Lloyd Wright *(p 191)*, the Prairie style "broke the box" of traditional residential architecture by creating low, horizontal compositions inspired by the flat Midwestern prairie. Roofs are very shallow in pitch and have long, overhanging eaves. Windows are casements rather than double-hung, and are often arranged in broad bands of stained and leaded glass. Roman brick with raked horizontal joints further emphasizes the horizontal, and entrances are no longer the organizing principle of the home's facade—indeed, the entrance is often hidden. Interior rooms flow into each other rather than being organized around corridors. Attics, basements and ancillary spaces are rare. Many of the style's premier examples are in Chicago and OAK PARK, including Wright's Robie House, Unity Temple, Heurtley House and Laura Gale House.

Arts and Crafts (1895-1920) – In response to the dehumanization of machines in the industrial age, Englishmen William Morris and John Ruskin called for a return to handcrafted articles of everyday life and reveled in simplicity. Frank Lloyd Wright and others responded to the movement, which in architecture is characterized by overhanging wooden beams, delicately mortised together to form the gable ends and porches of homes.

Art Deco or Moderne (1925-1940) – Rejecting the revivalist tradition, the Art Deco style first appeared as a style of decoration during the 1925 "Exposition Internationale des Arts Décoratifs et Industriels Modernes" in Paris. US zoning laws, which called for skyscrapers to "step back" to provide light and air to the street, helped define the architectural aspects of Art Deco, which favored setbacks and piers to emphasize verticality. Often designed in smooth stone or terra-cotta shiny surfaces, edifices featured highly stylized carved ornament in low relief with a pronounced muscularity and abstraction, recessed windows and spandrels. Chicago examples include the CHICAGO BOARD OF TRADE, 333 N. MICHIGAN AVENUE and the Field Building.

International Style (1930-1970) – Applied ornament is abandoned for sleek, sculptural lines in buildings, furniture and other designed objects, summarized by Mies' dictum "Less is more." Concrete, glass and steel are celebrated in buildings with box-like massing and raised lobbies surrounded by arcaded overhangs. Exterior walls of glass and steel minimize both ornament and modulation, deriving their design from proportion and materials alone, allowing the structures to express their function. 860-880 N. LAKE SHORE DRIVE and the FEDERAL CENTER by Mies, along with the RICHARD J. DALEY CENTER by C. F. Murphy Assocs. are some of the best examples in Chicago.

Post-Modern Style (1975-present) – This style is characterized by cavalier application of historical elements and references to buildings that express modern materials of mirrored glass, concrete and surfaces generally more colorful and modulated than the severe lines of the International style. Helmut Jahn brought the style to Chicago with his 1980 Xerox Centre, now 55 WEST MONROE BUILDING, and exposed both its ambition and failings in his 1985 JAMES R. THOMPSON CENTER and CITICORP CENTER. By 1990, the post-Modern style had adopted a sometimes eclectic mode with Art Deco homages like the 1989 NBC TOWER by Adrian Smith of Skidmore, Owings & Merrill.

Sports

Chicago's muscle-bound image is nowhere more apparent than in the fanaticism of its sports enthusiasts. The *Saturday Night Live* "Superfans" skit parodied supporters of "Da Bears" for years after their lone Super Bowl victory in 1986, and the team remains a paragon of old-style, smash-mouth ground-game football that eschews the ballet of long passes. In baseball, both White Sox and Cubs fans are devotedly loyal despite the fact that neither team has won a World Series since World War I. Although the nation's professional baseball and football leagues trace their origins to Chicago, it was basketball superstar **Michael Jordan** and three consecutive NBA titles (1991-93) that gave the city its most dominant sports team and a personality to outshine mobster Al Capone in worldwide notoriety.

Baseball – The **Chicago Cubs** are the oldest original franchise in professional sports, dating back to the founding of the National League by team president Walter A. Hulbert in 1876. Nicknamed the "lovable losers" of the North Side, the Cubs last played in a World Series in 1945 and last won one in 1908. In 1916, the team moved to their present home of WRIGLEY FIELD, which hosted several World Series in the 1920s and 30s. The 1969 season saw the first-place Cubs fade in the face of the New York "Miracle Mets," denying star slugger **Ernie Banks** a shot at the World Series. The team was purchased from the Wrigley family by the Tribune Company in 1981, and has had some moderate success with division titles in 1984 and 1989.

Members of the American League, the **Chicago White Sox** (founded in 1901) draw support from South Siders. In 1989, the State of Illinois built a new COMISKEY PARK, replacing a 1910 stadium that hosted the first All-Star game and the first Negro League All-Star game. White Sox fans are undying in their support of a team that last went to a World Series in 1959 and last won one in 1917. In 1920, the "Black Sox" scandal revealed that eight players in the 1919 World Series had conspired to "throw" the games for gamblers. The infamous episode is best remembered by a child's legendary confrontation with **"Shoeless Joe" Jackson**, when he sobbingly asked the star slugger to "Say it ain't so, Joe!" When the team advanced to the World Series in 1959, Mayor Richard Daley set off air-raid sirens, frightening a portion of the populace. Recently the team has reemerged as a contender, winning division titles in 1983 and 1993.

■ Legend of the Lovable Losers

The Chicago Cubs have not won a World Series since 1908 and have not appeared in the fall classic since 1945. Cub fans have wallowed in failure for so long that in 1989, newspaper columnist Mike Royko popularized a new baseball statistic invented by local writer Ron Berler: the ex-Cub factor. Essentially, the claim is that any baseball team with three or more former Cubs players cannot win the World Series, having been "infected" by association with the lovable losers. Each year, Royko points out which teams will be unable to triumph because they have too many ex-Cubs on their roster. To date, the ex-Cub factor has proved to be an accurate prognosticator. Another local legend began when Sam Sianis, owner of the Billy Goat Tavern *(p 78)*, was denied entry into Wrigley Field with his famous pet goat and placed a curse on the team to prevent its success. Years later, Sianis' son was invited by Cub management to attend a game with his goat to remove the curse, but even this bit of ungulate hoodoo has not brought success to the North Siders.

Football – The University of Chicago produced a Big Ten conference powerhouse in the early 1900s—the "Monsters of the Midway" under coach Amos Alonzo Stagg. Football was abolished there in 1939, leaving Northwestern University to carry on the Big Ten tradition at Dyche Stadium in Evanston. **George S. Halas** founded the Chicago Bears and the National Football League in 1920, pioneering the "T" formation and launching a team defined by defense and running plays. Known for ferocious tacklers like **Dick Butkus** and elusive runners like **Gale Sayers** and **Walter Payton**, the Bears won their only Super Bowl in 1986, a dominating victory that prompted tens of thousands of fans to celebrate in the streets despite the icy cold. In 1971, the Bears moved from Wrigley Field to SOLDIER FIELD for their home games, and now seek a new stadium.

Barry Gossage/NBA

Michael Jordan and the Chicago Bulls

Basketball – Professional basketball was a latecomer to this sports-minded city: the Chicago Bulls were formed in 1966, seventy years after the University of Chicago beat the University of Iowa in the first modern college basketball game in 1896. The Bulls' first championship came in stellar fashion in 1991 as **Michael "Air" Jordan** led the team to the first of three consecutive titles. Jordan retired in 1993 and dabbled in baseball before returning to Chicago in 1995 to try to help the team obtain another championship. The Bulls play in the new UNITED CENTER on the Near West Side.

Hockey – Like many North American cities, Chicago has a small but devoted cadre of hard-core hockey fans who regularly fill the seats of the United Center. The Blackhawks last won the coveted Stanley Cup in 1961 and earned a 1967 division title thanks to stars **Bobby Hull** and **Stan Mikita**.

Boxing – Chicago earned brief renown as a national boxing center in the early 20C, when Soldier Field was selected as the site for the "Long Count" championship, allowing heavyweight Gene Tunney to beat Jack Dempsey in 1927. Ten years later, Joe Louis began his string of victories with a triumph over Jim Braddock at Comiskey Park, while the Chicago Stadium hosted middleweight Sugar Ray Robinson's epic 1951 defeat of Jake LaMotta and Rocky Marciano's win over Jersey Joe Walcott in 1953. The city's heyday came to an end in the 1950s when the Supreme Court ruled that its International Boxing Club held an unfair monopoly.

Other – In 1895, the *Chicago Times-Herald* sponsored the first automobile race in America, a 54mi affair completed by only two vehicles. The Chicago Golf Club in suburban Wheaton built the first 18-hole course in the US, and the Chicago area hosts the second oldest US golf tournament, the **Western Open**, most recently at Cog Hill in Lemont. Every summer, colorful yachts ply the deep waters of Lake Michigan in the longest (333mi) freshwater race in the world—the **Chicago to Mackinac Island Race**. In 1994, Chicago hosted the first **World Cup** soccer match in the United States as Germany defeated Bolivia 1-0.

■ **Bear Weather**

Chicagoans can be proud of their harsh winters. Bears fans often speak of the advantages of "Bear Weather" to their home team, which has always played outdoors and has cultivated a tough, "smash-mouth" image. Recently, local journalists have exposed the "Bear Weather" myth, revealing that the team is just as likely to lose as win when the weather is inclement. Harder to dispute is the fact that the Bears are cursed on *Monday Night Football*, losing almost twice as often as winning. The 1985 Bears' only loss came on a Monday. The team's recent reliance on a passing game—in conflict with the Bears' earthy image—and the threat of a domed stadium in the future has many locals predicting the apocalypse.

Sights

Downtown

THE LOOP ★★★

Time: 1 day. **CTA** Brown or Orange line to Adams; Red or Blue line to Jackson.
Map pp 44-45

Source and center of Chicago, the Loop forms the heart of a commercial metropolis that invented the skyscraper and the department store. Culture, commerce and politics are focused in an area bordered on the north and west by the Chicago River, on the east by Lake Michigan and on the south by Congress Parkway. Originally a muddy swamp, today this bustling and hustling district is an outdoor museum of architecture and sculpture girdled by a loop of steel elevated tracks.

Historical Notes

A Prairie Grows Wild – Chicago began as a frontier trading post at the intersection of Lake Michigan and the Chicago River, hunkered in the shadow of Fort Dearborn. Set between the watersheds of the Great Lakes and the Mississippi, the site offered the possibility of an inland waterway connecting New York to New Orleans, and the canal planners laid out the original Loop city grid at the mouth of the river in 1830. The ILLINOIS & MICHIGAN CANAL opened in 1848, followed immediately by railroads. Soon Chicago became the largest railroad center and fastest-growing city in the world, expanding from barely 4,000 people in 1837 to 30,000 in 1850 and then tenfold to 300,000 by 1870. The city's growth reflected the nation's growth, as products and people passed through Chicago's formidable rail and shipping network, supplying lumber and steel to the emerging West and grain and meat to the established East. By the 1880s, a ring of cable car tracks linking neighborhoods to the downtown had created the "Loop" sobriquet, a nickname made official by the 1897 construction of the Union Loop Elevated, connecting transit lines running north, west and south.

A City Reborn – On October 8, 1871, began a devastating fire *(p 11)* that would, in two days, destroy the entire Loop. While it was a monumental tragedy, it was also an opportunity. The city's industry and continental rail connections had not burned, and its commercial future was never in doubt. Architects Daniel Burnham, John Root, Louis Sullivan and William Holabird & Martin Roche were drawn to Chicago by the prospect of rebuilding a metropolis. Skyrocketing land values encouraged ever-taller buildings that allowed for more rentable space on each parcel of land. The straight lines of the city's grid gave rise to rows of rectangular buildings set next to each other. Pioneering skyscrapers like the Rookery, Monadnock, Marquette and Reliance Buildings illustrated an aesthetic that celebrated functionalism and helped usher in the modern world. Chicago architects sank foundations into the swampy soils, developed wind-bracing and fireproofing techniques, and erected continuously rising steel frames. They developed an artistry based on engineering that would be emulated worldwide. The 1890s witnessed the sudden emergence of the city's cultural venues as it sought to dispel its frontier, money-grubbing image. The Art Institute, public library and opera provided stylish landmarks to the Loop, while the newly

> " Here, of all her cities, throbbed the true life–the true power and spirit of America; gigantic, crude with the crudity of youth, disdaining rivalry; sane and healthy and vigorous; brutal in its ambition, arrogant in the new-found knowledge of its giant strength, prodigal of its wealth, infinite of its desires."
>
> Frank Norris, *The Pit*, 1904

wealthy were drawn by the shopping attractions of State Street's palatial department stores and the ostentatious Palmer House Hotel. Prior to the Great Fire, real estate investor Potter Palmer determined that State Street should replace Lake Street as the retail thoroughfare, and he lured Field, Leiter & Co. (later Marshall Field & Co.) to move their substantial dry goods business to the street—then lined by a disparate collection of laundries and stables.

The new Loop had distinct areas—the Water Street Market fronted the river, while LaSalle and Clark Streets hosted banks, attorneys and government offices. Lake Street's retail strength was dealt a permanent blow by the construction of the "L" in 1897, while State Street grew rapidly to the benefit of Palmer. Wabash Avenue mixed retail with music businesses, and Michigan Avenue evolved into a cultural boulevard stretching from the auspicious Auditorium Building to the grand Public Library. The SOUTH LOOP around the various train stations became a red light district, while theater marquees lined Randolph Street on the north.

20C Development – The Loop thrived as the economic, political and cultural heart of Chicago for the first half of the 20C. State Street became "that Great Street" with eight department stores, some a full block long. LaSalle Street became synonymous with the financial district, a half-mile canyon of stock exchanges, banks and businesses. Michigan Avenue added Orchestra Hall, new offices and private clubs to its impressive facade overlooking GRANT PARK. The nature of the Loop began to change in the 1920s as the famous 1909 Plan of Chicago was implemented. Grant Park was redesigned as a Beaux-Arts promenade, the South Water Market was relocated, allowing for the creation of 2-level Wacker Drive, while the Michigan Avenue Bridge spurred the development of the North Side.

High-rise construction continued until the Great Depression, and stunning Art Deco landmarks like the Board of Trade dominated the skyline, but the end of World War II heralded drastic change. The new automobile culture, with its suburban housing developments and shopping malls, threatened the vitality of an area defined by steel rails. The Loop became the retail center for the urban poor, accelerating the decline of State Street, which was being rapidly supplanted by North Michigan Avenue *(p 77)* as the principal commercial thoroughfare. While business and commerce continued to prod the erection of new skyscrapers after 1955, the Loop lost many of its retail and entertainment functions and became a "daytime" environment. By the early 1970s, the city declared the North Loop "slum and blighted" and pushed for its redevelopment, a move seen as a reaction to the African-American clientele of North Loop retailers and theaters. State Street was transformed into a pedestrian mall in 1978, but retail activity remained in a slump. *Plans to open State Street to vehicular traffic once again are on the drawing board (expected completion date: end 1996).*

Architecture continued to flourish. World-famous architects such as Helmut Jahn, Philip Johnson and Cesar Pelli flocked to the "home of the skyscraper" to erect new office towers along Wacker Drive in the 1980s before the 1990 recession halted construction. Today the Loop strives for its origins, encouraging residential and institutional uses along the older commercial streets and continuing to attract tourists with its cultural venues, public places, shopping and architecture.

① **WALKING TOUR**   *distance: 3.3mi*

A walking tour of the Loop combines the hustle and vitality of a commercial hub with a wonderful collection of art and architecture, including the Chicago skyscrapers that revolutionized architecture in the late 19C, towers of the Art Deco, International and post-Modern styles, and a panoply of modern sculpture. The Loop bustles with pedestrians from the predawn opening of the stock, commodities and options markets until early evening. *Note that sights located in the western section of the Loop, including the Sears Tower, appear after the Walking Tour.*

　Begin at Congress Pkwy. and S. Michigan Ave.

South Michigan Avenue★ forms the eastern facade of the Loop, a mile of attractive historic buildings facing Grant Park and presenting an inviting front door to the City on the Lake. Unfortunately, it is almost impossible to admire the detailing adorning the high rises from the sidewalk. Several good vantage points—including the front steps of the ART INSTITUTE—on the east side of the avenue afford splendid views of the elaborate facades.

★★ **Auditorium Building** – *430 S. Michigan Ave. Theater may be visited by guided tour (45min) only, year-round Mon–Fri 10am–6pm. $4. Reservations required.* ♿ 🄿 ☎312-431-2354. This 1889 building launched the career of architects **Dankmar Adler & Louis Sullivan**. Influenced by H. H. Richardson's Marshall Field Wholesale Store (demolished), the building was the tallest and heaviest structure in Chicago when completed, the first constructed under electric lights at night and a pioneering multiuse building, combining a 400-room hotel, a 17-story office tower and a 4,000-seat theater. The Auditorium influenced the design of the Congress Hotel (1893, Clinton J. Warren) located immediately to the south and originally called the Auditorium Annex hotel *(p 104)*.

The design of the theater by the engineer Adler is still considered an acoustic marvel: a young draftsman on the project named Frank Lloyd Wright called it "the greatest room for music and opera in the world—bar none." The Chicago

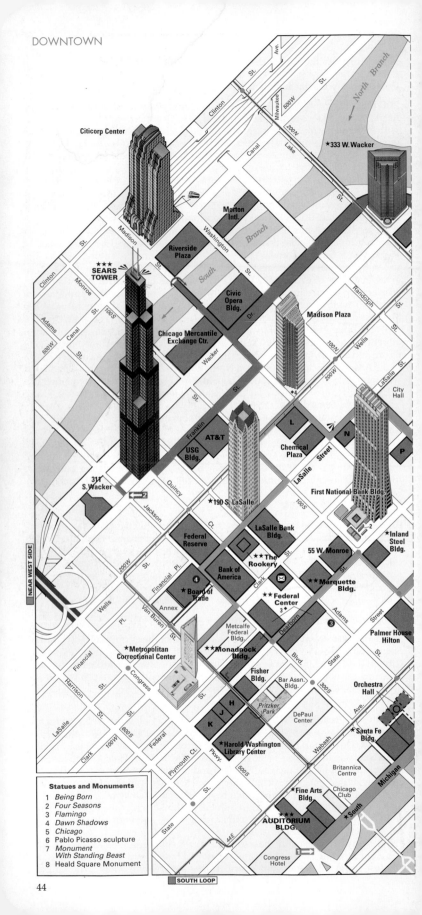

Citicorp Center

★333 W. Wacker

North Branch

Clinton St.

Milwaukee

500 W

200 N

Canal

Lake St.

Morton Intl.

Washington

Branch

Riverside Plaza

St.

South

Madison St.

Civic Opera Bldg.

Dr.

Madison Plaza

★★★ SEARS TOWER

Monroe St.

100 S

Chicago Mercantile Exchange Ctr.

Wacker

100 N

200 W

Wells

Randolph St.

LaSalle St.

City Hall

Adams St.

500 W

Canal

St.

Clinton

St.

AT&T

USG Bldg.

Franklin

L

Chemical Plaza

N

P

First National Bank Bldg.

311 S. Wacker

Quincy

★190 S. LaSalle

St.

LaSalle

Street

100 S

←2

Jackson

Ct.

LaSalle Bank Bldg.

St.

55 W. Monroe

★Inland Steel Bldg.

Federal Reserve

★★The Rookery

Clark

★★Marquette Bldg.

200 W

St.

Bank of America

✉

Financial Pl.

④

★Board of Trade

Federal Center

★★Federal Center

3★

Adams

③

Palmer House Hilton

Annex

Van Buren

St.

Metcalfe Federal Bldg.

Dearborn

State

Street

Wells Pl.

★Metropolitan Correctional Center

Congress

St.

★★Monadnock Bldg.

Blvd.

300 S

Orchestra Hall

Financial

St.

Fisher Bldg.

Bar Assn. Bldg.

Pritzker Park

DePaul Center

★Santa Fe Bldg.

Harrison

St.

H

LaSalle

600 S

J

Clark

100 W

K

Federal

★Harold Washington Library Center

Wabash

Britannica Centre

Michigan

Plymouth Ct.

Pkwy.

500 S

★Fine Arts Bldg.

Chicago Club

NEAR WEST SIDE

State

St.

44 E

★★★ AUDITORIUM BLDG.

★South

Congress Hotel

⊡

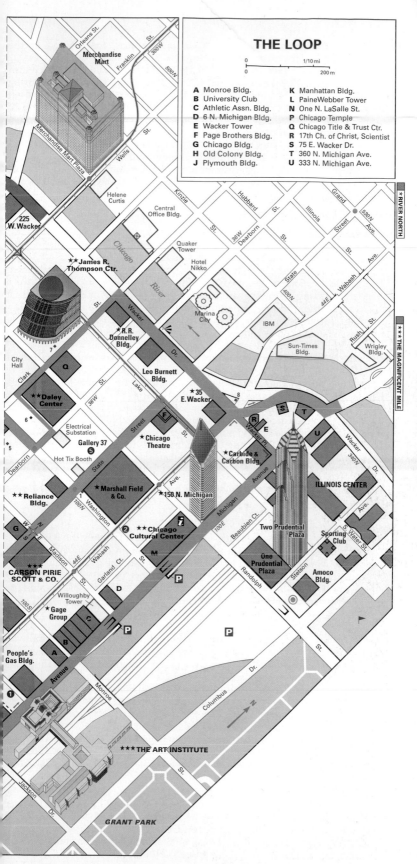

THE LOOP

0   1/10 mi
0   200 m

A Monroe Bldg.
B University Club
C Athletic Assn. Bldg.
D 6 N. Michigan Bldg.
E Wacker Tower
F Page Brothers Bldg.
G Chicago Bldg.
H Old Colony Bldg.
J Plymouth Bldg.

K Manhattan Bldg.
L PaineWebber Tower
N One N. LaSalle St.
P Chicago Temple
Q Chicago Title & Trust Ctr.
R 17th Ch. of Christ, Scientist
S 75 E. Wacker Dr.
T 360 N. Michigan Ave.
U 333 N. Michigan Ave.

Merchandise Mart

Merchandise Mart Plaza

Orleans St.
Franklin St.
300 W
500 N
Wells St.

Helene Curtis

225 W. Wacker

Chicago River

★★James R. Thompson Ctr.

Central Office Bldg.

Quaker Tower

Hotel Nikko

Kinzie St.
Hubbard St.
Illinois St.
Grand Ave.
530 N
36 W
Dearborn St.
State St.
400 N
Wabash Ave.
44 E
Rush St.

★RIVER NORTH
★★★THE MAGNIFICENT MILE

City Hall

★★Daley Center

Q

Clark St.

Wacker Dr.

★R.R. Donnelley Bldg.

Leo Burnett Bldg.

★ 35 E. Wacker

Marina City

IBM

Sun-Times Bldg.

Wrigley Bldg.

7 ★

6 ★
★ 5

Electrical Substation
Gallery 37 ⑤
Hot Tix Booth

Dearborn St.
36 W
Lake Street
State Street

F
★Chicago Theatre

R
E
S
T
U
Wacker Pl.
★Carbide & Carbon Bldg.

ILLINOIS CENTER

★★Reliance Bldg.

★Marshall Field & Co.

★150 N. Michigan

Michigan Ave.
100 E

W

Madison St.
144 E
Washington St.
700 N
100 S

①
★★ Chicago Cultural Center

J

M

Two Prudential Plaza

Sporting Club

★★★
CARSON PIRIE SCOTT & CO.

Wabash Ave.
Garland Ct.
State St.

P

One Prudential Plaza

Amoco Bldg.

Randolph St.
Beaubien Ct.
Stetson Ave.
S. Water St.

G

Willoughby Tower

★ Gage Group

D

C

B

A

P

People's Gas Bldg.

①

Avenue
Monroe St.

P

N

Columbus Dr.

★★★THE ART INSTITUTE

Jackson Dr.

GRANT PARK

45

Symphony Orchestra, headed by Theodore Thomas, first played at the Auditorium Theatre, eventually moving to the smaller ORCHESTRA HALL. Abandoned by the Civic Opera in 1929, the Auditorium would have been torn down but for its exceptional size and weight. It served as a USO center during World War II, with bowling alleys installed on the stage. In 1946, **Roosevelt University** converted the hotel and office areas for its use. The widening of Congress Parkway in the 1950s turned the southern bay of the first floor into a pedestrian arcade, destroying several rooms. In 1967, the Auditorium Theatre Council restored the theater, which now hosts major Broadway musicals and ballet. The facade is a symphony of design, rising from rough granite to smooth limestone in a series of Romanesque arcades. Walk into the lobby to admire some of Sullivan's intricate organic floriated design, as well as a small exhibit describing the building's history and construction.

Walk north on S. Michigan Ave.

★ **Fine Arts Building** – *410 S. Michigan Ave. Open year-round Mon–Fri 7am–10pm, Sat 7am–9pm, Sun 10am–4pm. Closed major holidays.* ♿ ☎*312-427-7602.* This 10-story structure (1885, Solon S. Beman) symbolizes the transition of South Michigan Avenue from a commercial and residential street to an artistic and cultural center. The "Studebaker" name inscribed above the first floor indicates its first use as a wagon showroom. In 1898 Beman redesigned it as the Fine Arts Building, adding theater and studio spaces and altering the roofline to match the Auditorium Building *(above).* The stone and terra-cotta structure, which features Romanesque windows, column capitals and arched entrances, hosted several luminaries: Frank Lloyd Wright, William Denslow, who prepared his illustrations for *The Wizard of Oz* in the building, and Harriet Monroe, whose *Poetry* magazine began here in 1911. From 1914 to 1917 Margaret Anderson's radical literary journal, *The Little Review,* was published here, introducing a reluctant America to James Joyce's *Ulysses.* Maurice Brown and Ellen Van Volkenburg's influential Little Theater (1912-1917) on the 4th floor helped define 20C art theater across the country. The building still houses dance and music studios. Take the old-fashioned, manually operated elevator to the 10th floor to view eight beautiful murals created by artists of The Little Room—a gathering of resident artists formed in 1892—including Frederic Clay Bartlett *(p 62)* and Ralph Clarkson.

The 1929 red Romanesque Revival Chicago Club *(corner of S. Michigan Ave. and Van Buren St.)* mimics the original Burnham & Root building that collapsed during renovation in 1929.

Cross Van Buren St. and continue north.

At 310 S. Michigan Avenue stands Britannica Centre, formerly the S.W. Straus Building, today home to the Encyclopedia Britannica Company. At night, six 1,000-watt light bulbs enclosed in a blue box illuminate the glass beehive adorning the roof. The imposing structure was erected one year after Chicago's 1923 zoning law, which allowed construction of buildings taller than 260ft, as long as setbacks were incorporated into the design.

Cross Jackson Blvd.

★ **Santa Fe Building** – *224 S. Michigan Ave.* Formerly known as the Railway Exchange Building, this 1904 design by D.H. Burnham & Co., finely detailed in pale terra-cotta, combines the structure of the Chicago school with the white Neoclassical ornament popularized by the 1893 World's Columbian Exposition. Burnham was both architect and developer, moving into the building and producing his famous 1909 Plan of Chicago here. Step in to see the 2-story atrium, reminiscent of Burnham & Root's ROOKERY with its grand staircase, balustraded mezzanine and elaborate metal light standards.

The not-for-profit **Chicago Architecture Foundation** bookstore and tour center offers some of the city's best neighborhood tours *(p 233),* as well as free lectures and temporary exhibits *(open year-round Mon–Sat 9am–6pm, Sun 11am–6pm; closed Jan 1, Easter Sunday, Thanksgiving Day, Dec 25;* ♿ ☎*312-922-8687).*

Orchestra Hall – *220 S. Michigan Ave.* The Georgian-style home (1905) of the world-famous Chicago Symphony Orchestra was planned by orchestra founder Theodore Thomas and completed after his death by D.H. Burnham & Co. In 1993 Daniel Barenboim succeeded the noted Sir Georg Solti as conductor of the prestigious orchestra. Begun in 1995, a 2-year, $105 million renovation and expansion will more than double the building's space to 291,000sq ft.

The private ninth-floor Cliff Dwellers Club (1908, Howard Van Doren Shaw) was formed by architects and artists, taking its name from the Henry Blake Fuller book depicting the occupants of an early skyscraper.

Dominating the Grant Park side of South Michigan Avenue, between Jackson Boulevard and Monroe Street, is the imposing facade of the **Art Institute** *(p 60)*. At the corner with Adams Street, look north to view **One Prudential Plaza** (1955, Naess & Murphy), the first high rise built after the Great Depression and the tallest in Chicago when completed. It is now dwarfed by **Two Prudential Plaza** (1990, Loebl, Schlossman & Hackl), with its dramatic needle-like spire and chevron roofline. Farther east, the **Amoco Building**, fifth tallest in the US, was designed in 1973 by Edward Durell Stone and Perkins & Will. The thin marble sheathing began to warp, and the entire building was refaced with thicker North Carolina granite in 1990 at a cost equal to the original construction.

> **1** **Russian Tea Time**
> *77 E. Adams St.* ☎ *312-360-0000.* Distinguished by red velvet furnishings, this elegant tea room buzzes with the polite chatter of classical music lovers when the symphony or opera performs. Fine caviar and champagne are *de rigueur* in the evening as is tea in the afternoon. The restaurant also offers a complete menu featuring Russian, Uzbek, Ukrainian and Baltic delicacies.

Cross Adams St. and continue north.

People's Gas Building *(122 S. Michigan Ave.)* is a massive Beaux-Arts high rise executed in 1910 by D. H. Burnham & Co. for the city's major natural-gas supplier. Here the steel framework characteristic of the Chicago school is almost entirely disguised with 2-story Ionic columns in granite, terra-cotta fretwork and stone lion heads.

Continue north to the corner of S. Michigan Ave. and Monroe St.

The **Monroe Building [A]** *(104 S. Michigan Ave.)* and **University Club [B]** *(76 E. Monroe St.)* were designed in 1912 and 1908 respectively by Holabird & Roche to cater to the eclectic tastes of the early 20C. The Monroe Building features Mediterranean columns, Gothic terra-cotta ornament and a gabled roof. Its narrow yet elegant L-shaped **lobby** incorporates vaulted ceilings and blind arcades of Rookwood tile. The Monroe was designed to complement the Gothic Revival University Club across the street, which also sports a gabled roof. The exterior of the private club is embellished with leaded glass windows, protruding bays, and Gothic spires and gargoyles at the crown.

Cross Monroe St. and continue north.

★**Gage Group** – *18-30 S. Michigan Ave.* Built for the Keith, Gage and Ascher millinery firms in 1899 by Holabird & Roche, this trio exemplifies the typical Chicago school facades that use a brick curtain wall to express the skeletal steel frame. With traditional construction, the walls supported the buildings. The Chicago school reversed architectural tradition by making the building (a steel frame) support the walls, which were draped on the iron skeleton like a curtain. Note at no. 18 the facade by Louis Sullivan, with his typical flowery ornament enlivening the spandrels and exploding from the piers at the cornice.

Adjacent to the Gage Building, the **Chicago Athletic Association Building [C]** (1893, Henry Ives Cobb) draws attention by the interweaving Venetian Gothic trefoil arches adorning its richly varied facade. The 1929 Willoughby Tower *(8 S. Michigan Ave.)* applies Gothic ornament to an Art Deco facade.

Cross Madison St. and continue north.

6 N. Michigan Building [D], executed in 1899 by Richard E. Schmidt, was the site of Montgomery Ward's nationwide mail-order business. Aaron Montgomery Ward performed a great service for Chicago when he sued to keep the lakefront (now Grant Park) *(p 108)* free of buildings. Dedicated to the art of designing, the Chicago Athenaeum's Museum of Architecture and Design *(entrance on Madison St.)* presents five rotating exhibits a year.

Cross Washington St.

■ *For a listing of the Loop's outdoor sculptures, see p 235.*

★★ **Chicago Cultural Center** – *78 E. Washington St. Open year-round Mon–Thu 10am–7pm, Fri 10am–6pm, Sat 10am–5pm, Sun noon–5pm. Closed major holidays. Guided tours (45min) available Tue & Wed 1:30pm.* ☎312-744-6630. This marvelous Neoclassical palazzo served as the city's first library when completed in 1897 after designs by Shepley, Rutan & Coolidge, who also designed the Art Institute. Noteworthy elements include a smooth limestone facade, recessed windows and elaborate Renaissance moldings at the entrance, cornice and balconies. Step inside to admire the inlaid marble grand stairway that leads from the Washington Street entrance up to **Preston Bradley Hall★**, with its Tiffany stained-glass dome. Visit any Wednesday at 12:15pm and Preston Bradley Hall reverberates with the classical sounds of the Dame Myra Hess Memorial Concert series. Another magnificent stained-glass dome is located on the north end of the second floor.

Chicago Cultural Center, Stairway

Chicago Photographic Co./Chicago Dept. of Cultural Affairs

A wide array of free public programs are offered here daily, including concerts, films, dances, lectures and art exhibits. This is also the home of the Chicago Department of Cultural Affairs, the Museum of Broadcast Communications and the **Chicago Office of Tourism Visitor Information Center** *(north side of building)*, a good place to start a Loop tour, with exhibits on the history of the Loop and a short video in 8 languages *(open year-round Mon–Fri 10am–6pm, Sat 10am–5pm, Sun noon–5pm; closed major holidays;* ☎312-744-2400). The Landmark Chicago gallery *(west side of building)* exhibits photographs of historic buildings throughout the city and its suburbs.

Museum of Broadcast Communications [M] – *Open year-round Mon–Sat 10am–4:30pm, Sun noon–5pm. Closed major holidays.* ☎312-629-6000. Located on the ground floor, this is one of two such collections in the country (the other is in New York City). The Kraft Television Center to the right of the Washington Street entrance provides an opportunity to don a news anchor's jacket and report news on video with a TelePrompTer *($19.95 cost includes a copy of the videotape; tapings are conducted every 20min)*. To the left of the entrance is the Radio Hall of Fame, which includes a radio studio and exhibits celebrating Jack Benny, Fibber McGee and ventriloquist Edgar Bergen's dummies, Charlie McCarthy, Effie Klinker and Mortimer Snerd.

Behind the main staircase is the television gallery, with video loops illustrating great moments in Chicago television history, including the famous Kennedy-Nixon debates of 1960, and entertainment staples like Kukla, Fran & Ollie and Garfield Goose. Early Chicago television personalities like Studs Terkel and Dave Garroway are lionized along with modern stars Oprah Winfrey and Siskel & Ebert. The adjacent room contains an interesting display on the history of broadcast advertising, with two mini-theaters presenting award-winning television advertisements and a wall of fame featuring the voices of famous advertising executives. The second-floor archives stores 10,000 television programs, 50,000 hours of radio programs, 2,500 newscasts and some 9,000 commercials, indexed on a computer catalog. After locating your video or radio selection, a $2 fee (free for MBC members) allows use of one of the 26 study booths.

Cross Randolph St. and continue north on N. Michigan Ave.

The unique roofline of **150 N. Michigan Avenue**★ (1984, A. Epstein & Sons), sliced at a beveled angle and set at a 45-degree angle to the street, marks the end of Michigan Avenue's Grant Park frontage.

Cross Lake St. and continue north.

Extending over 83 acres along the east side of North Michigan Avenue, **Illinois Center** *(between Michigan Ave., N. Lake Shore Dr., the river and Lake St.)* comprises more than a dozen buildings, grand in conception but muted and sterile in execution. One of the world's largest mixed-use projects was first envisioned in the 1920s for the air rights of the Illinois Central Railroad, which has run along the lakefront since the 1850s. Built in the 1970s and 1980s, mostly by the successor firms of Mies van der Rohe, the complex includes hotels, offices, shops, apartments, and the Illinois Golf Center, a 9-hole course reputed to be the first urban golf course. The small **Sporting Club** (1990, Kisho Kurokawa) is recognizable by its four white, framework towers that pay homage to Louis Sullivan and sport 17ft wind sculptures, called *Children of the Sun*, by Osamu Shingu.

Continue to Wacker Pl.

★ **Carbide & Carbon Building** – *230 N. Michigan Ave.* This Art Deco skyscraper (1929, Burnham Bros.), inspired by Raymond Hood's American Radiator Building in New York, is faced with dark green terra-cotta accented with gold leaf ornament, especially on the stepped-back tower. A 2-story lobby features curvilinear and geometric ornament with incised carving characteristic of the Deco style.

Turn left on Wacker Pl.

Designed in 1928 for the Chicago Motor Club by Holabird & Root, **Wacker Tower [E]** *(68 E. Wacker Pl.)* is a good example of the Art Deco style, defined by setbacks, continuous piers and recessed windows that emphasize the vertical. The **lobby**★ features a 1920s transcontinental highway map by John W. Norton.

Visible just north of the river are the "corn cob" towers of the MARINA CITY complex.

Turn left on Wabash Ave., right on Lake St. and continue to State St.

This section of Lake Street is located beneath the elevated Loop railway, first erected in 1897 to connect the various railroad lines serving the central business district. Marking the southeast corner of State and Lake Streets, the **Page Brothers Building [F]** (1872, John Mills Van Osdel) features a cast-iron Italianate facade *(Lake St. side)* and is a rare survivor of the building boom that followed the Great Fire of 1871.

Turn left onto State St. and continue south.

The **Chicago Theatre**★ *(175 N. State St.)*, designed by Rapp & Rapp in 1921, is one of the city's earliest and largest (4,000 seats) vaudeville movie palaces. French Renaissance in inspiration, the terra-cotta facade and multistory **lobby**★ were restored in 1985 after narrowly avoiding demolition.

Cross Randolph St.

★ **Marshall Field & Company** – *Bounded by State, Randolph and Washington Sts. and Wabash Ave. Open year-round Mon–Sat 9:45am–7pm, Sun noon–5pm. Closed Easter Sunday, Thanksgiving Day, Dec 25.* ✕ ᰔ ☎312-781-1000. Occupying an entire city

② Heaven on Seven
111 N. Wabash Ave., 7th floor. ☎ *312-263-6443.* Creole shrimp, soft-shell crab, po'boy sandwiches and jambalaya are just a few of the New Orleans-style dishes served in this bustling lunchroom. Most entrees are served plenty spicy, but connoisseurs of Cajun heat use the bottles of Louisiana hot sauces on the tables to season their food to taste. For a sweet ending, try a healthy serving of cinnamon-spiked bread pudding.

block, this building was constructed in several stages between 1892 and 1914 by D. H. Burnham & Co., combining the firm's structural engineering innovations with the Neoclassicism made popular by the World's Columbian Exposition of 1893. Marshall Field's career in commerce began in the dry goods business with partners Potter Palmer *(p 114)* and Levi Leiter. In the 1860s, Palmer left to focus on real estate, and Leiter split off shortly afterwards. Field became the preeminent department store retailer, succeeding under the dictum "Give the Lady What She Wants." The richly embellished clocks that ornament the corners on State Street are Chicago icons. The interior contains over one million square feet of retail space and features a Tiffany favrile dome *(near State and Washington Sts.)* as well as a new atrium resulting from a $110 million renovation.

Virginio Ferrari's *Being Born* **[1]** sculpture *(corner of State and Washington Sts.)* celebrates both the city and the precision metalwork of the "tool & die" industry that sponsored it.

★★ **Reliance Building** – *32 N. State St., at corner with Washington St.* Forty years ahead of its time, this building anticipated the glass and steel skyscrapers of Mies van der Rohe and the Second Chicago school of the 1930s through 1970s. In 1895, a decade after the invention of the skyscraper, **Charles B. Atwood** of D. H. Burnham & Co. realized the possibilities inherent in skeletal frame construction and designed the Reliance Building.

The facade is almost entirely glass. Extremely narrow piers and spandrels between floors, featuring Gothic ornamentation in a cream-white terra-cotta, reduce the solid exterior walls to a minimum. Projecting bays create a play of light across the facade and allow more light into the interior. Initially occupied by dentists and doctors, the structure was neglected for half a century. Restoration efforts have been underway since 1993.

Continue south on State St. to Madison St.

The corner of State and Madison is the heart of Chicago's rectilinear street grid, with all addresses to the north reading "North," to the south "South" and so forth. All four corner buildings exhibit the typical "Chicago window" *(p 34)*. The rusticated, brown **Chicago Building [G]** *(7 W. Madison St.)*, completed in 1904 by Holabird & Roche, is a textbook example of an early skyscraper divided into a base, shaft and crown *(p 33)*. Of note are the projecting bays of Chicago windows and the fancy cornice.

★★★ **Carson Pirie Scott & Co.** – *1 S. State St. Open year-round Mon–Fri 9:45am–7pm, Sat 9:45am–6pm, Sun noon–5pm. Closed Easter Sunday, Thanksgiving Day, Dec 25.* ✗ 占 ☎312-641-7000. Designed by **Louis Sullivan** in 1899, this is considered his greatest work. Sullivan said "Form follows function," yet he was the consummate 19C ornamentalist, and his gift is nowhere more apparent than here. The upper stories are white terra-cotta, plainly expressing the steel grid underneath, but the first two floors are bedecked with some of the most elaborate and plastic designs ever created by Sullivan. His ability to produce foliate ornament in three dimensions is best seen in the rounded corner, where the cast iron reaches out to create portholes that hover above the glass, making a

massive building seem light and airy. In a sense, form was following function, as the ornament was designed to attract shoppers to the goods in the windows.

Cross Monroe St.

The **Palmer House Hilton** (1927, Holabird & Roche), located at the southeast corner of State and Monroe Streets, is the fourth of this name founded by real estate mogul Potter Palmer. The luxurious interior features a grand Beaux-Arts second-floor **lobby★** and the Empire Ballroom.

Turn right on Monroe St. and continue to Dearborn St.

★ Inland Steel Building – *30 W. Monroe St.* This elegant high rise (1958, Skidmore, Owings & Merrill) must have been an apparition when it opened, its shining stainless steel facade surrounded by masonry buildings dark with soot. Bruce Graham designed a unique structural cage that supports the building outside of the wall plane, creating column-free floors. To achieve this, steel pilings were anchored 85ft deep into the bedrock, while

---

Most Chicagoans agree that the Loop is best explored on foot. However, the city offers some fun alternative ways of "looping the Loop."

- **By bus:** the Chicago Architecture Foundation *(p 233)* proposes an overview of the city, which includes a drive through the Loop. Or hop aboard a no. 151 bus at Wacker Dr. and Michigan Ave., grab a window seat and enjoy the view (the bus crosses the Loop, stops at Union Station, then returns to State St.)

- **By boat:** several tour operators *(p 234)* offer river and lake cruises, providing a fascinating look at the Loop's architectural diversity. In fact, a cruise is the best way to view the riverfront skyscrapers.

- **By "L":** the elevated Brown line (Ravenswood) circles the Loop, affording an intriguing if noisy glimpse into the bustling activity.

- **By tour train:** departing at the corner of Randolph St. and Wabash Ave., this "chartered" train offers the same views as the "L" *(runs July through September, Saturdays between 12:15– 3:35pm)*. Tickets are available daily at the Visitor Information Center in the Chicago Cultural Center *(p 48)*.

---

the mechanical and elevator systems were placed in a windowless steel tower to the east. In addition to innovative engineering techniques, Inland Steel also pioneered the use of air-conditioning and dual glazing for windows. The lobby is graced by Richard Lippold's *Untitled (Radiant I)*, a three-dimensional web of steel rods and wires.

At Dearborn Street, look north to the gracefully rising concave facade of the 60-story **First National Bank Building**, designed in 1969 by Perkins & Will. The edifice has extremely wide bays sheltering a large bank on the lower floors and offices above. The popular plaza, known for its lunchtime concerts in summer, surrounds the rectangular *Four Seasons* **[2]** mosaic created by artist Marc Chagall in 1974.

Walk south on Dearborn St.

The **55 West Monroe Building**, formerly the Xerox Centre (1980, C.F. Murphy Assocs.), sports the mirrored wall surfaces and curving facades favored by chief architect Helmut Jahn.

★ Marquette Building – *140 S. Dearborn St.* Considered one of Holabird & Roche's skyscraper masterpieces, this 1895 Chicago school design expresses the structural frame in the finely detailed terra-cotta and brick exterior. The piers project forward from the windows, creating a soaring grid best appreciated by looking up from the entrance. The corners are emphasized to suggest solidity. Four bronze panels above the entrance illustrate journal writings of French explorer-missionary Marquette, one of the first Europeans to visit the Chicago region. The hexagonal lobby features a stunning Tiffany glass **mosaic★** by J.A. Holzer illustrating Marquette's journey in the Mississippi River basin, as well as bas-reliefs of early French explorers and Native Americans by Edward Kemeys.

Cross Adams St.

★ Federal Center – *On Dearborn St. between Adams St. and Jackson Blvd.* Designed by **Ludwig Mies van der Rohe** in 1964 and completed ten years later, this 3-building complex is an excellent example of International-style architecture and urban space. The 1-story post office is as tall as the lobbies of the Dirksen and Kluczynski

Flamingo by Alexander Calder

Buildings, set at right angles to each other across Dearborn Street. All three buildings frame the beautiful plaza graced by Alexander Calder's 1973 **Flamingo [3]**, which seems to suggest steel beams that have leapt off the building to dance a bright red ballet. Mies' buildings appear stark and unadorned, but their beauty depends on rigid adherence to laws of proportion, and the edifices are ornamented by attached I beams that run up the facade like vertical ribs.

★★ **Monadnock Building** – *53 W. Jackson Blvd.* Behind the Federal Center rises a long, narrow building defining the architectural revolution that saw bricks replaced by steel. The northern half of the building (1891, Burnham & Root) is the tallest masonry structure in Chicago. Walls six feet thick at the base support 16 stories plus an attic of bricks piled on bricks. (The thickness of the walls can be seen in the window openings on the ground floor.) Peter and Shepherd Brooks developed the structure, insisting on brick, which they thought was more fireproof than the new steel technology. They also didn't want to pay for ornament. It must have shocked Victorian Chicagoans to see a naked building rising in this section of the Loop. Architect John Wellborn Root said its design, flared at the base and crown, was based on an Egyptian papyrus or the capital letter "I." Root's skills are apparent in the muscularity of the bays that ripple out of the wall plane along Dearborn Street. The southern half of the building (1893, Holabird & Roche) is partially braced by a steel frame and features more traditional ornament.

Walk south through the lobby of the Monadnock Building.

The **interior★** was painstakingly restored to its original 1890 design in the 1980s, including replication of the mosaic floor, fragments of which are preserved beneath glass at the north entrance and south elevators. The original marble ceiling and restored marble walls are ornamented by cast-aluminum light fixtures, mailboxes and a staircase in foliate forms reminiscent of the ROOKERY. The large interior shop windows provide a second "street" for retailers and bring precious light into the corridor from outside.

Exit the lobby at Van Buren St., turn left and walk east.

③ The Berghoff
17 W. Adams St.
☎ 312-427-3170.
Founded in 1898 by brewer Herman Berghoff, this spacious German restaurant is one of the oldest operating taverns in the city. The sauerbraten, schnitzel and creamed spinach draw huge lunchtime crowds. The adjacent stand-up bar (no seating), best known for its brats and potato salad, caters to diners on the run. The Berghoff sponsors a raucous outdoor Oktoberfest celebration every second weekend in September.

Located at 343 S. Dearborn Street, the Gothic-style **Fisher Building** (1896, D. H. Burnham & Co.), inspired by the Reliance Building *(p 50)*, is faced with light orange terra-cotta that includes playful references to the owner's name in the form of sculpted fish surrounding the edifice's former entrance in the center of the Van Buren Street facade.

Farther east, on the left, are the Chicago Bar Association Building (1990, Tigerman McCurry) with its spindly top, and tiny Pritzker Park, designed after René Magritte's *The Banquet*, housed at the Art Institute. Visible across the park, the block-long, white terra-cotta facade of the DePaul Center is a 1993 restoration of a 1912 Holabird & Roche department store.

★ **Harold Washington Library Center** – *Between Van Buren St., Congress Pkwy., State St. and Plymouth Ct. Open year-round Mon 9am–7pm, Tue & Thu 11am–7pm, Wed & Fri–Sat 9am–5pm, Sun 1–5pm. Closed major holidays. Guided tours (30min) available Mon–Sat noon & 2pm, Sun 2pm.* ♿ ☎312-747-4999. Hammond, Beeby & Babka won a competition to design Chicago's new library, a grandly scaled 1991 design that announces its public function with classical arcaded facades, ornamental garlands and an overachieving roofline of green metal and glass with looming owls. The building's rusticated base refers to landmarks such as the Auditorium and Marquette Buildings. Inside, a mosaic mural on the sterile first floor memorializes the city's first African-American mayor, the building's namesake. Reading rooms fill floors 3 through 8, and a large skylit "winter garden" tops out the structure. The western facade is a post-Modern glass wall, reflecting the historic structures across the street.

Backtrack on Van Buren St. and cross Dearborn St.

Look south on Dearborn to admire a trio of late 19C buildings. The **Old Colony Building [H]** (1894, Holabird & Roche), at 407 S. Dearborn Street, is the only downtown structure with rounded corners, a hallmark of the Victorian era. Located next door at no. 417, the **Plymouth Building [J]** (1899, Simeon B. Eisendrath) illustrates the use of Gothic ornament to illuminate high-rise towers. Briefly the tallest building in the world, the **Manhattan Building [K]** (1891, William Le Baron Jenney), at no. 431, is an experiment in decoration, with polygonal and rounded bays, a granite base and a variety of ornament such as the grotesque faces that stare at passersby from the bottom of each protruding bay.

Continue west on Van Buren St.

★ **Metropolitan Correctional Center** – *On Van Buren St. between Clark and Federal Sts.* Appearing almost two-dimensional, this unique concrete structure (1975, Harry Weese & Assocs.) resembles an old IBM punch card. The triangular layout affords an easily patrolled plan for the cells holding prisoners awaiting trial in the nearby FEDERAL CENTER. The cells also dictate the narrow beveled windows, which can only be 5in wide without bars. Unless the inmates are in the rooftop recreation area, it is easy to forget the building's purpose.

Turn right on Clark St.

Dominating the lobby of the Metcalfe Federal Building *(77 W. Jackson Blvd.)* is a huge Frank Stella sculpture, *The Town's Ho Story*, visible from the street.

Turn left on Jackson Blvd.

★ **Chicago Board of Trade Building** – *141 W. Jackson Blvd.* Deemed one of the city's best Art Deco skyscrapers, the 45-story Board of Trade (1930) was designed by Holabird & Root, successor to the Chicago school firm of Holabird & Roche. Soaring limestone piers terminating in sculptures are balanced by recessed windows and terra-cotta spandrels. The pyramidal roof is capped by John Storrs' 32ft aluminum sculpture of Ceres, the goddess of the harvest, and the clock in the center of the main facade is flanked by Father Time and a Native American cradling grain. The beautiful 4-story **lobby** is decorated with geometric forms in a variety of marbles, nickel-plated brass and platinum. The Board of Trade was founded in 1848 to regulate the trade of grain and commodities from Illinois and the Great Plains through Chicago to the eastern seaboard. In the upper floor **trading pits★**, which today include options as well as commodities, frenetic circles of traders in brightly colored jackets use elaborate hand signals and shouts to communicate their transactions *(open year-round Mon–Fri 8am–1:15pm; closed major holidays;* ✗ ♿ ☎312-435-3590). In 1980, Helmut Jahn of C.F. Murphy Assocs. designed a rear addition that defers to the older building in scale and form despite its reflective surfaces. Jahn's addition includes a love-ly 12th floor atrium with a sensuous 1930 mural of Ceres by John W. Norton. The Board of Trade is currently undergoing a third expansion to the east, scheduled for completion in 1997. The new, 4-story annex will be connected to the main building by a bridge spanning a land-scaped pedestrian mall.

Walk north on LaSalle St.

The **LaSalle Street** "canyon" stretches from the Board of Trade to the river, its walls formed by banks and brokerage institutions in a unity of architecture that belies the competitive financial world within. The **Bank of America Building** (1924) and **Federal Reserve Bank Building**

4 Everest

In Board of Trade Building.
☎ *312-663-8920. Reser-vations required.* Located on the 40th floor, this award-winning, upscale restaurant affords stunning views of the city. Chef Jean Joho uses seasonings and ingredients from his native Alsace in many dishes, and game is one of his specialties. Dine à la carte or sample several of Joho's favorite starters and entrees by ordering the "dégustation" meal.

(1922), both designed by Graham, Anderson, Probst & White, frame the end of LaSalle Street with classical grandeur. Ionic columns and an entrance pediment on the Bank of America are mirrored by a Corinthian portal on the Federal Reserve, the ensemble a fitting anchor for the LaSalle Street canyon. The Bank of America features a restored second-floor banking hall with a coffered ceiling and huge **murals** by Jules Guerin, illustrator of the 1909 Plan of Chicago. A small visitor center **Kids** in the Federal Reserve lobby affords the opportunity to see—but not touch—a million dollars in cash.

Continue north on LaSalle St. to Adams St.

As you pass Quincy Court on the left, note the SEARS TOWER looming before you, and the elevated train station a block west.

★★ **The Rookery** – *At the southeast corner of LaSalle and Adams Sts.* This 1888 structure is one of the earliest designs by Burnham & Root and the most impressive land-mark rehabilitation in the Loop. The building's name comes from a temporary city hall erected here in 1871 that attracted pigeons and other birds. A playful reference to this is found in carved birds (rooks) on either side of the entrance. Noted for the richness of John Wellborn Root's design and detailing, the 12-story facade of red granite, terra-cotta and brick is a combination of Romanesque Revival and Queen Anne elements, the former apparent in the large arched entrance. Two-story columns frame the lower retail floors, while arcades organized around the pro-truding entrance bay characterize the upper floors.

The square building is organized around a large **light court**★★, a device that brought natural light to interior offices in the era before gas and electric illumina-tion. Now enclosed by a domed skylight, the light court is considered a work of art in its own right. The interior was remodeled in 1906 by Frank Lloyd Wright, who covered Root's iron columns and staircases with white marble, incised and inlaid with gold leaf. One side of the column to the left as you enter the atrium is exposed to reveal the original Root design. This rare commercial work of Wright features Prairie-style urns framing the central staircase to the east. The west side is dominated by a graceful 8-story spiral staircase. The 1928 elevator lobby by Prairie school architect William Drummond includes whimsical elevator doors by Annette Cremin Byrne, which again play on the building's avian nomenclature. A $103 million restoration in 1992 brought the building back to its full glory.

★ **190 S. LaSalle Street** – *At the northwest corner of LaSalle and Adams Sts.* Inter-nationally renowned architects come to Chicago to realize their own work and to pay homage to the birthplace of the skyscraper. This 1987 building by Philip Johnson recapitulates Chicago's Masonic Temple (1892, Burnham & Root, demol-ished 1939) with its distinctive cross-gabled roof and elaborate iron cresting. The elegant white marble **lobby** is distinguished by red marble pilasters and oversized lanterns, surmounted by a gilded, vaulted ceiling. Art enlivening the lobby includes a tapestry depicting the Chicago Plan of 1909 and a 28ft steel sculpture by Anthony Caro, *Chicago Fugue.*

Located across the street at no. 135, the **LaSalle Bank Building** (1934, Graham, Anderson, Probst & White), erected by the estate of Marshall Field, was the last high rise built during the Great Depression. The edifice stands on the former site of the Home Insurance Building *(p 32)* erected by William Le Baron Jenney in 1885. Step inside the huge Art Deco structure to view the lovely 2-story lobby featuring chevroned skywalks, fluted chandeliers and an elevator panel in the shape of the building.

Continue north on LaSalle St., turn left on Monroe St. and walk west.

Look west to view the 1988 **AT&T Corporate Center** *(227 W. Monroe St.)*, linked to the 1992 **USG Building**, both designed by Adrian Smith of Skidmore, Owings & Merrill. The complex reinterprets Art Deco and marks a return to architecture organized around a hierarchy of detail, with ornamented window spandrels and light sconces shaped like the spires atop the structure.

Turn right on Wells St. and continue to Madison St.

At the corner of Wells and Madison Streets stands **Madison Plaza** (1982, Skidmore, Owings & Merrill), distinguished by an accordion wall of mirrored glass and steel typical of 1980s architecture. The facade, which creates numerous corner offices, provides a touchstone for Louise Nevelson's sculpture *Dawn Shadows* **[4]**, an intricate group of curving black forms. Marking the southeast corner of that intersection, **PaineWebber Tower [L]** *(181 W. Madison St.)* is another international contribution by Cesar Pelli, whose 1990 design refers to Eliel Saarinen's second-place entry to the 1922 *Chicago Tribune* Tower competition *(p 13)*, with extremely narrow bays and ribbing that dramatize its verticality. Colorful found-object sculptures by Frank Stella, *Loomings* and *Knights and Squires*, decorate the barrel-vaulted lobby.

Walk east on Madison St. to LaSalle St.

Chemical Plaza *(southwest corner of LaSalle and Madison Sts.)* features the original base of a 1912 building by Holabird and Roche surmounted by a sleek addition (1989) of blue and green aluminum and glass by Moriyama & Teshima. Designed in 1930, **One N. LaSalle Street [N]** *(northeast corner of LaSalle and Madison Sts.)* draws the eye to its 5th-floor panels depicting French explorer LaSalle, who is thought to have stayed here in the late 17C.

Walk north on LaSalle St. to Washington St. and turn right.

At the intersection of LaSalle and Washington, look back for an impressive **view** of the "canyon" culminating with the Board of Trade. The ornate City Hall/County Building *(bounded by Clark, Washington, LaSalle and Randolph Sts.)* was actually built in two sections, in 1907 and 1911, by Holabird & Roche. Huge, 75ft Corinthian columns (the tallest in the city) span the 5th to 9th stories.

Continue to the intersection of Washington and Clark Sts.

Chicago Temple [P] – *At the southeast corner of Washington & Clark Sts. Open year-round Mon–Fri 9am–5pm, Sat 9am–3pm, Sun 8:30am–noon. Sky chapel accessible by guided tour (45min) only year-round Mon–Sat 2pm, Sun 9:30am & noon.* ☎312-236-4548. When completed in 1923 by Holabird & Roche, this was the city's tallest building and remains the tallest church spire in the world at 568ft. The First United Methodist Church occupies the large, English Gothic-style sanctuary on the first floor, as well as the sky chapel, added to the steeple in the 1950s. Encompassing only 700sq ft, the tiny gem features lovely stained-glass windows and carvings on the oak walls.

East of the temple stands Joan Miró's celebrated *Chicago* **[5]** sculpture, resembling an elemental female form. A gift to the city from the artist, the 39ft statue was erected in 1981.

★★ **Richard J. Daley Center** – *Bounded by Washington, Randolph, Clark and Dearborn Sts.* In 1965 Jacques Brownson of C.F. Murphy Assocs. designed this fine example of Miesian architecture, bold and

5 **Gallery 37 and Skate on State**

For Gallery 37 information call ☎312-744-6630; *for Skate on State information call* ☎312-747-2200. This undeveloped block serves as an arts camp for public school children during the summer and as a skating rink during the winter. From June through August, wander through Gallery 37's tents and watch talented young artists at work. Bundle up and bring your blades (or be prepared to wait for a pair of rental skates) to brave the slick surface from November through March.

muscular as the city it represents. Massive bays 87ft wide are joined by huge, cross-shaped beams that narrow as they rise to the top. Only three bays span the main facade of tinted glass and Cor-Ten steel, designed to weather to a bronze patina resembling rust. Rising 648ft, the 31-story structure was named for the late Daley, "hizzoner da mare" *(p 20)*. Cor-Ten was also used to fabricate the untitled **Pablo Picasso sculpture [6]** in the plaza, which stirred controversy when unveiled in 1967 but has since become a beloved symbol of the city. The building houses courtrooms and offices while numerous cultural events and a farmer's market *(every second Thursday in summer)* take place in the plaza.

To the east of the plaza, an electrical substation boasting a vibrant relief by Sylvia Shaw Judson on the Dearborn Street facade is the only survivor of a failed redevelopment scheme from the late 1980s that destroyed several landmarks. The block currently serves as **Gallery 37** *(p 55). The Hot Tix booth, offering discount tickets to major shows, is located on the State St. side of the block.*

Continue north on Clark St. and cross Randolph St.

The unusual top of the **Chicago Title & Trust Center [Q]** *(111 W. Washington St.)*, built in 1992 by Kohn Pedersen Fox, suggests the bascule bridges *(p 77)* over the Chicago River. A second tower is planned for the vacant north half of the site.

★★ **James R. Thompson Center (formerly State of Illinois Center)** – *Bounded by Clark, LaSalle, Randolph and Lake Sts.* Named for the Illinois governor who chose the 1985 design by architect Helmut Jahn, this decidedly unusual building houses state agencies and a large lower-level food court. Note on the plaza Jean Dubuffet's *Monument With Standing Beast* **[7]**, a fiberglass sculpture of curvaceous black and white forms. The building's exterior skin of glass and pastel panels seems ethereal when compared to the stone and steel buildings around it, and its form ignores the street grid to create a sense of dramatic entry. The shape is a post-Modern reference to the classical domes of government buildings. A visit to the soaring **atrium★** is a must, since the building is all atrium, rising the full 17 stories with glass elevators to the beveled "dome within a dome." The effect of light filtering into the space creates a play of shadows that changes constantly. The open office floors and glass skin have caused heating, cooling and noise problems, but few visitors pass up a chance to see this quirky monument.

Continue north on Clark St. and turn right on Wacker Dr.

Across the river to the east, stand the QUAKER TOWER and HOTEL NIKKO development, erected in 1987. Adjacent to the Marina City complex, the IBM BUILDING forces its rectangular form into a curving riverfront site.

★ **R.R. Donnelley Building** – *77 W. Wacker Dr.* Celebrated Barcelona architect Ricardo Bofill designed this 1992 office tower in his "Modern Classical" style with a pedimented top and marble elements that suggest Greek and Roman temples. The firm of DeStefano & Partners supervised construction of the 50-story structure, one of the last skyscrapers to be erected in the Loop in the 20C. The elegant **lobby** in pure white marble from Thásos, Greece, features works by Catalan artists, including a wonderful Bofill fountain, *Twisted Columns,* and the rock-like *Three Lawyers and a Judge* by sculptor Xavier Corbero, set amid live bamboo.

Cross Dearborn St. and continue east on Wacker Dr.

At this point, take a moment to absorb the splendid **view★** east toward the WRIGLEY BUILDING and MICHIGAN AVENUE BRIDGE. Erected in 1989 by Roche & Dinkeloo and Shaw & Assocs., the **Leo Burnett Building** *(35 W. Wacker Dr.)* resembles a Prairie school column with its division into a base, shaft and capital. The corners protrude, creating more corner offices. The gray granite facade's square windows are ornamented with chrome. Lobby sculpture includes a semifigurative bronze fountain, *Rite of Spring,* by Bryan Hunt.

Cross State St. and continue east on Wacker Dr.

★ **35 E. Wacker Drive** – Reflecting the historical themes popular in the mid-1920s, this buff-colored terra-cotta high rise (1926, Thielbar & Fugard) is bedecked in a profusion of Beaux-Arts detailing. Originally called the Jewelers Building (note the "JB" initials carved in terra-cotta panels on the facade), it featured a car elevator until 1940 that allowed tenants to drive into the building. The top of the structure is distinguished by four, large Neoclassical lanterns at the corners, artfully disguising water tanks, as well as a 17-story central tower capped by a dome housing a presentation room for architect Helmut Jahn. In the 1920s, the 37th through 40th floors were home to Al Capone's Stratosphere, a popular watering hole. A whimsical addition to the building is the overhanging corner clock.

Adorning the island in the center of Wacker Drive, the Heald Square Monument **[8]** (1941, Lorado Taft and Leonard Crunelle) celebrates Haym Salomon and Robert Morris, financiers of the American Revolution. Both figures flank a statue of George Washington. Marking the corner of E. Wacker Drive and Wabash Avenue is the round **Seventeenth Church of Christ, Scientist [R]** (1968, Harry Weese & Assocs.). White travertine marble, the prominent site and unusual form give the small building a large presence.

Bear left and continue east on Wacker Dr.

75 E. Wacker Drive [S] (1928, H.H. Riddle), built by the descendants of Cotton Mather, is a pencil-thin Art Deco skyscraper sheathed in white terra-cotta.

Continue east on Wacker Dr. to N. Michigan Ave.

Distinguished by a curving Neoclassical entrance, **360 N. Michigan Avenue [T]** (1923, Alfred S. Alschuler) is built on a trapezoidal riverfront site. The building's English Renaissance ornament is capped with a Greek lantern. Across the street rises **333 N. Michigan Avenue [U]** (1928, Holabird & Root), a lovely Art Deco skyscraper with a dark granite base, stepped-back design and bas-reliefs that relate to the sculpted bridgehouses anchoring the Michigan Avenue Bridge. The building's design echoes the entry proposed by Eliel Saarinen for the *Chicago Tribune* Competition *(p 13)*, which won second prize.

★★ **The Magnificent Mile** – *Description p 77.*

> *The visitor who would like to return to Michigan Ave. and Congress Pkwy. is advised to walk south on the Grant Park side of Michigan Ave., for an interesting perspective of the different architectural styles lining the avenue.*

② ALONG THE RIVER

Begin at the corner of Jackson Blvd. and Franklin St.

★★ **Sears Tower** – *Bounded by Franklin St., Wacker Dr., Jackson Blvd. and Adams St.* Tallest building in the world for over 20 years, this 110-story feat of engineering cuts an unmistakable profile on the city's skyline. At the time of construction in 1968-74, the City did not require a zoning variance for the tower, allowing it to rise to an unsurpassed height of 1,454ft. In 1996, the tower was overtaken by architect Cesar Pelli's Petronas Towers in Kuala Lumpur, Malaysia, relegating the Chicago landmark to the rank of world's second tallest structure.

Designed by architect Bruce Graham and chief engineer Fazlur Khan for Skidmore, Owings & Merrill, the tower comprises nine rectangular tubes, resting on more than 100 steel and concrete caissons anchored into the bedrock hundreds of feet below ground. These 75ft-high bundled tubes provide solidity to the tower by maximizing resistance to wind loads: two tubes end at the 50th floor, two at the 66th floor, and three more at the 90th floor. Clad in black aluminum and bronze tinted-glass, the tower's structural skeleton required over 75,000 tons of steel. Redesigned in 1985, the Wacker Drive barrel-vaulted entrance is dominated by Alexander Calder's mobile **The Universe**, a collection of brightly colored forms turning and twirling.

Skydeck – 🄺 *Enter on Jackson Blvd. Open Mar–Sept daily 9am–11pm, rest of the year daily 9am–10pm. Final tickets sold 30min before closing. Brochures in Spanish, Chinese, Japanese, German, Polish, Korean,*

> **A lesson in size:**
> - height: 1,707ft (including the antennas), as tall as 16 city blocks
> - weight: 222,500 tons, covered by 28 acres of black aluminum
> - 103 elevators; only one travels to the top at a speed of 1,600ft/min or 18mi/hr
> - 6 automatic window-washing machines clean 16,000 windows 8 times/year
> - the tower contains enough phone wire to wrap around the earth 1 3/4 times and electrical wiring to run a power line from Chicago to Los Angeles
> - about 12,000 people work here; another 5,000 to 11,000 visit daily
> - even in high wind, the top of the tower never sways more than 6 inches

Italian and French are available. $6.50. ✗ & ☎312-875-9696. *Note that Skydeck may be closed due to high winds.* The visit to the Skydeck includes a multi-slide show, an exhibit of ten great Chicago buildings, and a one-minute narrated elevator ride to the 103rd floor. The entirely glassed-in 103rd floor affords spectacular **views★★★** of the city on the lake, while a taped commentary provides further insight. On clear days, the shores of Michigan are visible across the lake.

Exit Sears Tower on Franklin St.

Just south of the Sears Tower stands **311 S. Wacker Drive** (1990, Kohn Pedersen Fox), the world's tallest concrete frame skyscraper, built on speculation rights before the real estate depression of the 1990s. Planned as one of three buildings, the tower is topped by a huge illuminated crown resembling a circular fortress.

Continue north on Franklin St. to Madison St. Walk west to Wacker Dr. and across the bridge spanning the Chicago River to view sights to the west of the river.

Wacker Drive from across the River

Formerly known as the Northwestern Atrium Center, the deep blue and silver **Citicorp Center** *(500 W. Madison St.)*, rising like a giant jukebox, marks the intersection of Madison and Canal Streets. Another of Helmut Jahn's soaring atriums unites this combination commuter train station, retail arcade and office tower (1987), which takes its streamlined shape from 1930s "machine age" design.
Just east of Citicorp Center, **Riverside Plaza** (1929, Holabird & Root) was built for the now-defunct *Chicago Daily News*. The stately 26-story Art Deco high rise offers an expansive riverfront plaza, the first developed in Chicago. Built over active railroad tracks, this building incorporated ingenious foundations as well as vents for steam engines, a novelty at the time.
Visible to the north, the **Morton International Building** (1990, Ralph Johnson of Perkins & Will) is partly suspended over railroad tracks by means of an exposed rooftop truss that is reminiscent of the nearby bridges, just as the modern clock tower suggests older structures.

The bridge offers the best view of sights to the east of the river.

To the right, the **Chicago Mercantile Exchange Center** *(10-30 S. Wacker Dr.)*, established in 1919 as the Butter and Egg Exchange, has evolved like the Board of Trade from commodities to the fast-paced world of futures and options. The "Merc's" twin towers (1983, 1988; Fujikawa, Johnson & Assocs.) are linked by a windowless base that encloses two large free-span trading floors, open for public viewing from separate galleries. The frenetic activity on the floor is worth the **visit** *(open year-round Mon–Fri 7:30am–3:15pm; closed major holidays; guided tours available;* & ☎312-

930-8249). Some 3,000 people garbed in colorful jackets pack the large room, where eight transactions take place every second. The riverfront site has a modest walkway where the traders flock during lunchtime breaks.

To the left, the **Civic Opera Building** (*20 N. Wacker Dr.; 2hr backstage tours conducted in early spring Sun 11:30am-3:30pm, reservations suggested;* ✗ ⅙ ☎*312-332-2244 ext. 222*), built by utilities magnate Samuel Insull to house both offices and the Lyric Opera, combines Art Deco skyscraper design with a block-long Wacker Drive arcade that celebrates the classical origins of opera and theater. The building (1929, Graham, Anderson, Probst & White) was dubbed "Insull's throne" due to its armchair-like appearance from the river. The former Civic Theater has been incorporated into a complete modernization of the Opera House. The theater opened in November 1929 with a performance of Verdi's *Aïda* and still presents world-class opera.

Return to intersection of Madison St. and Wacker Dr. and walk north on Wacker Dr.

★ **333 W. Wacker Drive** – This edifice (1983, Kohn Pedersen Fox) set a new standard for downtown development as it began the 1980s building boom. The design takes full advantage of the triangular site—a mere parking lot at the time—where the South Branch of the Chicago River diverges from the main channel. The green mirrored-glass facade both suggests and reflects the river, with horizontal ribs that relieve the sheer height of the structure. The facade is stunning when clouds play across it. The building's base has more traditional green marble and gray granite accentuated by louvered "portholes," while the top folds the curving riverside facade into the flat walls of the Loop.

Notable for its masonry walls and four rooftop lanterns, **225 W. Wacker Drive** (*located across Franklin St.*) was completed by the same firm in a post-Modern style six years later.

Across the river rises the massive **Merchandise Mart**, commissioned by Marshall Field & Co. in 1928 (*1st, 2nd & 13th floors open to the public; 1hr 30min guided tour available year-round Mon–Fri noon; $8;* ✗ ⅙ 🅿 ☎*312-527-4664*). With 4.1 million square feet of space, the Mart is touted as the world's largest commercial building. Architects Graham, Anderson, Probst & White embellished their practical Art Deco design with simple geometric patterns incised and overlaid on the exterior. In the main lobby at the south entrance, murals by artist Jules Guerin depict trading activities around the world, which presaged the Mart's current international status as a "world trade center." Joseph P. Kennedy purchased the Mart in 1945, and the family still owns it today. A 5-year renovation project completed in 1992 included extensive exterior cleaning and the creation of a public retail mall on the first two floors. Wholesale showrooms on the 13th floor have recently opened to the public as well, but all other floors are closed to anyone but design professionals and authorized buyers.

Continue on Wacker Dr. and cross Wells St.

Located east of the Merchandise Mart, the red stone and green glass Helene Curtis Building was renovated from warehouse space to office building in 1984. Across LaSalle Street stands the Central Office Building (1914), topped by a clock tower, best known as Chicago's "traffic court."

Major Chicago thoroughfares are designated with a route number but are more commonly referred to by name:	
I-55	Stevenson Expressway
I-290	Eisenhower Expressway
US-41	Lake Shore Drive
I-294	Tri-State
I-88	East-West Tollway *(toll road)*
I-94 *(north of 290)*	Edens Expressway
I-94 *(south of 290)*	Dan Ryan Expressway
I-90 *(north of 290)*	Kennedy Expressway
I-90 *(south of 290)*	Chicago Skyway *(toll road)*

THE ART INSTITUTE OF CHICAGO★★★

Time: 1 day. S. Michigan Ave. at E. Adams St. 🚌 bus no. 151.
Map p 45 and plans p 61, 65 and 72

One of the great museums of the world and the preeminent arts institution of the Midwest, the Art Institute of Chicago is a comprehensive center for arts education and exhibition. Its collections span 5,000 years of visual expression, drawing on the cultures of Europe, Asia, Africa and the Americas, and featuring works in a wide range of media. The museum's reputation is primarily based on its collection of Impressionist and post-Impressionist paintings, one of the largest and most important outside of France.

Historical Notes

The Building – Founded in 1866 as the Chicago Academy of Design, the Art Institute was one of the first art schools in the US. Reorganized to incorporate a school and a museum in 1879, this institution by 1887 occupied its own building two blocks south of its current location. The institute's board of directors, determined to create a world-class center for art education and exhibition, used the occasion of the World's Columbian Exposition of 1893 to construct a new facility. Architecturally intended to embody the cultural attainments of Chicago, the Neoclassical edifice countered the city's tough, working-class reputation. The core structure, planned with its future as an art museum in mind, would be utilized by the World Congresses during the fair and then turned over to the Art Institute. It was the only World's Fair pavilion located off the fairgrounds in Jackson Park. Created by Shepley, Rutan & Coolidge, the building had initially been designed by architect John W. Root, who died before construction commenced.

The museum's monumental Indiana limestone facade on Michigan Avenue, inspired by Italian Renaissance designs, reveals its relationship with the other Beaux-Arts buildings of the fair's "White City." The broad staircase, today one of the favorite people-watching and meeting places in the city, makes a suitably grand entrance. From here, the view of the South Michigan Avenue facade *(p 43)* is splendid. The bronze *Lion* sentinels, cast by noted animal sculptor Edward Kemeys in 1894, have become popular symbols of the museum. Inside the original building, a grand staircase leads to the galleries on the second level. Skylights restored as part of an extensive rehabilitation of the museum in 1987 heighten the drama of the space with a warm, natural light. A large Renaissance-

---

■ *If you have only two hours to visit the Art Institute, spend them seeing the following masterpieces (listed in order of visit):*

- **Thorne Miniature Rooms** (Allerton lower level, gallery 11)
- **Archaic Chinese Jades** (Allerton first floor, galleries 131A-132)
- **Tomb figures, Tang Dynasty** (Allerton first floor, gallery 105)
- **Mrs. Daniel Hubbard,** John Singleton Copley (Rice first floor, gallery 167)
- **Cotopaxi,** Frederic E. Church (Rice first floor, gallery 175)
- **The Bath,** Mary Cassatt (Rice first floor, gallery 179A)
- **Rubloff Paperweight Collection** (Rice lower level, gallery 69)
- **Augsburg Cabinet** (Rice lower level, gallery 71)
- **America Windows,** Marc Chagall (Rubloff first floor, gallery 150)
- **Ayala Altarpiece** (Rubloff first floor, gallery 157)
- **Trading Room of the Chicago Stock Exchange** (Rubloff lower level)
- **Architectural fragments** (Allerton second floor, gallery 200)
- **Mater Dolorosa,** Dieric Bouts (Allerton second floor, gallery 207)
- **The Assumption of the Virgin,** El Greco (Allerton second floor, gallery 215)
- **Old Man with a Gold Chain,** Rembrandt van Rijn (Allerton second floor, gallery 216)
- **Arrival of the Normandy Train, Saint-Lazare Station** (Allerton second floor, gallery 201) and six versions of **Wheatstacks,** Claude Monet (Allerton second floor, gallery 206)
- **Paris Street; Rainy Day,** Gustave Caillebotte (Allerton second floor, gallery 201)
- **A Sunday on La Grande Jatte–1884,** Georges Seurat (Allerton second floor, gallery 205)
- **Nighthawks,** Edward Hopper (Allerton second floor, gallery 238B)
- **Mother and Child**, Pablo Picasso (Allerton second floor, gallery 243)
- **Time Transfixed**, René Magritte (Allerton second floor, gallery 246)
- **American Gothic**, Grant Wood (Allerton second floor, gallery 247)

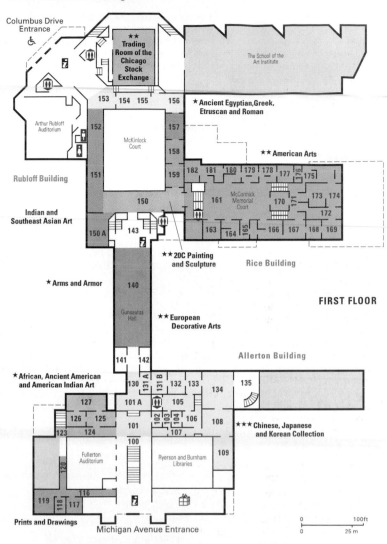

inspired arcade should surround the upper level of the stair court; however, financial problems during the depression of 1893 prevented its completion. From the original 50,000sq ft of the Allerton Building, the Art Institute has expanded to over 400,000sq ft. Coolidge & Hodgdon designed McKinlock Court (1924), the open-air garden to the east, today used for jazz concerts on Tuesday evenings during summer. Subsequent additions included the Goodman Theatre (1926), by Howard Van Doren Shaw; the Ferguson Building (1958) to the north of the Allerton Building, by Holabird & Root & Burgee; the Morton Building (1962), by Shaw, Metz & Assocs.; the Rubloff Building (1976) and a new facility for the School of the Art Institute by Skidmore, Owings & Merrill; and the Rice Building (1988), designed by Hammond, Beeby & Babka. Also of note is the reconstruction of Louis Sullivan's Trading Room from the Chicago Stock Exchange (1893).

The museum houses many facilities for arts education, including study rooms for prints, textiles, architectural drawings and photographs. The Kraft Education Center, opened in 1992, presents demonstrations of artistic techniques related to current exhibitions in the museum in addition to display galleries and a resource center. The Ryerson and Burnham Libraries were founded by Martin Ryerson, an art collector who donated his books on the fine and decorative arts, and by architect Daniel Burnham, whose architectural journals, drawings and letters formed the nucleus of the library collections. The Film Center at the School of the Art Institute offers a variety of cinema, and the Goodman Theatre *(p 113)* a full season of live performances.

The Collections – The museum's seminal holdings flourished thanks to the enthusiasm of civic leaders whose wealth—derived from railroads, manufacturing, real estate and lumber—enabled them to amass personal collections. Their financial and material donations established the museum's reputation for large-scale, high-quality acquisitions. Among the earliest material donations to the Art Institute was the Henry Field Collection of 41 paintings of the Barbizon School. The museum made its first large purchase in 1894, acquiring the Demidoff Collection of 14 Dutch and Flemish masterpieces.

Chicago's early art collectors reveled in their independence; they built their collections based on personal taste, in spite of criticism for ignoring expert advice. Because of this radical independence, by 1890 more collectors of French Impressionist and post-Impressionist paintings lived in Chicago than in Paris. Succeeding generations of Chicago collectors continued to challenge prevailing tastes and many of the museum's finest collections, including those of Asian, African and 20C art, have their roots in this determined acquisition style.

The Art Institute's prominent donors include Bertha Honoré Palmer, socialite and wife of Potter Palmer, one of Chicago's most successful real estate developers. Palmer established her role as collector and advocate of the Impressionists through her friendship with the artist Mary Cassatt. Her bequest of the Potter Palmer Collection of 52 Impressionist paintings in 1922 helped secure the Art Institute's reputation in this field. Lumber baron Martin Ryerson bequeathed an amazing 227 American and European paintings, as well as drawings and Asian and European decorative arts to the museum. The donations of Clarence Buckingham and his sister, Kate Sturges Buckingham, featuring Chinese and Japanese prints, paintings, sculpture and ceramics, form the foundation of the department of Asian art. The collection of avant-garde post-Impressionist paintings donated by Frederic Clay Bartlett in memory of his wife Helen Birch includes many of the treasures of the museum, in particular George Seurat's *A Sunday on La Grande Jatte–1884* (1884-86). The Edwin & Lindy Bergman Collection, donated in 1987 and 1991, brought the museum 78 significant paintings, collages, constructions and works on paper by noted American and European Dada and Surrealist artists.

Principal sections of the museum

19C European Painting★★★ .... (*p 63*)	African, Ancient American and American Indian Art★ .... (*p 74*)
European Painting and Sculpture★★ .... (*p 65*)	Arms and Armor★ .... (*p 74*)
20C Painting and Sculpture★★ ...... (*p 67*)	Ancient Egyptian, Greek, Etruscan and Roman★ .... (*p 75*)
American Arts★★ .... (*p 68*)	Prints and Drawings .... (*p 75*)
Chinese, Japanese and Korean Collection★★★ .... (*p 70*)	Indian and Southeast Asian Art ..... (*p 75*)
European Decorative Arts★★ .... (*p 72*)	Photography .... (*p 76*)
Thorne Miniature Rooms★★ .... (*p 74*)	Architecture .... (*p 76*)
Trading Room of the Chicago Stock Exchange★★ .... (*p 74*)	Textiles .... (*p 76*)

Collection highlights are indicated in tan boxes in the order of the visit.

How to visit the museum

Open year-round Mon–Fri 10:30am–4:30pm (Tue 8pm), Sat 10am–5pm, Sun & holidays noon–5pm. Closed Thanksgiving Day, Dec 25. $7. Guided tours available. Introduction to the Collections tour (45min) daily 2pm at Grand Staircase. ✗ ⅋ ☎312-443-3600.

The main entrance is on Michigan Avenue, across from Adams Street. You will enter a foyer which houses an information desk and ticket booth, a checkroom and the museum store. The collections are displayed in the Allerton Building and its two major additions, the Rubloff and Rice Buildings to the east. The buildings are connected only on the first floor. We suggest you begin your visit at the foyer information desk for materials on temporary exhibits, lectures and special events or tours. Just beyond the foyer is the grand staircase, the point of departure for the "Introduction to the Collections" tour (*see above*). Recorded tours of major special exhibits are available for rent near special exhibition areas. Some galleries have brochures available near their entrances which describe the works on display. Certain galleries may be closed (*inquire at the information desk*) and specific works of art may be exhibited in locations other than those indicated here.

The Garden Restaurant—a favorite for outdoor summer dining—and the Court Cafeteria are located in the Rubloff Building, lower level. Visitors who wish to dine without paying museum admission can enter the secondary entrance facing Grant Park on Columbus Drive, south of Monroe Street.

The museum's regularly changing temporary exhibits draw from its own collections and from other sources and are supplemented by lectures and demonstrations. These exhibitions build on the museum's varied holdings, providing an in-depth and detailed experience of the work on view. In addition to special exhibits, the Art Institute offers a comprehensive program of classes for all ages, gallery tours and films through the Film Center of the School of the Art Institute. Check for times and topics at the information desk.

■ From July 22 through November 26, 1995, the Art Institute of Chicago mounted a hugely successful retrospective, "Claude Monet: 1840-1926." The blockbuster exhibit included 159 works by the French Impressionist painter, some of which had never been shown outside of France. Some 965,000 visitors attended the show, generating $389 million in economic benefits to the city. AIC membership soared to 158,000, surpassing for the first time the Metropolitan Museum in New York.

★★★ 19C EUROPEAN PAINTING   *Galleries 221-226, 201-206, Allerton 2nd floor.*

The Art Institute's 19C European paintings are the heart of its prodigious body of works. Its collection of Impressionist and post-Impressionist paintings is one of the largest, most comprehensive and highest in quality outside of France. Chicago collectors, in particular the Potter Palmers, Martin Ryersons and Frederic Clay Bartletts, began acquiring works by Monet, Renoir, Degas and Cézanne as early as the 1880s, and their gifts to the museum form the core of its holdings. The **Helen Birch Bartlett Memorial Collection★★** of post-Impressionist and early 20C masters on exhibit in gallery 205 comprises an imposing assemblage of painterly genius.

Neoclassicism, Romanticism and Realism – Out of the humanitarian ideals of the Enlightenment grew two major schools of artistic thought: Neoclassicism and Romanticism. In very different languages, both sought to express the idealism and nationalism of the new world order. Inspired by archaeological discoveries at Pompeii and Herculaneum in the mid-18C, the Neoclassicists—preeminently **Jacques Louis David**—viewed the quiet grandeur, heroic subjects and precise proportions of antiquity as fitting counterpoints to the petty dalliances of their Rococo predecessors. His superb draftsmanship and crisp, classical lines made **J.A.D. Ingres** the finest portrait painter of the era. Rejecting such precision, the painters of the Romantic movement reveled in a freer attitude toward brushstroke and color, relying on historic events and settings for their exoticism, drama and allegory. In a portent of Impressionism, **Eugène Delacroix**, master Romantic, declared, "I do not paint a sword but its sparkle." The treatment of atmosphere and light by Englishmen John Constable (*gallery 222*) and **Joseph Mallord William Turner** is also prophetic. Toward the middle of the 19C, a new movement grounded in reality began to emerge. Forsaking classical ideals and romantic bravura, the Realists observed and recorded the world around them. Inspired by Camille Corot (*gallery 223*), their palette tended to be dark, and, like **Gustave Courbet** and **Jean-François Millet**, their subjects ordinary people. Their leaves and landscapes reveal an interest in light and shade that would blossom with the Impressionists.

Francisco Goya	*The Capture of the Bandit El Maragato by Friar Pedro de Zaldivia*, c.1806 (gallery 221)
Jacques Louis David	*Madame de Pastoret and Her Son*, c.1792 (gallery 221)
J.M.W. Turner	*Fishing Boats with Hucksters Bargaining for Fish*, c.1837 (gallery 221)
J.A.D. Ingres	*Amédée-David, The Marquis of Pastoret*, 1823-26 (gallery 222)
Eugène Delacroix	*The Combat of the Giaour and Hassan*, 1826 (gallery 222)
Jean-François Millet	*French Peasants Bringing Home a Calf Born in the Fields*, 1864 (gallery 222)
Gustave Courbet	*Mère Grégoire*, 1855-59 (gallery 223)

Impressionism – The segue from Realism to Impressionism took place at the hand of **Edouard Manet** who employed the dark tones and ordinary subjects of his contemporaries to explore the opposition of light and shadow. Indeed, as it evolved, Impressionism sought to define its subjects in terms of their color and reflected light, thereby dissolving the hard outlines that traditionally delineated the painted form and, in the extreme, recasting subjects as an arrangement of colors and light. The Impressionists understood the ephemeral nature of their quest and painted rapidly to record moments in time with quick brushstrokes that would give a spontaneous "impression" of a scene. They often worked outdoors

Two Sisters (On the Terrace), by Pierre Auguste Renoir

attempting to capture the fleeting effects of sunlight, and the movement acquired its name, coined derogatorily by an unimpressed critic, from **Claude Monet's** 1872 painting *Impression, Sunrise* (housed in Paris' Musée Marmottan). So radical did these works seem in subject, palette and technique that they were roundly rejected by the art establishment and refused admission to the annual exhibitions of the prestigious Paris salon. Undaunted, the Impressionists mounted eight of their own exhibitions between 1874 and 1886, eventually gaining critical acclaim. From the smoky railway stations and wintery grainstacks of Monet, to the soft, summery aura of **Pierre Auguste Renoir**, the Impressionists observed and painted a colorful and luminous world.

Edouard Manet	*The Mocking of Christ*, 1865 (gallery 224)
Claude Monet	*Arrival of the Normandy Train, Saint-Lazare Station*, 1877 (gallery 201) and six versions of *Wheatstacks*, 1890-91 (gallery 206)
Gustave Caillebotte	*Paris Street; Rainy Day*, 1877 (gallery 201)
Pierre Auguste Renoir	*Two Sisters (On the Terrace)*, 1881 (gallery 201)
Edgar Degas	*Dancers Preparing for the Ballet*, c.1876 (gallery 202)

Post-Impressionism – Because of its very nature and the diversity of its practitioners, the Impressionist phenomenon, though short-lived, opened the floodgates of artistic interpretation. Arising both out of and in opposition to its precepts, the artists of post-Impressionism pushed the formal aspects of painting in new emotional, compositional, coloristic, symbolic and scientific directions. At the heart of the activity were several artists who had practiced as Impressionists, including **Paul Cézanne**, **Paul Gauguin** and **Georges Seurat**. In general, they shared a desire to turn from the spontaneity of Impressionism to explore more enduring forms of expression. Individually, each came to represent a different artistic vision. In rejecting the atmospheric realism of the Impressionists, these artists freed themselves to explore new perspectives on color, symbolism, composition and form. Cézanne's interest, for instance, in structure and composition set him apart from the Impressionists and strongly influenced Matisse, Picasso and the Cubist works of the next generation, earning him the epithet "father of modern painting." Tahitian symbolism lends the work of Paul Gauguin a certain spirituality, and his bold planes of color bespeak permanence rather than impression. Seurat, in perhaps the ultimate departure, reduced his images to a near molecular level, only to build them up again using dot patterns of color. This technique, known as Pointillism, had its basis in the idea that points of color mixed more brilliantly in the

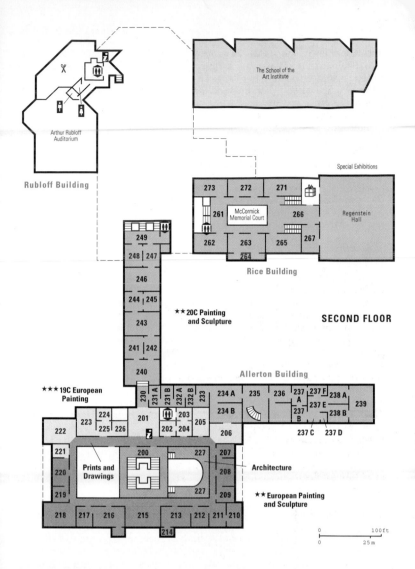

observer's eye than did paint on the artist's palette. Other post-Impressionist directions can be seen in the work of **Vincent van Gogh, Henri de Toulouse-Lautrec** and Alfred Sisley.

Vincent van Gogh	*The Bedroom at Arles*, 1889 (gallery 205) and *Self-Portrait*, c.1887 (gallery 206)
Georges Seurat	*A Sunday on La Grande Jatte—1884*, 1884-86 (gallery 205)
Pablo Picasso	*The Old Guitarist*, 1903 (gallery 205)
Paul Cézanne	*The Basket of Apples*, c.1895 (gallery 205)
Henri de Toulouse-Lautrec	*At the Moulin Rouge*, c.1895 (gallery 205)
Paul Gauguin	*Day of the Gods (Mahana No Atua)*, 1894 (gallery 206)

★★ EUROPEAN PAINTING AND SCULPTURE

Galleries 207-220, Allerton 2nd floor.

This portion of the European painting and sculpture collection features work by masters from all of the major centers of artistic activity from the 15C to 1800. The art in these galleries takes religion, historic events, portraits, ancient myths, still-life and landscape as all its subjects, demonstrating the evolution of media and style from the early Renaissance through the Age of Reason. Small contemporary paintings, works on paper, and objects are installed in the connecting hallways.

65

Renaissance – As the Middle Ages came to an end after 1300, European arts and sciences flourished. The styles, subjects and media of Renaissance art vividly reflect the quickening quest for knowledge and an expanding curiosity about the world. Artists came to understand perspective, and flat landscapes of the medieval era gave way to works with depth and dimension. Human faces took on an expressiveness, and subjects grew increasingly secular. Flanders, in present-day Belgium, and Florence, Italy, burgeoned as artistic centers, developing distinctly different styles but trading influences. The Flemish discovered that oil, as a painting medium, imparted to their work a translucent warmth missing in the bright and distinct colors of egg tempera, which remained popular in Italy for some time. Oil paint made possible the rendering of nuance, and the northerners—**Dieric Bouts** and Hans Memling *(gallery 207)* among them—became masters of depth and detail. In Florence, painters experimented with perspective and studied anatomy and classical sculpture, while Sienese like **Giovanni di Paolo** continued to work in the flattened spatial field of their predecessors. In northern Italy, painters rendered lush canvases; even their Biblical subjects assumed an increased sensuality as in the works of **Sandro Botticeli**. Some artists of the High Renaissance like **Corregio** adopted Leonardo da Vinci's pyramidal composition and blending of light and shade, experimenting with new ways to unify their works by softening the rules of perspective and composition. Others, having mastered the human form, began to twist and manipulate it, working from intellectual preconception rather than observable reality. Called Mannerists, they took many cues from Michelangelo—whose influence can be seen in the works of both **Tintoretto** and Titian *(gallery 211)*—often producing large, dramatically lit works filled with complicated juxtapositions of humanity. With typical Mannerist zeal, **El Greco's** animated and elongated figures capture the essence of religious ecstasy, contrasting with the severe Sevillian styles of Bartolomé Murillo and Francisco de Zurbarán *(gallery 215)*.

Dieric Bouts	*Mater Dolorosa,* c.1475 (gallery 207)
Giovanni di Paolo	*Six Scenes from the Life of St. John the Baptist,* c.1460 (gallery 208)
Sandro Botticelli	*Virgin and Child with Angel,* c.1485 (gallery 208)
Corregio	*Virgin and Child with the Young St. John the Baptist,* c.1515 (gallery 211)
Tintoretto	*Tarquin and Lucretia,* c.1590 (gallery 211)
El Greco	*The Assumption of the Virgin,* 1577 (gallery 215)

Baroque – Baroque painting would eventually encompass a variety of styles, but by 1600, the new realism that distinguished it from Mannerism was emerging. The often tortured forms of the 16C resolved themselves in the sharply illuminated, realistic tableaux of Caravaggio and the gentle luxuriance of **Peter Paul Rubens**. By contrast, **Nicolas Poussin** cultivated a heroic Neoclassicism based on the principles of geometry and a vision of the ideal landscape. Baroque style took another turn in Holland, culminating in the work of **Rembrandt**, whose masterful use of light, after Caravaggio, imbued his portraits with poignant realism. As the 17C waned, a stylistic ostentation inspired by the opulence and ceremony of the pre-Revolutionary court was becoming fashionable in France. Largely popular for their applications in interior design, ornate rococo forms found expression in the fanciful portrayals of a pastoral world painted by **François Boucher**, Jean Antoine Watteau *(gallery 219)* and Jean Honoré Fragonard *(gallery 219)*. The murals of Giovanni Batista Tiepolo *(gallery 218)* exuberantly epitomize both the decorative and artistic flamboyance of the rococo. In the revolutionary atmosphere of the late 18C, however, artists rejected the Baroque and rococo traditions as they had come to represent the hated exorbitance of the nobility.

Peter Paul Rubens	*The Holy Family with SS. Elizabeth and John the Baptist,* c.1615 (gallery 212)
Nicolas Poussin	*Landscape with St. John on Patmos,* 1640 (gallery 213)
Rembrandt van Rijn	*Old Man with a Gold Chain,* c.1631 (gallery 216)
François Boucher	*Are They Thinking About the Grape?,* 1747 (gallery 219)
Antonio Canova	*Bust of Paris,* 1809 (gallery 220)

★★ 20C PAINTING AND SCULPTURE

Paintings, sculpture and objects produced from 1900 to 1935 are arranged chronological-
ly from gallery 234B to gallery 249, Allerton 2nd floor. To continue with art produced
from 1935 to 1950, retrace your steps to gallery 235 and continue to gallery 239, also
Allerton 2nd floor. Additional galleries: 150, Rubloff 1st floor; and 261-267, 271-273,
Rice 2nd floor.

The significant and diverse collection of modern art at the Art Institute encompasses American and European painting, sculpture and mixed media works
produced since 1900. Galleries on the second floor of the Rice Building house
recent works but are sometimes occupied by temporary exhibits.

Early Modernism – Experimentation and progress into the abstract characterize
much of 20C art. Artists turned from rendering what they saw to expressing what
they felt and finally to creating "subjectless" works reliant only on themselves for
meaning. The accelerating pace and increasing complexity of the industrial age
hastened the process, constantly challenging artists to respond anew. The free use
of shockingly bright colors earned a small group of painters led by **Henri Matisse**
the name *les Fauves* "the wild beasts" when they exhibited together in 1905.
Largely concerned with the decorative qualities of color, the short-lived movement inspired reaction from **Pablo Picasso**. Like post-Impressionist Cézanne,
Picasso experimented with representing three-dimensional forms on a flat surface.
When he and Georges Braque *(gallery 233)* first dissolved the bonds of perspective
around 1908, unfolding and flattening their subjects, the results were dubbed
Cubism. The concept exerted a powerful influence on the course of modern art.
The faceted works of Juan Gris *(gallery 232B)* and Fernand Léger's *(gallery 243)*
curvilinear forms demonstrate further developments in the Cubist style. Meanwhile, artists in pre-World War I Germany were thinking along very different
lines. As the Cubists searched for new ways to render form, the Expressionists
turned inward for inspiration. From the prismatic, mystical visions of Franz Marc
(gallery 232A), to the nervous brushwork of Oskar Kokoschka *(gallery 233)*, the
Expressionists charged their work with emotion, capturing spirit, if not form. It is
not surprising that Expressionist **Wassily Kandinksy** would be the first painter to
create completely abstract canvases.

Contemptuous of these serious currents, a group of young artists in 1915 promoted an irreverent anti-art known as Dada (a randomly chosen French word
meaning "hobbyhorse"). Using nonsense words, collages of chance materials and
"ready-made" objects, Dadaists like **Marcel Duchamp**, Man Ray and Francis
Picabia *(all in gallery 241)* jabbed mercilessly at society. Spent by 1922, the remnants
of Dada fit well into the growing Surrealist movement, which practiced an art
governed by the subconscious mind. Unexpected juxtapositions, distortions of
time and space and eerie dreamscapes haunt the works of Surrealist painters
like **Salvador Dalí** and Giorgio de' Chirico *(gallery 240)*. The Surrealist influence
can be seen in the works of **Joan Miró** and **René Magritte,** and even the folk fantasies of **Marc Chagall.**

Pablo Picasso	*Daniel Henry Kahnweiler*, 1910 (gallery 233) and *Mother and Child*, 1921 (gallery 243)
Wassily Kandinksy	*Painting with Green Center*, 1913 (gallery 232A)
Henri Matisse	*Bathers by a River*, 1907-16 (gallery 240)
Joan Miró	*The Policeman*, 1925 (gallery 244)
Alberto Giacometti	*Couple*, 1926 (gallery 244)
Salvador Dalí	*Inventions of the Monsters*, 1937 (gallery 246)
René Magritte	*Time Transfixed*, 1938 (gallery 246)
Marc Chagall	*America Windows*, 1977 (gallery 150)

American Trends – Although Modernism evolved mainly in Europe, painters
like **Georgia O'Keeffe** and Joseph Stella helped to Americanize it. But the representational impulse was strong, and much early-20C American art developed
along realistic lines, delighting in the American landscape, both urban and rural.
Around 1907, the new Realists began to look to city streets for inspiration, but the
art establishment, disturbed by their graphic realism, derisively dubbed them the
Ash Can school. George Bellows *(gallery 231A)* is well known for his works in this
vein, and the lonely urban vistas of **Edward Hopper** owe a strong debt to the Ash

Can school. In the 1930s, American painters looked again at the landscape, this time celebrating the countryside in an overt rejection of modernism. The uncomplicated, figurative styles of **Grant Wood** appealed to Americans beset by the Great Depression.

In dramatic contrast came Abstract Expressionism in the 1940s, a movement that combined subjectless abstraction with the emotion of Expressionism. The Action Painting of Jackson Pollock *(gallery 239)* epitomized the concept: the artist dripped and hurled paint onto the canvas hoping to create patterns reflecting pure emotion. **Willem de Kooning** worked his painted surfaces over and over to achieve the right effect, and the massive color fields of Mark Rothko *(gallery 239)* vibrate with intensity. Many consider this the first truly influential American movement, its typically large and energetic canvases reflecting something of the national psyche.

Grant Wood	*American Gothic*, 1930 (gallery 247)
Georgia O'Keeffe	*Black Cross, New Mexico*, 1929 (gallery 248)
Joseph Cornell	series of boxed constructions, 1935-69 (galleries 237 A-D, F)
Edward Hopper	*Nighthawks*, 1942 (gallery 238B)
Willem de Kooning	*Excavation*, 1950 (gallery 239)

★★ AMERICAN ARTS
Galleries 161, 163-182, Rice 1st floor; galleries 158-159, Rubloff 1st floor.

American galleries at the Art Institute exhibit furniture and decorative arts since the 17C, and painting and sculpture to 1900. Beginning with the simple household objects of Puritan New England, the collection chronicles the development of American taste.

Colonial America – Pilgrim-style furniture in gallery 164 shows the influence of medieval forms and somber Renaissance design. Makers favored carving, turning, and painting for decoration, although little of the painting has survived. Carving on a chest made near Plymouth, Massachusetts, gracefully blends the stylized design elements popular at this time. Furnishings in galleries 165-168 reflect an increasing refinement of form and finish that began with the William and Mary style around 1690. Pieces grew tall and elegant; high chests came into vogue. By around 1725, the curvaceous and sturdy cabriole leg distinguished the Queen Anne style, to which mid-century Chippendale designers added claw-and-ball feet. American cabinetmakers introduced undulating fronts to desks and bureaus. Note the bombe-style Bostonian **chest of drawers** in gallery 167 and the block front of the **desk** in gallery 168 made in Norwich, Connecticut.

Colonial **silverwares** include arcane receptacles and containers: caudle cups, porringers and patch boxes for storing false beauty marks fashionable in the early 18C. Look for works by several fine Boston and New York artisans—Jeremiah Dummer and Edward Winslow among them. Cornelius Kierstade's **two-handled cup** in gallery 165 is a lovely example of early American baroque design.

The New Republic – Post-Revolutionary Americans adopted English Neoclassicism, calling it Federalism to honor the new republic. Examples of this slender style furnish galleries 169 and 172. Popularized in England by George Hepplewhite and Thomas Sheraton, the style tends toward fine proportions, clear lines and Classical motifs. Another Neoclassical movement, known as Empire, came by way of Napoleonic France, its massive forms and heavy antique flourishes replacing the delicate shapes of Federalism. American Neoclassicism reached its apex in the shop of Duncan Phyfe, likely maker of a **settee** and a lyre-backed mahogany **armchair** in gallery 173.

American painting matured with the new nation. Colonial portraitist **John Singleton Copley** painted with volume and luminescence in contrast to the flat, primitive works of his predecessors. **Raphaelle Peale**, son of Charles Willson Peale *(gallery 172)*, became the country's first virtuoso still-life painter, while **William Sidney Mount** rendered his genre scenes of American life with a classical rigor. Soon the drama of light and a heroic sense of landscape captured the imaginations of American artists. Awed by the vastness of the continent, painters of the Hudson River school like **Thomas Cole**, and others, including **Frederic Church**, Albert Bierstadt and **George Inness** (to whom gallery 170 is devoted), exulted in the wonder of nature. For **Winslow Homer**, heroism came with human endeavor. And, with a different sence of grandeur, American sculptors of the 19C like Hiram

Powers, Daniel Chester French and **Lorado Taft** *(gallery 161, McCormick Memorial Court)* used Neoclassical allegory to describe the ennobling power of art and the glory of the young republic.

Lorado Taft	*Solitude of the Soul*, date unknown (gallery 161)
John Singleton Copley	*Mrs. Daniel Hubbard*, 1764 (gallery 167)
Raphaelle Peale	*Strawberries, Nuts, etc.*, 1822 (gallery 172A)
Thomas Cole	*Niagara Falls*, 1830 (gallery 173)
William Sidney Mount	*Walking the Line*, 1835 (gallery 173A)
George Inness	*Catskill Mountains*, 1870 (gallery 170)
Frederic Church	*Cotopaxi*, 1857 (gallery 175)
Winslow Homer	*The Herring Net*, 1885 (gallery 175A)

Victorian Era – Furniture styles between 1840 and 1920 proliferated in a series of concurrent revivals, including Gothic, rococo and Renaissance. Victorians delighted in their eccentric shapes, decorations and blends of materials. The rosewood **étagère** in gallery 175 represents in form, fabric and function the spirit of the Rococo revival, and indeed, the excesses of the Victorian era. Silver of the period erupted with florid surface patterns. In gallery 178, Tiffany's magnificent Greek Revival candelabra and **punch bowl** shimmer with the opulence of the age.

Pieces in galleries 179 and 180 signal a shift away from the historicism and exorbitance of the Victorian era and a return to handcrafting. The strong Japanese influence on such "art furniture" can be seen in the lovely **sideboard** and Tiffany **pitcher** in gallery 179A. Born of the same ideals, furniture of the Arts and Crafts Movement is exhibited upstairs in gallery 158.

American painting of the late 19C took many forms, informed by currents in Europe where several influential American artists studied, lived and worked. **James Abbott McNeill Whistler**, an expatriate since 1855, renounced realism to experiment with compositions of light and color, an effort even his titles reflect. The flattering high society portraits of **John Singer Sargent** contrast with the penetrating realism of **Thomas Eakins**. **Mary Cassatt**, a protege of Edgar Degas in France, bathed her intimate views of women and children in the light and color of Impressionism.

Galleries 181 and 182 feature folk, naive and vernacular arts and crafts, including Shaker furniture and a beguiling array of ship's figureheads made between 1790 and 1860.

John Singer Sargent	*Mrs. George Swinton*, 1897 (gallery 177)
Thomas Eakins	*Mary Adeline Williams*, 1899 (gallery 178A)
Mary Cassatt	*The Bath*, 1891-92 (gallery 179A)
James Abbott McNeill Whistler	*An Arrangement in Flesh Color and Brown (Arthur Jerome Eddy)*, 1894 (gallery 180A)

20C – American furniture and decorative arts of the 20C continue a half flight up in galleries 158-159. Prairie school furniture inherited the aesthetic ethos of the British Arts and Crafts movement. Called by innovator Frank Lloyd Wright his "architectural sculpture," pieces like the **oak desk** of c.1909 echo in miniature the geometry of Prairie school buildings. The 1920s, by contrast, heavily influenced by the advent of Modernism, embraced the smooth streamlining of Art Deco. Inventive forms, industrial materials and minimal decoration characterize the post-1940 International style which had its roots in the German Bauhaus. Molded **chairs** by Eero Saarinen and Charles Eames *(gallery 159)* have become icons of this eclectic modern movement.

Sights described in this guide are rated:
- ★★★   *Highly recommended*
- ★★   *Recommended*
- ★   *Interesting*

★★★ CHINESE, JAPANESE AND KOREAN COLLECTION
Galleries 101-109, 130-134, Allerton 1st floor.

This part of the Art Institute's Asian collection covers nearly 5,000 years, from the Neolithic Age to the 20C, including works in stone, bronze, jade, paint and print, pottery and porcelain. Particularly strong in Chinese ceramics, the museum has also accumulated one of the most significant collections of woodblock prints outside of Japan.

China – The geometric precision of the Neolithic **jade prisms** *(cong)* dating to the third millenium BC *(gallery 131A)* testifies to the craftsmanship of the earliest Chinese cultures as well as to their ancient reverence for jade. Indeed, the **Sonnenschein Collection of Archaic Chinese Jades★**, mounted in a wall case that spans the length of galleries 131A-132, illustrates the beauty of Chinese jade craft. Although difficult to work, jade was believed to possess life-preserving properties, making it the ideal material for the manufacture of grave goods.

Artifacts in galleries 131B and 132 date back to the Bronze Age, which began in China around 2,000 BC. A stunning array of bronze vessels made to contain ritual offerings of wine and food traces the beginnings of Chinese surface decoration, from the tightly wound spirals of the Shang Dynasty to the robust relief work of the Zhou. In gallery 131B, compare the 12C tripod **wine vessel**, or *jia*, with a pair of 9C **wine jars**, called *hu*. These variously shaped containers signified the social status of their owners and mark the height of Chinese bronzeworking skill.

Gallery 133 introduces works from early imperial China. As a growing middle class demanded less costly tomb furnishings of clay and wood, items like ceramic burial models—to make the deceased feel at home in the afterworld—became popular. Note the Han dynasty **pigsty and latrines**. *Mingqi*, or spirit objects representing mortals and animals to attend the departed, also illustrate this increasingly wordly view of the afterlife. A particularly evocative ensemble of carved wooden **tomb figures** dates to the 4-3C BC burials in the Kingdom of Chu. **Earthenware vessels** of the 3C foreshadow the virtuosity of later Chinese ceramics.

■ **Highlights of the Chinese Dynasties:**

Neolithic Period (5th millenium BC-18C BC): an era of emerging regional cultures with distinct craft traditions in clay, stone, bone, basketry and textiles.

Shang Dynasty (1766-1111 BC): transition to the Bronze Age accompanied by the rise of cities and rival clans. Invention of remarkable piece-mold technique for casting shapely bronze vessels, whose artistry is unmatched in other contemporary cultures.

Zhou Dynasty (1111-221 BC): an unsettled period of statemaking, but increasing prosperity creates a market for objects of extreme technical refinement and splendor. Decorative patterns on stone and bronze become lavish and complex.

Qin Dynasty (221-206 BC): established by the first emperor, this dynasty represents the beginnings of imperial China. The Great Wall is begun.

Han Dynasty (206 BC-AD 221): a major dynasty, marked by expansion and the coming of Buddhism. The decorative dragon becomes prominent, along with layered and inlaid bronzework.

AD 221-264: 3 kingdoms split the empire.

Western Jin Dynasty (AD 265-317): a nominal reunion in a time of rebellion and rivalry, this short-lived dynasty produced an early celadon-glazed stoneware.

Six Dynasties (AD 317-580): the celadon technique is refined.

Sui Dynasty (AD 581-618): the empire is reunited and potters improve glazing techniques.

Tang Dynasty (AD 618-906): a time of power and international prestige with a taste for splendor. Aristocratic burial rites become increasingly elaborate and tomb furnishings proliferate in quality and quantity.

AD 907-960: breakdown of the empire into individual states.

Song Dynasty (AD 960-1279): humanistic age of extreme aesthetic richness renowned for fine and varied ceramics.

Yuan Dynasty (AD 1279-1368): this Mongol dynasty favored blue and white porcelains to trade with Islamic nations.

Ming Dynasty (AD 1368-1644): marked by a return to native rule, this classic age of blue and white wares featured a proliferation of glazing and decorating techniques.

Qing Dynasty (AD 1644-1911): foreign rule under the Manchus introduced delicate ceramics of brilliant color and eggshell translucency.

The extensive collection of ceramics in **gallery 134★** demonstrates the incredible profusion of styles, colors and techniques that characterizes Chinese pottery through 1,800 years, from the Han to the Ming dynasties. Kilns proliferated during the cultural flowering of the Song dynasty, and various wares came to be known by their places of manufacture. Note the celadon-glazed stoneware of Longquan, precious because it resembled jade, and the creamy white Ding ware, bound with metal to cover its unglazed edge. A group of **ceramic pillows**, by contrast, typifies the exuberant decorative style of the 10-11C Cizhou potters, whose work was intended largely for a popular audience. Among the Ming ware, ceramics made for the emperor's use include a striking mid-16C **plate** in brilliant yellow (the imperial color) and blue. In spite of their diversity, the pieces share an exquisite integration of form and surface design. The abundant collection overflows into gallery 108, where delicate and colorful porcelain work of China's last dynasty is exhibited along with furniture and hanging scrolls. An *Ogre* mask in glazed terra-cotta and an intricately carved 10C *Seated Guanyin* marble figure are also installed here.

Tang Dynasty Tomb Figure

Another highlight of the Chinese collection consists of the elegant earthenware retinue of Tang Dynasty funerary statues in gallery 105; most are decorated with polychrome glazes known as *sancai*, or three-color. Dating from the 8C, they reflect the life and fashion among the aristocracy during this golden age. The **equine statues**, for instance, convey the imperial love of fine horses; note the matronly equestrienne and her elegant mount, particularly unusual because it is unglazed.

Korea – Long overshadowed in the West by Chinese wares, Korean ceramics blend Chinese and original elements. The pottery in gallery 106 demonstrates the artistry of Korean celadon-glazed stoneware, which the 12C Chinese are said to have admired. The pieces are touched by whimsy; even the elegant 12C **celadon vase** *(maebyong)* carries a carefree image of playing children. Later Korean pottery, made by simpler techniques, became even more casual and spontaneous.

Japan – Japanese Buddhist art is presented in galleries 102-104, designed to evoke the serenity of a Japanese interior. Buddhism—with its host of deities—began to replace Shintoism in Japan in the 6C, taking strong hold in the 8C when the Japanese embraced the religious culture of the Tang Chinese. The **Seated Bosatsu** (bodhisattva) was made at the new Japanese capital of Nara around 775 during a time of intensive temple building and statue production. In contrast to his peaceful visage, other figures depict dramatic personifications of the guardians of Buddhist virtues and laws—note the **Thunderbolt Deity** in the same gallery—who derive the force of their emotional expression from fierce facial features and exaggerated poses.

The **Clarence Buckingham Japanese Print Collection★** occupies gallery 107. The donor's original gift of 2,000 prints has grown to 12,000 produced over the last 40 years, with an emphasis on the 19C. Because of their light sensitivity, exhibits change every six weeks and are likely to include the 18C Kabuki portraits of Toshusai Sharaku, the vistas of Ando Hiroshige or the works of 19C master Katsushika Hokusai. In gallery 109, a subtle combination of painted screens and pottery complements the room's interior, designed by architect Tadao Ando to convey a sense of Japanese spatial aesthetics.

★★ EUROPEAN DECORATIVE ARTS

This section occupies 13 galleries arranged chronologically in four sections. Begin with Gallery 140, Allerton 1st floor; then on to gallery 157, Rubloff 1st floor. Continue to galleries 60-61, 63-69, 71, Rice lower level. End the visit in gallery 50, Rubloff lower level.

The institute's European Decorative Arts collection comprises a trove of household, ornamental and religious objects produced since 1100 and made more interesting by the wide variety in their materials and manufacturing techniques. To view the collection chronologically is a journey through the evolution of Western design and tastes.

The western end of the wall case in Gallery 140 contains medieval devotional objects in metal, ivory, wood and enamelwork. Eight pieces come from the Guelph Treasure of the Cathedral of St. Blaise in Brunswick, Germany; the most arcane are several reliquaries with transparent chambers still containing the relics of saints. The adjacent aisle cases include sculpture in stone and intricately woven chasubles in linen, wool and silk.

Farther on, an inventively decorated **wine cistern** (1553) highlights a considerable collection of Italian majolica, a tin-glazed, brightly painted earthenware. One of the prizes of the textile collection, a Spanish **retable and altar frontal**, adorns a freestanding panel across the aisle. This 1468 masterpiece of embroidered linen, silk and gilt metal-wrapped thread from the altar of the Cathedral of Burgo de Osma, catalogues an array of needlework styles and materials.

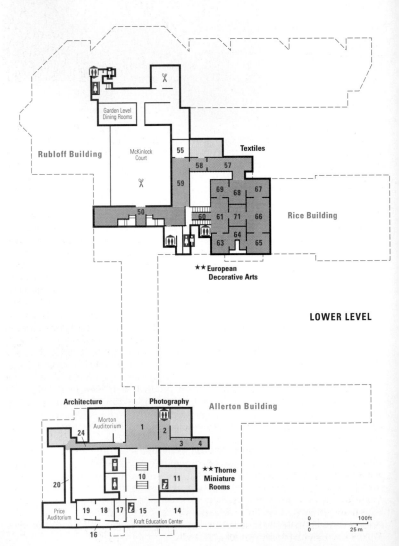

The wall case continues with German and Czech glass, vessels of all shapes and sizes, Dutch and English silver, and intricately carved wooden sculptures, including a fine Flemish boxwood *Corpus* of Christ dating to around 1650. Tableware from the 17-18C predominates at the end of the case, including plates, cups, salt cellars and pitchers, as well as a Chinese porcelain vessel transformed into a ewer with the addition of an English silver mounting (1610). Aisle cases at the end of the gallery contain a lovely gilded silver **rosewater ewer and basin** (1596) from Germany and a collection of Mexican earthenware ceramics that reveal the Spanish, Islamic and Chinese influences exported to Mesoamerica by Europeans during the contact period.

A shimmering exhibit of **European jewelry** (1450-1650) occupies part of the Alsdorf Gallery of Renaissance Jewelry *(gallery 157)*. Baroque pearls, devotional jewels and cameos, among other stunning pieces, illustrate the variety of techniques used in the production of jewels during the Renaissance period. The jewels are beautifully displayed and illuminated, many of them suspended so

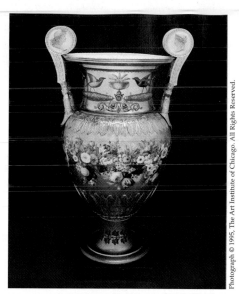

Londonderry Vase

as to reveal both sides. In the adjacent space hangs the **Ayala altarpiece**, one of the largest intact medieval altarpieces in America. Commissioned in 1396 to house a reliquary in the funerary chapel of a Castillian family, the work portrays various members of the family in scenes from the lives of Christ and the Virgin Mary. Stairwell gallery 60 contains two wall boxes featuring 18C English boxes. Pass through gallery 61 to the left and enter gallery 69 to view the **Rubloff Paperweight Collection★**, a superb assemblage of 1,000 glass paperweights dating from the 19C and 20C, manufactured by Baccarat, Clichy, St. Louis and others. The exhibit also presents a display on the making of "mushroom" and *millefiori* weights. Italian for "thousand flowers," millefiori involves encasing decorative glass canes in crystal for a kaleidoscopic effect.

Exhibits in galleries 68 through 61, arranged roughly by period and place of origin, include furniture as well as decorative items. Notable are the Mühsam Collection of engraved glass in gallery 68 and the Meissen porcelain **centerpiece and stand** (1737) in gallery 67. The amusing *Monkey Band* (1765-66)—a Meissen grouping of 15 clad music-making monkeys—reflects a contemporary fascination with simians. Marie Antoinette's **corner cupboard** (1785), which may have graced her 2-room shepherdess' cottage on the grounds of Versailles, stands in gallery 64, and the famous Sèvres porcelain **Londonderry Vase** (1813), originally commissioned by Napoleon in 1805, in gallery 63. An unusual Florentine **chair** (1876) in gallery 61 boasts a cupid sleeping on each of its armrests. Gallery 71, at the center of these galleries, features the stunning **Augsburg Cabinet** produced in Nuremberg around 1640, a masterpiece of craftsmanship in ebony with inlaid ivory and carved wood relief.

Gallery 50, in the Rubloff Building, presents works from the late 1800s to the present, including striking examples of the British Arts and Crafts, Art Nouveau, Art Deco and Modernist movements. The **tall case clock** (1906) represents the ethos of the Vienna Secession movement which rejected historicism and sought to blend the best of fine and applied arts into the creation of everyday objects. The collection also includes chairs designed by modern masters Marcel Breuer, Le Corbusier, Josef Albers and Ludwig Mies van der Rohe. A display of post-World War II furniture focuses on new materials and designs, with examples from Scandinavia, England, Italy and Austria (note the 1966 *Malitte Seating System* by Roberto Matta and the shapely English holly and hide chair).

★★THORNE MINIATURE ROOMS Kids *Gallery 11, Allerton lower level.*

Of international renown, the 68 rooms in this unique collection display a gamut of interior decorative styles ranging from 13C Europe to 20C America. Arranged in chronological fashion, some of these rooms re-create historic interiors, while others blend stylistic elements in typical, if imaginary, period arrangements. Naturalistic lighting and an occasional glimpse up a staircase or through an open door add to the realism of each setting, from a pre-Revolutionary Connecticut Valley tavern to a chic French library of the 1930s.

Mrs. James Ward (Narcissa Niblack) Thorne's childhood interest in miniature decorative objects began when her uncle, an admiral in the navy, sent her objects he found in his many ports-of-call. Mrs. Thorne (1882-1966) married the son of a founder of Montgomery Ward and Co. and traveled extensively, adding to the collection. Combining a love of miniatures with studies in the history of architecture and the decorative arts, Mrs. Thorne completed her first rooms in the early 1930s. Between 1937 and 1940, she hired skilled craftsmen to reproduce them in exceptional detail at a scale of 1in to 1ft. She even commissioned artists to paint the diminutive canvases that decorate the walls. Their technical excellence, delicate scale and charming variety lend the rooms a romantic sense of history. Mrs. Thorne donated the rooms to the Art Institute in 1941 where they went on permanent display in 1954.

★★TRADING ROOM OF THE CHICAGO STOCK EXCHANGE
Rubloff lower level; balcony access from gallery 153.

In its innovative structural design and ornamental detail, the old Chicago Stock Exchange (1893-94) was one of the most important buildings created by world-renowned architects Dankmar Adler and Louis Sullivan *(p 33).* In spite of intense efforts to save it, the structure fell victim to the wrecker's ball in 1972, but its entrance arch and Trading Room were carefully dismantled and preserved. The arch now stands outside the Institute's Columbus Drive entrance. The colorful Trading Room, reconstructed inside the Rubloff Building in 1977, features Sullivan's organic decorative scheme in painted stencils, plaster ornament and art glass. One of Chicago's earliest and most ardent preservationists, photographer Richard Nickel, was killed when part of the structure collapsed on him as he was documenting the building's demolition.

★AFRICAN, ANCIENT AMERICAN AND AMERICAN INDIAN ART
Galleries 123-127, Allerton 1st floor.

These galleries display an elite selection of artifacts representing the quintessential artistic traditions of Africa and ancient and native America. Ceremonial and festival objects are the focus of the small but choice installation of West African art in galleries 123 and 124. The masks, headdresses and sculptures in wood, ceramic and metal are arranged by culture and region, with many items from Ghana, Ivory Coast, Nigeria and Zaire. Note in particular the elaborately crafted statuary, from the early Malian **kneeling figure** (13C) to a 20C Yoruban **veranda post**, that well illustrate the complicated mythologies and symbolic systems of these cultures.

Mesoamerican and Peruvian objects occupy galleries 125 and 126, which display ceramics, jewelry, ritual implements and an outstanding collection of beautifully presented **Moche portrait vases** (100 BC-AD 500). Of particular historic importance is the commemorative **coronation stone of Moctezuma II**, which marked the ascendance of the last Aztec emperor in 1503.

Gallery 127 presents pre-Columbian figures and ceramic objects from the southwestern US. Many of these items were buried with the dead and illustrate the relationships between the community, nature and the spirit world. The human forms among the **cache of ritual figures** of New Mexico's Salado culture (14-15C) represent the spirits of the earth and sky. The ensemble relates to the interconnectedness of all life. Also on exhibit in this gallery are artifacts of the Plains Indians, including plant fiber baskets, bead-worked clothing and accessories and a fascinating series of Comanche drawings from the 1880s.

★ARMS AND ARMOR *Gallery 140, Allerton 1st floor.*

The Harding Collection ranks among the most important collections of historic military arms and armor in the US. It is particularly strong in examples fabricated in Germany, Austria and Italy from the 14C to 17C, an era when armaments were as important for aesthetic and ceremonial purposes as for defensive or offensive reasons. Note the decorative richness of the later pieces, especially the gilded and etched steel work of the 16C Italian armorers. The collection includes chainmail, plated armor and equestrian equipment, some designed for battle and some for tournament—note in particular the 15C **Burgundian parade saddle** of wood, staghorn and pigskin. Early weapons are represented by polearms, battle-axes, swords, maces, daggers and crossbows. Three stately German two-hand swords (16C) stand as tall as a person. Historic firearms such as matchlock, flintlock and rare wheel-lock rifles with richly carved and inlaid stocks of wood and ivory, a set of 19C French dueling pistols and an ornate ivory-handled **Remington revolver** (1870) complete the exhibit.

★ANCIENT EGYPTIAN, GREEK, ETRUSCAN AND ROMAN
Galleries 153-156, Rubloff 1st floor.

Egyptian ceramic vessels, mummy head covers, carved stone wall fragments and small art objects are exhibited in galleries 153, 154 and 154A. Most were found in tombs dating from 2600 BC through AD 200. Greek artifacts in gallery 155, from the Bronze Age to the Roman conquest, comprise works in stone, ceramic and metal, including jewelry, military helmets and coins. Among the collection of black- and red-figure vessels is a wine jar (stamnos) by the anonymous Chicago painter, so called because this is his signature piece. Produced in Periclean Athens, it represents the height of the red-figure technique. Two beautifully carved **funerary stele**, dated respectively to 380 and 330 BC provide an excellent comparison of the styles prominent before and during the age of Alexander the Great.

The Theodore W. and Frances S. Robinson collection of **antique glass** from around the Mediterranean occupies gallery 155A. These delicate bottles and ornaments in blown and core-formed glass are as remarkable for their longevity as for their beauty. Gallery 156A houses the Etruscan collection, which includes an incised bronze mirror (c.470 BC) and several lovely pieces of granulated gold jewelry, all testaments to Etruscan metalworking skill. A lifelike terra-cotta **votive head** represents a penchant for realistic funerary portraiture.

The Etruscans passed their love of the portrait bust on to the Romans, who applied the Greek figurative style to it to create a dynamic new form of sculptural portraiture, as in the marble **portrait of Hadrian** (AD c.100). A variety of Roman art—stone and bronze sculpture, fresco painting, jewelry, mosaic and glass—fills gallery 156. One case contains fine silver objects from the *Tivoli Hoard* dating from c.50 BC. These examples of late Republican craftsmanship were hidden, probably during time of war, and never retrieved by their owners. On nearby pedestals are sculptural fragments in relief and in the round from AD 1C to the 3C, and a fragment of a mosaic floor from the 5C.

PRINTS AND DRAWINGS
Galleries 116-120, Allerton 1st floor; galleries 202A-226A and galleries of 20C art, Allerton 2nd floor.

This collection includes around 69,000 works on paper from Europe and the Americas dating from the 15C to 20C. The Dutch and French Baroque are extensively represented with works by Rembrandt, Lorrain, Watteau, Boucher and Fragonard. The substantial 19C and 20C holdings include drawings by Goya, Turner, Delacroix, Daumier, Picasso, De Kooning, Miró and Johns. Because of their fragility, prints and drawings rotate on and off exhibit in the side galleries of the European Painting and Sculpture Collection and in the halls of 20C art *(both Allerton 2nd floor)*. Galleries 116-120 host special exhibits.

INDIAN AND SOUTHEAST ASIAN ART
Galleries 150-152, Rubloff 1st floor.

Dominated by works associated with the Hindu faith, the collection of Indian art in these three galleries features sculptural reliefs, statuary and temple fragments dating from AD 5C to the 12C, representing the gods, their servants and the forces of nature they control. In gallery 150, for instance, a bronze *Shiva Nataraja* of AD c.1000 presents the deity as the cosmic dancer who set the universe and the forces of life and death in motion.

Other objects showcase the Buddhist heritage of India, Tibet and the Southeast Asian countries. The collection includes freestanding representations of the Buddha in stone and bronze and several portrait head fragments from large votive figures and temple reliefs. These are accompanied by paintings depicting scenes of the Buddha's life on silk panels, ceremonial objects and intricately detailed private devotional articles, such as pilgrim's boxes for offerings.

PHOTOGRAPHY
Galleries 1-4, Allerton lower level; galleries of 20C art, Allerton 2nd floor.

The photography department has amassed over 25,000 images dating from 1839 to the present and representing many of the world's most famous artists. The collection includes photos by Gustave Le Gray, Eugene Atget, Ansel Adams, Man Ray, Edward Weston, André Kertész and Diane Arbus. The Alfred Stieglitz collection, which includes images by Paul Strand, Edward Steichen, Stieglitz and others, forms an essential part of the museum's holdings. Works by 20C photographers are featured in the galleries of modern art *(p 67)*, where they are installed along with contemporary paintings, constructions and books. Rotating exhibits occupy galleries 1-4.

ARCHITECTURE
Gallery 200, top of the Grand Stairs; gallery 227, Allerton 2nd floor; gallery 24, Allerton lower level.

Chicago's best-known contributions to modern art have come in the field of architecture. Following the 1871 Fire, architects created a revolutionary approach to commercial architecture using steel-frame construction as the basis for the structural and aesthetic expression of a new building type—the skyscraper. The collection reflects the innovative work of the Chicago school and documents other architectural movements since the 18C. **Fragments★** of now-demolished buildings by such famous Chicago architects as William Le Baron Jenney, Daniel Burnham and Louis Sullivan encircle the second-floor balcony like pieces of ancient temples *(gallery 200)*. Represented by windows and other decorative elements are the designers of the Prairie school, led by Frank Lloyd Wright. Architects' works on paper (including Daniel Burnham's 1909 Plan of Chicago and blueprints for the entries in the 1922 *Chicago Tribune* competition) rotate in gallery 24, while gallery 227 features special exhibits.

TEXTILES
Galleries 57-59, Rubloff lower level; also in galleries of American Arts, European Decorative Arts and the Chinese, Japanese and Korean collection.

Presented in three temporary exhibitions each year, the museum's textile holdings span the period from 500 BC to the present, with objects from Africa, Asia, Europe and the Americas. The 15,000-piece collection includes woven and printed fabrics used as tapestries, wall hangings, quilts, clothing and religious vestments, as well as 20C fiber art. The only textile on permanent exhibit—made possible by special low-light levels in gallery 140—is the exquisite 1468 Spanish retable and altar frontal *(p 72)*. Recent developments in fiber art are represented in works by Ed Rossbach, Lenore Tawney and Chicagoan Claire Zeissler.

Addresses, telephone numbers, opening hours and prices published in this guide are accurate at press time. We apologize for any inconvenience resulting from outdated information, and we welcome corrections and suggestions that may assist us in preparing the next edition. Send us your comments:

Michelin Travel Publications
Editorial Department
P.O. Box 19001
Greenville, SC 29602-9001

THE MAGNIFICENT MILE ★★★

Time: 1 day. **cta** bus no. 151.
Map pp 80-81

Champs Elysées of Chicago, this flower- and light-filled promenade along North Michigan Avenue is the city's most prestigious thoroughfare. Lined with exclusive shops and boutiques, luxury hotels, and premier residential and office high rises, the "Magnificent Mile" lies between Chicago's most important waterways, the Chicago River on its south border and Lake Michigan on its north. Just to the east, bustling Streeterville abounds in trendy restaurants and entertainment venues.

Historical Notes

Chicago's first permanent settler, **Jean Baptiste Point du Sable** *(p 10)*, built his cabin here in 1779, on an unpromising flat plain. In 1804, **John Kinzie**, a fur trader, situated his cottage on the north bank of the river close to the present site of the Equitable Building. Yet almost half a century later, when Chicago was incorporated as a city, the area remained a muddy patch of Lake Michigan sediment. By 1860 (the year Abraham Lincoln was nominated as the Republican candidate for President at the Wigwam a few blocks away), various mercantile establishments and ordinary 2-story houses bordered the avenue, then called Pine Street. The Great Fire of 1871 leveled all of the buildings on the street except the Water Tower and Pumping Station, still standing proudly at Chicago Avenue.

By the turn of the century numerous businesses, including loft manufacturing establishments, warehouses, sign companies and taverns, transformed the street into a major traffic artery. The 1920 opening of the Michigan Avenue Bridge, which joined the south and north sides of the city, catalyzed an incredible building boom. Most of the landmarks on the avenue, including the Wrigley Building, Tribune Tower, Medinah Athletic Club, Lake Shore Bank, Woman's Athletic Club, Allerton Hotel, Fourth Presbyterian Church, Palmolive Building and the Drake Hotel were constructed during the decade that followed. A profusion of Art Deco and Neoclassical elements adorned the modestly scaled, limestone edifices, lending the avenue a sophisticated "European boulevard" look that would last until the 1970s. Although the Great Depression and World War II interrupted development, in 1947 Chicago developer Arthur Rubloff dubbed North Michigan Avenue "The Magnificent Mile," forecasting a commercial revival during the 1950s and 60s.

Construction of two extraordinary mixed-use complexes contributed to the retail boom of the 1970s that changed the face of Michigan Avenue. Erected in 1969, the landmark John Hancock Center ushered in a new era of skyscrapers along the avenue. Completed seven years later, Water Tower Place included one of the first and most successful vertical shopping centers in the US, and began a shift in retail focus from downtown State Street to the more glamorous Michigan Avenue location. The upward spiral continued through the 1980s and 1990s as fashionable retailers multiplied each year, creating one of the most affluent shopping districts in the country. Recently, however, the slick and elegant image has been dealt a blow, as large-scale developers begin to invade the avenue, often demolishing historic structures to make way for mass-market shops. Long-time residents and architectural purists argue that the stores and their gaudy signage are gradually "cheapening" the area, transforming it into a "magnificent mall" of suburbia. Immediately east of the Magnificent Mile lies **Streeterville**, an area originally settled in the 1880s by the infamous Captain George Wellington Streeter. When his ship ran aground on a sand bar near present-day Chicago Avenue, Streeter built a causeway to the mainland and encouraged contractors to dump debris around his ship. The land grew to reach 180 acres and Streeter declared it the "District of Lake Michigan," separate from the city of Chicago and answerable only to the federal government. He and his wife battled police to a standoff, and his claim for independence wasn't dismissed from the courts until 1918. Most of the buildings east of Michigan Avenue are built on Streeter's landfill.

WALKING TOUR   *distance: .8mi.*

Begin at the corner of N. Michigan Ave. and E. Wacker Dr.

★ **Michigan Avenue Bridge** – *Corner of Wacker Dr. and N. Michigan Ave.* This monumental, double-leaf trunnion bascule, 2-level bridge is the gateway to the Magnificent Mile. Like the seesaw for which it is named, the bascule is a kind of drawbridge counterweighted so that it can be raised and lowered easily. Built to designs by Edward H. Bennett (co-author with Daniel Burnham of the 1909 Plan of Chicago), the bridge was completed in 1920. Four corner bridgehouses, each almost 40ft in height, showcase bas-reliefs in Bedford limestone designed by J.E.

Fraser and Henry Hering that celebrate important episodes in Chicago history. Michigan Avenue Bridge affords some of the most spectacular **views**★★ of the gleaming Loop high rises towering over the river.

Walk north across the bridge on the west side.

★★ **Wrigley Building** – *400-410 N. Michigan Ave.* Set majestically on the north bank of the Chicago River, this sparkling edifice heralded the 20C development of the North Michigan Avenue business district. Designed by Graham, Anderson, Probst & White as the headquarters for William Wrigley Jr.'s successful chewing-gum company, the structure was built in two stages (the 30-story south section in 1920 and the 21-story north section in 1924); the two towers are connected by an arcaded walkway at street level and on the 3rd and 14th floors. Modeled after Seville Cathedral's Giralda Tower in Spain, the structure represents a fine example of the French Renaissance style. The white terra-cotta cladding dazzles, especially at night when the building is illuminated. Chicagoans use the soaring, four-sided clock atop the south tower for time checks from several blocks away in every direction. A handsome little plaza between the two structures leads to another miniature park next to the Sun-Times Building.

❶ The Billy Goat

430 N. Michigan Ave. (lower level). ☎ *312-222-1525.* The gruff grill chefs at the Goat inspired John Belushi's famous "cheeseboorger, cheeseboorger, cheep, cheep, no Coke, Pepsi" skit from *Saturday Night Live*. Its proximity to the *Chicago Sun-Times* and *Tribune* offices makes this underground tavern a favorite with journalists, printers, delivery drivers and advertising executives. Framed newspaper clips and photos on the walls provide interesting slices of obscure Chicago history.

Cross to the east side of Michigan Ave.

On the northeast bank of the Chicago River rises the **Equitable Building** at no. 401 (1965, Skidmore, Owings & Merrill; Alfred Shaw & Assocs.), a 40-story granite and glazed bronze solar-glass office tower. The Channel Garden, immediately north of the building and reminiscent of Rockefeller Center's Channel Gardens in New York, offers a pleasant rest stop. Pioneer Court, a spacious plaza in front of the Equitable's entrance, provides a scenic outlook to the adjacent buildings and those on the avenue beyond. The plaza's sweeping stairway to the south leads to **River Esplanade**★, a pleasant walkway extending along the north bank of the Chicago River. Affording fine **views** of Loop skyscrapers looming above the turquoise-green waters of the Chicago River, the esplanade leads to McClurg Court and the Centennial Fountain, which emits a jet of water across the river every hour on the hour (except 3 and 4pm) during summer. Plans are under way to expand the walkway to Lake Shore Drive.

Continue east along the promenade.

University of Chicago Graduate School of Business Downtown Center – *450 N. Cityfront Plaza Dr.* Designed by Lohan Assocs. in 1992, this 8-level glass, steel and precast concrete structure features a glassed front facade overlooking the Chicago River and an angled back with cantilevered pods. Its stark, windowless western wall was dictated by the university, which did not want the architectural beauty outside to distract its students from their scholarly pursuits.

★ **NBC Tower** – *455 N. Cityfront Plaza Dr.* Reminiscent of New York's GE Building at Rockefeller Center, this 38-story Art Deco office tower (1989, Skidmore, Owings & Merrill), topped by a 130ft steel spire, rises in a series of setbacks that strengthen its vertical progression. Limestone constitutes most of the building's skin except for the dark green precast concrete spandrels and the green, gray and black granite of its base.

The tower is set on the western edge of **Cityfront Center**, a 60-acre development extending east of Michigan Avenue and north to Grand Street that includes office, hotel, entertainment, retail and residential development. The integration of this project with the surrounding city and the river provide a marked contrast with the stark monoliths of ILLINOIS CENTER directly across the Chicago River.

Return to Michigan Ave.

Wrigley Building and Tribune Tower

Don & Pat Valenti/Tony Stone Images

★★ **Tribune Tower** – *435 N. Michigan Ave. Guided tours (1hr) of the Freedom Center printing facilities (777 W. Chicago Ave.) are conducted year-round Tue–Fri 9:30, 10:30, 11:30am, 1:30pm. Closed major holidays. 2-week advance reservations required. Children under 10 not admitted. & (with advance notification)* 🅿 ☎312-222-2116. A suitable monument to the Tribune Company's vast communications and sports empire and its corporate headquarters, this soaring, crenellated, Gothic-style tower (1925, Howells & Hood) was the first-place winner of the 1922 *Chicago Tribune* international competition to erect "the most beautiful and distinctive office building in the world." The 36-story, 456ft limestone structure adorned with floodlit flying buttresses, sculpted fleur-de-lis and numerous gargoyles and grotesques echoes the Butter Tower in Rouen, France, and the Tower of Malines in Mechelen, Belgium. Fragments from more than 120 of the world's famous structures—the Parthenon, the Great Wall of China, Westminster Abbey, the Berlin Wall and Notre Dame Cathedral in Paris, among others—were collected by *Tribune* correspondents and are embedded in the exterior walls of the building.

A richly ornamented, 3-story arch adorned with a stone screen carved with figures from Aesop's fables marks the entrance to the **lobby**. This harmonious space, restored in 1990 by architect John Vinci, is known to journalists as the Hall of Inscriptions: a series of quotations expressing the ideals and obligations of the press is carved in its travertine marble walls. The east wall is dominated by a papier-mâché map of North America, originally constructed in 1925 by noted geographic sculptor George Robertson. On the south wall are copper engraved *Chicago Tribune* front pages commemorating significant moments in history, while the north wall features seven television monitors showing news and weather.

■ The Tribune Company publishes six daily newspapers, operates seven TV and six radio stations (Chicago-based WGN radio—**W**orld's **G**reatest **N**ewspaper—broadcasts from a street-level, glass-enclosed studio in the building). In addition, it produces and syndicates information and programing, publishes books and information in print and digital formats, owns the Chicago Cubs baseball team and has an interest in newsprint manufacturing.

Cross Illinois St.

★ **Hotel Inter-Continental Chicago** – *505 N. Michigan Ave.* This 41-story eclectic building (Walter W. Ahlschlager), erected in 1929 as the Medinah Athletic Club for members of the Shrine organization, was restored for $130 million in 1990 by Harry Weese & Assocs. In 1994, the hotel expanded to include its northern neighbor, the Forum Hotel Chicago, and is now contained in two towers connected by a glass lobby. Carved into the Indiana limestone facade, a large Egyptian-style frieze depicts architects and builders parading in front of the pharaoh.

Inside the historic tower, public spaces are adorned with superb inlays of marble, intricately detailed bronzed and brass trimming, murals and frescoes. Step through heavy bronze doors to admire the ornate **entryway**★ whose beamed ceiling is painted with colorful Celtic and Mesopotamian motifs—the lion, fish, eagle and peacock—representing the highest powers of nature. Marble stairways flank the arched greeting, *Es Salamu Aleikum* (Peace Be To You), and are crowned with squat, Moorish-style columns sporting hooded, sleeping knights. The Hall of Lions *(2nd floor)*, King Arthur Foyer and Court *(3rd floor)*, the Spanish Court and the Renaissance Room Foyer *(both 5th floor)* have all been opulently restored. The 25m, junior Olympic-size swimming pool on the 14th floor is the last remaining feature of the original Athletic Club (a 23rd floor miniature golf course no longer exists). An onion-shaped dome and minaret atop the building complete the fantasy below.

Across the street to the west stands the 16-story Art Deco **520 N. Michigan Avenue** built in 1929 as the McGraw-Hill Building by architects Thielbar & Fugard, who had an office there. Clad in limestone on a granite base, the building displays a variety of exterior detail including sculpted mythological figures and ornamental panels.

Cross overpass spanning Grand Ave.

The intimate scale and decorative architecture of the 5-story, lilliputian gem at **543-545 N. Michigan Avenue** (1929, Philip B. Maher) was originally constructed to house the luxurious Jacques dress shop. The sculptured female figures above each doorway, characteristic of the Art Deco style of the building, also served the practical purpose of attracting customers.

Cross Ohio St.

The 4-story Lake Shore Bank at no. 605 (1922, Marshall & Fox), taken over by the **First National Bank of Chicago** in 1994, is noteworthy for its temple-like appearance and massive Corinthian columns. A recent renovation produced a new banking center on the 2nd and 3rd floors, while the first floor was given over to retail shops. On the west side of the street is the former site of 612 and 620 N. Michigan Avenue. After a bitter preservation battle, the historic structures fell victim to the wrecking ball—along with the Arts Club of Chicago, which featured an interior space designed by Mies van der Rohe—to make way for a 9-screen cinema complex and mall *(scheduled completion: late 1996).*

Continue north.

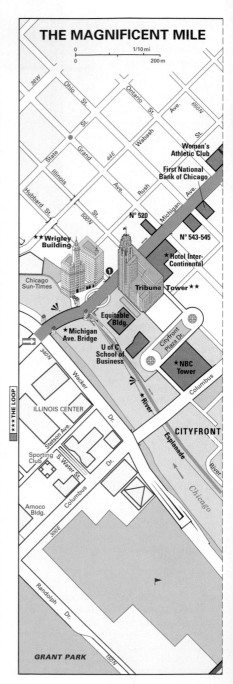

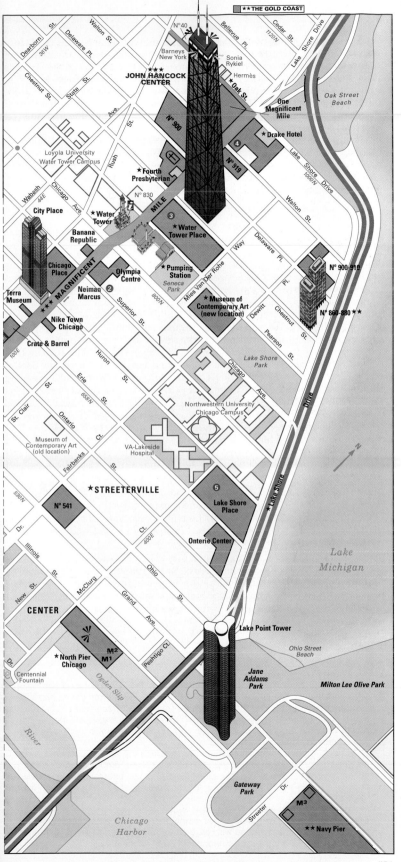

N°40

Barneys
New York

Sonia Rykiel

Bellevue Pl.

Cedar St.

1120N

Lake Shore Drive

★★★
JOHN HANCOCK
CENTER

Hermès

★ Oat St.

Oak Street
Beach

Walton St.

Delaware Pl.

N° 900

One
Magnificent
Mile

★ Drake Hotel

4

Lake Shore Drive

1060N

Chestnut St.

State St.

Dearborn St.

36W

Loyola University
Water Tower Campus

Rush St.

Ave.

N° 319

Wabash

44E

Chicago

Ave.

★ Fourth
Presbyterian

N° 830

MILE

Walton
St.

★ City Place

★ Water
Tower

3

★ Water
Tower Place

Way

Delaware Pl.

N° 900-910

Banana
Republic

Mies Van Der Rohe

N° 860-880 ★★

Chicago Place

Olympia
Centre

★ Pumping
Station

Dewitt

Chestnut

Pl.

Terra
Museum

★★★ Neiman
Marcus

2

Seneca
Park

★ Museum of
Contemporary Art
(new location)

St.

Pearson
St.

MAGNIFICENT

800N

Nike Town
Chicago

Superior St.

Chicago
Ave.

Lake Shore
Park

100E

Crate & Barrel

Huron

St.

St.

Erie

658N

St.

Northwestern University
Chicago Campus

Lake Shore

St. Clair

Ontario

Ct.

St.

Museum of
Contemporary Art
(old location)

Fairbanks

VA-Lakeside
Hospital

Drive

530N

★ STREETERVILLE

Ct.

5

Lake Shore
Place

Dr.

N° 541

400E

Onterie Center

Lake
Michigan

Illinois

St.

Ohio

St.

New

St.

CENTER

McClurg

Grand

St.

Ave.

Lake Point Tower

Ohio Street
Beach

M²

★ North Pier
Chicago

M¹

Peshtigo Ct.

Jane
Addams
Park

Milton Lee Olive Park

Dr.

Centennial
Fountain

Ogden Slip

River

N

Gateway
Park

Streeter

Dr.

M³

Chicago
Harbor

★★ Navy Pier

On the northwest corner of Ontario and Michigan Avenues at no. 626, the 9-story **Woman's Athletic Club** (1928, Philip B. Maher), one of the oldest, private athletic and social facilities for women in the US, provides a stately legacy of the avenue's 1920s understated, low-rise look. The Bedford limestone and pressed brick exterior, mansard roof, second-floor Palladian windows separated by carved ox skulls, and the winged griffins in the seventh-floor niches reflect its French inspiration and the elegance of its interior. Upscale retail shops occupy the first floor on Michigan Avenue.

Its neighbor to the north, **Crate & Barrel** (1990, Solomon Cordwell Buenz & Assocs.) at no. 646, makes a contrasting modernist statement with the stark white aluminum and luminous glass of its exterior and the high-tech trappings of its interior. The northern curved corner of this flagship housewares emporium echoes the famed rotunda of Louis Sullivan's CARSON PIRIE SCOTT store on State Street.

Cross to the west side of Michigan Ave. and cross Erie St.

Terra Museum of American Art – *664-666 N. Michigan Ave. Open year-round Tue noon–8pm, Wed–Sat 10am–5pm, Sun noon–5pm. Closed Jan 1, Jul 4, Thanksgiving Day, Dec 25. $4 (Tue free). Guided tours (30min) available Tue–Sun noon & 2pm.* ☎312-664-3939. Fitting snugly among the Magnificent Mile's retail emporiums, this modest museum presents a bite-size overview of over two centuries of American art history. Many major artists are represented, albeit by lesser-known works. Daniel J. Terra, appointed by President Reagan as ambassador for cultural affairs, founded the museum in suburban Evanston in 1980 to showcase his collection of 800 works. (In 1992, he opened a sister institution in Giverny, France.) In an effort to increase exposure, the Evanston museum moved to its present location in 1987, and occupies the three top floors of 664 N. Michigan (1927, Philip B. Maher) as well as the adjacent glass and marble edifice at no. 666. Erected in 1987 by Booth/Hansen & Assocs., the latter building contains the entrance lobby and a sweeping staircase connecting the three exhibit floors in no. 664. The museum collections highlight 19C portraiture, romantic landscapes and domestic scenes by artists such as John Singleton Copley, Thomas Cole, George Caleb Bingham, George Inness, William Merritt Chase and Winslow Homer. 20C works by Ash Can-school artists Stuart Davis and Maurice Prendergast and Expressionists such as Reginald Marsh, Milton Avery and George Tooker are also displayed. The museum frequently hosts traveling exhibitions featuring individual artists. Lectures and educational programs supplement the permanent collection.

Across the street to the east at no. 669, **Nike Town Chicago** Kids, a 5-level retail theater showcase for Nike's footwear and apparel collections, has become one of the city's more popular tourist attractions *(open year-round Mon–Fri 10am–8pm, Sat 9:23am–5:50pm, Sun 10am–6pm; closed Thanksgiving Day, Dec 25; guided tours available, advance reservations required;* ☎312-642-6363).

Set perpendicular to the avenue, granite **City Place** (1990, Loebl, Schlossman & Hackl) at no. 676 resembles a giant jukebox. Red vertical lines and pink spandrels provide a dramatic contrast to the smoky blue windows whose arrangement demarcates the varied purposes of the building—retail streetside with a hotel and offices above. The "bootlike" design with a lower mass at the sidewalk and a tower setback is typical of the skyscrapers built on the avenue in the 1980s and 1990s.

Cross Huron St.

■ **Chicago-style Pizza**

Chicago undoubtedly ranks as one of the country's greatest spots for pizza. Pizza aficionados rave about the city's deep-dish pizza, sometimes called pizza-in-the-pan, a savory concoction of tomatoes, cheese, sausage and vegetables ladled over a thick, doughy crust. Over 2,000 restaurants serve a variety of this mouth-watering dish, with toppings ranging from the simple to the exotic, from mushrooms to clams and artichokes.

The dough remains an essential ingredient in preparing an old-fashioned deep-dish pizza. A mixture of water, yeast and flour can be embellished by adding sugar, cornmeal, oil and even milk. Once the dough has risen and been kneaded down, place it in a pan, prick it with a fork and bake it at 475°F for about 5 minutes. Layer slices of mozzarella directly on the dough. Then spoon canned tomatoes, combined with oregano, basil, salt and pepper, over the cheese. Top with freshly grated Parmesan. Next come the various meat and vegetable toppings. Drizzle the mélange with olive oil and bake the pizza in a preheated 475°F oven until the crust is browned, about 30 to 45 minutes.

Chicago Place – *700 N. Michigan Ave. Open year-round Mon–Fri 10am–7pm, Sat 10am–6pm, Sun noon–5pm. Closed Easter Sunday, Thanksgiving Day, Dec 25.* ✗ ₺ ▣ ☎*312-642-4811.* Distinguished by a varicolored 2-story base in green and pink granite, this multi-purpose structure (1990, Skidmore, Owings & Merrill; Solomon Cordwell Buenz & Assocs.) also adopts the boot-shaped scheme. Eight floors of retail, including Saks Fifth Avenue and 50 other upscale shops, are topped by a 43-story residential tower setback to the west. Its windows are designed in the "Chicago style," and its curved southern facade honors Sullivan's Carson Pirie Scott store. Step inside the huge **lobby** to view the 23x32ft Thomas Melvin murals depicting Chicago history. Soaring over the atrium is a barrel-vaulted roof whose skylights illuminate the charming garden and food court located on the 8th floor.

Look north across Michigan Avenue at the **Neiman Marcus** store *(no. 737)*, occupying the low-rise section of **Olympia Centre** (1986, Skidmore, Owings & Merrill), whose 63-story tapering office and residential tower looms over Chicago Avenue to the northeast. On the Sullivanesque arch over Neiman's main entrance, a whimsical glass panel replaces the keystone.

> **2 Gino's East**
> *160 E. Superior St.* ☎*312-943-1124.* Graffiti covers almost every surface of this renowned deep-dish pizzeria. Peruse the hand-drawn love declarations, song lyrics and doodles while waiting for one of Gino's signature two-inch-thick pies. Call ahead and order your pizza, or be prepared to wait at least 30min for it to cook. At lunch-time, Gino's offers smaller, deep-dish pizzas (ready in 5min) at a take-out window just east of the main entrance.

Cross Superior St.

The freestanding, 2-story **Banana Republic** (1991, Robert A.M. Stern) at no. 744 lends a hint of the tropics to its urban setting with the gray, lead-coated copper panels and wooden windows of its facade. The lighted eyebrow window centered in its barrel-vaulted roof adds a fanciful note.

Cross Chicago Ave.

Visions of another era, the **Chicago Water Tower★** (1869, William W. Boyington) and **Pumping Station★** (1866) stand like sentinels on the west and east sides of Michigan Avenue, solid reminders that they were the only two buildings in the area to survive the Great Fire. Both are built of Joliet limestone in the castellated Gothic style. The still active Pumping Station now houses the multimedia show "Here's Chicago" *(visit by 1hr guided tour only, year-round daily 9:30am–5pm; closed Jan 1, Easter Sunday, Dec 25; $5.75;* ₺ ☎*312-467-7114).* Rising across the street, the Water Tower contains a visitor information center *(open Memorial Day–Labor Day Mon–Fri 9:30am–7pm, Sat 10am–7pm, Sun 11am–6pm; rest of the year Mon–Fri 9:30am–6pm, Sat 10am–6pm, Sun 11am– 5pm; closed Jan 1, Dec 25;* ☎*312-744-2400).* Horse-and-carriage rides of the Magnificent Mile and environs, as well as double-decker bus and trolley tours *(p 234),* depart from the charming park adjoining the Water Tower.

Chicago Water Tower and John Hancock Center

Stephen Graham/DPA

The small downtown campus of Loyola University (Water Tower Campus) begins at the southwest corner of "little" Michigan Avenue and Pearson Street, at no. 820.

Continue north.

Occupying the former I. Magnin building *(830 N. Michigan Ave.)*, Filene's Basement, Victoria's Secret and Borders Books & Music advertise their wares in tall, red and pink aluminum letters plastered over the facade.

★ **Water Tower Place** – *No. 845. Open year-round Mon–Fri 10am–7pm, Sat 10am–6pm, Sun noon–6pm. Closed major holidays.* ✗ ⅍ ▯ ☎312-440-3165. Located on the east side of Michigan Avenue, this square-block complex (1976, Loebl, Schlossman & Hackl) salutes its neighbor, the historic Water Tower, in name only. The stark, almost windowless, white-veined marble face it presents to the avenue accommodates a 12-story shopping complex and office space while a 62-story tower to the east houses the Ritz-Carlton Hotel and luxury condominiums. Its more than 150 shops, boutiques, services, restaurants and cinemas, as well as anchor tenants Lord & Taylor and Marshall Field's, moved the center of retail action to this area from State Street downtown. A prominent tourist attraction, Water Tower Place is recognized as one of the most successful mixed-use projects in the US.

Cross Chestnut St.

★ **Fourth Presbyterian Church** – *N. Michigan Ave. at Delaware Pl. Open year-round Mon–Sat 11:30am–1:30pm, Sun 8am–8pm. Closed major holidays.* ⅍ ☎312-787-4570. Dedicated in 1914, this sanctuary is an elegant reminder of Michigan Avenue's character before the myriad tour buses and shopping malls. It was designed by Ralph Adams Cram, in association with Howard Van Doren Shaw, in the Gothic Revival style (Cram also designed the Cathedral of St. John the Divine in New York City). The church and parish house were fully restored and renovated in 1994. Although originally built for a wealthy and large congregation (the church seats 1,500), the interior is subdued and somber. Stained-glass windows set high on the west and east walls provide color and drama and were designed by Charles J. Connick of Boston, while the intricately painted ceiling is the work of native Chicagoan Frederic Clay Bartlett. Fourteen lifesize musicians at the base of each ceiling arch gaze down upon the worshippers.

The church is known throughout the city for its organ, and concerts are often given *(Mar–Jun Fri 12:10–12:40pm)*. Outside, the charming cloister and fountain that lie between the church and its ivy-covered parish house provide a serene oasis amid the clangorous activity of the avenue.

Cross to the east side of Michigan Ave.

③ FoodLife
In Water Tower Place, mezzanine level. ☎312-335-3663. Create an eclectic, healthful meal from the Chinese, Mexican, Middle Eastern, sandwich, burger and pizza stands housed in this bustling food court. At the entry, pick up a coded card and wooden tray and select entrees and drinks from a variety of stands. (The nutritional value of every item is clearly posted.) After you visit a stand, FoodLife staffers add the cost of your food to the electronic tally on your card; you pay the grand total when you leave. For those who prefer traditional restaurant service, the **Mity Nice Cafe** (at the back of the complex) offers the same fare as FoodLife.

④ Palm Court
In Drake Hotel. ☎312-787-2200. The potted-palm dotted lobby of the Drake Hotel is a perfect spot to take a break after a shopping spree along Michigan Avenue or Oak Street. An elegant British-style high tea complete with scones, finger sandwiches and petit fours is served every afternoon *(reservations recommended Jan–Nov, not accepted in Dec)*.

★★★ **John Hancock Center** – *875 N. Michigan Ave.* Nothing represents Carl Sandburg's epithet for Chicago—"the city of big shoulders"—more than this 1,127ft skyscraper (1969, Skidmore, Owings & Merrill). It is the third tallest building in Chicago, the sixth tallest in the US and, because of its huge cross-bracing steel members, one of the most recognizable in the city. Its 100 stories of black anodized aluminum and tinted glass are divided between office and residential space.

The tower was constructed at half the cost of a building of comparable height thanks to engineer Fazlur Khan's efficient design. Applying the braced tube concept to his structure, Khan developed an obelisk-shaped structural framework, which functions as a large-scale truss. Comprising some 46,000 tons of steel, the cross braces, columns and beams efficiently carry gravity and wind loads. The tapering tower rises from a 265ft by 165ft base to a top floor measuring 100ft by 160ft, offering an interior space of 2.8 million square feet.

Wide steps descending into a large sunken **plaza** frame colorful planters and a wall waterfall. The plaza affords interesting views of the Magnificent Mile skyscrapers looming to the north and south. The CHICAGO ARCHITECTURE FOUNDATION's recently opened center offers guided tours of the area *(open year-round daily 10am–8pm; closed Jan 1, Easter Sunday, Thanksgiving Day, Dec 25;* ♾ ☎312-922-8687).

Observatory – Kids *Open year-round 9am–midnight. $5.75.* ✗ & ▯ ☎312-751-3681. In 39 seconds, the elevators ascend to the 94th-floor observatory. One almost feels airborne while experiencing panoramic **views**★★★ of the city in every direction—particularly the spectacular eastern one of Lake Michigan. To the north, Lake Shore Drive winds lazily along the lake, leading to the NORTH SHORE suburbs.

Cross Delaware St.

Rising 871ft on the west side of Michigan Avenue, the 66-story **900 N. Michigan Avenue** (1989, Kohn Pedersen Fox) is best known for its anchor tenant, Bloomingdale's, the Four Seasons Hotel and the four illuminated lanterns atop the building. The spacious 6-story atrium ringed by gallery shops offers a restful retreat from the bustling streetscape.

The 37-story, 468ft **919 N. Michigan Avenue** office building (1929) ascends gracefully in a series of symmetrical setbacks topped by the now-dimmed 150ft Lindbergh Beacon, whose two billion-candlepower beam could be seen 500mi away by airplane pilots. Sheathed in Bedford limestone above the first two retail floors, which are clad in ornamental cast iron and metal, it was initially called the Palmolive Building for the company that commissioned Holabird & Root to design it as its headquarters. From 1967 to 1989 it was known as the Playboy Building when the magazine's headquarters were located here.

Cross Walton St.

★ **The Drake Hotel** – *140 E. Walton St.* Listed on the National Register of Historic Places, this 535-room luxury hotel (1920, Marshall & Fox) built on landfill at the edge of Lake Michigan provides an elegant transition to the East Lake Shore Drive Historic District, which begins at its back door and marks the northeastern border of the Magnificent Mile. Covered in limestone, its plain exterior is unadorned except for a majestic colonnade on its northern face that looks out over LINCOLN PARK, Oak Street Beach *(p 115)* and the lake. Its simplicity bespeaks the elegance of a grand hotel. Set on a rectangular base, the structure changes to an H-shape at the 3rd floor to suit hotel room layouts. Step up into the dignified lobby and public rooms to admire the plush red velvet wall coverings, the wooden caisson ceiling and the elegant Palm Court *(p 84)*.

Cross to the west side of Michigan Ave.

The northwestern border of this area is marked by **One Magnificent Mile** at nos. 940-980 (1983, Skidmore, Owings & Merrill), a 58-story mixed-use building comprising three hexagonal concrete tubes clad in rose-colored granite, which rise 57, 49 and 21 stories respectively. The three structures are joined together as a bundled tube to resist wind loads, a design originally conceived by engineer Fazlur Kahn and architect Bruce Graham for the SEARS TOWER.

Turn left onto Oak St.

★ **Oak Street** – *Between N. Michigan Ave. and Rush St.* In a single turn one is transported from high-rise shopping flurry to a tree-lined streetscape reminiscent of New York's Upper Madison Avenue—sophisticated, but understated. This is a wonderful block for browsing or buying, and each doorway heralds another upscale boutique: Hermès *(no. 110)*, Sonia Rykiel *(no. 106)*, Gianni Versace *(no. 101)*, Jil Sander *(no. 48)* and others reflect the wealth of the GOLD COAST neighborhood just to the north. At no. 40, a vintage 20-story apartment building erected in 1929 by Drake Hotel architect Ben Marshall conjures up images of a pampered past. Barneys New York *(no. 25)* anchors the western edge of this pleasant area.

★ STREETERVILLE

Bordered by Lake Michigan, the "Mag Mile" and the Chicago River, and dominated by NORTHWESTERN UNIVERSITY's Chicago Campus—including its medical, dental and law schools and several hospitals of its McGaw Medical Center—Streeterville exudes a cosmopolitan atmosphere enhanced by upscale residential high rises, the Museum of Contemporary Art, the renovated North Pier Chicago and Navy Pier and the headquarters of several prestigious national associations (American Bar, American Dental and American Hospital Associations).

★ **Museum of Contemporary Art** – *237 E. Ontario St. until July 1996. After that date: 220 E. Chicago Ave. Open year-round daily 10am–6pm (1st Fri of the month 9pm). Closed Thanksgiving Day, Dec 25. $6.50. Guided tours (1hr) available.* ✗ & ▣ ☎312-280-2660. Founded in 1967, the museum presents a wide range of contemporary visual and related arts from established international artists and less familiar names experimenting with new media and concepts. Exhibits, mounted on a rotating basis from the museum's 7,000-plus-piece permanent collection, include works by Marcel Duchamp, Max Ernst, René Magritte, Joan Miró, Jean Dubuffet and Andy Warhol. Since its inception, the museum has fostered Chicago and Illinois artists, including Ed Paschke, June Leaf, Leon Golub and Jim Nutt.

Having outgrown its limited quarters on Ontario Street, the museum will be moving to a 2-acre site located between the historic Water Tower and Lake Michigan in July 1996. The new building, the first in the US designed by Berlin architect Josef Paul Kleihues, will include permanent collection galleries *(3rd and 4th floors)*, temporary exhibition spaces *(2nd floor)*, and a library and education center with a 300-seat auditorium *(ground floor)*. A 16ft-high staircase leads to the building's grand entrance, framed by glass and aluminum panels. Facing Lake Michigan is a one-acre terraced outdoor sculpture garden. The museum's former location was the first building in the US to be wrapped by environmental artist Christo in 1969.

541 N. Fairbanks (formerly Time & Life Building) – Harry Weese & Assocs. (1968) combined the traditions of the Chicago school—the exposed metal curtain wall, regular bay spacing and horizontal window emphasis—with the austere simplicity of the Miesian idiom in this 28-story office building. Two environmentally correct and functional designs were incorporated into the building: the architect chose bronze-tinted exterior glass to reflect the sun and reduce the need for air conditioning. The interior elevator cabs were double-decked so that they could service two floors simultaneously during morning and evening rush hours (an arrangement since discontinued).

Onterie Center – *446-448 E. Ontario St.* Completed in 1986 by architect Bruce Graham and engineer Fazlur Khan, best known for their collaboration on the Sears Tower and the John Hancock Center, this building is distinguished by concrete cross-bracing expressed in blank window panels on each facade. A 2-bay inset notch runs the length of the south facade.

★ **North Pier Chicago** – **Kids** *435 E. Illinois St. Open year-round Mon–Thu 10am–9pm, Fri–Sat 10am–10pm, Sun & holidays 11am–7pm. Closed Thanksgiving Day, Dec 25.* ✗ & ▣ ☎312-836-4300. Built originally as the Pugh Terminal Warehouse in 1905, North Pier Chicago was artfully rehabilitated in 1990 by Booth/Hansen & Assocs. to house office spaces on the upper four floors and a retail and entertainment center on the lower three. The latter, a 170,000sq ft festival marketplace arranged around an attractive central rotunda, boasts more than 60 shops, clubs, restaurants and entertainment venues, including two museums, a miniature golf course, two interactive virtual reality centers and a boat company that offers Chicago architectural and historical tours *(departs Jun–Sept daily 9am–3pm; May & Oct Mon–Fri noon, weekends noon–2pm; $16;* ✗ & ▣ *Chicago From The Lake* ☎312-527-1977). Striking **views★** of the city can be observed from its southern glass galleries or the dockside promenade.

The Bicycle Museum of America [M¹] – **Kids** *Lower level, east end. Open year-round Mon–Thu 10am–6pm, Fri–Sat 10am–8pm, Sun noon–5pm. $1.50. Guided tours (1hr) available.* & ☎312-222-0500. The only such institution in the US, the museum presents an extensive collection of 50,000 items related to the bicycle: 600 2-wheelers dating from the mid-1800s through the 1990s as well as catalogs, clothing, advertisements and vintage movies. The introductory video presentation provides a short, yet complete, history of the bicycle. Revolving exhibits and special cycling clinics are scheduled each month. Valet parking for bicycles is available for $1, and the popular Lake Shore Drive bike path *(p 244)* is a few blocks away.

The Nature Museum of the Chicago Academy of Sciences [M²] – Kids *Third level, east end. Open year-round Mon–Fri 9:30am–4:30pm, Sat 10am–6pm, Sun noon–6pm. Closed Easter Sunday, Thanksgiving Day, Dec 25. $3.* ♿ ☎*312-871-2668.* The academy has been collecting and preserving pieces of the natural environment since 1857, making it one of the oldest scientific museums in America. Formerly located in Lincoln Park, the museum is temporarily housed here, awaiting completion of its new, 74,000sq ft museum at the corner of Fullerton Parkway and Cannon Drive *(scheduled completion: 1998).*

Near the entrance, **Waterworks** invites visitors to build a riverbed and pump water through it to see how rivers sculpt the land. Microscopes and other instruments are on hand to help explore the chemistry of the Chicago River, using real river water. In the **Children's Gallery**, kids can try on stag horns, make leaf impressions, handle fossils and bones and use any of the computers, puzzles, books and art materials for a grand introduction to the particularities of living beings.

★ **Lake Shore Drive** – This thoroughfare bordering the lake is lined with an array of high rises, several of which were designed by renowned German architect **Ludwig Mies van der Rohe** *(p 35).*

★★ **860-880 N. Lake Shore Drive** – The completion of these apartment towers in 1951 by Mies van der Rohe established his reputation as a master of Modernism and prefigured the design of steel-and-glass skyscrapers throughout the 1960s and 70s. Their prominent location, substantial scale and elegance of proportion were the first realization of steel-and-glass curtain wall designs that Mies had been developing for over 30 years. Here, he used steel piers encased in concrete and created a strong vertical dynamic by attaching I beams to the exterior between the window frames. A transparent lobby space creates an elegant effect. The two buildings are angled to each other and the street, providing many lake views for the apartments. The success of these two towers led to another commission two years later at **900-910 N. Lake Shore Drive**. Distinguished by dark glass and window frames, these structures represent a more monochromatic design.

Lake Shore Place – *No. 680.* Visible from many places in the area is the blue pyramidal roof of this office and residential complex, formerly known as the American Furniture Mart (1926). The 30-story tower and its four corner tourelles are embellished with Victorian Gothic designs, including 3-story arches and an ornamental lantern at the top.

Lake Point Tower – *No. 505.* Lonely sentinel on the east side of the drive, this unusual high rise was built in 1968 by Schipporeit-Heinrich, students of Mies van der Rohe who adapted an unexecuted 1920 design by the master. All of the exterior surfaces of the Y-shaped tower are rounded, creating a flowing surface studded with vertical steel piers.

5 **Gold Star Sardine Bar**
680 N. Lake Shore Place; use entrance on McClurg Ct. ☎*312-664-4215.*
Top local jazz combos and up-and-coming torch singers from across the country entertain in this tiny jazz boîte. The aptly named Sardine Bar's typically chic patrons sip champagne and nibble White Castle hamburgers and elegant little chicken salad sandwiches late into the evening. Liza Minnelli, co-owner Bobby Short, Tony Bennett and other celebrities have been known to give surprise, unbilled shows.

★★ **Navy Pier** – Kids *600 E. Grand Ave. at Lake Michigan. Open May–Sept Mon–Thu 10am–10pm, Fri–Sat 10am–midnight, Sun 10am–9pm; rest of the year Mon–Thu 10am–9pm, Fri–Sat 10am–10pm, Sun 10am–7pm.* ✗ ♿ 🅿 ☎*312-595-7437. Local cruise ships dock on the south end of the Pier: year-round, Odyssey* ☎*630-990-0800 and Anita Dee* ☎*312-281-1300; seasonally, The Spirit of Chicago* ☎*312-836-7899 and Shoreline Marine* ☎*312-222-9328.* Designed by Charles S. Frost in 1916, the 3,000ft-long pier was the largest in the world at the time. With an upper level for passengers and streetcar tracks and a lower level for freight, it was an important terminal for several decades. Long freight sheds (since demolished) connected the Head House (now known as the Family Pavilion) to the Auditorium building at the far end. The pier was used for naval training during World War II, and then by the University of Illinois until 1965, at which time it was affectionately known as "Harvard on the Rocks." Renovated in 1959 for the opening of the St. Lawrence

Navy Pier at Night

Seaway and again in 1976, the pier fell into disrepair until 1991, when the City proposed a $190 million redevelopment plan, which foresaw the pier as an extension of the MCCORMICK PLACE Convention Center.

Today encompassing more than 50 acres of shops, eateries, gardens and attractions, the pier has regained its fame as one of the largest entertainment piers in the country. A bustling and festive place that draws throngs of fun-seekers, the Pier features an IMAX Theater, the Chicago Children's Museum, boutiques, restaurants and office space in its Family Pavilion. Adjoining the pavilion to the east, the Crystal Gardens house an indoor tropical park, embellished with Arizona palm trees. At the center of the pier is Navy Pier Park which showcases a 150ft-high Ferris Wheel, a musical merry-go-round and a 1,500-seat outdoor amphitheater, Skyline Stage. With its taut, sail-like roof, the popular venue rises above a 1-story retail level. Festival Hall, a series of 3-story structures designed for conventions, trade shows and meetings, connects the central area to the Terminals Building, with its splendidly restored ballroom. A seasonal beer garden welcomes weary strollers, who enjoy some of the city's best views of the lake and the famed skyline.

★ **Chicago Children's Museum [M³]** – 🧒 *Open Memorial Day–Labor Day daily 10am–5pm (Thu 8pm), rest of the year Tue–Sun 10am–5pm (Thu 8pm). $5.* ♿ 🅿 ☎312-527-1000. Founded in 1982 as the Express-Ways Children's Museum, this 3-story, hands-on facility is designed to activate the intellectual and creative potential of children approximately one to twelve years old. Interactive exhibits invite youngsters to build bridges, recycle trash, appreciate grandparents, climb aboard a replica 1850 schooner, respond to prejudice and discrimination, go to the hospital and create news broadcasts, all in a fun, safe, colorful environment monitored by trained supervisors.

Be sure to don a raincoat before entering **Waterways**, to direct the world's most abundant resource through a system of rivers, locks and bridges. Prejudice and discrimination are explored in **Face to Face** *(not recommended for children under seven)*; exhibits here help kids identify offensive behavior and practice ways of responding constructively. In **The Stinking Truth About Garbage**, walk through a landfill and find out how to reuse and recycle trash. Other popular permanent exhibits include "City Hospital," designed to demystify children's fears about medical care; the "Inventing Lab," where you create your own flying machine; and "On Camera," a state-of-the-art broadcasting studio.

At the entrance to Navy Pier, 19-acre **Gateway Park** includes a modern water fountain—splashing allowed!—and artworks inspired by the ILLINOIS & MICHIGAN CANAL NATIONAL HERITAGE CORRIDOR. To the north, bordering Ohio Street Beach, **Jane Addams Park** and **Milton Lee Olive Park** provide a welcome respite from busy Streeterville with flower gardens, lush trees and pleasant walkways.

THE FIELD MUSEUM OF NATURAL HISTORY★★★

Time: 1 day. Roosevelt Rd. at Lake Shore Dr. [CTA] bus no. 146 (museum bus).
Map p 111 and plan p 91

This world-class natural history museum commands a suitably grand presence at the south end of GRANT PARK. Indeed, there is nothing small about this institution. Nine acres of exhibit halls and over 20 million artifacts inhabit the vast Neoclassical edifice where collections, exhibits and public programs specialize in anthropology, geology, botany and zoology. Dinosaur bones, ethnographic materials and animal taxidermy are among the museum's traditional strengths; today all have been incorporated into modern interpretive exhibits.

Historical Notes

"A Grand Museum" – By the time work was begun on the present-day Field Museum in 1915, the institution already had a long history. Harvard anthropologist Frederick Ward Putnam was determined that the vast ethnographic and zoological collections he had amassed for display at the World's Columbian Exposition *(p 12)* in 1893 would have a permanent home after the fair, envisioning for "this great city… a grand museum of natural history." He enlisted the aid of Edward E. Ayer, a collector of Native American artifacts, to persuade department store magnate Marshall Field to contribute the million dollars it would require to establish such an institution. That endowment funded the Field Columbian Museum, which was to be housed in the fair's Palace of Fine Arts in Jackson Park. Never intended as a permanent structure, the palace would not be suitable for long, and the Field soon required another home.

Before his death in 1906, Marshall Field hired architect Daniel Burnham to create a new natural history museum in the august Beaux-Arts style of the World's Columbian Exposition, bequeathing money to pay for and endow it. Burnham's vision of a museum in Grant Park raised a furor with advocates of a lakefront free and clear of building *(p 108)*, and it wasn't until the Illinois Central Railroad offered a muddy and desolate parcel of land just south of the park that plans for the Field could be finalized. Begun in 1915, landfilling alone took a year to complete. The museum's doors finally opened in May 1921.

The Building – The monumental scale of the museum is at once awe-inspiring and exhausting. Burnham based the 706ft-long, colonnaded facade on the Ionic order, and even included caryatids modeled by sculptor Henry Hering on those at the Erechtheion on the Acropolis in Greece. Thanks to exterior conservation and an extensive cleaning in 1988, the crisp white Georgia marble cladding once again glows. A pedestrian walkway under Lake Shore Drive leads to the JOHN G. SHEDD AQUARIUM.

No less impressive are the inside spaces, the most dramatic of which is **Stanley Field Hall**, a 300ft, 2-story expanse where visitors can get their bearings. Behind stately arches and columns on either side, exhibit spaces unfold deep into the

Stanley Field Hall

symmetrical wings. Female statues (also the work of Henry Hering) representing the four purposes of the museum—science, dissemination of knowledge, research and recording—gaze down from each of the four upper corners of the hall.

The Collections – Equally grand in scale are the museum's collections, only about four percent of which are on display in over 20 exhibits. Since the mid-1980s, as part of a $40-million, 10-year effort, many exhibits have been thoroughly renovated and now include computer and video elements, detailed interpretation and modern exhibit techniques. Some, notably in the Native American wing, are old and represent a more traditional, "study collection" exhibit approach—case after unvarying case of artifacts accompanied by very few labels. Behind the scenes, millions of artifacts, many from the World's Columbian Exposition and others collected over years of field work or purchased from private collectors, serve as the basis for research projects and publications by scholars from around the world.

VISIT

Open year-round daily 9am–5pm. Closed Jan 1, Thanksgiving Day, Dec 25. $5 (there is a separate $2 charge for entry to dinosaur galleries). ✕ ♿ ▯ ☎312-922-9410.
Since the museum offers enough to fill several days, visitors should focus on the subjects of interest to them by consulting the floor plan and FieldNotes, *a listing of daily activities available at the admissions desk.*

The Field's exhibits can be categorized into three groups: introductory exhibits, of special interest to children, presenting basic ideas in simple ways—**Sizes** Kids *(1st floor)* and **Families at Work** Kids *(2nd floor)*, for instance; comprehensive thematic exhibits, dealing with culture groups, botany, earth sciences and evolution; and resource centers, where visitors can extend their learning by doing further research on their own. A good orientation to the museum's overarching purpose can be had by beginning with the four huge displays in Stanley Field Hall. Labels accompanying a replica **Brachiosaurus★ [A]** Kids (the largest mounted dinosaur in the world), a pair of taxidermied bull elephants **[B]**, two Haida totem poles **[C]** and a globe of the earth **[D]** explain the organization and mission of the museum.

Begin in the southwest corner of Stanley Field Hall on the first floor.

First Floor – Particularly interesting for children, the lively **What is an Animal?** exhibit Kids presents a colorful array of animal life, from head lice to giant squid, arranged so that visitors can contrast and compare sizes, colors, habitats, survival techniques and other animal behaviors and characteristics. Just outside this exhibit, **Inside Ancient Egypt** begins with a tour through the **mastaba tomb★** of Unis-ankh, son of the last pharaoh of the Fifth Dynasty (2428-2407 BC). Part replica and part authentic, this is the largest full-size reconstruction of a tomb outside of Egypt. In the original chambers, tomb paintings are preserved under glass. A stairway leads to the roof for a good view into the tomb, and from here a spiral staircase winds down to the ground floor of the museum where the exhibit continues into the depths of the tomb's burial chamber. The Field's strong collection of Egyptian **burial and mortuary artifacts** fills the next rooms with some 20 mummies, sarcophagi, papyrus scrolls and other funerary objects arranged by dynasty. Admire the tiny **diorama** illustrating the embalmer's art before exiting through an ancient Egyptian marketplace.

Also on the ground floor is **Bushman [E]** Kids, LINCOLN PARK ZOO's legendary gorilla, now stuffed. Bushman captured the hearts of Chicagoans upon his arrival from the French Cameroons in 1930. He died in 1951 and has resided at the Field ever since. Sea mammals cavort in dioramas lining the walls of nearby vending areas. Temporary exhibit galleries occupy the opposite end of the ground floor.

Return to the first floor.

Just beyond the Egyptian tomb, on the west side of Field Hall, is a kaleidoscopic new exhibit entitled **Africa★★**. From the streets of Dakar, Senegal, decked out for the Muslim feast day of Tabaski (which celebrates an Islamic story of Abraham and Isaac), to the sand dunes of the Sahara, where the Tuareg people live and trade, this sweeping presentation investigates African politics, art, environment, wildlife, geography, commerce and family life by focusing on representative regions and peoples. Note especially the **ritual regalia★** and beautifully crafted tools of the Bamum people of Cameroon in the section on art and society. In conspicuous contrast, a segment on the slave trade compels visitors to walk through a dimly lit slave ship's hold and consider such artifacts of slavery as shackles and

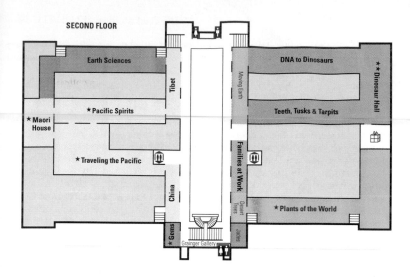

SECOND FLOOR

Earth Sciences

Tibet

DNA to Dinosaurs

★★ Dinosaur Hall

Moving Earth

★ Maori House

★ Pacific Spirits

Teeth, Tusks & Tarpits

★ Traveling the Pacific

China

Families at Work

★ Gems

Grainger Gallery

Jades

Desert Trees

★ Plants of the World

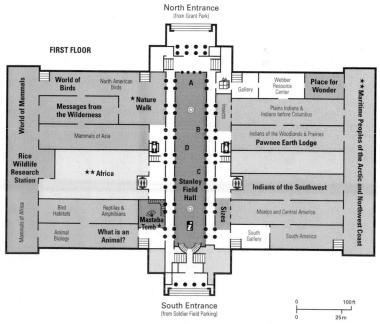

North Entrance
(from Grant Park)

FIRST FLOOR

World of Mammals

World of Birds

North American Birds

★ Nature Walk

Messages from the Wilderness

Mammals of Asia

Rice Wildlife Research Station

★★ Africa

Mammals of Africa

Bird Habitats

Reptiles & Amphibians

Mastaba Tomb ★

Animal Biology

What is an Animal?

A

B

D

C

Stanley Field Hall

Sizes

Gallery

Webber Resource Center

Place for Wonder

★★ Maritime Peoples of the Arctic and Northwest Coast

Insects

Plains Indians & Indians before Columbus

Indians of the Woodlands & Prairies

Pawnee Earth Lodge

Indians of the Southwest

Mexico and Central America

South Gallery

South America

South Entrance
(from Soldier Field Parking)

0   100 ft
0   25 m

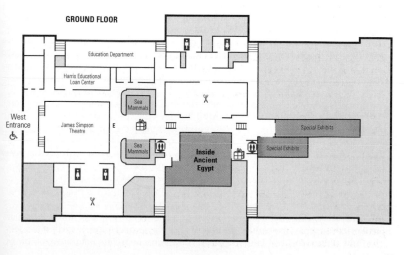

GROUND FLOOR

Education Department

Harris Educational Loan Center

James Simpson Theatre

West Entrance

E

Sea Mammals

Sea Mammals

Inside Ancient Egypt

Special Exhibits

Special Exhibits

a restraining collar. Blending words, videos and artifacts, this exhibit is designed to appeal to every age group. At its conclusion, a resource center offers books and other reference materials for further study.

The northwest corner of this floor is devoted to mammals, birds and their habitats. These galleries show off to great advantage the elaborate taxidermy and dioramas—largely the legacy of Carl Akeley—for which the Field is famous. Akeley, who worked at the museum between 1896 and 1909, was a sculptor and pioneer in the field of taxidermy and diorama making, setting the standards for realism and detail that would inform those crafts for 50 years. His most recognizable work is the pair of bull elephants in Stanley Field Hall, but his **Four Seasons★**, on display continuously at the museum since its creation in 1902, represents the height of his art. The four-part tableau depicts deer in their habitat throughout the year. It can currently be seen in **Nature Walk★**, an exhibit that takes visitors on a trek through woods, wetlands and other wild places. This exhibit combines historic dioramas with contemporary interactive devices and computers. Interpretive labels engage viewers of all ages to reflect on what they see in each detailed diorama, or invite them to turn over a log for a peek underneath. A computer offers detailed information on local and regional nature areas and organizations; another gives visitors a chance to "manage" a herd of deer. To complement Nature Walk, **Messages from the Wilderness** employs dioramas to deliver timely messages about environmental issues and extinction. In the **World of Birds** and the **World of Mammals**, hundreds of birds and mammals are mounted in old-fashioned display cases. To this traditional approach have been added interpretive graphics, sound effects (such as bird calls) and environmental notes. At the far end of that exhibit is the **Rice Wildlife Research Station**, a large, comfortable space where visitors can use books, computer programs and other resources to study specific subjects.

The galleries to the east of Stanley Field Hall are devoted to the culture groups of North and South America. With the exception of the **Pawnee Earth Lodge** (one of several full-scale dwellings reconstructed throughout the museum) and the section on maritime peoples, these exhibits represent a past generation of museum display techniques. The artifacts are no less stunning for it, however. Kachina dolls, ancient pottery and Pima and Papago basketry highlight the **Indians of the Southwest** gallery. The dense **Maritime Peoples of the Arctic and Northwest Coast★★** exhibit, opened in 1984, contains a seemingly exhaustive catalogue of materials contrasting life on the Northwest Coast and in the Arctic. Especially impressive are a case of Northwest Coast **masks** and a forest of stately cedar **totem poles★** (most collected by anthropologist Franz Boas for the World's Columbian Exposition in 1893), which towers above the display. In the northeast corner of this wing, the **Place for Wonder** 🄺🄸🄳🅂 offers young visitors their own resource center where they can commune up close with bones and stones, objects and artifacts.

Ascend to second floor.

Second Floor – Ten years in the making, a 3-part exhibit entitled **Life Over Time★** was an ambitious undertaking for curators and proves equally so for visitors. Divided into three major halls, the exhibit covers life before the dinosaurs, the reign of the dinosaurs and life after their demise and into the Ice Age. Truly interested visitors can lose themselves for a day in these halls, but the exhibit challenges the casual observer because it is so dense with information and materials. Throughout the exhibit, video "newscasts" starring local broadcasters provide effective summaries of the events of each time period covered. The first part, **DNA to Dinosaurs**, offers a comprehensive look at the prehistory of the earth over 3.8 billion years, from primordial soup to the emergence of four-legged creatures, investigating along the way mutation, evolution, adaptation and extinction, the processes by which life comes and goes and changes on our planet. **Dinosaur Hall★★** 🄺🄸🄳🅂, the highlight of the exhibit, bridges the first and last sections with breathtaking skeletons (replica and genuine) of those enormous beasts: long-necked *Apatosaurus*, delicate *Pteranodon* and primeval-looking *Triceratops* among them. **Teeth, Tusks and Tarpits** opens with a cleverly contrived multimedia presentation entitled **Fossil Lake Adventure★** about the scientific value of fossils. Fast-paced, entertaining and stagy, the balance of the exhibit covers the rise of mammals, particularly in the Americas, and concludes with the origins and evolution of the human species.

In a completely different vein, the serene and beautifully crafted exhibit **Plants of the World★** occupies the southeastern corner of the second floor. Including models of a third of the world's plant species, it is the most complete botanical exhibit in existence. It succeeds in dazzling the visitor with the incredible variety of form, color and function among the world's plants. Made through a process pioneered by Carl Akeley at the turn of the century, each model was meticulously formed of wax or plastic from molds of living plants. A single model may have taken two or three months to complete. Accompanying label text is no less detailed, describing fruits, flowers and leaves for family after family of plants. Interesting facts are highlighted, and visitors learn, for instance, that as members of the poison ivy family, cashews must be removed from the poisonous juices in their husks before they can be eaten.

Tucked into a small gallery just west of the south staircase, an exhibit of **Gems**★ presents a shimmering collection of precious and semiprecious stones. Careful lighting in a darkened room brings out the best of the opals, moonstones, rubies and others on display from among the museum's collection of 60,000. (More mineralogy can be found in the **Earth Sciences** hall in the northwest corner of the second floor.)

The remainder of this side of the second floor is devoted to Asia and the Pacific. Small exhibits on **China** and **Tibet** showcase ritual and secular artifacts from those cultures. Particularly noteworthy are examples of Tibetan ceremonial paraphernalia—prayer wheels, wands, shell trumpets and the like—all forms unfamiliar to the Western eye, each exquisitely tooled and ornamented. Equally fascinating are the Tibetan anatomical and medicinal charts. By way of introduction, a video makes good use of historic footage of monastic life in Tibet.

Two full-scale exhibits focus on separate aspects of the cultures of Oceania: navigating the waters and ceremonial life. To evoke the essence of the islands, **Traveling the Pacific**★ uses modern "stage settings"—a lava flow, a deserted beach—alongside traditional glass case displays. Hundreds of elaborately decorated artifacts related to canoes, canoe building and canoe ornamentation—including a wonderful assortment of paddles—form the core of the exhibit. Next door, **Pacific Spirits**★ again draws on the museum's vast Oceanic collection to explore the religious beliefs of the peoples of Polynesia, Micronesia, Melanesia and New Guinea. The highlight of this journey around the Pacific is Ruatepupuke, an authentic **Maori meeting house**★ that has been reconstructed here piece by piece. The only such meeting house in the Western Hemisphere, it is a sacred place to New Zealand's Maori people, and curators collaborated with Maori consultants to follow ancient protocols in its installation and re-consecration. The house, which dates from 1881, is 55ft long, 23ft wide and 15ft high, and represents both an ethnographic treasure and a work of art, as its intricate incised surfaces and complex carvings are unique to the Maori.

JOHN G. SHEDD AQUARIUM★★★

Time: 1/2 day. 1200 S. Lake Shore Dr. 🚌 bus no. 146 (museum bus).
Map p 111 and plan p 95

Located appropriately at the very edge of Lake Michigan, the Shedd Aquarium is one in the triumvirate of museums devoted to earth (FIELD MUSEUM), sea and sky (ADLER PLANETARIUM) clustered at the south end of GRANT PARK. The world's largest indoor aquarium, the Shedd includes some 8,100 aquatic animals comprising 650 species, from tiny, jewel-like spiny lobsters to 1,500lb beluga whales. A strong emphasis on conservation and the environment pervades all of the aquarium's exhibits and programs; its remarkable animals make the message come to life.

Historical Notes

Ocean by the Lake – When John Graves Shedd, who rose from stock boy to chairman of Marshall Field & Company between 1872 and 1926, donated $3 million for the construction of an aquarium in Chicago, he intended it to house "the greatest variety of sea life on display under one roof." Architects Graham, Anderson, Probst & White designed a fitting edifice to complement the stately Field Museum across Lake Shore Drive. It opened in 1930, one of the last Beaux-Arts buildings in Chicago, and perhaps the final nod to city planner Daniel Burnham's vision of the "City Beautiful," an aesthetic outgrowth of the World's Columbian Exposition of 1893. The octagonal structure, clad in shimmering white Georgia marble, resembles at every turn a monument to Poseidon. Indeed, the sea god's trident

Coral Reef

surmounts the building's dome. The aquarium's nautical decor is among its most remarkable features: inside and out repeating wave and shell patterns decorate doorways, cornices, tiles and pediments; bas-reliefs of elegant sea creatures embellish walls and even lighting fixtures mimic piscine forms. All blend into a delightful aquatic paraphrase of a classical Doric temple. The building was awarded National Historic Landmark status in 1987.

The aquarium is equally remarkable for its state-of-the-art mechanical systems. Original plans called for the latest in materials, piping (75mi of it), water storage (enough for two million gallons—four times larger than any of that day) and environmental controls that made life in the aquarium's 200 tanks possible. Salt water was imported by barge and train from Key West and the Gulf of Mexico until 1973 when the aquarium began mixing its own using water from Lake Michigan.

A pioneer in the re-creation of aquatic habitats, the Shedd is in the midst of transforming its old-fashioned stacked rock tank environments into mini-ecosystems supporting not only fish but plants and microscopic life as well. This approach to aquatic exhibition makes habitats as handsome and interesting as their inhabitants. And, in keeping with the Shedd's focus on conservation, these habitats convey the idea and importance of biodiversity and the interrelationships of species with each other and with their surroundings. Of particular interest are endangered and degraded environments, and several displays offer visitors a look at ecosystems that may already no longer exist in the wild.

In 1991 the much-heralded 170,000sq ft oceanarium opened to the southeast of the original building to house marine mammals and an expansive replication of the endangered Pacific Northwest Coast ecosystem. Completed at a cost of $45 million, the addition (Lohan & Assocs.) is covered in marble peeled from the side of the old building now shared by the oceanarium. Its most distinguishing feature, a broad "curtain of glass" barely seems to separate the interior from Lake Michigan. Inside, oceanarium planners created a habitat as close to nature as possible—down to the shape of the pools—after considerable study of the needs and behaviors of the animals that would live there.

VISIT

🄺🄸🄳 *Open Jun–Aug daily 9am–6pm; rest of the year Mon–Fri 9am–5pm, weekends & holidays 9am–6pm. Closed Jan 1, Dec 25. $4 each for aquarium and oceanarium (aquarium free on Thu). Guided tours available.* ✗ ⅋ 🄿 *($5)* ▥▥▥ ☎ *312-939-2483.*
Morning is the best time to visit the Shedd Aquarium, especially in summer when a line is likely to form around the block by 11am. Early visitors can expect immediate admission to the oceanarium; those who come later often must wait to enter. No matter what the time, the galleries seem to swim with children and school groups.

Main Building – Laid out in the shape of a cross, the main exhibit areas in the original building fan out from the centerpiece, the 90,000gal **Coral Reef★** exhibit situated beneath the rotunda. The huge tank harbors 500 tropical fishes from

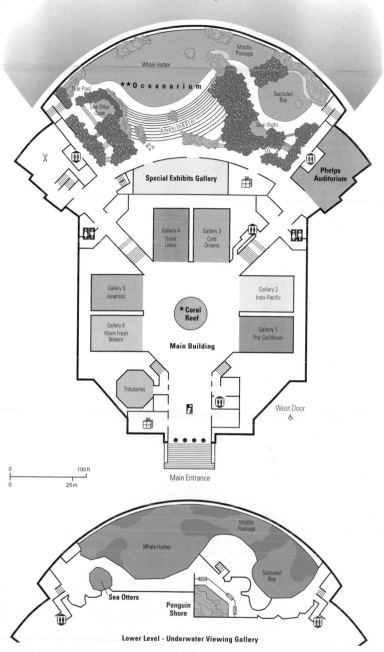

**Oceanarium

Whale Harbor

Middle Passage

Tide Pool

Sea Otter Cove

Amphitheater

Secluded Bay

Seal Bight

Special Exhibits Gallery

Phelps Auditorium

Gallery 4
Great Lakes

Gallery 3
Cold Oceans

Gallery 5
Americas

Gallery 2
Indo-Pacific

★Coral Reef

Gallery 6
Warm Fresh Waters

Gallery 1
The Caribbean

Main Building

Tributaries

West Door

Main Entrance

0   100ft
0   25m

Middle Passage

Whale Harbor

Secluded Bay

Sea Otters

Penguin Shore

Lower Level - Underwater Viewing Gallery

nurse sharks to moray eels. Daily feedings by scuba-diving animal caretakers are engrossing; the divers narrate their actions from underwater as they work. Radiating from the reef, six 90ft rectangular galleries flow one into the other, each focusing on a different type of aquatic system. The darkened spaces contrast with the brightly lit tanks to provide optimum viewing.

The Caribbean exhibits in gallery 1 introduce visitors to the many layers of life in that region, from island-dwelling rock iguanas, to leopard sharks of the pelagic zone and beyond into the reaches of the deep reef. The sparkling clarity and colorful inhabitants of Indo-Pacific waters make gallery 2 a visual delight. Here, a particularly stunning exhibit of **"marine jewels"** showcases feathery and delicate denizens of the deep—elegant shrimp, potbellied sea-horses and the like—which contrast dramatically in size and aspect with the rotund Queensland grouper in its neighboring barrier reef habitat. Behind a darkened screen, flashlight fish dart and glow. These furtive creatures harbor luminescent bacteria under each eye to find and lure food.

In gallery 3, a **Northwest Coast "surge zone"**—created by "dump buckets" above the tanks that release 100gal of water every 15sec—teems with starfish and other tide-tossed life. At the river otter display in gallery 4, interpretive graphics and visitor-activated videos introduce the lively animals behind the glass. The **alligator snapping turtle** in gallery 5 is celebrated for its inactivity. Visitors wait patiently to see it rise for air about once an hour. The 50-year-old barnacle-encrusted beast weighs in at 220lbs.

In gallery 6, a school of **piranhas** dwells in its Venezuelan river habitat. Their silvery backs and scarlet stomachs lend them an elegance that belies their reputation. Although capable of devouring a small animal in minutes with their razor-sharp teeth, this school lives contentedly on its diet of krill, smelt and pellets.

Across the gallery, the large **Asian River habitat** faithfully reproduces an endangered riverine system in Thailand, including a Thepa giant catfish, whose habitat in the wild has virtually disappeared. Also in gallery 6 lurks the prehistoric-looking Australian lungfish. The original of this group was collected by the aquarium in 1933, making it more than 60 years old.

Throughout the exhibit areas, a smattering of interpretive graphics with strong ecological overtones offer informative and sometimes humorous data on such diverse topics as fish senses and Chicago's changing shoreline.

★★ **Oceanarium** – In contrast to the darkened halls of the older building, light floods the airy and open oceanarium, the world's largest indoor marine mammal pavilion. A visit here amounts to a walk through a huge diorama, complete with living marine animals, that is a faithful reproduction in steel and epoxy—down to the last rock and pine needle—of a Northwest coastal ecosystem. Life along this coast lends itself particularly well to exhibit as the ranges of many marine mammals overlap here, and the Sitka spruce forest could be successfully simulated in an exhibit setting. Depicting this region also offers an unequaled opportunity to demonstrate the dynamics of an entire ecosystem, and an endangered one at that, as the harvesting of North American temperate rain forests proceeds at a devastating pace.

Did You Know?

■ A large Caribbean parrot fish excretes a ton of sand a year. Using two oversized front teeth, it nibbles on seagrass and scrapes algae. Another set of teeth in its throat grinds up coral it ingests.

■ Fish have excellent senses of hearing and smell and rely very little on eyesight.

■ It takes two weeks for a pair of elegant shrimp to devour a starfish 100 times their size.

■ Some sea anemones grow microscopic gardens inside their bodies to produce oxygen and nutrients when outside food is scarce.

■ The largest-known American lobster on record weighed 48lbs.

■ A hundred years ago, 12 million pounds of whitefish were fished from Lake Michigan. Today the annual take is 3 million pounds.

■ A sunflower sea starfish can travel along the bottom at 5ft per hour. Some sea anemones move at 4in per hour by somersaulting.

■ Adult electric eels 5 to 7ft long produce enough electricity—600 volts—to stun a horse.

The self-guided stroll "along the coast" follows the edge of the oversized pools where **beluga whales**, Pacific white-sided **dolphins** and **harbor seals** carouse. Around each bend loom islands, a tide pool, a fault line and other geologic features. The wide expanse of Lake Michigan stretches beyond, a vista barely interrupted by the oceanarium's glass wall. Throughout the day, animal care specialists work in unscheduled sessions with the whales and dolphins to encourage natural behaviors, accustom the animals to human contact and provide them with play time. These sessions can be observed up close from the nature trail. Formal 15min demonstrations of natural behaviors are presented several times daily (*check presentation times at entrance*) and can be viewed from an amphitheater carved into the "rocks" above the pools. Demonstrators stress that the animals are not performing tricks but doing what comes naturally on hand cues from a poolside trainer. A "spy-hopping" dolphin, for instance, stands straight up on its tail for a better view above the water.

One level below the habitat, an **Underwater Viewing Gallery** offers glimpses into the depths of the huge pools. **Penguin Shore** houses colonies of rockhopper, magellanic and gentoo penguins, three of the world's seventeen penguin species. These creatures—found only in the frigid reaches of the Southern Hemisphere—are perfectly suited to their environment, combining the best of bird, marine mammal and fish. Strong "wings" allow them to "fly" through the water. Blubber and a complex layering of feathers keep them warm in water 70 degrees colder than their bodies. And, their dolphinlike shape streamlines their swimming. The **sea otter** habitat can be viewed from both levels. These smallest of marine mammals lack the bulk and blubber their relatives rely on for keeping warm; instead, their dense fur must act as insulation. Clean fur is therefore essential, and the otters spend much of the day grooming. To an otter, an oil spill can be devastating. Four of the aquarium's otters were rescued from the *Exxon Valdez* spill in 1989.

A series of interactive exhibits presents topics related to the marine mammals such as breathing and diving, beluga populations, locomotion through water, and otters and oil spills. One display explains the workings of the oceanarium, mechanical as well as human, and an intriguing video provides a look at the animals "after hours."

One level above the oceanarium is the **Special Exhibits Gallery**, which presents two exhibits each year on matters marine and maritime, recently including model ships, endangered species, life among the Inuit along with the gallery's first live animal exhibit featuring a rare white alligator from the Louisiana bayous. In the **Phelps Auditorium**, short videos on a variety of aquatic topics run continuously. The aquarium's two restaurants and library are also located here.

Consult the Practical Information section (pp 218-245) for travel tips, useful addresses and phone numbers, and a wealth of details on shopping, recreation, entertainment and annual events.

RIVER NORTH★

Time: 1/2 day. **CTA** Brown or Orange line to State; Red line to Grand.
Map p 101

Nestled in the crook between the Chicago River and its north branch, with Wabash Avenue on the east and Division Street on the north, River North is an eclectic neighborhood of historic buildings, modern skyscrapers and churches that punctuate endless blocks of ordinary city. Site of Chicago's earliest industries, River North is today most famous for its art galleries, celebrity-owned restaurants and trendy clubs.

Historical Notes

From Factories to Flophouses – River North encompasses one of Chicago's oldest areas, Wolf Point, a small promontory around which the river turns north. Here in the 1830s, early settlers, French-Canadian fur traders and Potawatomi Indians mingled at trading posts and taverns while small industries sprang up nearby. By mid-century, factories crowded the water's edge. Grain elevators, lumber mills, brickyards, tanneries and breweries bustled and spewed. Between the north and the main branches of the river, insalubrious shantytowns spread, housing laborers and their families. Waves of immigrants—Irish, Norwegians, Danes,

Swedes and later Italians—settled south of Division Street, while in the blocks around Washington Square Park and just west of Michigan Avenue, Chicago's elite established an early North Side enclave.

In 1871, the Chicago Fire devastated shanties and mansions alike as it leapt the river and raged northward. Rebuilding began immediately, and the area reemerged as before: a corridor of elegant homes flanking the eastern edge of a working-class neighborhood. By 1900, the blighted and lawless northwestern corner was known as Little Hell. The population continued to increase as industry burgeoned. Around World War I, the newest immigrants—blacks moving up from the South in the Great Migration (p 154)—took their place in the melting pot that characterized River North.

In 1920, the completion of the Michigan Avenue Bridge ensured the destiny of that boulevard as the fashionable MAGNIFICENT MILE. The desirable neighborhoods along the avenue attracted wealthy residents from the blocks between Wabash Avenue and LaSalle Street to the west, leaving the old homes there to be subdivided into apartments and rooming houses. Washington Square Park, nicknamed "Bughouse Square," became the center of Chicago's bohemia, an open forum for soapbox orators, hobo poets and a parade of characters expounding on everything from Nietzsche to free love. Clark Street north of the river became the magnificent mile of the demimonde, lined with flophouses, bars and dance halls. In the old Little Hell, massive urban-renewal efforts throughout the 1940s and 1950s produced the controversial Cabrini-Green housing projects, now a sad reminder of good intentions gone awry.

1 Ontario Street

Between Dearborn and Wells Streets, this neon-lit artery forms the hub of River North nightlife drawing hordes of tourists to such popular chain restaurants as the **Hard Rock Cafe** (63 W. Ontario St.; ☎ 312-943-2252), **Rock 'n' Roll McDonald's** (600 N. Clark St.; ☎ 312-664-7940) and **Planet Hollywood** (633 N. Wells St.; ☎ 312-266-7827). **Ed Debevic's** (640 N. Wells St.; ☎ 312-664-1707), a Chicago institution, is known for its sassy waitstaff, often dressed as characters from 1950s movies and TV shows. A huge basketball atop **Michael Jordan's Restaurant** (a few blocks south of Ontario St. at 500 N. LaSalle St.; ☎ 312-644-3865) beckons visitors. An enormous video screen dominates the first-floor sports bar while magazine covers of the world's favorite basketball star decorate the upstairs dining room.

Art Brings a New Start – In the 1970s, art dealers frustrated by rising costs on Michigan Avenue sought less expensive gallery spaces. The deserted warehouses in the old industrial district south of Superior Street and west of Wells Street offered a perfect alternative, and they soon swarmed with artists, buyers and lookers. After a decade of prosperity, tragedy struck in 1989 when fire destroyed the entire block between Orleans and Sedgwick Streets south of Superior Street, consuming nine galleries. On its heels, the economic downturn of the early 1990s caused several more galleries to close or leave, some for River West—the next reviving neighborhood to offer reasonable rents. Around 65 remain, however, sustaining River North's reputation as Chicago's center of contemporary art.

This quarter seems also to be a favorite location for celebrity-owned restaurants and clubs. Since the 1980s, such popular spots as the Hard Rock Cafe, Excalibur, Harry Carey's, Michael Jordan's and Planet Hollywood have been attracting city folk, suburbanites and tourists alike.

SIGHTS

River North covers a large area, which can be roughly divided into six sections. Of most interest are the first three areas: the eastern corridor, stretching from the river to Pearson Street; the Washington Square neighborhood, primarily along Dearborn Street; and the gallery district concentrated around Wells, Orleans, Superior and Huron Streets. In addition, River North contains the Mart District, including the behemoth MERCHANDISE MART, the Ohio-Ontario corridor of trendy restaurants (see above) and the cathedral district, centering around Holy Name Cathedral (p 101).

★ Eastern Corridor

Located across the river from the Loop's bustling business district, this area offers a varied blend of architecture and purpose, including modern office buildings, 19C residences and religious edifices.

Begin at the intersection of N. State St. and Wacker Dr.

★ **Marina City** – *300 N. State St.* From the river's edge rise the twin "corncob" towers of Bertrand Goldberg's prototype urban community. Revolutionary when conceived in 1959, the columnar apartment buildings were an attempt to encourage young professionals to resist the lure of the suburbs by providing not only living space but entertainment and services as well. Above the 18-story parking garages, pie-shaped units radiate from each tower's central core, where most of their load is borne. The cast-concrete construction and undulating surfaces of the towers contrast dramatically with the Miesian "glass boxes" so popular at the time.

Across State Street, for example, stands the **IBM Building★** (1971), the last American work of Ludwig Mies van der Rohe. Although still on the drawing board when the architect died in 1969, the edifice is quintessential Mies in its purity of form and function. Wrapped in a bronze-tinted curtain wall, its rectangular mass ascends from a spacious plaza.

Marina City and IBM Building

Walk west along the river, then cross the river on the Dearborn St. bridge and continue to the Hotel Nikko; descend stairs at northwest corner of the bridge to the riverfront promenade and continue west.

An unlikely duo—**Quaker Tower** (*321 N. Clark St.*) and the **Hotel Nikko Chicago** (*320 N. Dearborn St.*)—are connected by a riverbank promenade called Riverfront Park. For Quaker Tower (1987), architects Skidmore, Owings & Merrill invoked the spirit of their own Lever House (built 30 years earlier in New York) in this 35-story rectangular tower. The lines of the much smaller hotel (1987, Hellmuth, Obata & Kassabaum) next door seem soft by comparison. The serenity of the Nikko's lobby, decorated with Asian art, is enhanced by the lovely riverside garden that it overlooks.

At the western corner of Quaker Tower, ascend stairs to Clark St. and walk north; turn right on Hubbard St.

Courthouse Place (Cook County Criminal Courts Building) – *54 W. Hubbard St.* Identifiable by its stern Romanesque Revival facade, this quiet professional building (1892) was for years the center of much judicial and journalistic hubbub. Celebrated defense attorney Clarence Darrow successfully defended Chicago murderers Nathan Leopold and Richard Loeb here in 1924, and journalists Ben Hecht and Charles MacArthur were inspired enough by the press room to write *The Front Page* in 1928. The courts moved out in 1929, leaving the building to the more mundane city agencies that occupied it until its renovation in the mid-1980s.

Walk east on Hubbard St. and turn left on State St.

2 Gold Coast Dogs

418 N. State St. ☎ *312-527-1222.* The Chicago-style hot dog ranks with the deep-dish pizza as a source of local culinary pride, and this busy stand serves up some of the best in town. Though topping choices vary depending on individual taste, the basic architecture of the Chicago-style dog (also known as a "red hot") consists of a Vienna beef frank served on a poppyseed bun. Mustard, relish and onions are a must, and tomatoes, pickle slices and hot peppers are acceptable. Ketchup, however, has absolutely no business on a red hot!

3 Jazz Record Mart

444 N. Wabash Ave. ☎ *312-222-1467.* Impresario Bob Koester has been a fixture on the local scene for decades, and his commitment to and enthusiasm for jazz and blues make his record store one of the most popular in town. While the Mart's comprehensive selection of albums, CDs and cassettes includes everything from Bix Biederbeck to Thelonious Monk to Kenny G., serious jazz aficionados flock to the shop in search of vintage vinyl, imports and other rare recordings Koester and his staff are renowned for finding.

4 Pizzeria Uno and Pizzeria Due

Uno: 29 E. Ohio St.; ☎ *312-321-1000. Due: 610 N. Wabash Ave.;* ☎ *312-943-2400.* These sister restaurants located in converted Victorian mansions always rank at the top of local "best deep-dish" polls. Both restaurants are very popular on weekends, and the staff will take your pizza order before you're seated to help reduce your wait. At lunchtime, Uno and Due offer express service, which guarantees that a miniature deep-dish pie will be at your table in 20 minutes.

The slab-like building at **515 N. State Street★** is Japanese architect Kenzo Tange's first Chicago work (1990). The razor-sharp, 45-degree angle that bisects the building on the west and the 4-story cutout near the top lend the 30-story headquarters of the American Medical Association a most unusual profile.

Continue walking north on State St. to the intersection with Ohio St.

Built in three stages between 1894 and 1913, **Tree Studios** (*601-623 N. State St.*) were the inspiration of Judge Lambert Tree, who, as a prominent patron of the arts, wished to persuade artists to settle and work in Chicago by providing them an inexpensive place to live. Today artists continue to live and work in the historic studios.

Walk east on Ohio St. to Wabash Ave.

Medinah Temple, the curious mosque-like edifice at 600 N. Wabash Avenue, was built for the Shriners in 1913 to house fraternal meetings and ceremonials. Today it accommodates the annual Shrine Circus, as well as a variety of civic events. Textured brickwork and interlocking line designs around the doors and windows add to its exotic Arabian look. Its immense auditorium seats 4,200 (*guided tours available* ☎ *312-266-5000*).

Walk north on Wabash Ave. to Erie St.

At the corner of Wabash Avenue and Erie Street stand two remnants of the gracious living that once characterized the eastern corridor of River North: the **Ransom R. Cable House★** (1886, Cobb & Frost) at 25 E. Erie Street and the **Samuel M. Nickerson House★** (1883, Burling & Whitehouse) diagonally across the street. The two imposing residences display the Victorian tendency toward extravagance, stylistic eclecticism and mass. The Cable house, built by the president of the Chicago, Rock Island & Pacific Railway Company, exhibits the hallmarks of the Richardsonian Romanesque style, fusing a variety of architectural elements and design motifs into a uniform whole. Of particular interest are the turret, dormers, recessed windows, arches, surface decoration and steeply sloping slate roof. The rectangular symmetry of the Nickerson house is more traditionally Italianate. But the dark, brooding exterior belies the Baroque luxuriance of its renowned **interior★**, often referred to as the "marble palace." Samuel Nickerson, president of the First National Bank when he commissioned the home, clearly spared no expense. A dazzling mélange of woods, marbles, tile and glass decorates each

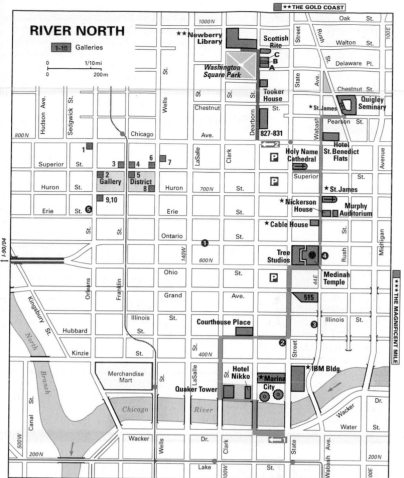

room on the mansion's three floors. Nickerson House is now a lavish gallery space for the R. H. Love Galleries, who restored it in 1991 *(open year-round Mon–Sat 9am–5pm; closed major holidays; ♿ ☎312-640-1300 or 800-437-7568, US only)*. Next door at 50 E. Erie Street, the incongruous facade of the **John B. Murphy Memorial Auditorium** (1926) looms over the sidewalk. Named for a prominent physician, the structure houses an auditorium-library for the American College of Surgeons.

Continue north on Wabash Ave. to Huron St.

★ **Episcopal Cathedral of St. James** – *N. Wabash Ave. at E. Huron St. Open Apr–Oct Mon–Fri 11am–2pm, Sun 9am–1pm; rest of the year Sun 9am–1pm. ♿ ☎312-787-7360.* From the outside, this Victorian-style cathedral (1857, Edward J. Burling; 1875, Burling & Adler; restored 1985, Holabird & Root) appears typical of the Chicago churches built of local limestone around the time of the Great Fire. The original structure of 1857 was destroyed in the Fire; only the 1867 bell tower remains standing, still bearing telltale char marks. The Civil War memorial in the narthex also survived the Fire and served as a temporary altar until the church could be rebuilt in 1875. The **interior★** of the church is truly breathtaking; its meticulously restored stencilwork, originally applied in 1888, draws heavily on the naturalistic designs and colors of the Arts and Crafts movement.

Continue north on Wabash Ave. to Superior St. and turn left.

At the corner of Superior and State Streets, **Holy Name Cathedral** *(735 N. State St.)*, an impressive structure dating back to 1875, serves as the Cathedral of the Catholic Archdiocese of Chicago. Renovated twice in 1914 and 1968, the Gothic Revival edifice was the site of Pope John Paul II's visit to Chicago in 1979.

Return to Wabash Ave. and continue north to Chicago Ave.

At Chicago and Wabash Avenues, note the **Hotel St. Benedict Flats** (1882). These apartments were designed to attract upper-middle-class residents—an unprecedented concept since apartment living was then considered déclassé. To dispel that image, architect James J. Egan devised the facade to resemble attached row houses.

Continue north on Wabash Ave., turn right on Pearson St. and continue to Rush St.

At 831 N. Rush Street, the Gothic-style **Archbishop Quigley Preparatory Seminary** (1919), named for the archbishop most dedicated to building Catholic schools in Chicago, bears testament to the heyday of Catholic architecture in the city. At the southwest corner, the **Chapel of St. James★**, modeled after Sainte-Chapelle in Paris, features stunning windows, each comprising 45,000 pieces of antique English glass that is truly "stained" (the glass, while molten, is mixed with pigment) and not merely painted *(open mid-Jun–mid-Sept Mon–Sat 11am–3pm, rest of the year Mon–Tue, Thu, Sat noon–2pm; guided tours available; & ☎312-787-8625).*

Washington Square

The establishment of Washington Square Park in 1842 stimulated residential development in the neighboring blocks. Today, the homes along Dearborn Street between Chicago Avenue and Maple Street give a sense of the area as it must have looked in the late 19C.

Begin at the intersection of Dearborn St. and Chicago Ave. and walk north.

North Dearborn Street – The row houses at **nos. 827-831** sport bas-relief portraits rescued from Adler & Sullivan's downtown Schiller Theater at its demolition in 1961. (Others can be seen at The Second City, *p 123.*) At no. 863, the **Robert N. Tooker House** was designed by William Le Baron Jenney and William A. Otis in 1886. But the Tooker name may be more famous for Tooker Place, the alley next door, where in later years, the denizens of bohemia flocked nightly to the Dill Pickle Club, located in a since-razed brick barn. Between 1916 and 1931, indigent artists, poets, playwrights and philosophers rubbed elbows and raised glasses here with thieves and gangsters, lawyers and professors.

The buildings in the next block north are owned by the Oriental Consistory (Scottish Rite Bodies), a Masonic lodge with headquarters at no. 915, the former **John Howland Thompson House [A]**. Designed by Henry Ives Cobb and Charles S. Frost in 1888, the mansion features a lively roofline balancing the massive quality of its rusticated sandstone surface. The 1895 **George H. Taylor House [B]** *(no. 919)* is purely Georgian in style, while the adjacent **George B. Carpenter House [C]** *(no. 925)* combines massive stone with elegant, rounded bays. The **Scottish Rite Cathedral** *(no. 929)* began life in 1867 as Unity Church. The Fire destroyed all but its Gothic limestone walls, and it was rebuilt in 1873 by the architectural firm of Burling & Adler. Dankmar Adler, who established his reputation for superior acoustics with this commission, would go on to become Louis Sullivan's *(p 33)* partner and an expert in theater and auditorium design. The church was eventually sold to the Oriental Consistory, which renovated the inside to meet its needs *(not open to the public).*

Walk west on Walton St.

Washington Square Park is Chicago's oldest surviving park, donated to the city by developer Orasmus Bushnell who hoped it would attract wealthy home builders to his subdivision. Perhaps more famous as "Bughouse Square" *(p 98)*, the park is still occasionally the site of speeches and debates during the summer.

★★ **Newberry Library** – *60 W. Walton St. Exhibits open year-round Tue–Thu 10am–6pm, Fri–Sat 9am–5pm. Reading rooms open year-round Mon, Fri–Sat 8:15am–5:30pm; Tue–Thu 8:15am–7:30pm. Guided tours available. & ☎312-943-9090.* Established in 1887 with a bequest from merchant, banker and land speculator Walter L. Newberry (1804-1868), this venerable institution ranks among the top independent research libraries in the country for scholars in the humanities. Its collections are impressive both in quality and quantity: 1.5 million volumes and 5 million manuscript pages include materials as diverse as a 1481 edition of Dante's **Divine Comedy** and a 17C Mexican manuscript on tree bark. Its map, music, American Indian and Midwestern literature holdings are unparalleled. Researchers come from around the country to use its genealogical resources. Architect **Henry Ives Cobb** designed the Spanish Romanesque edifice in 1893. A 10-story stack and storage wing by Harry Weese & Assocs. was added in 1982. For the casual visitor, a look around the lobby, with its tall ceilings, grand staircase, terrazzo floors and lovely reproduction light fixtures, imparts a sense of the building's grandeur. Rotating exhibits in the galleries located just off the lobby draw heavily on the collections, offering the nonresearching public a chance to sample the library's treasures.

River North Gallery District

Briefly dubbed "SuHu" (for Superior and Huron Streets), this bustling district in River North features galleries devoted to contemporary and ethnic art; 19C and 20C American works; ceramics and furniture; Chicago artists; photography; and a sampling of European paintings, sculpture and prints. On occasional Friday evenings throughout the season *(Sept–Jun)*, galleries sponsor concurrent opening receptions, drawing Chicago art lovers out for an evening of "gallery-hopping." *Most galleries are open Tue–Sat 10am–5:30pm; gallery hours during the summer may be limited and it is always best to call ahead. Gallery opening celebrations are often held Friday evenings 5–8pm. The public is welcome; call* ☎312-640-0064 *for gallery schedules.*

⑤ Mr. Beef

660 N. Orleans St. ☎312-337-8500. Tonight Show host Jay Leno put this place on the map. He discovered it as a struggling stand-up comic working the nightclub circuit and has been recommending it to his Hollywood pals for years. Don't go to Mr. Beef just to catch a glimpse of a visiting celebrity; go for the Italian beef sandwiches, consisting of a soft Italian roll piled high with thinly-sliced marinated beef garnished with *giardinere* (pickled peppers, celery and spices). Variations on the basic sandwich are: "hot" (topped with chili peppers), "sweet" (with roasted red and green peppers) and "wet" (dipped in the beef's juices).

A Sampling of River North Galleries *(map p 101)*

■ **Perimeter [1]**, *750 N. Orleans Street*, features contemporary painting, sculpture and master crafts.

■ **Phyllis Kind [2]**, *313 W. Superior Street*, offers contemporary American works with a specialty in Chicago artists.

■ **New van Straaten [3]**, *300 W. Superior Street*, specializes in contemporary works on paper, prints and lithographs from around the world.

■ **Marx-Saunders [4]**, *230 W. Superior Street*, is known for its contemporary American and European collection and art glass.

■ **Robert Henry Adams Fine Art [5]**, *715 N. Franklin Street*, specializes in American regionalists and other 20C schools.

■ **Carl Hammer Gallery [6]**, *200 W. Superior Street*, focuses on "outsider" and self-taught artists.

■ **Roy Boyd [7]**, *739 N. Wells Street*, features abstract American works.

■ **Mongerson Wunderlich Gallery [8]**, *704 N. Wells Street*, focuses on American western art.

■ **Rhona Hoffman [9]**, *325 W. Huron Street*, shows contemporary American and European works.

■ **Zolla/Lieberman Gallery [10]**, *325 W. Huron Street*, the first gallery to come to River North in 1975, showcases emerging and established artists.

SOUTH LOOP

Time: 2 hours.   Red line to Harrison or bus no. 146.
Map below

Bordered by Congress Parkway, 16th Street, the lakefront and the South Branch of the Chicago River, this small neighborhood was taken over by industry after the Fire of 1871 and remained the grimy underbelly of the Loop's business district until its recent rebirth as a community of rehabbed loft buildings, new apartments and town houses. Today, young urbanites frequent the various clubs, cafes and bookshops that have ensconced themselves in the historic structures along Michigan Avenue and Printer's Row, creating a lively, vibrant atmosphere. In addition to offering convenient access to Loop shopping, this district is only a hop, skip and a jump away from the city's best museums in GRANT PARK and from the lakefront stadium, SOLDIER FIELD.

Historical Notes

In the pedestrian city of the 1850s, Michigan and Wabash Avenues south of the Loop were lined with fine town houses and churches catering to the upper middle class. Following the 1871 Fire, however, the wealthier classes moved away from the Loop to Prairie Avenue (p 155) and the NEAR WEST SIDE. When the Dearborn Street railroad station was built in 1883-85, the streets south of Van Buren between Wabash and LaSalle quickly turned into an industrial district. Printers, attracted by convenient railroad access and narrow Dearborn Street lots (which allowed more light into the buildings), moved in, creating an international center for the printing industry. At the same time, hotels expanded along South Michigan Avenue near the Illinois Central Railroad passenger station at Roosevelt Road. The printing industry changed and moved out of the area after World War II, and many buildings were abandoned. Congress Parkway was widened in the 1920s and again in 1957, creating further separation from the Loop. State Street became a skid row area, and even South Michigan Avenue went into decline. Two events led to the rebirth of the South Loop in the late 1970s. The first was the construction of the Dearborn Park community on vacant railroad land south of Dearborn Station. The second was the creation of the South Loop Printing House Row Historic District north of the station and subsequent rehabilitation of printing lofts as apartments and offices. Within ten years almost every building in the district had been redeveloped and a new neighborhood was born, spreading west to the Chicago River with the 1986 construction of the River City apartments and marina. While State Street has not shed its seedy image, the 1986 renovation of the Chicago Hilton & Towers and the creation of residential buildings on Wabash Avenue, and in the Central Station development south of Grant Park, have given the South Loop a new urbane character.

SIGHTS

Congress Hotel – 520 S. Michigan Ave. This hotel was built in 1893 as the Auditorium Annex. The Clinton J. Warren design in limestone mimicked its namesake (p 43) with arcaded windows and a third-floor balcony. Polygonal bays rib the facade, which was extended to the south in 1902 and 1907 by Holabird & Roche. Step inside the Congress Parkway lobby to see the lovely mosaic tile arches.

Known for its arts curriculum, especially broadcast media and photography, **Columbia College** occupies several South Loop buildings, including the Harvester Building at 600 S. Michigan Ave. The 1907 structure features a limestone base, red brick facade, and oversized brackets at the cornice. Today, its ground floor houses a museum of photography.

Museum of Contemporary Photography [M¹] – *Located in Columbia College, 600 S. Michigan Ave. Open Jan–Jul, Sept–Dec Mon–Fri 10am–5pm (Thu 8pm), Sat noon–5pm. Closed major holidays. Guided tours available, reservations suggested.* ☎312-663-5554. The only Midwestern museum dedicated exclusively to this visual art began in 1976 as the Chicago Center for Contemporary Photography. Since then, the museum has amassed an impressive permanent collection of 4,000 works by 460 contemporary American imagemakers, focusing on American photography since the 1959 release of Robert Frank's seminal work, *The Americans*. Masterpieces by Larry Clark, Diane Arbus, Aaron Siskind, Dorothea Lange and Irving Penn as well as temporary exhibits are featured on a rotating basis in the main gallery. The second floor houses the Print Study Room and museum offices.

Spertus Museum [M²] – *618 S. Michigan Ave. Open year-round Mon–Thu, Sun 10am–5pm, Fri 10am–3pm. Closed Jan 1, Memorial Day, Jul 4, Labor Day and major Jewish holidays. $4.* ☎312-922-9012. Located within the Spertus Institute of Jewish Studies, this small museum comprises some 6,000 pieces of Jewish art, making its collection the largest of its kind in the Midwest. Scholars from around the world come to consult the Institute's 90,000-volume Asher Library, located on the 5th floor. The winding first-floor galleries house selections from the museum's permanent collection displayed in a series of small exhibits, each dedicated to a Jewish holy day or ritual. By juxtaposing objects from different eras and cultures, the displays highlight both diversity and tradition within the Jewish faith. Enclosed in a small, dark room, the **Zell Holocaust Memorial** features videos, displays and an installation that lists Chicagoans' relatives who died during the Holocaust. Visitors can honor the dead by placing a stone atop a symbolic gravestone at the entrance to the memorial. The Spertus has hosted several important temporary exhibits, including Judy Chicago's "Holocaust Project: From Darkness into Light," "Biblical Images: Chagall and Tissot," and "Being There: The Life and Works of Jerzy Kosinski."

Minor temporary exhibits are mounted in the museum's second-floor gallery. The Rosenbaum **ArtiFact Center** Kids is located, appropriately, in the museum's basement. Dedicated to archaeology, this wonderful center for children features a mock excavation where kids can literally dig up reproductions of Jewish artifacts from different periods.

A mansard roof punctuated by dormers and white terra-cotta trim distinguish the **Blackstone Hotel** *(626 S. Michigan Ave.)*, designed in 1908 by Marshall & Fox in the Second Empire style. What the lobby lacks in size, it makes up for in style, with large chandeliers, curving staircases, marble balustrades and an ornate ceiling. Marshall and Fox also designed the French-inspired Blackstone Theater *(60 E. Balbo Ave.)* in 1910, now the Merle Reskin Theater of DePaul University.

Erected in 1927 by Holabird & Roche, the 25-story **Chicago Hilton & Towers★** *(720 S. Michigan Ave.)* was at the time of construction the largest hotel in the world, containing 3,000 rooms, an 18-hole rooftop miniature golf course and a hospital. French in inspiration, the design features a limestone base and cornice framing a red brick facade. The main lobby's ceiling is painted with clouds and angels bordered by ornate bands of gold and platinum leaf. Winding staircases on the left lead past a lion's-head fountain to the grand ballroom. Known for years as the Conrad Hilton Hotel, the structure was renovated in 1985 and maintains its luxurious tradition.

The formerly run-down area around State Street and Roosevelt Road has been given new birth by the development of modern residential complexes. Organized around small interior parks and

1 Buddy Guy's Legends
745 S. Wabash Ave. ☎312-427-1190. Owned by blues guitar great Buddy Guy, this is one of the largest and most well-appreciated blues bars in town. Guy's status as a local legend ensures that the performers are top-notch (Eric Clapton gave several concerts here in 1994), and that visiting rock stars will sit in for impromptu jams (live music nightly).

courtyards, the **Dearborn Park I** apartments and town houses were built from 1979 to 1987 between State and Clark Streets north of Roosevelt Road. South of Roosevelt Road the newer town homes of **Dearborn Park II**, begun in 1988, exhibit more traditional urban design.

★ **Dearborn Station Galleria** – *47 W. Polk St. Open year-round Mon–Fri 7am–7pm, Sat 7am–5pm. Closed major holidays.* ✗ ♿ 🅿 ☎312-554-4400. Loop skyscrapers rise to the north beyond the square tower of downtown's oldest surviving train station. Designed by Cyrus L.W. Eidlitz in the Romanesque Revival style, the 1885 building features red brick and stone with nicely detailed cornices and round-arched arcaded window and door openings. The original steeply gabled roof gave way to a third story following a 1922 fire. The train sheds were demolished in 1976 and the edifice renovated in 1986 to contain offices, shops and restaurants.

On the northeast corner of Plymouth Court and Polk Street, the **Lakeside Press Building**★ **[A]** *(731 S. Plymouth Ct.)* was designed in 1897 by society architect Howard Van Doren Shaw for the R. R. Donnelley Company,

1883 Flyer

(vertical caption:) Chicago Historical Society (ICHi-05257)

the world's largest commercial printer. Shaw's first nonresidential building sports metallic bays surrounding a richly detailed entrance arch and a top story of semicircular windows alternating with stone medallions. Redeveloped as apartments in 1986, the building now serves as a dormitory for Columbia College *(p 105)*.

★ **Printing House Row Historic District** – *Along Dearborn St., between Polk St. and Congress Pkwy.* This stretch of late 19C and early 20C structures experienced a colorful history. First used by printing and other book-related industries, the buildings were eventually abandoned and some stood empty for years. In the late

1970s, architects Larry Booth and Harry Weese and industrialist Theodore Gaines realized the district's potential and began a massive restoration effort. Today, the entire row has become a coveted residential area dubbed Printer's Row. At no. 720 stands the **Second Franklin Building**★ **[B]** (1912, George C. Nimmons), ornamented with colorful terra-cotta panels depicting the various steps in bookmaking. Redeveloped into residential lofts in 1988, the building also contains various shops.

Across the street, the **Donohue Building [C]** at no. 711 (1883, Julius Speyer) was redeveloped for commercial and residential lofts in the 1970s. A 1913 annex to the south continues the simplified Romanesque Revival style. Farther north, the red brick **Rowe Building [D]** (1892) at no. 714 was the first to be rehabilitated in 1978 and features a cast-iron entrance and Luxfer prisms on the staircase, which allow light to filter into the basement.

Grace Place [E] *(no. 637)*, a 1915 loft building, was renovated in 1985 by Booth/ Hansen & Assocs. as a multidenominational worship space. Light floods the simple wood interior upstairs, streaming in from the circular skylight. The restoration of the once-abandoned **Transportation Building [F]** *(no. 600)*, a massive 1911 structure in light-colored brick, was crucial in securing the area's redevelopment. Today the building contains 294 apartments as well as restaurants and shops. Visible to the right, on Plymouth Court, cantilevered balconies jut out from the side of the **Mergenthaler Linotype Building [G]** *(531 S. Plymouth Ct.)*. Built in 1886, the edifice was restored as luxury living spaces in 1980 by Kenneth A. Schroeder & Assocs. Mergenthaler invented the modern Linotype machine in 1884; within ten years all the daily newspapers were using it.

The **Pontiac Building★ [H]** *(no. 542)*, designed in 1891 by Holabird & Roche, exemplifies the firm's Chicago school design with its skeletal frame and brick sheathing reminiscent of the contemporaneous MONADNOCK BUILDING with bays that flow rather than project from the surface. At no. 537, the **Terminals Building [J]** (1892, John M. Van Osdel & Co.) is an elegant design featuring a rusticated limestone base below red brick Romanesque-style bays. The **Hyatt on Printer's Row [K]** at no. 500 occupies three structures: two late-19C buildings and a modern northern addition designed by Booth/Hansen & Assocs. in 1987. The Old Franklin Building at no. 525 (1887, Baumann & Lotz) sports the iron windows and spandrels seen in the Lakeside Press Building *(p 106)*.

② Gourmand Coffeehouse
728 S. Dearborn St.
☎*312-427-2610.* Relax with a cup of gourmet coffee or a Ghirardelli hot cocoa in this friendly coffee shop. Quiches, soups, bagel sandwiches and several vegetarian dishes are available and the shop's muffins, cookies and breads are baked fresh every day.

③ Sandmeyer's Bookstore
714 S. Dearborn St. ☎*312-922-2104.* The wooden floors will creak comfortably beneath your feet as you browse through Sandmeyer's aisles. The store stocks a thorough collection of fiction and poetry by local authors and books on Chicago history, but its main focus is the extensive travel section, which features guidebooks as well as creative works about life on the road.

④ Prairie Avenue Bookshop
711 S. Dearborn St.
☎*312-922-8311.* This loft-style bookstore is a mecca for architecture buffs. The shop's floor-to-ceiling shelves carry everything from glossy coffee-table books to arcane volumes only a grad student could love.

⑤ Prairie
In the Hyatt on Printer's Row.
☎*312-663-1143.* The name of this highly acclaimed restaurant says it all: the furniture and decorations are inspired by Prairie school architect Frank Lloyd Wright, and the inventive menu features such regional Midwestern foods as buffalo, coho salmon, pheasant, duck and wild rice.

Additional Sights

Central Station – *East of Indiana Ave. between Roosevelt Rd. and 16th St.* Although this new development south of Grant Park will not be completed for decades, several homes have been occupied, including that of Mayor Richard M. Daley *(p 20)*. The modern, Victorian-style town houses feature copper finials, turrets and window surrounds. Almost half of Central Station's projected 79-acre development will be built on air rights over the railroad tracks located to the east.

River City – *800 S. Wells St.* Revolutionary Chicago architect Bertrand Goldberg designed this 1985 development—his most famous since the similarly inspired MARINA CITY executed 20 years earlier. Undulating walls ripple along the riverfront marina, while eyelid windows in the white facade suggest a futuristic space colony.

American Police Center and Museum [M³] – [Kids] *1717 S. State St. Open year-round Mon–Fri 9am–4:30pm. Closed Jan 1, Memorial Day, Thanksgiving Day, Dec 25. $3. & ⊞ ☎312-431-0005.* Located in a plain brick warehouse, the museum was opened in 1974 "to promote understanding of law enforcement methodology and educate citizens in the prevention of crime." A large, 3-story hall features graphic exhibits geared toward youth—including a coffin full of drugs—and gives the daring an opportunity to sit in an electric chair. Popular displays include Gangster Alley, with numerous photos of Big Jim Colosimo, Johnny Torrio, Al Capone, Frank Nitti and others. The Haymarket Tragedy of 1886 is recalled in historic photographs and lithographs. Several interactive exhibits and displays of police uniforms from all over the world complete the collection.

GRANT PARK★

Time: 2 hours
Map p 111

In Grant Park, Chicago's physical characteristics and urban personality converge. The city's 319-acre "front yard," located between Randolph Street on the north and Soldier Field on the south, marks roughly the midpoint in the swath of parks that trims Chicago's 30mi shoreline. From Lake Michigan on the east to Michigan Avenue on the west, the park is a segue from lakefront to bustling central city. Despite its checkered history and sometimes haphazard development, the park exudes a sense of the grand urban landscape that turn-of-the-century city planners envisioned for Chicago. Today, though bifurcated by busy streets, it offers tranquil corners, peaceful walkways, picnic spots and lovely vistas of the city and lake.

Historical Notes

In the 1830s, while selling land to finance the construction of the Illinois Michigan Canal, state commissioners designated a thin strip of shoreline east of Michigan Avenue between Madison and Eleventh Streets as "public ground—a common to remain forever open, clear and free of any buildings, or other obstruction whatever." In the ensuing decades, Lake Park, as it was then called, would be encroached upon by erosion from Lake Michigan on the east and, from the west, by city dwellers anxious to build on the prime real estate. In 1852, the city promised the Illinois Central Railroad the right to a trestle just offshore in exchange for financing the construction of a breakwater. The narrow basin created between the railroad tracks and the park was filled in with debris from the 1871 Fire, widening the land considerably and initiating a series of landfills that would eventually enlarge the park to its present size.

Railroad tracks, stables, an armory, storage sheds, squatters' huts and a city dump crowded park grounds. In 1890, mail-order magnate **A. Montgomery Ward** (1843-1913), whose offices overlooked this eyesore, decided he had had enough. For 20 years Ward battled the city and various private interests to clear and keep clear the lakefront park, basing his suits on the commissioners' original declaration. After a long and arduous fight, he prevailed, vilified by city officials who accused him of impeding progress.

McCormick Place Convention Center

Covering almost 100 acres at the southern end of Burnham Park, at S. Lake Shore Dr. and 23rd St., McCormick Place is the largest convention and trade show center in the US. When completed in 1997, the complex will boast three large buildings encompassing convention space and meeting rooms, hotels and restaurants. Some figures for 1994:

- **Number of conventions:**
  37,535 (including those held at Navy Pier)

- **Number of people attending conventions:** 4 million

- **Largest attendance at public event:**
  1,000,000 (Chicago Auto Show)

- **Exhibition floor space:** 1.6 million square feet (will increase to 2.2 million by 1997)

- **Number of hot dogs sold in a year:**
  436,000

- **Gallons of soft drinks sold in a year:**
  1,800,000

- **Gallons of coffee sold in a year:**
  461,000

In 1901, the park's name was changed to honor President Ulysses S. Grant, an Illinois native, and in 1907, the first real plans for its development as a park were published by the Olmsted Brothers, whose architectural firm succeeded that of Frederick Law Olmsted. Their scheme, based on the gardens of Versailles, called for symmetrical divisions of the space defined by paths and alleys of stately trees, promenades, formal gardens, fountains and sculpture. These landscaping principles worked nicely into Daniel Burnham's 1909 Plan of Chicago, which envisioned Grant Park as "the formal focal point, the intellectual center of Chicago." The actual execution of the design would take another 20 years, largely guided by the Plan's coauthor Edward Bennett. The FIELD MUSEUM was given a home at the south end, and by the 1933-34 Century of Progress International Exposition, the park had assumed much of its modern form.

Since then, Grant Park has both suffered and profited from its central location. As a result of a 1919 city ordinance, the Illinois Central Railroad agreed to depress its tracks. The rise of the automobile brought the intrusion of major thoroughfares that inelegantly sliced through the park and eliminated much of its open plaza space. An underground parking garage skewed the plan again, although today, landscaping and recreational facilities above the garage help to mitigate its presence. To the southeast of Grant Park across Lake Shore Drive, an interesting parcel of land juts into Lake Michigan. This is the northern end of **Burnham Park**, which stretches the rest of its 598 acres south along the lakefront. In 1930, after ten years of landfilling, the city created an offshore island, dubbed Northerly Island, intended to be the first in a manmade archipelago proposed in the 1909 Plan of Chicago. The ADLER PLANETARIUM took up residence on the northeastern corner of the island first; a bridge connected it to the mainland where Solidarity Drive is now located. The 1933-34 Century of Progress International Exposition spread from Northerly Island three miles south. After the fair, plans surfaced to turn the island into an airport, and in 1945, it contended to become the home of the newly formed United Nations. Finally, in 1948, Northerly Island Airport opened to serve private air traffic. Its name was changed to Merrill C. Meigs Field in 1950 to honor a pioneer Chicago aviator. Today, the number of flights in and out of Meigs has greatly declined. Plans are being developed to close the airport and return the land to a park-like setting.

Visiting Grant Park

Getting There – Grant Park is accessible by several 🚌 bus lines; the closest rapid transit stations are: Red and Blue line to Monroe or Jackson; Brown and Orange line to Adams (☎ 312-836-7000). Underground parking on Monroe St. *(map p 221)*; metered parking on Columbus St.

Park Information – Visitor Center at Daley Bicentennial Plaza *(337 E. Randolph St.; open year-round Mon–Fri 7am–10pm; weekends 8am–5pm; ☎ 312-742-7648)*. Information by mail: Lakefront Region Office, South Shore Cultural Center, 7059 South Shore Dr., Chicago IL 60649 *(☎ 312-747-2474)*.

Recreation – Public sports venues located throughout the park include soccer fields, volleyball courts, softball fields, tennis courts and ice-skating at Daley Bicentennial Plaza *(p 245)*. The park also houses Soldier Field, home of the Chicago Bears *(ticket information p 245)*. A bicycle/running **path** *(p 244)* runs along the lakefront. **Boat tours** depart near Buckingham Fountain at the Lake Shore Promenade and on the north side of Shedd Aquarium and Adler Planetarium *(Chicago Architecture Foundation ☎ 312-902-1500, Mercury ☎ 312-332-1368, Wendella ☎ 312-337-1446)*. **Walking tours** are conducted by the Chicago Architecture Foundation in the summer *(☎ 312-922-3432)*.

Special Events – Music and drama at the Petrillo Music Shell include: free performances sponsored by the Grant Park Music Festival *(Jun–Aug, ☎ 800-588-4443, worldwide)*; the lively **Blues Festival** held for three nights in June; the two-night **Gospel Festival** also in June; and the Labor Day weekend **Jazz Festival**. Independence Day celebrations include **fireworks** over Monroe St. Harbor the evening of July 3, exploding to the music of the Grant Park Symphony. **Taste of Chicago**, one of the city's largest annual events, offers live music and an opportunity to sample the fare of restaurants from around Chicago. In August, **Venetian Night** features a parade of decorated boats through Monroe St. Harbor, a concert and fireworks display.

VISIT

Grant Park is divided roughly into large rectangles, each with its own character and purpose. Its center and visual focal point is Buckingham Fountain, which is aligned on an east-west axis with East Congress Parkway.

★ **Grand Entrance** – The main entry to the park at Congress Parkway and Michigan Avenue retains only vestiges of its original grandeur. When built in 1929, its 100ft-wide staircase, flanked by two heroic equestrian statues—**Indians** (*the Bowman* and *the Spearman*) by Yugoslavian sculptor Ivan Mestrovic—welcomed visitors to the park. Burnham had envisioned an expansive plaza at the top of the stairs leading all the way east to the fountain. But by 1929, automobile traffic was already determining the shape of such spaces, and the plaza had evolved into a roadway. In 1956, with the Eisenhower Expressway under construction to the west, Congress was extended into the park, at the expense of the grand staircase, to link Lake Shore Drive with the new expressway. Today the mounted Indians [1, 2] remain, elegantly framing Buckingham Fountain to the east. Each bronze statue weighs 27,000lbs and stands 17ft high.

Abraham Lincoln (The Seated Lincoln) – East of the grand entrance and one block north of Congress Parkway, *The Seated Lincoln* presides over the *Court of the Presidents*, a lonely post as the other works park planners intended never materialized. Augustus Saint-Gaudens' Lincoln was cast in 1908 (a year after the sculptor's death) and installed in the park in 1926. This work resembles Daniel Chester French's figure in the Lincoln Memorial in Washington, DC because both artists used as models the life masks of Lincoln taken by Chicagoan Leonard Volk in 1860.

★★ **Buckingham Fountain** – The centerpiece of Grant Park, the Clarence Buckingham Memorial Fountain is truly a lakefront jewel. Donated to the city by philanthropist Kate Sturges Buckingham to honor her brother, the fountain was completed in 1927 at a cost of $750,000. A $2.8 million restoration completed in April 1995 returned the fountain to its original splendor. Architect Edward Bennett modeled it on the Latona Basin at Versailles, enlarging it to nearly twice the size of the original. Intended to represent Lake Michigan, the fountain pumps 1.5 mil-

Buckingham Fountain at Night

lion gallons from the lake, recirculating all but what's lost through spray and evaporation. Three basins of Georgia pink marble rise from a main pool that measures 280ft across; gargantuan carvings of seaweed and shells encircle the outside of each basin. In the large pool, four bronze sea horses, each 20ft in length, represent the states that border the lake.

As spectacular as its monumental scale are the water and light shows that emanate from the fountain throughout the summer. The fountain's 133 jets pump water at a rate of 14,000gal a minute, and the central jet shoots water skyward to 150ft. At night, a carefully orchestrated show of lights plays off the cascading water to create a dazzling effect (*May 1–Oct 1 9–11pm; call ☎312-747-2474 to confirm*). Once controlled entirely by hand, the choreography of water and light is today regulated by a computer.

Petrillo Music Shell – Originally located south of Buckingham Fountain at 11th Street, the first band shell was erected in 1931 in anticipation of the Century of Progress Exposition. This "temporary" structure hosted nearly half a century of free musical entertainment. In 1935, James C. Petrillo, president of the musicians' union, saw park concerts as a way to employ musicians suffering the effects of the Depression. Working with the Chicago Park District, he used union funds to bring in the finest artists, including Lily Pons, Andre Kostelanetz, Yehudi Menuhin and Benny Goodman. Several orchestras, including the Chicago Symphony, appeared in the early years, and in 1944 the Grant Park Symphony was formed. The park district moved the enormously popular venue to a new band shell at its present location in 1978.

Prairie Garden (Chicago Wildflower Works I) – In 1985, 1.5 acres above the Monroe Street parking facility were transformed into two oval plots of prairie wildflowers that bloom profusely during the summer months. A dramatic contrast to the formal plantings elsewhere in the park, the garden was at first the source of intense controversy, a "visual disaster" to some officials who lobbied to have it removed. Today, fully established and matured, the garden thrives thanks to the efforts of volunteers.

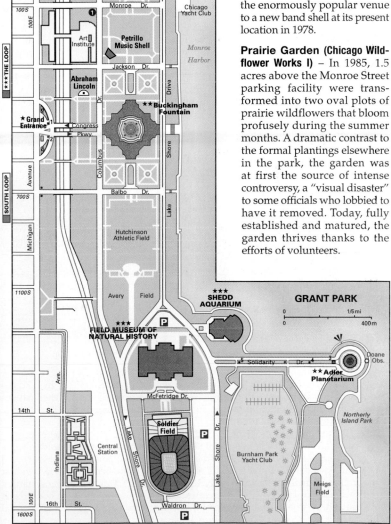

Soldier Field – At the southern end of Grant Park stands this famous athletic field, designed by Holabird & Roche to harmonize with the Field Museum to the north. The formal dedication of the field, named to honor the soldiers of World War I, took place on the occasion of the 29th annual Army-Navy football game, November 27, 1926. Since then concerts, religious festivals, and, in 1994, World Cup Soccer, have packed the stadium.

MUSEUMS IN GRANT PARK

★★★ **The Field Museum of Natural History** – *Description p 89.*

★★★ **John G. Shedd Aquarium** – *Description p 93.*

★★ **The Adler Planetarium & Astronomy Museum** – Kids *1300 S. Lake Shore Dr. Open year-round daily 9am–5pm. Closed Thanksgiving Day, Dec 25. $4 (free admission on Tue).* ✗ & 🅿 ☎312-922-7827. Occupying a beautiful vantage point, the Adler Planetarium offers commanding **views★★** up and down the lakefront. The oldest planetarium in the Western Hemisphere, it is renowned for its fine collection of historic astronomical instruments and its splendid sky shows.

Historical Notes – Intrigued by a German device known as a Zeiss projector for re-creating the night sky on an enclosed dome, philanthropist Max Adler (1866-1952) decided in 1928 that Chicago ought to have one "to emphasize that under the great celestial firmament there is order, interdependence and unity." Adler, a retired officer of Sears, Roebuck and Company (of which his brother-in-law Julius Rosenwald was president), donated $1 million to the city to establish a planetarium, and acquired a substantial collection of astronomical instruments for its museum. Architect Ernest A. Grunsfeld, Jr. designed a compact, Art Deco jewel for the dramatic setting at the tip of Northerly Island *(p 109)*. When it opened in 1930, the planetarium's modern style contrasted with the Beaux-Arts edifices that housed Chicago's other cultural institutions. Bronze bas-reliefs depicting signs of the zodiac punctuate the smooth reddish granite of the 12-sided, 3-tiered exterior. The whole is crowned by the dome of the planetarium theater where the original Zeiss projector operated until 1970, when a new model took its place.

Adler Planetarium

The building was extended underground to the west in 1973, and a new entryway added in 1981. In 1977, the Doane Observatory opened, offering the public a firsthand view of the heavens through its 20" reflecting telescope. The planetarium achieved National Historic Landmark status in 1987.

Three important sculptures surround the planetarium. At the main entrance, Henry Moore's 12ft working **Sundial [3]**(1980) commemorates the "golden years of astronomy" from 1930 to 1980. To the west, a seated **Nicolaus Copernicus [4]** holds an open compass and a model of the solar system. Bertel Thorvaldsen cast the bronze original (in Warsaw) in 1823. Farther down Solidarity Drive (so named in 1980 by Mayor Jane Byrne at the request of the Polish community to honor Lech Walesa and the Polish labor movement) stands the **Tadeusz Kosciuszko Memorial [5]**, sculpted by Kasimir Chodzinski in 1904.

Visit – Oddly enough for an institution focused skyward, the planetarium's entrance leads down to the subterranean main level. Here, the Robert S. Adler Hall of Space Exploration features displays about the solar system and space flight. Many of the exhibits are designed to be interactive and fun for children: step-in "capsules" compare bodyweight on various planets; a lively video describes a trip through the solar system in terms relative to distances around the Chicago area.

Also on this floor is the Kroc Universe Theater, the venue for the slide-show introduction to all of Adler's spectacular **sky shows★**. After this presentation, the 77ft "Stairway to the Stars" escalator spirits the audience up two levels through a tunnel of "stars" to the Sky Theater under the 68ft dome. Here, the Zeiss Mark VI can reproduce the night sky of a millenium past or future by projecting nearly nine

> ### 1 Goodman Theatre
> 200 S. Columbus Dr.
> ☎ 312-443-3800. Founded in 1925, the Goodman is considered the first regional theater company in the US. Its quality productions draw notices from critics in both New York and Los Angeles. The theater's six annual mainstage productions usually include a Shakespeare play, a splashy musical and a world-premiere work by a renowned playwright such as August Wilson. Every November and December, families flock to the Goodman's "A Christmas Carol."

thousand stars, as well as planets and other heavenly phenomena. Daily sky shows focus on various aspects of astronomy, such as the skies of Africa, the nature of stars and a preview of that evening's sky. New presentations debut each March and September. Lively narration accompanies the special effects created by the projector, making the programs appeal to young and old alike. On Friday evenings the sky show includes a look at live or recorded images beamed in from the Doane Observatory telescope.

Galleries surrounding the Sky Theater on the upper level house the **Universe in your Hands** exhibit, showcasing the planetarium's extensive collection of historic astronomical, navigational, timekeeping, surveying and measuring instruments. Case follows case of intricately decorated metal objects, arcane and curious in appearance and name: orrery, astrolabe, compendium, eclipsometrium. Note in particular a remarkable assemblage of sundials in ivory, brass, wood, silver and stone dating from the 14-18C. A model of a medieval university lecture hall allows visitors to don scholars' robes and pretend to be astronomy students. Stairs lead down to the middle level where other instruments are exhibited, including a wooden **telescope** (1775) reportedly used by William Herschel to discover Uranus. Additional displays explain navigation and optics. An exhibit entitled **Seeing the Universe** demonstrates the most modern astronomical tool of all—the computer. As one of seven institutions around the country hooked into the observatory at Apache Point, New Mexico, the Adler is the only one to offer public access to its views via computer. Its "substation" is part of the exhibit.

■ It Happened in Grant Park:

1880s: Aldermen "Hinky Dink" Kenna and "Bathhouse" John Coughlin stage riotous masquerade balls in the old armory building to honor popular prostitutes from the city's Levee neighborhood (p 18).

1904: The park is considered as a site for the Olympic Games that eventually went to St. Louis.

1911: Between 3 and 4 million people flock to the International Aviation Meet held in the park.

1933: 70,000 fans attend the first national tournament of 16in softball in Soldier Field. This gloveless version of America's most popular team sport is a Chicago institution.

1968: Grant Park is the scene of demonstrations and anti-Vietnam War activity during the National Democratic Convention.

1979: Pope John Paul II says mass here in front of a crowd of 350,000 worshipers. The service features a 30ft altar and 370 bishops.

1980s: Grant Park becomes the site for a series of summertime music and food festivals, including Taste of Chicago and blues, jazz and gospel fests.

THE GOLD COAST★★

Time: 2 1/2 hours. **CTA** Red line to Clark/Division or bus no. 151.
Map p 116

This slice of Chicago's lakefront has been home to the city's most prominent and wealthiest citizens for over a century. Nestled between the nightlife district of Oak and Division Streets on the south and LINCOLN PARK on the north, the most expensive residential property in Chicago encompasses the towering apartment buildings of Lake Shore Drive and the quaint Victorian town houses of Astor Street. To the west, LaSalle Street and Sandburg Village mark the transition to the recently gentrified OLD TOWN Historic District, while the MAGNIFICENT MILE lies just a short walk to the south.

Historical Notes

Lifestyles of the Rich and Famous – The young city's moneyed classes first settled in the Prairie Avenue district *(p 155)* south of the Loop. By the end of the 19C, they had relocated to present-day Gold Coast. Two events contributed to the rise in fame of this patch of land located just south of Lincoln Park. In the 1860s, the city's municipal cemetery—established on marshy swampland north of the city limits—was removed to create Lincoln Park, and in 1875, **Lake Shore Drive** opened, improving transportation to the area. Five years later, the Roman Catholic Archbishop's lavish residence was built at North Avenue. And in 1882, **Potter** and **Bertha Honoré Palmer**, the city's real estate king and society queen, erected an ostentatious mansion on Lake Shore Drive, striking the decisive blow in the battle to win the homes and haunts of Chicago's rich and famous. Abandoning Prairie Avenue en masse, the wealthy elite soon followed Palmer, who had wisely purchased much of the land, which quadrupled in value within a decade. Bertha Palmer entertained without pause, exhibiting her collection of French Impressionists (later donated to the ART INSTITUTE) in the home's famed 75ft-long picture gallery. By 1900 the Archbishop had subdivided and sold his land as well, and the Gold Coast quickly filled with mansions and extravagant stone town houses, detailed in the popular styles of the period: Romanesque, Queen Anne and Beaux-Arts.

Return of an Era – Developers began to erect apartment high rises in the 20C, most featuring full-floor, 18-room units with servants' quarters and all the amenities of a private home. Many Victorian houses were razed in the 1920s, especially on Lake Shore Drive, as a rash of luxurious high-rise construction increased the density of the area without diminishing its prestige. While the Gold Coast was thriving, the area to the west of LaSalle Street was settled by working-class Irish, German and Swedish immigrants, followed by Italians. In 1929, Harvey Zorbaugh documented the contrast in *The Gold Coast and the Slum*, a benchmark in urban sociology.

Palmer's Lake Shore Drive "castle" was demolished in 1950 during another spate of high-rise development. More town houses were mown down and replaced by hundreds of apartments with the most precious of Chicago commodities—a view of the lake. Urban redevelopment in the 1960s targeted the deteriorating

Peter Pearson/Tony Stone Images

Gold Coast Town Houses

area to the west by erecting Carl Sandburg Village *(p 125)* along Clark Street, from Division Street to North Avenue, initiating the gentrification of the nearby Old Town and Lincoln Park areas. In 1962, Butch McGuire opened the first singles bar on Division Street, turning the southern edge of the Gold Coast into a raucous nightlife district, while a surgeon's stately home became Hugh Hefner's first *Playboy* mansion. In 1973 the city designated **Astor Street** a landmark, and limited building heights to help stem the high-rise trend and preserve the turn-of-the-century ambience. Four years later, the entire Gold Coast from North Avenue south to Oak Street and Dearborn Street east to Lake Shore Drive, was listed on the National Register of Historic Places, and in 1990, the city designated as landmarks the last seven houses on Lake Shore Drive. Today many mansions that had been divided into apartments are being restored as single-family homes, ushering in a new era of gentility and luxury in this park-like enclave.

WALKING TOUR *distance: 2.3mi*

Tucked below the skyscrapers of the Magnificent Mile, the area exudes a sense of elegance and luxury. An early Sunday morning stroll is probably the best way to enjoy this lovely district, where stately town houses fronted by tiny, manicured lawns bring to mind visions of a bygone era. End your walk by grabbing a pastry at the St. Germain Bakery and Cafe *(p 119)* and, in the summer, heading to the popular Oak Street Beach.

Begin at Bellevue Pl. and Lake Shore Dr. and walk west.

Bellevue Place – This charming, tree-lined street exhibits an array of Victorian architectural styles. The handsome, 3-story **Bryan Lathrop House** *(120 E. Bellevue Pl.),* designed by McKim, Mead & White in 1892, created quite a contrast to the picturesque facades of Queen Anne and Romanesque Revival architecture dominating the Gold Coast in the late 19C. This Chicago landmark brought the comparatively sedate Georgian Revival to the area, and it became the most popular style by 1900. Graceful rounded bays

1 Oak Street Beach
The most chic beach in Chicago is (appropriately) situated at the intersection of Oak Street and Michigan Avenue. In the summer, the tanned and toned soak up the rays and swim in the shadow of the Drake Hotel. To get to the beach (and the bike path, which winds along the lakefront from Hyde Park to Hollywood Avenue), use the underground tunnels at Walton or Division Streets.

frame a symmetrical brick facade with an expansive porch and Beaux-Arts detailing. A 1972 restoration by Perkins & Will replicated the original cornice. Built for a real estate magnate who helped found the Chicago Symphony Orchestra, it has been the Fortnightly of Chicago, a women's literary club, since 1922.

Note the 1887 **Lot P. Smith House** at no. 32, a rare surviving home by Burnham & Root, and the looming, 4-story, Georgian Revival Chandler Apartments at no. 33, designed in 1911 by Schmidt, Garden & Martin.

Turn right on Rush St.

The tiny, pie-shaped Mariano Park contains a 1900 pavilion designed by Birch Burdette Long, a student of Frank Lloyd Wright. The bustle of commercial Rush Street contrasts with the surprisingly quiet residential streets of the Gold Coast.

Turn right on Cedar St.

The 1920s high-rise boom in this tony area led to buildings like the Gothic-style **20 E. Cedar Street** (1924, Fugard & Knapp), which takes the lavish ornament and picturesque rooflines of a Gold Coast town house and stretches them out over fifteen stories. The streetscape ranges from well-preserved Romanesque and Georgian Revival town homes to faceless modern high rises. The highlight of the street is the Romanesque Revival **60 E. Cedar Street** (1890, Curd H. Gottig), a confection of turrets, arches and protruding bays in rusticated Georgia marble. Note the lovely stained glass punctuating the facade.

Turn left on Lake Shore Dr.

Lake Shore Drive had witnessed $25 million worth of apartment high-rise development by 1928, mostly in the form of elegant structures such as no. 1120 (1926, Robert S. DeGolyer) and no. 1130 (1911, Howard Van Doren Shaw), one of the first cooperatives, featuring full-floor apartments and a Tudor Revival design with medieval motifs. Marshall & Fox followed in 1913 with the luxurious **Stewart Apartments** *(no. 1200)*, in the Adamesque style with large bay windows. Look south for an impressive **view★** of the DRAKE HOTEL and East Lake Shore Drive, a row of luxury high rises developed before 1929.

Turn left on Division St. and continue to Astor St.

Renaissance Condominiums – *1200 N. Astor St.* Originally the McConnell Apartments, this 1897 Holabird & Roche design is one of the earliest high rises in the area. This is an excellent example of a Chicago school apartment building, combining Victorian rounded corners with modern brick wall planes and massing. The OLD COLONY BUILDING downtown is another example of this combination.

Turn right on Astor St.

Early high-rise apartments give way to quaint graystones with delicate wrought-iron railings and miniature front gardens on historic **Astor Street★★**, named for John Jacob Astor, whose American Fur Company traded in the area before the settlement of Chicago. Note how the attached town houses are staggered along the angled street so that each facade projects forward as you walk north. While other wealthy neighborhoods boasted large lots, many Gold Coast mansions are squeezed into parcels only 25ft wide.

Turn right on Scott St. and left on Lake Shore Dr.

Four of the seven homes on Lake Shore Drive designated Chicago landmarks by the city in 1990 are located side by side in this block. The Carl C. Heisen House at **no. 1250** (1891, Frank B. Abbott) and Mason B. Starring House at **no. 1254** (1891, L. Gustav Halberg) are heavy Romanesque Revival structures that were joined in 1990 to create four luxury condominiums. Holabird & Roche designed the flowery Venetian Gothic home at **no. 1258** in 1898 for Arthur Aldis, while the same firm exhibited Georgian restraint in 1910 at **no. 1260** next door.

Turn left on Goethe St. and right into Astor St.

Goudy Park provides a pocket of recreation for Astor Street children. Philip B. Maher designed the nearly identical buildings at **1260** and **1301 N. Astor Street** in 1931-1932. The sleek Art Deco towers retain the full-floor luxury of earlier apartment buildings; note the elegant canopy at no. 1260. Potter Palmer, II and his wife occupied three floors in no. 1301 when it opened. The modern design at **no. 1300** (1963, Bertrand Goldberg) presents a sharp contrast with slender posts supporting the building above the automobile-oriented ground level.

★**James L. Houghteling Houses [A]** – *1308-1312 N. Astor St.* Designed in 1887 by John Wellborn Root of Burnham & Root, the three surviving houses have a beautiful sculptural quality created

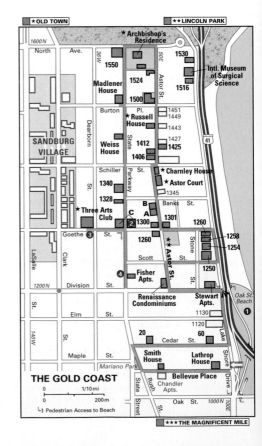

THE GOLD COAST

116

by variegated massing and polychromatic wall treatments. A rusticated base of red sandstone supports tawny brick walls and metal bay windows, rising to a picturesque roofline of turrets, gables and dormers. Root himself lived at no. 1310 until his untimely death in 1891 during the planning of the World's Columbian Exposition. Root's sister-in-law, Harriet Monroe (p 30), lived here as well. Monroe was first in the country to publish Vachel Lindsay, Carl Sandburg and T. S. Eliot.

The Romanesque Revival row houses at **1316-1322 N. Astor Street** **[B]** were designed in 1889 for real estate mogul Potter Palmer. The walls of the houses gradually progress from heavy rustication to smooth surfaces. Note the huge Romanesque arch framing the entrance at no. 1322.

Cross Banks St. and continue north on Astor St.

More 1960s high rises on the left overwhelm tiny Victorians on the right, such as the multicolored checkerboard at 1345 N. Astor Street (1887, Treat & Foltz). William O. Goodman, who endowed the GOODMAN THEATRE, lived at **Astor Court★** *(1355 N. Astor St.)*, a stately Georgian mansion (1914, Howard Van Doren Shaw). A small courtyard is visible at the southern entrance behind a gate ornamented with golden door knockers in the shapes of hands holding apples.

★ **James Charnley House** – *1365 N. Astor St.* **Frank Lloyd Wright** *(p 191)* designed this 1892 home while in the employ of Adler & Sullivan. Wright, who immodestly called it the first modern building, managed to create a horizontal composition by employing his trademark Roman bricks and minimizing decoration. Sullivanesque ornament covers the protruding balcony and front door, while the limestone base and broad eaves hint at Wright's future work. The house has only eleven rooms organized around a central skylit stair.

Cross Schiller St. and continue north on Astor St.

At the northeast corner of Schiller and Astor Streets, note the polychromatic stone treatments of the row houses, especially the greenstone at no. 38. The corner unit was given a Georgian facade at the turn of the century. On the west side, **1406 N. Astor Street** was built for steel scion Joseph T. Ryerson (grandson of philanthropist Martin A. Ryerson) in 1922 by David Adler, who excelled in French stylings. Adler added the slate mansard roof in 1931 to enclose a gallery exhibiting local memorabilia now at the CHICAGO HISTORICAL SOCIETY. The Thomas W. Hinde House at **no. 1412** boasts an unusual facade embellished with English Renaissance motifs and diamond-paned windows.

William D. Kerfoot gained fame in 1871 when his was the first Loop business to reopen the day after the Chicago Fire destroyed all of his real estate holdings. The sign on his wooden shanty—now at the Chicago Historical Society—read, "W. D. Kerfoot. Everything gone but wife, children, and energy." By 1895 his energy afforded him the 8,000sq ft graystone Georgian at **1425 N. Astor Street**. Skyscraper pioneer William Le Baron Jenney and Sullivan collaborator J.L. Silsbee erected the adjacent Romanesque Revival homes at nos. 1427 and 1443 around 1890.

★ **Edward P. Russell House** – *1444 N. Astor St.* Perhaps the most elegant Art Deco construction in the Gold Coast, the building (1929, Holabird & Root) features a facade of stone from Lens, France, a gently curved 3-story metal bay with incised floral decoration and a carved panel depicting graceful peacocks. Delicate oval windows flank a door covered with grillwork.

The French Chateau style, ill-suited to narrow lots, was nonetheless attempted at 1449 N. Astor Street, while Howard Van Doren Shaw's John L. Fortune House *(no. 1451)* used a corner lot to accommodate the Jacobethan style that replaced the Georgian Revival around 1910.

Cross Burton St.

1500 N. Astor Street – The huge Renaissance-style palazzo (1893, McKim, Mead & White) at the corner of Astor and Burton Streets was built by *Chicago Tribune* publisher and former mayor Joseph Medill as a wedding gift for his daughter Elinor Patterson. A 2-story front porch supported by Doric and Ionic columns is flanked by orange Roman brick walls with elaborate terra-cotta trim and capped by a cornice and balustrade that exhaust the Classical vocabulary. Cyrus Hall McCormick, II purchased the home in 1927 and employed David Adler to double its size, a fact visible on the walls of the structure, which became a school and was then divided into $8 million condominiums in 1978.

Continue north on Astor St.

The rounded corner and brick facade of **1524 N. Astor Street** (1968, I.W. Colburn & Assocs.) harmonizes this modern high rise with the Beaux-Arts and Georgian town houses that first defined the block in the 1910s.

★ **Residence of the Roman Catholic Archbishop of Chicago** – *1555 N. State Pkwy.* The oldest Gold Coast home (1880, Alfred F. Pashley), this Queen Anne fantasy in red brick with limestone trim is distinguished by 19 chimneys punctuating the roofline and an uncharacteristic expanse of surrounding land. The mansion was built prior to the rapid rise in real estate values in the 1880s and 1890s.

At the edge of Lincoln Park turn left on North Ave., and left again on N. State Pkwy.

★ **1550 N. State Parkway** – When it opened in 1912, this Beaux-Arts apartment building set the standard for Gold Coast gentility with 9,000sq ft, 15-room apartments organized around expansive sun parlors. Its architect, **Benjamin Marshall** of Marshall & Fox, grew up rich and stayed rich by designing Chicago's most prestigious homes and hotels in the 1910s and 1920s, including the nearby Drake Hotel. From its rusticated base to the large urns atop the balustrade, no. 1550 is a tour de force of white terra-cotta ornament and French grillwork with balconies overlooking Lincoln Park and the Archbishop's mansion.

Walk south on N. State Pkwy. and turn right on Burton Pl.

Albert F. Madlener House – *4 W. Burton Pl.* An epochal 1902 work of Prairie school architect Hugh Garden, this mansion was built for a local brewer. Roman brick and coursed limestone create an austerity broken by the beauty of the **entrance★**, framed by oversized Prairie-style urns and wonderfully intricate coursing and grillwork. The former mansion is home to the Graham Foundation for Advanced Studies in the Fine Arts, an architectural endowment.

Return to N. State Pkwy. and continue south.

The 1400 block of N. State Parkway contains many lovely town houses, but the **George A. Weiss House** at no. 1428 (1886, Harald M. Hansen) gathers the most attention with its pink Romanesque Revival stone facade, dramatic corner spire and a gabled chimney bay thrusting toward the street. Note the gargoyles and slate mansard roof.

Cross Schiller St. and continue south on N. State Pkwy.

A Queen Anne graystone with a prominent corner tower heralds a series of attached row houses at State and Schiller Streets. More stately town houses with English antecedents give way to the oversized but orderly French-inspired facade of **1340 N. State Parkway**, designed in 1899 for surgeon George S. Isham by James Gamble Rogers, the architect of Yale University. A steep slate roof is broken by three dormers surrounded by garlanded urns. These noble walls enclosed the after-dark lifestyle of *Playboy* founder and Chicago native **Hugh Hefner** throughout the 1960s and 1970s. The building was given to the School of the Art Institute of Chicago in the mid-1980s and served as classrooms and dorms until its 1993 conversion into several condominium units. The famous Playboy Mansion underground pool and grotto were demolished in the rehabilitation.

A little farther south, **1328 N. State Parkway** presents a rounded glass-block corner with a deep, low entry into what are actually two homes on either end of a long, narrow lot. Built in 1938 by Andrew N. Rebori, who designed the similar FRANK F. FISHER APARTMENTS, the buildings were joined into a single home and studio for artist Lillian Florsheim in 1956 by her son-in-law, architect Bertrand Goldberg.

Continue south to Goethe St.

Framing N. State Parkway at Goethe Street are the **Ambassador East and West [C]**, two prestigious hotels that have catered to the Gold Coast for generations. Booth 1 at the Ambassador East's **Pump Room** *(p 119)* was the most glamorous seat in town for entertainers and other luminaries from the 1940s to the 1970s.

Walk west on Goethe St. to Dearborn St.

At the corner of Goethe and Dearborn Streets, a stately brick palace surrounding an enclosed courtyard has provided living space for female art students since its opening in 1914. Designed by **Holabird & Roche**, the facade of the **Three Arts Club★** features large bas-relief sculptures and other eclectic ornament.

Return to N. State Pkwy. and continue south.

Frank F. Fisher Apartments – *1209 N. State Pkwy.* In 1937 architect **Andrew N. Rebori** designed the white brick and glass-block Art Moderne facade leading to 13 apartments organized around a very narrow atrium. Artist Edgar Miller, famous for his "handmade houses" on West Burton Place *(p 125)*, contributed the facade's sculptural plaques.

Rows of late-19C Italianate and Victorian town houses frame N. State Parkway south of Goethe Street, before giving way to the contemporary restaurants and noisy bars of bustling Division and Rush Streets.

Additional Sights

International Museum of Surgical Science – *1524 N. Lake Shore Dr. Open year-round Tue–Sat 10am–4pm, Sun 11am–5pm. Closed major holidays. $2.* ☎*312-642-6502.* Located on Lake Shore Drive in a landmark mansion (1917, Howard Van Doren Shaw), this museum features an idiosyncratic and sometimes bizarre collection of surgical instruments, art and artifacts devoted to the history of medicine and surgery. The museum was opened in 1952 by the International College of Surgeons, headquartered next door at no. 1516 *(p 120)* and founded in 1935 in Geneva by the Hungarian-born Chicago surgeon Max Thorek.

First floor – Located to the left of the grand entry hall is a room chock-full of 19C medicines and implements ranging from speculums to ear trumpets. Highlights include an interesting display on Civil War amputation illustrated with instruments, period photos and text conveying the enormity of the conflict (30,000 amputations).

In the back of the room, a reconstructed turn-of-the-century pharmacy is completely outfitted with medicines, flasks, pill cutters and a prescription book proving that doctors' handwriting is immune to the advances of medicine. An automated pharmacist relates how he made pills and provided other necessities of life. P.T. Barnum got his start hawking patent medicines like those on display, many of which carried labels boasting of their high alcohol content.

Second floor – The "Hall of Immortals" features 12 statues by Louis Linck and Edouard Chassaing, who also sculpted *Hope and Healing* on the front lawn. A working iron lung recalls the war against polio in this century. The 5,000-volume wood-paneled library is an original interior feature of the house. Greek and Roman fragments illustrate ancient medical techniques. Note the

② The Pump Room

In the Ambassador East Hotel. ☎ *312-266-0360.* In its heyday during the 1940s, this restaurant was *the* place to see and be seen for Chicago's swell set and visiting Hollywood stars. They undoubtedly came for the outrageous service— many dishes were delivered to patrons on flaming swords, and guests' dogs could dine in the adjacent Pup Room. While it's no longer the center of Chicago society, the Pump Room remains a charming, elegant restaurant. Don't miss the impressive gallery of photographs of celebrities in the bar area.

③ The Third Coast

1260 N. Dearborn St. ☎ *312-649-0730.* Sip cappuccino or claret in this warm, comfortable coffeehouse and wine bar open 24hrs/day. The Third Coast's clientele ranges from well-dressed Gold Coast matrons to bohemian art students who board at the Three Arts Club across the street. Soups, sandwiches and salads are available as are several of Chicago's free arts publications, including *The Third Word*, a magazine founded by the cafe's owners and habitués.

④ St. Germain Bakery and Cafe

1210 N. State St. ☎ *312-266-9900.* The murals in this cavernous cafe and deli depict a Parisian street scene and the menu offers such French bistro staples as escargots, steak frites and croque monsieur, as well as some of the best pastries in town. Create a picnic from the baguettes, jambon cru, foie gras and other Gallic goodies sold at the patisseries counter and head toward the lake for a wonderful meal.

bearded Aescilipius, leaning on the snake and staff, which still symbolize medicine. A series of paintings depict great moments in surgical science.

Third floor – Rooms devoted to South American, Dutch, Egyptian and Canadian surgery are illustrated by paintings, books, clippings and more surgical instruments. There is a nice collection of old microscopes and a large exhibit tracing the development of X-ray machinery.

Fourth floor – Highlights include a disquieting display of large "stones"—the kind that form in kidneys and bladders—and the primitive alloy tools used by the Incans for trephination (brain surgery), shown next to their patient's skulls. There is also a model of the first anatomy theater, built in Padua, Italy, in 1594. Rotating exhibits of several months' duration can also be found here, part of an effort to update and reinterpret the museum.

Lake Shore Drive Mansions – *1516 and 1530 N. Lake Shore Dr.* Built of gray Indiana limestone in the Beaux-Arts style, these two mansions form bookends to the International Museum of Surgical Science. To the south, the Edward T. Blair House *(no. 1516)* was designed by New York's McKim, Mead & White in 1914. Designed in 1916 by Benjamin H. Marshall, the Bernard A. Eckhart House *(no. 153)* is now occupied by the Polish Consulate. Howard Van Doren Shaw's creation, now housing the museum, was modeled on Versaille's Petit Trianon at the client's behest.

OLD TOWN★

Time: 1/2 day. **CTA** Brown line to Sedgwick and North.
Map p 121

Vintage cottages and elegant row houses share tree-lined streets with modern apartments in this upscale residential neighborhood bounded by Division, Halsted and LaSalle Streets and Armitage Avenue. Bustling Wells Street, home to the renowned Second City comedy club and a variety of shops, bars and restaurants, cuts a colorful path through the charming Old Town Triangle Historical District north of North Avenue.

Historical Notes

German Broadway – In the 1840s and 1850s, German immigrants began to settle just north of the city's border at North Avenue. These working-class families built modest homes and started their own businesses or took jobs as semi-skilled laborers. Mostly Catholic, they established St. Michael's parish in 1852, and the church at Eugenie Street and Cleveland Avenue soon became the focal point of the German community. In 1871, their wooden cottages burned like kindling during the Great Chicago Fire, but immediately following the conflagration, "relief shanties" began to spring up. In no time, older residents had rebuilt their homes and, as factories crowded the banks of the Chicago River directly west, workers flocked to North Town, later called Old Town. In 1874, the city extended its strict fire ordinance to the community, forcing builders to abandon wood for more fireproof materials. Stone Italianate and Queen Anne row houses, as well as brick cottages and coach houses commingled with the older wooden structures, giving Old Town the variegated architectural look it retains today. By 1900, North Avenue, then known as the German Broadway, was alive with shops, bakeries, taverns and delicatessens. Surviving testaments to Old Town's German heritage include the House of Glunz wine shop at Wells and Division Streets and the Germania Club at North Avenue and Clark Street, which was built in 1888 as headquarters of the German Maennerchor singing club.

A Century of Progress? – Growth of the community slowed in the early 20C as post-Fire buildings began to deteriorate. Impoverished neighborhoods to the west and south teeming with Eastern Europeans, Italians and African Americans pressed in on Old Town while the Germans moved north. By the late 1920s, the dilapidated tenements and boardinghouses southwest of LINCOLN PARK contrasted dramatically with the glittering GOLD COAST to the east. Gradually, attempts were made to refurbish the blighted neighborhood. In 1927, a group of artists led by **Sol Kogen** and **Edgar Miller** bought run-down buildings along Carl Street (now Burton Place) and transformed them into fanciful Art Deco-style homes. Wealthy industrialist Marshall Field, III tried his hand at urban renewal in 1928 by financing ten 5-story buildings on Sedgwick Street. Few poor families could afford the

$35 to $63 monthly rents, however, and the managers let most of the flats remain vacant. In 1934, the Chicago Housing Authority's first effort to clean up the slum in western Old Town failed. When the CHA announced plans to clear 67 acres along Halsted Street, residents protested so vehemently that the city backed down. (Between 1943 and 1962, the CHA succeeded in establishing the huge housing project known as Cabrini-Green at the southern edge of Old Town.) In another form of urban renewal, the development of Carl Sandburg Village beginning in the 1960s along Clark and LaSalle Streets south of North Avenue heralded the influx of thousands of young singles and families.

A Community Reborn – By the late 1950s, Asian and Hispanic immigrants had joined the ethnic mix in Old Town, and inexpensive rents attracted artists and musicians. In 1947, a group of neighbors decided to raise money to spruce up a small park on Eugenie Street. They invited "anyone who painted, sculpted, wove or baked" to display and sell their work. The event evolved into the **Old Town Art Fair** *(p 220)*, which today attracts artists from around the world and draws thousands of spectators every second weekend of June. The Old Town School of Folk Music opened in 1957 on North Avenue to preserve America's tuneful traditions and introduce music from around the world. (It has since moved to Armitage Avenue.) In 1959, comedians Paul Sills and Bernie Sahlins relocated their fledgling theater company from HYDE PARK to Wells Street and renamed it "The Second City." The troupe, which performs comedy skits based on improvisation, earned rave reviews for its irreverent fast-and-loose style. Over the years, The Second City has trained such great comic actors as Alan Arkin, Joan Rivers and its most famous alumnus, John Belushi.

Old Town's "artsy" reputation and affordable housing made it a natural choice for the hippies of the late 1960s and early 1970s, and political bookstores and psychedelic shops sprouted up all along Wells Street. As part of an urban-renewal project in the early 1970s, the city vacated broad Ogden Avenue from North Avenue to Lincoln Park—only 40 years after it had been slashed through the neighborhood. Housing developments for low-income families shared the newly vacant land with stunning single-family homes designed by Stanley Tigerman and other prominent Chicago architects. In 1976, the **Old Town Triangle**, bordered roughly by the former Ogden Avenue, North and Lincoln Avenues, was declared a Chicago Landmark District, and in 1984 the area was listed on the National Register of Historic Places, well-deserved recognition for the revived neighborhood.

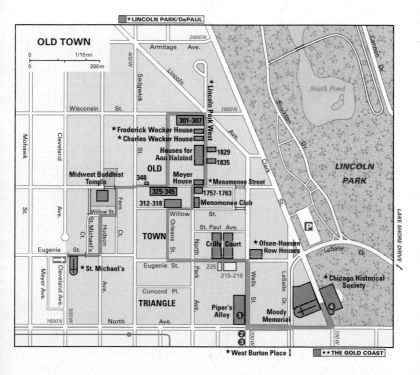

121

WALKING TOUR *distance: 1.4mi*

A walk through the Old Town Triangle offers a compact glimpse into Chicago's architectural history and gives a sense of the city's mid- to late-19C residential landscape, down to the narrow streets. Indeed, were it not for the high rises that loom on the perimeter of the neighborhood, it would be easy to lose track of the modern city.

Begin at St. Michael's Church between Hudson and Cleveland Aves.

★ **St. Michael's Church** – *447 W. Eugenie St. Open year-round daily 8am–7pm.* ♿ 🅿 *☎312-642-2498.* This is the third church building to serve St. Michael's parish since its formation in 1852. When the Fire destroyed all but the east, south and west red brick walls of the second structure finished in 1869, parishioners rallied to rebuild the interior in just a year's time. The steeple was added in 1888, and in 1913, an 8ft statue of St. Michael was placed in a niche high up on the facade. The church's ornate Bavarian Baroque interior is the result of years of renovation.

When exiting the church, walk east (right) to Hudson Ave., turn left on Hudson and continue to Willow St.

In temporal, architectural and cultural contrast to St. Michael's stands the **Midwest Buddhist Temple** *(435 W. Menomonee St.)* built in 1971. Its simple, pagoda-like lines and low profile evoke a Japanese shrine.

Continue east on Willow St., turn left on Fern Ct., right on Menomonee St. and cross Sedgwick St.

★ **Menomonee Street** – This quaint street in particular evokes the essence of historic Old Town. The nine cottages on its south side, **nos. 325-345**, are good examples of the type built in the area during its original settlement, although these were constructed in the years immediately following the Fire. These small wooden cottages could be erected in no time using "balloon framing" *(p 32)*, a Chicago building innovation partially accountable for the rapid growth and combustibility of the city. The tiny house at **no. 348** on the north side of the street is a rare example of a fire relief shanty, one of 3,000 one-room dwellings donated by the Chicago Relief and Aid Society to families left homeless by the Fire.

Proceed north on Orleans St. and turn right on Wisconsin St.

The brick row houses at **301-307 W. Wisconsin Street** typify the Italianate style popular in late 19C Chicago. Incised sandstone lintels ornament their tall, narrow, bayed fronts.

Turn right on Lincoln Park West.

★ **Lincoln Park West** – The well-to-do residents of eastern Old Town built their homes in the open land adjacent to the developing Lincoln Park. Completed in 1874, before the strict fire laws took effect, the ornate **Frederick Wacker House★** at no. 1838 was built by a brewer who embellished its basic form with incised woodwork and other Victorian detail. Next door is the **Charles H. Wacker House★** *(no. 1836)*, erected by Frederick's son Charles—the city planner for whom Wacker Drive was named—who relocated and remod-

Henry Meyer House

eled his father's coach house in 1884. To the immediate south, a very different facade spans nos. 1826-1834, the **Houses for Ann Halsted**. These red brick town houses were designed and built as rental property in 1884 and 1885 by Louis Sullivan and Dankmar Adler in a simplified Queen Anne style. They represent an early commission for Sullivan, a master of elaborate organic ornamentation, and his hand is especially evident in the terracotta stringcourses that top each unit. Across the street, note the handsome and well-preserved Italianate detail on **nos. 1829** and **1835**, both built around the mid-1870s. At the end of the block, the **Henry Meyer House** *(no. 1802)* dates from the same year. Although built as a farmhouse, simple decorative touches around the windows lend it a sophistication befitting this prosperous neighborhood.

Cross Menomonee St. and continue south on North Park Ave.

Nestled among the town homes and cottages of Old Town are garages and coach houses of the type seen at **1757-1763 North Park Avenue**. As Chicago's wealthy Gold Coast residents to the east acquired cars in the burgeoning age of the automobile, they built garages and lodgings for chauffeurs on the empty lots in Old Town. This example, which today houses the Old Town Triangle Association, was built for Philip D. Armour in 1915.

The **Menomonee Club for Girls and Boys** *(no. 244)* offers a nondescript wall along North Park Avenue, but the Willow Street facade erupts into an oriel of fanciful woodwork and stained glass, including a lovely etched-glass window reading "North End Bowling Club."

Turn right on Willow St. and continue to Orleans St.

Built in 1974, a century after Old Town's post-Fire building boom, the row houses at **312-318 W. Willow Street** represent the continuing effort to design efficient and comfortable city residences in close quarters. Architect Harry Weese modeled these multistory units on London row houses, adding garages at street level.

Turn left on Orleans St., left again on Eugenie St., and continue to Crilly Ct.

① The Second City

1616 N. Wells St. ☎ *312-337-3992.* Scan the list of Second City "alumni" posted in the theater's lobby and you will find hundreds of familiar, famous names. Since 1959 comic actors have traveled to The Second City to learn the art of improvisational comedy. Today the company's best students perform comedy revues featuring skits created from improv games. The scenarios in each show are the same every night, but the actors vary their performances based on feedback from the audience.

② Up-Down Tobacco Shop

1550 N. Wells St. ☎ *312-337-8505.* Since the 1960s, this shop has featured fine smokes from tobacconists from around the world. Hand-carved pipes, unusual lighters, chic cigarette cases and other smoking paraphernalia are available, and the store's staff is helpful and will recommend cigar- and pipe-friendly clubs and restaurants to the aficionado. Each year the shop sponsors a pipe-smoking contest; the winner is the one who can keep a pipe lit longest.

③ Zanie's

1548 N. Wells St. ☎ *312-337-4027.* The oldest comedy club in the city, this well-worn venue has outlasted a dozen glitzier competitors. Name a stand-up comedian, and chances are he or she has performed at Zanie's. The club features three comics a night: two up-and-coming performers and a well-known headliner.

In 1885, developer Daniel F. Crilly bisected this block with a north-south street and spent the next ten years erecting residential and commercial space around it. The centerpiece of his **Crilly Court Development** are the Queen Anne row houses (1885) that line the street's west side. The apartment buildings (1895) across the court bear Crilly's children's names above the entryways. Across Eugenie to the south are four Chicago cottages *(nos. 215-219 and 225)*, all built prior to 1874. Each has the characteristic high basement, steep front staircase and Italianate detail. The wall around no. 225 was added during its renovation.

Continue east on Eugenie St. to Wells St.

Across Wells Street, elegant and elaborate Queen Anne row houses flank the north side of Eugenie Street at nos. 164-172. A sharp contrast to the simpler Queen Anne houses in the interior of the Triangle, the **Olsen-Hansen Row Houses★** (1886) represent the style at its most flamboyant. Irregular rooflines, turrets and a variety of textures, materials and colors adorn the exteriors.

Turn right on Wells St.

Beginning with an existing bakery, architect Stanley Tigerman developed **Piper's Alley** as a multiuse mall between 1974 and 1977. Movie theaters, restaurants, ice-cream shops and gift stores move in and out, but The Second City has prevailed at 1616 N. Wells Street since 1959. The theater seems to transcend change in this neighborhood where so many other entertainments and diversions—from head shops to peep shows—have come and gone. Note the terra-cotta heads that ornament the facade; these German philosophers and poets were salvaged from Adler & Sullivan's downtown Schiller Theater when it was demolished in 1961.

Turn left on North Ave. and left again on Clark St. two blocks later.

A wide-open town like mid-19C Chicago attracted its share of evangelists and reformers. Among the revival movement's most powerful voices was that of Dwight Moody, who had come to Chicago in 1856. In 1893, he attracted more than two million people to his meetings at the World's Columbian Exposition. The **Moody Memorial Church** *(1609 N. LaSalle St.)* testifies to his lasting influence on fundamental Christianity. Built in 1925, the brick edifice blends elements of Byzantine and Romanesque design, and is said to have been partially inspired by Hagia Sophia in Istanbul.

Cross Clark St. to the Chicago Historical Society, where the walking tour ends.

★ THE CHICAGO HISTORICAL SOCIETY

1601 N. Clark St. at North Ave. Open year-round Mon–Sat 9:30am–4:30pm, Sun noon–5pm. Closed Jan 1, Thanksgiving Day, Dec 25. $3. Guided tour (1hr) available, reservations required. ✗ ⅋ ☎312-642-4600.

Sited at the southwestern corner of Lincoln Park, the city's oldest cultural institution reflects the evolution of history museums from storehouses of memorabilia to institutions actively engaged in making sense of history to a diverse audience. The society's collections and exhibits cover America until 1865 and Chicago since the arrival of explorers and settlers.

Historical Notes – Organized in 1856 by a group of prominent businessmen, the collections (then stored in the offices of one of the founders) were damaged in the Great Fire of 1871 and again by fire in 1874. In 1896 the Society moved into a Richardsonian Romanesque structure designed by Henry Ives Cobb at Dearborn and Ontario Streets. In 1927, the Society purchased the vast Gunther Collection of materials primarily relating to the Civil War. To house it, Graham, Anderson, Probst and White designed the institution's present home, a Georgian-style building completed in 1932. A 1971 addition on Clark Street doubled the original space. Aesthetic concerns and the need for yet more room in the 1980s inspired Holabird & Root to create the wraparound facade and the 3-story rounded glass-and-steel atrium through which visitors now enter.

Visit – Artifacts representing the seven collections—costumes, prints and photographs, decorative arts, library, architecture, paintings and sculpture and manuscripts—occupy a grid of niches on either side of the main lobby. The unexpected juxtaposition of such objects as the steering wheel from the ill-fated steamer *Eastland* and a grouping of Lava Lites makes this a lively display. The second floor houses the museum's highlights.

Second Floor – With an emphasis on interpretation, the permanent exhibits on this floor go beyond the traditional chronological approach. In the **American Galleries** on the right, "We The People: Creating a New Nation 1765-1820" examines the roles of ordinary Americans in the Revolution. Highlights include first printings of the Declaration of Independence and the Constitution—newsprint versions that most citizens of the period would have actually read. "A House Divided: America in the Age of Lincoln" uses the Society's rich Civil War collection—including Lincoln's deathbed and John Brown's Bible—to explore the economic and social impact of slavery. On the left of the hall, six **Chicago History Galleries** illustrate themes in the city's growth: commerce, culture, public works, architecture, world's fairs and daily life. Here children can climb aboard the **Pioneer locomotive** 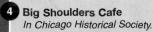, Chicago's first train and the Society's largest artifact. Also of interest is Chicago's first fire engine, enlivened by bright red trim, purchased in 1835 and in service until 1860. These modern exhibits contrast revealingly with eight dioramas displayed in a small room just off the central hall. Created by WPA workers in the 1930s to represent moments in Chicago history, the beautifully crafted dioramas have themselves become artifacts of an earlier age of museum exhibition.

④ Big Shoulders Cafe
In Chicago Historical Society.
☎ *312-587-7766.* Located in a sunny corner of the venerable institution, the cafe is a great place to stop on a walk through Old Town, a trek through the park or a visit to the museum. The cafe's light, healthy menu features a variety of salads, sandwiches and pasta dishes.

First floor – A small exhibit entitled "Fort Dearborn and Frontier Chicago" offers an intimate glimpse into early-19C life in the lakeshore village using personal artifacts, letters and daguerreotypes of Indians and the earliest settlers. Logs from the original Ft. Dearborn form one wall of the exhibit.

At the south end of the museum, tucked away in the Big Shoulders Cafe, looms a re-creation of the massive archway that once marked the entrance to the Chicago Stock Yards. Its bas-reliefs of cattle and cowboys recount a closed chapter in Chicago's history.

ADDITIONAL SIGHTS

Several sights along LaSalle Street, south of North Avenue, are worth noting. The 1927 Art Deco renovations of Sol Kogen and Edgar Miller crowd the cul-de-sac that is **West Burton Place★**. This unusual collection of apartments began as Victorian houses that the two artists refitted with modern elements such as tile work, contemporary windows and mosaics.

In a complete change of visual scale, **Carl Sandburg Village** looms across LaSalle Street. This expansive agglomeration of high rises, town houses and ground-hugging apartment buildings that extends from North Avenue to Division Street was developed between 1960 and 1975.

A series of restored houses in the 1300 and 1400 blocks of LaSalle Street conjures up the elegant late-19C profile of this boulevard. A block farther south, at **no. 1211**, stands a fitting sentinel on the southern edge of Old Town. This 1929 hotel was renovated in 1981 as an apartment building. On its eastern and southern walls, artist Richard Haas has painted a trompe-l'oeil entitled *Homage to the Chicago School of Architecture*. The work's primary elements include, at the top, a depiction of a Louis Sullivan window, and, at the bottom, his golden doorway from the Transportation Building at the 1893 World's Columbian Exposition. Between the two, Haas painted an imaginary reflection of the CHICAGO BOARD OF TRADE BUILDING, visible two miles south down LaSalle Street in the heart of the financial district.

Throughout 1996, new area codes are being introduced in the Greater Chicago region. In this guidebook, all phone numbers are preceded by these latest area codes. Note that numbers preceded by the 773 area code should be dialed with the 312 area code until October 1996.

Chicago downtown:	*312*
Chicago other areas:	*773 (in effect Oct. '96)*
Northern suburbs:	*847*
Southern suburbs:	*708*
Western suburbs:	*630*

Hugging its namesake greensward to the east, the eclectic Lincoln Park/DePaul neighborhood is a checkerboard of lovely residential streets crisscrossed by lively commercial boulevards. From Armitage Avenue on the south to Diversey Parkway on the north, and west to Racine Avenue, the nucleus of Lincoln Park/DePaul is well suited to a pleasant day of walking, window-shopping and noshing. Evenings here draw colorful crowds attracted to the area's diverse offerings in music, food and theater.

Historical Notes

From Celery to City – Green Bay Road (present-day Clark Street) ran northwest through this territory along the marshy lakefront as early as the 1830s. To the west, German farmers established celery and other vegetable farms. By 1853, the land between North and Fullerton Avenues to the river had been annexed by the city, and the natural sprawl of the growing metropolis began to shape the area's development. Frame houses supplanted celery gardens, a horsecar line linked the area to downtown, and a public park began to unroll up the lakefront. The Great Fire in 1871 devastated the incipient neighborhood before burning itself out at Fullerton Avenue, but the area's location outside the city's strict new fire codes invited speedy recovery. As industry marched up the north branch of the river, German, Irish and Polish workers built cottages in the western reaches of the neighborhood. In a parallel progression to the east, well-to-do Germans commissioned fine homes along the edge of the increasingly lovely lakefront preserve known since 1865 as LINCOLN PARK.

Catholic Cornerstone – The Presbyterian Theological Seminary had located at Fullerton Avenue and Halsted Street in 1863. Surviving the fire, the seminary (later renamed McCormick in honor of its benefactor, the famous industrialist) attracted settlers to this distant corner of Chicago, spawned the establishment of several churches and even, in 1882, constructed row houses to let for the income. Despite the seminary's influence, the more lasting effect on the neighborhood would be wrought by the Vincentian order, which founded St. Vincent de Paul parish in

UPI/Bettman

Biograph Theater, 1934

■ Two neighborhood addresses figure prominently in Chicago's gangland history: 2122 N. Clark Street, the site of the garage (since demolished) where the St. Valentine's Day Massacre *(p 13)* took place in 1929; and 2433 N. Lincoln Avenue–the **Biograph Theater**–where federal agents gunned down "public enemy number one" John Dillinger on July 22, 1934.

1875 to serve the local Irish population. In 1898, the fathers established St. Vincent's College, from which would grow DePaul University, today a cornerstone of the Lincoln Park community.

Location, Location – Over the years, the neighborhood continued to grow in both area and population. The blocks between Fullerton Avenue and Diversey Parkway were annexed by the city in 1889. Ethnic diversity increased as working-class Romanians, Greeks, Italians, Poles, Hungarians, Serbs and African Americans discovered the convenience and affordability of the neighborhood. However, new housing didn't keep pace with the swelling population and the existing buildings suffered from overuse. Except for the luxury residences east of Clark Street, Lincoln Park grew dilapidated.

The area's intrinsic advantages, however, served it well. Location, accessibility and a basic architectural soundness stimulated an interest in the neighborhood, and conservation associations formed to encourage renovation efforts. In 1956, the community was designated an urban-renewal area. Rehabilitation, and the companion phenomenon dubbed "gentrification," proceeded so successfully that Lincoln Park today is one of Chicago's most desirable, attractive, high-priced— and congested—neighborhoods.

SIGHTS

Few of the residential blocks in the neighborhood will disappoint the visitor on foot, each one offering a variety of architectural and landscaping surprises. They are difficult to negotiate by car, however, as parking can be hard to find. The major commercial boulevards—particularly Armitage Avenue and Diversey Parkway, Halsted Street and the two diagonals, Lincoln Avenue and Clark Street—are chock-full with bookstores and boutiques, bars and bistros.

Lincoln Avenue and Clark Street slice the neighborhood roughly in pie-shaped thirds. To their west, the university serves as a major focus, and the surrounding blocks are known as the DePaul neighborhood. Chartered in 1907 as **DePaul University** from St. Vincent's College , the campus grew outward from the limestone church buildings in the 1000 block of W. Webster Avenue, where the Romanesque Revival **St. Vincent de Paul Church** (1897, James J. Egan) towers over the block. Today, DePaul's 30-acre campus extends between Fullerton and Webster Avenues and Clifton and Halsted Streets. Major buildings face a pedestrian mall created in the 2300 block of Seminary Avenue in 1992. The concrete Brutalism style of the **Arthur J. Schmitt Academic Center [A]** and the **Harold L. Stuart Center [B]** (2323 and 2324 N. Seminary Ave.), both designed by C.F. Murphy Assocs., contrasts with the more fitting brick construction of the **Richardson Library [C]** (2350 N. Kenmore Ave.), completed in 1992 by Lohan Assocs.

DePaul acquired the land east of the elevated tracks from the Presbyterian Theological Seminary when it moved to HYDE PARK in 1973. Embedded in the property is **Chalmers Place★**, a verdant

1 Kingston Mines
2548 N. Halsted St.
☎ *773-477-4646.*
Frequented by top-notch musicians and regular folk, this ramshackle blues club features live music until 4am (5am on Saturday). Seven nights a week, two top local bands take turns playing on the club's two stages. The place fills up quickly, and at 2am fans pour in from B.L.U.E.S. across the street, so arrive early to get a good seat.

2 B.L.U.E.S.
2519 N. Halsted St.
☎ *773-528-1012.*
You feel like you can reach out and touch the performers in this tiny, smoky club. Quality players from across the city and a down-and-dirty atmosphere make this one of the most popular blues bars in town.

3 Steppenwolf Theater
1650 N. Halsted St.
☎ *312-335-1650.*
John Malkovich, Laurie Metcalf and Gary Sinise are members of this acclaimed local troupe which is renowned for the intensity of its performers as well as its impressive state-of-the-art theater. Steppenwolf presents five or six mainstage plays a year. Several workshop productions, staged readings and smallscale shows are mounted in the company's studio theater.

block of privately owned town houses that were originally built by the seminary to generate income. An unembellished blend of Queen Anne and Romanesque Revival styling, their facades of smooth brown brick face each other with no-nonsense solidarity on either side of a park-like square. The two freestanding houses at the eastern end of the square *(834 and 835 W. Chalmers Pl.)* were constructed in the 1880s for faculty members. Another series of row houses backs up to Chalmers Place along W. Belden Avenue just south. These brick homes, the **McCormick Row Houses [D]** *(nos. 832-840, 844-858)*, built between 1884 and 1889, appear somewhat less heavy than their counterparts, with livelier rooflines, stained glass and decorative brickwork. Similar row houses also line the 900 block of Fullerton Avenue; the seminary originally built more than 50 in all.

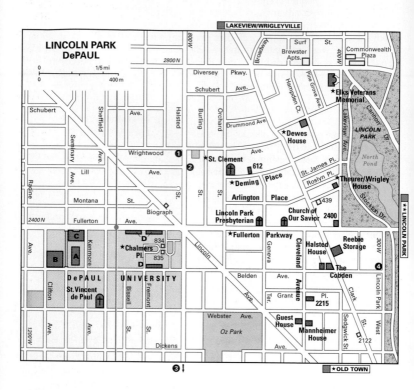

Between Lincoln Avenue and Clark Street are some of the area's most interesting private homes, apartment buildings and churches. Along **Cleveland Avenue**, for instance, note the variety of styles and eras represented. At no. 2147, the **Leon Mannheimer House** bears the unmistakable decorative hallmarks of Louis Sullivan, whose firm designed it in 1884. Across the street at no. 2150, the **Walter Guest House** was remodeled in 1932 by the artistic hand of Edgar Miller, whose other Art Deco renovations grace WEST BURTON PLACE. Incised chevrons decorate the expansive leaded-glass windows, and a close look at the front door reveals a frolic of Miller's favorite animals. In the next block, Bruce Graham of Skidmore, Owings and Merrill designed himself an impenetrable home at **no. 2215** in 1969 that reveals little of itself except its debt to the concrete hulks of the Brutalism style popular in the 1960s.

Several blocks north, the **Ann Halsted House** (1883) at 440 W. Belden Avenue is another Adler & Sullivan commission decorated along its gable with the firm's signature lotus motif. **The Cobden** apartment building (1892, Charles S. Frost) spans 418 to 424 W. Belden and bends around the corner along Clark Street, where the ground level houses shops. The Belden Avenue facade is particularly interesting for its surface decoration, undulating bays and crowning gable. At 2325 N. Clark Street, the whimsical **Reebie Storage and Moving Company** warehouse was designed in 1923 in an unabashed celebration of the opening of King Tut's tomb in 1922. The two sentinel statues of Ramses II are said to represent the Reebie brothers; hieroglyphics below the right one read, "I give protection to your furniture"!

Since the 1980s, **Fullerton Parkway**★ between Clark Street and Lincoln Avenue has been a pleasant street of elegant homes, trees and gardens. Two hearty Romanesque-style churches dominate adjacent blocks, but blend genteelly with their surroundings: the Episcopal **Church of Our Savior** (1888) at no. 530 and the **Lincoln Park Presbyterian Church** (1888) at no. 600. Two blocks north, at Deming Place and Orchard Street, **St. Clement Roman Catholic Church**★ (1918), constructed of smooth limestone with the twin towers and rose window of the French Romanesque style, underwent a thorough interior renovation in 1989 to restore the spectacular mosaics and murals of its Byzantine dome. Set back from the street, the houses along **Deming Place**★ recall an elegant era; the oldest were built in the 1880s and 1890s by successful German businessmen. A montage of elements from the Romanesque, Queen Anne, Gothic and Classical styles characterizes these residences. Note the Sullivanesque detail that trims the porch at **no. 612**.

East of Clark Street, high-rise apartment buildings of every description cluster along the edge of Lincoln Park, all vying for the best view of Lake Michigan beyond. The 30-story glass and steel structure at **2400 North Lakeview Avenue** (1963) is the last residential high rise to be designed by Ludwig Mies van der Rohe in Chicago. At no. 2466, the **Theurer/Wrigley House**★ (1897) dominates the corner of Arlington Place. Italian Renaissance elegance swaddles its sturdy steel and concrete underpinnings, and a glimpse into the **solarium**★ at the southwest corner hints at the decorative detail inside. Chewing-gum magnate William Wrigley, Jr. purchased the home from brewer Joseph Theurer around 1910. The Wrigley family occupied it until the 1930s when, supposedly, threats of kidnapping necessitated the move to a more secure apartment residence. The home lay virtually unused for 50 years until the specter of a high-rise replacement galvanized preservationists, politicians and developers to save it in the early 1980s. Other lovely homes line **Arlington Place** and, where it meets Clark Street, walkers are greeted by the cacophony of birdsong that emanates from the privately maintained bird sanctuary adjacent to no. 439.

The fairy-tale quality of the **Francis J. Dewes House**★ (1896) at 503 W. Wrightwood Avenue is perhaps exaggerated by the surrounding modern city. Crisp white Bedford limestone contrasts with a dark slate mansard roof and cast-iron railings. The house's zest, however, derives from its extravagant Baroque detailing, particularly the two disproportionate figures that flank the front door and the elaborate variety of window decoration. Dewes was a German brewer who no doubt hired his architects, German Adolph Cudell and Hungarian Arthur Hercz, partly for their familiarity with European decorative traditions.

At 2750 North Lakeview Avenue, an entirely different architectural spectacle commands the corner at Diversey Parkway. The **Elks Veterans Memorial**★ *(open year-round Mon–Fri 9am–4pm;* ☎773-528-4500*)* was completed in 1926 to honor Elks brethren who had served in World War I. It has since been re-

4 Ambria

2300 Lincoln Park West.
☎ *773-472-5959.*
This elegant, romantic restaurant consistently ranks at the top of both critics' and diners' lists. Chefs Gabino Sotelino (who owns and manages the restaurant) and Takashi Yagihashi prepare delicious, exquisitely presented French cuisine. To complement the chefs' creations, Ambria boasts an extensive, award-winning wine list. Located across the lobby, the renovated dining room of the old Belden Stratford hotel houses **Un Grand Café** *(*☎ *773-348-8886)*, best known for its bistro atmosphere and classic French fare, including steak frites and onion soup topped with Gruyère.

dedicated to veterans of all succeeding American military conflicts. Inside the relatively sedate Neoclassical Indiana limestone exterior, not a square inch of wall, window or ceiling surface remains undecorated. In the rotunda and reception room, 26 varieties of marble and lavishly carved oak paneling dazzle the visitor, while gilded statuary, elaborate murals and art-glass windows illustrate the fraternal order's cardinal virtues of charity, justice, brotherly love and fidelity, along with other allegories. A video on view in the reception room discusses the memorial and the order's history.

LINCOLN PARK ★★

Time: 1 day
Map p 133

Unlike so many urban areas whose waterfronts have been taken up by industry, Chicago provides its residents with unlimited access to the lake via its numerous lakefront parks. Among the finest of these is Lincoln Park. Belying its origins as a soggy cemetery, this sweeping expanse is today one of Chicago's most compelling landscapes. Stretching 6mi and 1,200 acres along the shoreline of Lake Michigan, from Ohio Street north to Ardmore Avenue, Lincoln Park trims the city's watery edge with a pleasant and peaceful greenbelt. Millions of Chicagoans flock here year-round to enjoy the zoo, conservatory, picnic groves, beaches and playing fields. At North Avenue, the park forms the northern edge of the affluent GOLD COAST and at Clark Street, the eastern boundary of the lively LINCOLN PARK/ DEPAUL neighborhood, where theaters, restaurants and shops abound.

Historical Notes

Back from the Dead – In typical Chicago fashion, Lincoln Park was the product of years of grass-roots activism, a rivalry with New York and copious amounts of landfill. In 1837, the Illinois General Assembly granted the city a large parcel of sand dunes and marshes, between present-day North Avenue and Webster Street, for use as a municipal burial ground. As development crept north toward this once remote location, the cemetery's new residential neighbors began to lobby for its closure and conversion into a greensward to be called Lake Park.

Formation in 1869 of several regional park boards charged with encircling the city with green space gave the North Side park movement its much needed impetus. Inspired by Frederick Law Olmsted's Central Park in New York (begun in 1857) and, ironically, by the beautifully landscaped cemeteries on the city's edge, the local citizenry, developers and civic leaders banded together and clamored for completion of their lakefront park. Work progressed slowly, since moving the thousands of bodies buried south of Menomonee Street—including Confederate dead from the prisoner-of-war stockade at Camp Douglas on the city's South Side—proved nearly impossible. Shifting sands, poor records and politics hindered the townspeople in their efforts to locate and identify all the graves, and still today, stray bones turn up during excavations in the area.

Northward, ho – Renamed shortly after the assassination of President Lincoln in 1865, the park grew in stages, at the hands of at least six landscape architects between 1864 and 1957. One of the first sectors to take shape was the old cemetery—today the heart of Lincoln Park. Most bodies had been moved by 1875, and the park's naturalistic style began to emerge: winding pathways, flower beds and ponds, which landscapers **Swain Nelson** and **Olaf Benson** believed would enhance the park's lushness by reflecting the surrounding greenery. One by one, other elements of the modern park appeared: the zoo in 1868, Ridge Drive in 1878, the Lagoon in the 1880s. As the adjacent neighborhoods became more and more populous, landfilling was begun to extend the park northward to Montrose Avenue by 1925, to Foster Avenue by 1936 and lastly, to Ardmore Avenue by 1957. Much of this portion of the park is landscaped with native plants, the work of Ossian C. Simonds, and later, **Alfred Caldwell**, who also designed the serene Lincoln Park Zoo Rookery in the Prairie school style.

Such extensive landfilling was not undertaken strictly for the recreational enjoyment of the populace, however. The development of Lake Shore Drive, which today cuts a swath up the lakefront from south to north side, is closely linked with the history of Lincoln Park. The park's promenades and boulevards, designed for quiet strolls and leisurely carriage rides, had been conceived before the advent of the automobile. By the 1920s, the park's bucolic atmosphere was in jeopardy as daily commuters began to overburden its thoroughfares and scenic routes. Lake Shore Drive, today an 8-lane highway, unrolled inexorably up the lakefront, sharing landfill with the park and posing new challenges for planners bent on maintaining a harmonious co-existence of parkland and expressway.

Today, some balance has been achieved on that score through pedestrian bridges and underpasses, and in recent years the drive itself has been softened by median landscaping. The rush of traffic seems not to affect the tremendous popularity of this pleasure ground, where throngs of visitors savor lake breezes against a stunning skyline backdrop.

The 🚊 *symbol indicates Chicago Transit Authority rapid transit or bus lines .*

Visiting Lincoln Park

Getting There – Lincoln Park is accessible by several ᴄᴛᴀ bus lines including no. 151 (☎312-836-7000). Parking in northern section of park near Diversey Harbor or in southern section, adjacent to North Ave. Beach *(map p 133)*.

Park Information – Visitor Center at Lincoln Park Cultural Center *(2045 N. Lincoln Park West; open year-round Mon–Fri 9am–9pm, Sat 8am–4pm;* ☎312-742-7726*)*. Information by mail: Lakefront Region Office, South Shore Cultural Center, 7059 South Shore Dr., Chicago IL 60649 (☎312-747-2474).

Recreation – Public sports venues (located primarily in the South Field, Waveland and Montrose areas of the park) include baseball/softball fields, basketball courts, soccer field and tennis courts. The Waveland area also features **ice-skating** and **archery** (rentals available). A bicycle/running **path** *(p 244)* runs along the lakefront. Miniature and 9-hole **golf** courses are located near Diversey Harbor.

WALKING TOUR   *distance: 2.8mi*

Begin on the east side of the Chicago Historical Society (p 124).

Gazing out over the garden in front of him, Augustus Saint-Gaudens' **Standing Lincoln★** (1887) is a masterpiece of monumental art and likely the sculptor's finest work. Imbued with humanity and dignity, Lincoln seems on the verge of imparting a great thought. The exedra surrounding the statue was designed by architect Stanford White, with whom Saint-Gaudens often collaborated. Another of the sculptor's Lincoln statues resides in GRANT PARK.

Take the path heading northwest of the Lincoln statue.

On a small bluff rising behind the Chicago Historical Society stands the **Couch Mausoleum**, an anomalous reminder of the cemetery that once covered these acres. Deemed too difficult to move when the land was converted into a park, the tomb is the resting place of Ira Couch, proprietor of the Tremont House, Chicago's fashionable mid-19C hotel.

Continue under LaSalle St. and take the path northeast of the Franklin statue.

The only way to view the front of **Benjamin Franklin** (1896, Richard Henry Park) is on foot since he stands with his back to LaSalle Street. The playing fields to the east are generally alive with softball and other games on summer weekends and evenings.

Continue up Ridge Dr.

At the crest of Ridge Drive (once a main north-south thoroughfare), a mounted **General Ulysses S. Grant [1]**, the 1891 work of Louis T. Rebisso, surveys the park and Lake Shore Drive from atop a massive Romanesque base. Owing to the monument's height off the ground, it is best viewed from a distance rather than up close.

1   North Avenue Beach
Access via overpass in park, just north of North Ave.
This broad stretch of sand is Chicago's volleyball mecca. In summertime, the Park District and several private clubs set up dozens of nets. Many courts are reserved for league play, but pick-up games are common. To organize your own game or outing, call the Park District six days in advance to rent a net, boundary line tapes and a ball.

The **Air and Water Show**, an annual festival of aviation and boating, takes place along the lakefront on the last weekend in July and is best viewed from North Avenue Beach. Past shows have included exhibitions by precision military flight squadrons, acrobatic stunts performed in vintage planes and rescue drills executed by the Coast Guard and Chicago Fire Department.

Continue on Ridge Dr., crossing over South Pond.

The splendid **view★★** south from the bridge over **South Pond** breathes life into the city's epithet *Urbs in Horto* ("City in a Garden"). From here, downtown skyscrapers seem an afterthought to the park's towering trees.

Enter the Farm in the Zoo, to the left.

★ **Farm in the Zoo** – *1901 N. Stockton Dr. Open year-round daily 9am–5pm.*♿ ☎312-742-7707. This peaceful 5-acre haven, a working farm constructed as part of Lincoln Park Zoo in the 1960s, offers city children a chance to commune with rural life. In five well-kept barns dwell cows, poultry, horses and other livestock. Demonstrations of butter churning, horse grooming and goat milking go on throughout the day *(times are posted)*. Particularly interesting is the **Dairy Barn**, where cows are milked by hand and by machine, yielding 16 to 20gal of fresh milk daily, which goes to feed the other animals. Both simple labels and interactive computers explain the milk production process. In the **Poultry Barn**, fertilized eggs in all stages of hatching are on view in incubators. Lucky visitors might see chicks pipping, or breaking through their shells.

Exit Farm to the west and head north on Stockton Dr.

To the west stands the Matthew Laflin Memorial, a 3-story Renaissance Revival building financed in 1893 by the Chicago entrepreneur who was disappointed that he could not be buried in the park that was once a cemetery. The Lincoln Park Zoo is renovating the building for office use.

Walk across Stockton Dr. to the east.

★ **Café Brauer** – *2021 N. Stockton Dr. Open Mar–Oct daily 10am–5pm, rest of the year daily 10am–3pm.* 🍴♿ 🅿 ☎312-280-2767. Architect Dwight Perkins, whose other credits include several of the animal houses at Lincoln Park Zoo, designed this refectory in 1908 at the behest of restaurateurs Paul and Caspar Brauer. A striking example of the Prairie school style, it hugs South Pond with its main pavilion and two flanking loggias. Arts and Crafts details—chandeliers, tiles, mosaics and windows—lend the interior a suitably rustic charm. A popular gathering place until it closed in the 1940s, the cafe underwent a $4.2 million restoration in 1989 and today once again offers parkgoers a quiet spot to snack and relax.

In a grove to the northwest of the cafe sits a bronze **Hans Christian Andersen [2]**, sculpted by John Gelert in 1896.

Enter zoo along path north of Café Brauer.

★★ **Lincoln Park Zoological Gardens** – *2200 N. Cannon Dr. Open year-round daily 9am–5pm.* 🍴♿ 🅿 ☎312-742-2000. This wonderfully accessible zoo, convenient and free of charge, is best enjoyed in an afternoon of wandering. Founded with the gift of a pair of swans from New York's Central Park in 1868, the zoo has grown to encompass 35 acres, house over 1,000 animals and attract 4 million annual visitors in the intervening years. The zoo has evolved from a typical 19C "menagerie," so that today its collection and agenda reflect its strong conservation mission. Forty-four of the zoo's species are endangered; interpretive graphics and labeling focus sharply on ecological issues.

Over the past decade, the zoo has meticulously renovated its historic buildings—Primate House (1927, renovated 1984), Lion House (1912, renovated 1986) and Bird House (1900, renovated 1986)—adapting them to accommodate the realistic habitats typical of modern zoos while retaining their architectural charm and detail. New habitats, such as the Great Ape House (1976), the Crown-Field Center (1979) and the Penguin and Seabird House (1981), burrow unobtrusively into landscaped hillocks, creating a pleasingly unobstructed terrain.

Entering the zoo from Café Brauer, note the **Waterfowl Lagoon** directly north. Although renovated in 1978 with the addition of the Flamingo Dome, the lagoon itself is one of the few remaining original elements of the park designed by Swain Nelson in 1865. It provides a lovely, naturalistic setting for local and migratory waterfowl. Farther along, a major center of zoo activity is the Lester E. Fisher **Great Ape House★**. Of particular interest are families of endangered lowland gorillas, of which the zoo has birthed more than 38 since 1970, winning it the nickname "gorilla capital of the world." The zoo's most famous gorilla, Bushman, arrived in 1930 and lived 21 years to delight millions of visitors. Today he is on display, stuffed, at the FIELD MUSEUM. The newly renovated Helen Brach **Primate House★** shows off gibbons, marmosets, mandrills and their relations in a rain-forest environment. Just northeast of the Primate House, note the *Eugene Field Memorial* **[3]** (1922) by sculptor Edward McCartan, a gentle tribute to the children's works of that Midwestern humorist. The large **Lion House [A]** features the zoo's collection of big cats that are not as docile as the ones cleverly incorporated into the exterior brickwork. The **McCormick Bird House★** presents a variety of avian species in intimate, sometimes open habitats.

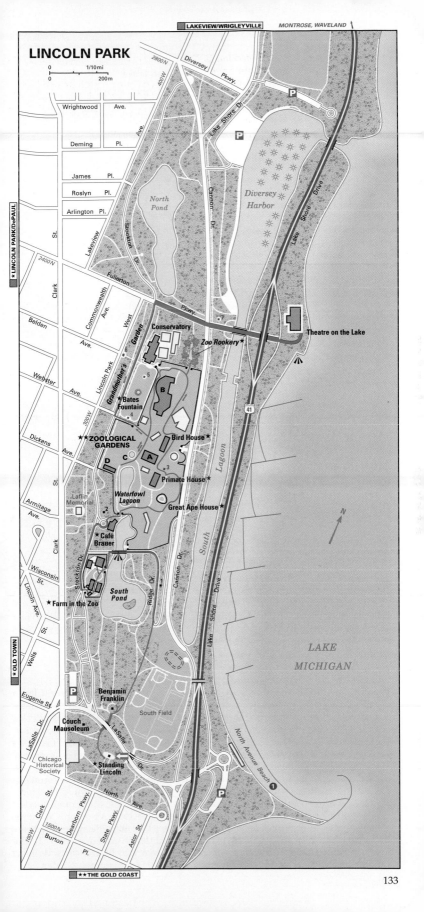

LINCOLN PARK

0   1/10mi
0   200m

LAKEVIEW/WRIGLEYVILLE
MONTROSE, WAVELAND

Wrightwood   Ave.

Deming   Pl.

James   Pl.

Roslyn   Pl.

Arlington   Pl.

North
Pond

Diversey
Harbor

Lakeview   Dr.

Stockton   Dr.

Fullerton

★LINCOLN PARK/DePAUL

2400N

Clark   St.

Belden   Ave.

Commonwealth   Ave.

West   Garden

Webster   Ave.

Lincoln   Park

Dickens   Ave.

Grandmother's   Garden

Conservatory

Zoo Rookery ★

Theatre on the Lake

★ **Bates Fountain**

B

★★ **ZOOLOGICAL GARDENS**

Bird House ★

A

D   **C**

Primate House ★

Laflin Memorial

Waterfowl Lagoon

Great Ape House ★

South Lagoon

Armitage   Ave.

Clark   St.

Stockton   Dr.

★ **Café Brauer**

Wisconsin   St.

Lincoln   Ave.

★ **Farm in the Zoo**

South Pond

Ridge   Dr.

Cannon   Dr.

Lake Shore   Drive

N

Wells   St.

LAKE
MICHIGAN

Eugenie   St.

Benjamin Franklin

South Field

Couch Mausoleum

LaSalle   Dr.

Chicago Historical Society

★ **Standing Lincoln**

North Avenue Beach

★OLD TOWN

Clark   St.

Dearborn   Pkwy.

North   Ave.

State   Pkwy.

Astor   St.

1500N

Burton   Pl.

★★ THE GOLD COAST

133

At the far north end of the grounds, the **Zoo Rookery**★ provides an interesting counterpoint to the Waterfowl Lagoon. Designed by Prairie school disciple Alfred Caldwell in 1937, this wooded grove, planted thickly with native trees surrounding a large pond, provides a tranquil enclave for zoo visitors and migrating birds alike. Interpretive labels elaborate on bird-watching, migration patterns and the various species that visit the rookery throughout the year. Low-slung, Japanese-style pavilions and stacked rockwork evoke the site's Prairie school inspiration *(the rookery can also be entered from the north off of Fullerton Pkwy.; open year-round daily 10am–4pm; closed during inclement weather;* **P** ☎*312-747-2200).* The return trail south passes the **Large Mammal Area [B]**, housing perennial favorites such as elephants and giraffes. Beyond the **Sea Lion Pool [C]**, the **Pritzker Children's Zoo [D]** incorporates a nursery behind large windows and an outdoor petting area. Docents offer kids of all ages a chance to hobnob with turtles, hedgehogs, parrots and other hearty creatures.

> **Zoo facts:**
>
> ■ Biggest animal:
> Binti, an African elephant
> weighing over 6,500lbs
>
> ■ Smallest animal:
> the poison dart frog,
> the size of a dime
>
> ■ Total number of lowland gorillas
> born at the zoo: 38
>
> ■ Number of endangered species
> at the zoo: 44
>
> ■ Zoo's annual grocery bill:
> $350,000

Exit zoo at west entrance and continue north to the Lincoln Park Conservatory.

Western Lowland Gorilla

Susan Reich/Lincoln Park Zoo

The approach to the Lincoln Park Conservatory is marked by a broad lawn dominated by a formal garden nearly a block in length. In its center, the **Bates Fountain**★ *(Storks at Play)* presents a joyful tableau of water play between storks, boys and fish *(covered in winter).* The fountain (1887) is the work of Augustus Saint-Gaudens and his assistant Frederick MacMonnies, although since Saint-Gaudens was then busy on the *Standing Lincoln*, the credit for *Storks at Play* goes largely to MacMonnies. Eli Bates, the Chicago lumber merchant for whom the work was named, left a bequest in his will for both the Lincoln statue and the fountain. South of the garden stands *Johann Christoph Friedrich von Schiller* **[4]**, fashioned in bronze by German sculptor Ernst Bildhauer Rau in 1886. The traditionally styled statue of the German playwright and poet is a copy of one in Marbach, Germany. A bust of Sir Georg Solti **[5]**, renowned conductor of the Chicago Symphony Orchestra from 1969 to 1991, was dedicated north of the garden in 1987. To the west, across Stockton Drive, a bronze *William Shakespeare* **[6]** (1894) by William Ordway Partridge rests thoughtfully in the informal **Grandmother's Garden**.

Lincoln Park Conservatory

Lincoln Park Conservatory – *2400 Stockton Dr. Open year-round daily 9am–5pm.* ☎*312-742-7736.* Modeled by architect Joseph Lyman Silsbee on London's Crystal Palace, the conservatory (1892) and its 18 propagating houses, cold frames and hotbeds now cover three acres. Three main galleries in the glass and copper structure display extensive collections of palms, ferns, cacti and related flora, including a grouping of cycads, which are among the oldest-known plants. In the Show House, four major exhibits take place each year: in November, chrysanthemums; a holiday poinsettia display; azaleas and camelias in late February; and flowering bulbs in the spring. Many of the flowers that enliven Chicago's parks are germinated in the conservatory's greenhouses.

Continue along Stockton Dr. and turn east on Fullerton Pkwy.

On the north side of Fullerton Parkway stands Ellsworth Kelly's monolithic stainless steel *I Will* **[7]**, commissioned in 1981, the first new sculpture in Lincoln Park in 30 years. According to the artist, the work, bearing as its name Chicago's unofficial post-Fire motto, represents the city as the birthplace of the skyscraper. Farther east, at the water's edge, the 384-seat **Theatre on the Lake** mounts eight productions each summer *(2nd Tue Jun–Labor Day,* ☎*312-742-7994).* The Prairie school building (1920) first served as the *Chicago Daily News* Fresh Air Sanitarium, located where tuberculosis patients might take full advantage of the lake's breezes. The **view★** to the south from this vantage point imparts a real sense of the harmonious relationship between lake and city, nature and urban center.

Addresses, telephone numbers, opening hours and prices published in this guide are accurate at press time. We apologize for any inconvenience resulting from outdated information, and we welcome corrections and suggestions that may assist us in preparing the next edition. Send us your comments:

Michelin Travel Publications
Editorial Department
P.O. Box 19001
Greenville, SC 29602-9001

MILWAUKEE AVENUE CORRIDOR

Time: 1/2 day
Map p 137

A broad, bustling and colorful artery, Milwaukee Avenue has been the spine of a working-class immigrant community on the Northwest Side since its first settlement in the mid-19C. Historically Polish and currently Hispanic, the neighborhood extending from Chicago Avenue to Belmont Avenue remains a melting pot of diverse cultures and rich streetscapes, confirming Chicago's image as a city of neighborhoods and attracting a wide cross section of residents.

Historical Notes

Lured by industries along the North Branch of the Chicago River, immigrant laborers from Germany began to settle the West Town neighborhood along Milwaukee Avenue following the revolutions of 1848, and the street became known as "Dinner Pail Avenue." Polish immigrants arrived in the 1860s and soon created St. Stanislaus Kostka parish near Division Street. While simple laborers' cottages mushroomed along the avenue, the area around Wicker Park, donated to the city by real estate developers Joel and Charles Wicker in 1870, became an enclave of grand mansions constructed by German and Scandinavian businessmen. As the number of Poles steadily increased, Germans and Scandinavians left, following the avenue north and west and establishing the migratory pattern for other immigrant groups. The development of the West Side Parks and Boulevard System—designed to ring the city with broad avenues and greenswards—after 1871 attracted many successful Norwegian and Swedish immigrants who settled around Humboldt Park and Logan Square after the turn of the century. By 1900 more than eight Polish parishes filled the dense corridor, and over 5,000 families attended St. Stanislaus alone. Some 250,000 people, including Russian Jews, Ukrainians, Slovaks and Italians in addition to Polish residents, lived within walking distance of the intersection of Milwaukee and Ashland Avenues, dubbed the Polish Downtown, home not only to local groups but also to all of the major Polish-American organizations in the nation.

By the 1930s the lower portion of the Milwaukee Avenue Corridor had fallen into decline. Chicago author **Nelson Algren** *(p 31)* documented the sordid street life around Wicker Park in the 1940s in his novels and short stories. By the 1960s Hispanics, especially Puerto Ricans, were the dominant ethnic group in West Town and Humboldt Park, pushing other immigrants to the northwest to follow the pattern of migration established back in the late 19C. "Urban pioneers" began rehabilitating the Victorian mansions of Wicker Park and Logan Square in the late 1970s, when both communities were listed on the National Register of Historic Places. In the following decade, Wicker Park came to the forefront as an artists' mecca, attracting galleries and theaters that had been priced out of LINCOLN PARK/DEPAUL and River West. Today, the lively neighborhood is home to one of the largest artist communities in the nation.

Milwaukee Avenue Window Display

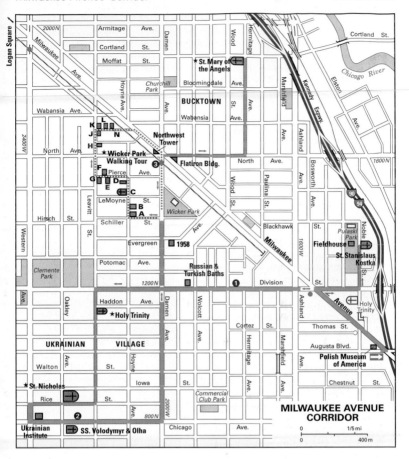

DRIVING TOUR   *distance: 5.8mi (including 1mi walking tour)*

The tour covers a variety of ethnic neighborhoods and an eclectic mix of architecture, cultural sights and shops. Although long sections of the avenue resemble most urban streetscapes with nondescript buildings, discount warehouses and fast-food restaurants, the visitor will discover hidden gems lurking behind unassuming structures. The Wicker Park neighborhood has become the city's most popular night spot, teeming with cultural venues and quirky boutiques ranging from the occult to the antique, and giving rise to several alternative bands, including the Smashing Pumpkins and Liz Phair. As the drive covers great distances, it is best to visit this area by car; however, we have included a walking tour of the Wicker Park neighborhood.

Begin at the intersection of Milwaukee Ave. and Augusta Blvd.

Polish Museum of America – *984 N. Milwaukee Ave. Open year-round daily 11am–4pm. Closed Jan 1, Easter Sunday, Dec 24–25, 31. $2. Guided tours available, advance reservations suggested. Library and archives by appointment. &* 📮 *☎773-384-3352.* Located on the upper floors of the Polish Roman Catholic Union of America headquarters, one of the oldest and largest ethnic museums in the US encompasses an extensive collection of fine arts and historical artifacts.

Sculptures and drawings by Stanislaw Szukalski (1893-1987) line the steps to the third-floor entrance. The main exhibit space is a 2-story hall. Along the east wall stands a massive stained-glass piece, followed by Hussar armor and exhibits on Tadeusz Kosciuszko and Casimir Pulaski, heroes of the American Revolution. A wood-paneled room dedicated to Polish Kings features royal documents. The west wall displays folk artifacts, crucifixes, silverware and wooden sculptures. Early-20C murals decorate the south wall, and cases on the north exhibit costumes and church relics.

Outside of the main room, an 8ft-long **sleigh**★ carved from a single log in the form of a dolphin was given by King Stanislaus Leszczynski to Princess Maria, future wife of the Grand Dauphin of France, later Louis XV. A staircase lined with modern art leads to a gallery on the fourth floor, devoted to paintings representing landscapes and portraits. A highlight of the museum is the **Paderewski Room**★ *(2nd floor)*, which presents a large collection of artifacts from the life of the Polish pianist (1860-1941), including the living room where he spent his last years. The museum hosts about six temporary exhibits annually.

Continue northwest on Milwaukee Ave. to Division St. Turn right on Division St., then left on Noble St.

At 1255 Noble Street rises **St. Stanislaus Kostka Catholic Church**, a large brick structure covered with stucco. Following extensive community protest, the Kennedy Expressway was routed around the edifice, thereby saving the city's oldest Polish church (1876). Across the street, Pulaski Park is one of a series of green spaces developed in the 1910s to provide recreational facilities for the poor. Its most prominent feature, the 1912 **Pulaski Park Fieldhouse**, was designed by William Carbys Zimmerman and incorporates elements of the Tudor and Prairie styles. Visible to the south, the spires of Holy Trinity Roman Catholic Church *(1120 N. Noble St.)* tower over the neighborhood.

1 Andy's Deli
1737 W. Division St.
☎ *773-486-8870.* Dozens of sausages, breads, cheese and an assortment of knick-knacks vie for shelf space in this cramped and bustling Polish delicatessen.

2 Galans
2210 W. Chicago Ave.
☎ *773-292-1000.* Aside from the nearby churches, this restaurant is one of the few places where you can experience the neighborhood's Ukrainian flavor. The menu features stuffed cabbage, borscht, sausages, dumplings, potato pancakes and chicken Kiev. For a wide sample of Ukrainian cuisine, try the hearty Kozak feast.

Return to Division St. and turn right.

The intersection of Milwaukee Avenue and Division Street marks the heart of the former Polish Downtown. West of the intersection, Division Street retains the urban seediness depicted by Nelson Algren in the 1940s. Just west of Wolcott Street, the **Division Street Russian & Turkish Baths** *(no. 1916)* still offer the old-world sauna treatment in a 1907 terra-cotta building *(open to men: year-round Mon–Thu 8am–10pm, Fri & Sat 7am–10pm, Sun 6am–10pm; women: year-round Wed, Fri–Sat 10am–10pm; $17; ✗ ▯ ☎773-384-9671).*

Turn left on Leavitt St.

The neighborhood of simple, red brick 2-flats with neatly groomed lawns, located south of Division Street between Damen and Western Avenues, is known as the **Ukrainian Village**. Built and settled by Ukrainian immigrants after 1900 and still occupied by their descendants, the district reveals a variety of Ukrainian shops and restaurants along Chicago Avenue, as well as the Ukrainian Institute of Modern Art *(p 139)*.

★ **Holy Trinity Russian Orthodox Cathedral** – *1121 N. Leavitt St.* This tiny jewel, designed by Louis Sullivan in 1899, combines his decorative aesthetic with the form of a rural Russian church. The tower topped by an onion dome is trimmed in yellow while the building's walls are covered in white stucco. The edifice was constructed with a donation of $4,000 from Czar Nicholas II and became a base for Patriarch Tikhon, who was recently beatified.

Turn right on Rice St. and continue to Oakley Ave.

At Oakley and Rice stands **St. Nicholas Ukrainian Catholic Cathedral**★, the mother church for Ukrainian Catholics in Chicago. The soaring structure features 13 domes symbolizing Christ and his disciples. Built in 1915 by architects Worthmann, Steinbach & Piontek, St. Nicholas was restored in 1975 and glimmering mosaics were added in 1988.

Continue on Rice St. to Western Ave. Turn left on Western Ave. and left again on Chicago Ave.

At 2320 W. Chicago Avenue stands the **Ukrainian Institute of Modern Art** *(open Jan–Jun & Sept–Dec Tue–Sun noon–4pm; Jul–Aug weekends noon–4pm; contribution requested; guided tours available, reservations required;* ♿ 🅿 ☎*773-227-5522).* Founded in 1971 and presenting work by artists of Ukrainian descent, the respected museum is located in a white one-story building in the heart of the Ukrainian Village. Rotating exhibits occupy the large gallery to the left of the entrance, while three connected galleries to the right display the permanent collection of drawings, paintings, sculpture and multi-media artworks.

Continue east on Chicago Ave.

In the 1960s the Ukrainian Catholic congregation was split by reforms of the second Vatican council, and the traditionalists built a new edifice two blocks south of St. Nicholas Cathedral—**SS. Volodymyr & Olha Church** *(739 N. Oakley Ave.)* opened in 1975. Much simpler in design, the massive edifice is crowned by a huge gold dome. Here services are still held in Ukrainian and worshippers follow the Orthodox (Gregorian) calendar. The arched mosaic above the entrance depicts Saint Volodymyr and his mother Olha blessing the Rus people in the Dnieper River in AD 988.

Drive east on Chicago Ave. and turn left on Damen Ave. Continue north on Damen Ave. to Schiller St. and park to tour the Wicker Park neighborhood on foot.

A small, 3-acre triangle, Wicker Park is lined with impressive stone Victorian mansions as well as early-20C apartment buildings along Schiller Street and Wicker Park Avenue. One block south, a plaque marks the 3-flat at **1958 W. Evergreen Avenue** where author Nelson Algren lived for three decades.

Walk west on Schiller St. and turn right on Hoyne Ave.

A city and national landmark, the **Wicker Park★** neighborhood contains numerous mansions commissioned by prosperous German and Scandinavian immigrants in the late 19C. Occupying a spacious corner lot at the intersection of Schiller Street and Hoyne Avenue, the **John H. Rapp House★ [A]** *(1407 N. Hoyne Ave.),* built in 1879 by a wine merchant in the Second Empire style, sports a mansard roof, domed tower, elaborate wood brackets and trim and a cast-iron porch and fence. Built in the 1880s for a Norwegian furniture maker, **no. 1427 [B]** is an eclectic design reflecting Romanesque as well as Victorian detailing; note the workmanship of the wood and pressed-metal porch.

Cross LeMoyne St. and continue north.

The **Wicker Park Lutheran Church [C]** *(2112 LeMoyne St.)* was built in 1906 with granite salvaged from a brothel in the Levee *(p 154).* The pastor reportedly defended the material, saying the stones had "served the devil long enough, now let them serve the Lord." At **no. 1520 [D]**, golden hands rising from the stairs hold the banisters on the Second Empire mansion, built in 1886 for Russian lumberman Henry Grusendorf. Note the unusual double-gabled porch, with its intricate wood carvings, and the sculpted woman's head embellishing the facade.

Turn left and walk west on Pierce Ave.

John H. Rapp House

Peter Pearson/Tony Stone Images

The **Hermann Weinhardt House★ [E]** at no. 2135 (1889, William Ohlhaber) defines ostentation with its unflinching use of architectural detail. The gabled roof is encrusted with pressed-metal bargeboards, and every element of the facade seems to drip with decorative forms in brick, metal or wood. The profusion of balustrades on the **John D. Runge House★ [F]** at no. 2138 (1884, Frommann & Jebsen) helped advertise the owner's wood-milling firm. The home later served as the Polish Consulate and hosted a veranda concert by the Polish pianist Ignacy Paderewski in 1930. The Romanesque Revival **Theodore Juergens House [G]** at no. 2141 (1895, Henry T. Kley) features gargoyles and a third-floor ballroom.

Turn right on Leavitt St. and walk north to Concord Pl., one block past North Ave.

The two short blocks of Concord Place and Caton Street were developed by wealthy Scandinavians after 1890. Today, their incongruous location behind discount shops and elevated rail tracks belies their former elegance. Built in 1893, **2156 W. Concord Place [H]** features a conical tower and gabled dormer.

Continue north to Caton St. and turn right.

The large mansion at **2159 W. Caton Street [J]** was erected two years earlier in the Queen Anne style. Norwegian merchant Ole Thorp developed Caton Street and lived in the large home distinguished by a domed turret at **no. 2156 [K]** (1891, Faber & Pagels), where he reportedly entertained the Queen of Norway. The same architectural firm also designed **no. 2146 [L]**, a Romanesque Revival home in red brick with carved column capitals, and the pink sandstone and orange brick Queen Anne structure at **no. 2142 [N]**.

Turn right on Milwaukee Ave. and walk south to North Ave.

The heart of artistic Wicker Park is the intersection of Milwaukee, Damen and North Avenues, defined by the 12-story Art Deco **Northwest Tower** (1929, Perkins, Chatten & Hammond), centerpiece of the annual "Around the Coyote" tour of galleries and artists' lofts (*p 220*). The 2-story terra-cotta **Flatiron Building** on the southeast corner of Milwaukee and North Avenues contains a bewildering array of restaurants, galleries and shops. In recent years, new coffeehouses, bookshops

---

■ Cafes and Bookstores

The artsy inhabitants of greater Wicker Park have mastered the art of hanging out, and this neighborhood's various haunts deserve a peak inside, if just for people-watching. Booklovers should check out **Myopic Books** (*1726 W. Division Ave.*), which has its own cafe and stays open until 1am; **Quimby's Bookstore** (*1328 N. Damen Ave.*) specializing in gay and lesbian literature and offering a wide selection of underground magazines; and the **Occult Book Store** (*1561 N. Milwaukee Ave.*) for its works on witchcraft, tarot and all things eerie. Cafe culture in Wicker Park runs the gamut from boho-student to BMW-banker. A spacious, loft-like coffeehouse, **Urbus Orbis** (*1934 W. North Ave.*) serves strong java to an artsy crowd. **Earwax** (*1564 N. Milwaukee Ave.*)—cafe in front, used record shop in back—is the preferred meeting place for struggling musicians, while the neighborhood's well-dressed denizens frequent the **Mad Bar** and **The Northside Tavern** (*1640 and 1635 N. Damen Ave.*).

■ Nightclubs

At night, people from across the city flock to the neighborhood's clubs and taverns. Originally a polka lounge, the **Rainbo Club** (*1150 N. Damen Ave.* ☎ 773-489-5999) now claims a varied clientele including the likes of Liz Phair, Urge Overkill and the Smashing Pumpkins. Struggling rock bands perform at **Phyllis' Musical Inn** (*1800 W. Division St.* ☎ 773-486-9862) with its vintage musicians' mural, while **The Bop Shop** (*1807 W. Division St.* ☎ 773-235-3232) presents jazz combos. On the fringes of the Ukrainian Village, the **Empty Bottle** (*1035 N. Western Ave.* ☎ 773-276-3600) books an eclectic mix of experimental jazz, hot local rock acts and bands on the brink of national renown. **Red Dog** (*1958 W. North Ave.* ☎ 773-278-5138) is Wicker Park's dance club, where house and techno music rule. Decorated in kitschy Vegas-supper-club style, **Holiday** (*1471 N. Milwaukee Ave.* ☎ 773-486-0686) caters to stylish martini drinkers. The **Double Door** (*1572 N. Milwaukee Ave.* ☎ 773-489-3160) is the premier live-music venue in the area. The owners book bands that are just breaking onto the national scene and the small V-shaped room is a great place to see future stars up close and personal.

and antique stores catering to artists have joined the discount furniture stores and fast food restaurants lining Milwaukee.

Return to car along Damen Ave. Drive north on Damen Ave. and turn right on North Ave.; turn left on Hermitage Ave.

Located north of North Avenue between Milwaukee and Ashland Avenues, **Bucktown** was a largely Polish working-class community that experienced a sudden real estate boom in the late 1980s as hundreds of yuppies and artists moved into the quaint brick homes and quiet streets. Stately **St. Mary of the Angels Catholic Church★** *(1850 N. Hermitage Ave.)* dominates the streetscape of Bucktown. The brown brick and white terra-cotta edifice, completed in 1920 by Polish Catholics in a Roman Baroque style, features a twin-towered facade with an elaborate portico, 9ft-high terra-cotta angels ringing the parapet, and a huge dome and cupola modeled on St. Peter's Basilica in Rome. Parishioners and neighbors led a successful 5-year fund-raising effort that saw the church restored and reopened in 1992. The interior paintings and elaborate decoration well illustrate the exuberant Baroque style.

> **3 Busy Bee**
> *1546 N. Damen Ave.*
> ☎ 773-772-4433. This Polish restaurant/coffee shop is one of the last bastions of ethnicity in a rapidly "gentrifying" neighborhood. Sit at the horseshoe-shaped lunch counter and listen to the waitresses chatter in Polish while the "L" rumbles by overhead. Huge portions of pierogis (dumplings) and potato pancakes please both palate and wallet.

LOGAN SQUARE AREA

Begin at the intersection of Milwaukee Ave. and Logan and Kedzie Blvds.

The 1918 **Illinois Centennial Monument [1]** marks the intersection of Logan and Kedzie Boulevards with Milwaukee Avenue. An eagle surmounts a fluted pillar that rises from a base ringed by marching Native Americans, French explorers, farmers and workers.

Turn right on Logan Blvd., on the frontage road, and continue to Washtenaw St.

The most beautiful stretch of Chicago's 28-mile boulevard system is also the best place to view the city's finest **graystones**, houses that incorporate Romanesque-style stonework with Victorian and Neoclassical details in durable Indiana limestone. Stone stairs, turrets, battlements and stained glass lend many of these buildings a picturesque quality. The **John Rath House★** *(2701 Logan Blvd.)* is a Chicago Landmark designed in 1907 by George W. Maher. Broad eaves and recti-linear forms of the Prairie style combine with Maher's distinctive flattened arches and floral motifs repeated in windows, brackets and doors. The porch seems carved out of the side of the house, set back to take advantage of the boulevard.

Turn left and return west on the frontage road of Logan Blvd. to Kedzie Blvd.

The **Apartments for John Gerson** (1909, Frederick R. Schock) at 2934-36 Logan Boulevard, feature a fascinating, bowed-arch doorway flanked by Prairie urns with Craftsman-style detailing. At 2614 N. Kedzie Boulevard, the red brick Norwegian Lutheran Memorial Church, known as **"Minnekirken"** (1908, Charles Sorenson), boasts a large central tower and beveled edges that make the 30ft-wide building appear monumental.

Drive south on Kedzie Blvd.

141

More grand mansions line Kedzie Boulevard south of Logan Square, such as the 1897 **William Nowaczewski House** *(no. 2410)* with its elaborate porch, tower, gargoyles and stepped gables. Just south of Fullerton Avenue, the **Norske Club** *(no. 2350)* was designed in 1916 by Giaver & Dinkelberg as a lodge hall with dragon-head eaves that recall Norwegian architecture.

Additional Sight

Humboldt Park – *Between W. North Ave., W. Augusta Blvd., N. Kedzie Ave. and N. California Ave.* Covering 200 acres, this expansive park was created in 1871 by William Le Baron Jenney as part of the West Side Parks and Boulevard System. It was redesigned in 1906 by Prairie architect Jens Jensen, who added a "prairie river" extension of the lagoon and three large meadows on the western edge. Sights of interest in the park include the triple-arched **Boat House** (1907, Hugh Garden) overlooking the lagoon and Jensen's formal **Rose Garden** on the east side, guarded by two bronze buffalo (1911) by sculptor Edward Kemeys and restored Prairie-style lanterns (1907, William Carbys Zimmerman). The massive, half-timbered **Stables Building** (1896, Frommann & Jebsen) appears as a series of sloping roofs and turrets above a stone base. Extensively damaged by fire in 1992, the structure is being rebuilt as a Latino-American museum, expected to open in late 1997.

LAKEVIEW/WRIGLEYVILLE and UPTOWN

Time: 2 hours
Map p 145

A dense residential district on Chicago's North Side lakefront, this popular area is known for its upbeat restaurants and theaters and offbeat shops and nightclubs. Its most famous landmark, Wrigley Field, has lent its name to the northern part of Lakeview, which extends from Diversey Boulevard to Irving Park Road. Uptown stretches north to Foster Avenue. Lying between the two areas, Graceland Cemetery provides a unique slice of the city's history, art and architecture.

Historical Notes

A farming community settled by Germans in the 1830s, Lakeview began, as did its southern neighbor LINCOLN PARK/DE PAUL, as the celery basket of Chicago. Incorporated in 1857, the township was named for the 1854 Lake View House Hotel, a glamorous resort hotel built on the shores of Lake Michigan at present-day Grace Street. The late 19C witnessed the gradual transformation of the quiet lakefront community into a residential neighborhood, spurred by real estate developers who offered cheap frame houses outside Chicago's fire district. Swedish immigrants followed the Germans to the remote area, working in steel plants, brickyards and tanneries along the Chicago River and relaxing in numerous beer gardens and saloons—for which Lakeview is still famous today. Incorporation into Chicago in 1889 and the completion of the elevated line in 1900 led to intensive development. The 1920s boom in population and construction spread north to the roaring nightlife district of Uptown.

The fledgling film industry produced hundreds of silent movies—starring the likes of Charlie Chaplin and Gloria Swanson—at the neighborhood's **Essanay Studios** before moving west to milder climes. Following the Depression years, Uptown fell upon hard times, losing its appeal as Chicago's entertainment district. With its stock of inexpensive apartments, the neighborhood became the "port of entry" for immigrants from Appalachia, the Far East, Latin America and even American Indian reservations.

By the 1960s, much of the North Side was in decline, but the opening of several theaters, clubs and restaurants in the 1970s helped fuel intensive reinvestment. The neighborhood around historic Wrigley Field, promoted as "Wrigleyville" by apartment redeveloper Seymour Persky, attracted a young crowd in search of affordable digs. Large Victorian homes on Hawthorne Place, Hutchinson Street and in the Buena Park area were restored. Gleaming high rises sprouted along the lakefront, which was gradually gentrified north to Irving Park Road.

Today, Lakeview/Wrigleyville, home to the city's largest gay population, is best known for its plethora of entertainment options. Uptown retains a seedier image, exacerbated by many transient residents. Nonetheless, popular concert venues near Lawrence Avenue and Broadway, redevelopment of the Sheridan Park Historic District and the emergence of Chicago's Vietnamese Chinatown along Argyle Street have ended Uptown's decline. In addition, the Ravenswood and Lincoln Square neighborhoods located west of Uptown have experienced a surge in popularity, attracting a young and eclectic clientele.

SIGHTS

The far-flung sights in this area do not lend themselves to a walking tour. The area is best seen by car.

The southern section of Lakeview/ Wrigleyville continues the genteel neighborhood feel of Lincoln Park/ DePaul, with a densely built-up lakefront sheltering quiet residential streets. Of note here, the rusticated stone **Brewster Apartments** building *(2800 N. Pine Grove Ave.)* was designed in 1891 by Enoch Hill Turnock. This early high rise, distinguished by a rounded corner and rooftop penthouse, provides a vivid contrast to the stark aluminum **Commonwealth Plaza** *(330-340 W. Diversey Pkwy.)*, a Mies van der Rohe creation dating from 1956.

★ **Hawthorne Place District** – *Between Broadway and Lake Shore Dr.* This landmark district of sprawling homes and gardens was developed as Lake View's showpiece by Benjamin and John McConnell in 1883. Victorian mansions include the **George E. Marshall House [A]** *(no. 574)*, completed in 1886 by Burnham & Root, and the 1884 **Benjamin F. McConnell House [B]** *(no. 568)*, clad in shingles and clapboards. Dating from the 1890s, the Queen Anne **Herman H. Hettler House [C]** *(no. 567)* owned by the adjacent Chicago City Day School, retains its original corner turret, curving veranda and boulder stone foundation. The **John McConnell House [D]** *(no. 546)*, built in 1885 for the developer and mayor of Lake View, was extensively renovated in 1993.

Just around the corner, at 3480 N. Lake Shore Drive, stands **Temple Sholom**★, a Byzantine-style octagon clad in yellow ashlar limestone that is covered with intricate ornamentation. Designed in 1930 by the firm of Loebl, Schlossman & Demuth, this large structure provides an elegant break in the seemingly unending wall of lakefront high rises.

1 Argyle Street

Between Sheridan Road and Broadway, this bustling strip of Argyle Street (5000N) is the focal point of Chicago's Southeast-Asian community. Take the time to browse among the dozen of Vietnamese, Laotian and Cambodian shops and restaurants, as well as numerous Thai, Chinese and Filipino establishments. Seafood, hearty soups and wrap-it-yourself cellophane-noodle dishes rank among the house specialties at **Nha Trang Restaurant** *(1007 W. Argyle St.* ☎ *773-989-0712)*. The Laotian **Cafe Nhu Hoa** *(1020 W. Argyle St.* ☎ *773-878-0618)* is known for its good food and budget-friendly lunch specials. Dried tamarind candy, pink pearl tapioca, leechee honey, fresh persimmons and other Asian delicacies fill the shelves of the **Viet Hoa Plaza** market *(1051 W. Argyle St.* ☎ *773-334-1028)*. **Vinh Tho** *(1112 W. Argyle St.* ☎ *773-275-2985)* offers herbal remedies and a wide assortment of medicinal teas.

2 Lincoln Square

This predominantly German neighborhood is located where Lincoln, Lawrence and Western Avenues converge. The stretch of Lincoln Ave. between Leland and Lawrence encompasses a pedestrian mall where German culture thrives, from the Stieff stuffed animals at Timeless Toys *(4740 N. Lincoln Ave.)* to the Birkenstock shoes at Salamander *(4762 N. Lincoln Ave.)*. **Enisa's European Pastry and Cafe** *(4701 N. Lincoln Ave.* ☎ *773-271-7017)* offers petit fours, tarts and cookies baked daily. Founded in 1875, the **Merz Apothecary** *(4716 N. Lincoln Ave.)* stocks a huge selection of European and eco-friendly cosmetics as well as homeopathic herbs and remedies. Facing the square's small plaza, **Cafe Selmarie** *(2327 W. Giddings St.* ☎ *773-989-5595)* serves mouth-watering pastries by day and exotic dishes by night. Whole smoked eels, homemade wursts and schnapps galore can be found at **Meyer Delicatessen** *(4750 N. Lincoln Ave.)*. Feast on a plate of sauerbraten and hoist a stein of Stiegl at the boisterous **Chicago Brauhaus** *(4732 N. Lincoln Ave.* ☎ *773-784-4444)*, which features live German music nightly.

★ **Wrigley Field** – *1060 W. Addison St. See p 245 for additional information.* Built as Weeghman Field for the Chicago Whales of the Federal League before being occupied by the Cubs *(p 38)* of the National League in 1916, this stadium (1914, Zachary Taylor Davis) is a North Side icon. Famous for its ivy walls and lovable losing teams, the stadium has a backdrop of turn-of-the-century 3-flats rather than the usual sea of parking lots. Many of the adjacent buildings on Sheffield Street boast rooftop clubs where members watch the game over the outfield walls. The community stonewalled the addition of lights for night baseball until 1988.

Addison Street, near Wrigley Field, 1915

Chicago Historical Society (ICHi-24343)

★ **Alta Vista Terrace** – *3800 block, between Grace and Sheridan Sts.* The city's first protected landmark district was designed in 1904 by Joseph C. Brompton as a single work of architecture. Each side of the street contains 20 homes mirrored diagonally on the facing side. The Roman brick homes are 20ft wide and two stories high, except for the four central, 3-story limestone structures. Basically Georgian in style, the homes nevertheless exhibit a rich variety of details from the Byzantine, Neoclassical, Gothic and Renaissance styles as well as colorful rooflines. The street was built by the prolific neighborhood real estate developer **Samuel Eberly Gross** (1843-1913), whose inspiration came from several trips to London.

★★ **Graceland Cemetery** – *4001 N. Clark St. Sightplan available at entrance ($.25). Open year-round daily 8am–4:30pm.* ☎773-525-1105. One of Chicago's most evocative sites contains notable architecture and sculpture, marking the final resting places of many of the city's movers and shakers. The wealthy neighbors of Prairie Avenue *(p 155)* and the GOLD COAST, including the Palmers, Fields, McCormicks and Pullmans, are once again neighbors here, joined by renowned architects William Le Baron Jenney,

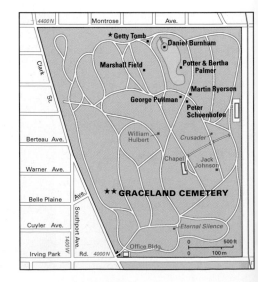

Daniel Burnham, John W. Root, Louis Sullivan and Mies van der Rohe. Developed in 1860, Graceland received many re-burials from the site of LINCOLN PARK. Its 119 acres were designed after 1883 in a picturesque, naturalistic style by Ossian Cole Simonds.

Lorado Taft sculpted the haunting *Eternal Silence* memorial for hotel owner Dexter Graves in 1909, and the heroic *Crusader* in 1931 for the grave of *Daily News* founder Victor F. Lawson. Louis Sullivan's masterful **Getty Tomb**★ (1890), designed for merchant Henry Harrison Getty following his wife Carrie Eliza's death, features intricate grilles (exhibited at the Paris Exposition of 1900), delicate acanthus leaf ornamentation, and windows in a round-arched composition of exquisite balance and plasticity. Sullivan's earlier **Martin Ryerson Tomb** (1887) takes the form of an Egyptian mastaba with a pyramid top in black polished granite. Daniel Chester French and Henry Bacon created the **Marshall Field Tomb** prior to their joint design of the Lincoln Memorial in Washington,

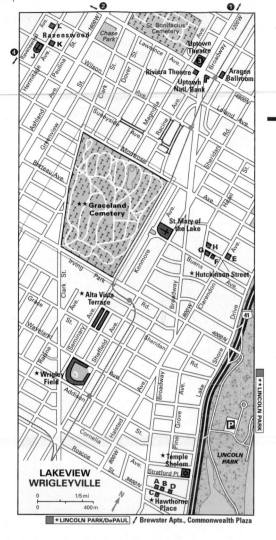

DC. Socialites **Potter and Bertha Palmer** rest in twin sarcophagi in a Neoclassical temple (McKim, Mead & White) overlooking a small, winding lagoon dotted with an island where **Daniel Burnham** is buried. Brewer **Peter Schoenhofen's** tomb is a miniature pyramid guarded by a sphinx and a Victorian angel. **George Pullman's** Corinthian column and exedra by Solon S. Beman cover a maze of concrete and steel designed to prevent angry workers from disinterring the railroad magnate (*p 187*). Sports legends buried here include boxing great Jack Johnson and National League founder William Hulbert, who lies beneath a large baseball.

St. Mary of the Lake Catholic Church – *4200 N. Sheridan Rd.* This 1917 design by Henry J. Schlacks draws on various churches in Rome, including St. Pudentiana for the dramatic campanile tower, and St. Paul's Outside the Walls for the main, Neoclassical facade. The light terra-cotta facade and red tile roof reinforce the appearance of a Roman basilica.

★ **Hutchinson Street District** – *Between Lake Shore Dr. and Hazel St.* Several designs by Prairie school architect George Washington Maher together with a range of eclectic, single-family homes provide a welcome diversion from the high-rise lakefront. The **Edwin J. Mosser House [E]** (1902) at no. 750, features oversized urns and a Sullivanesque entrance facing Clarendon Street. At no. 817, the 2-story **Claude Seymour House [F]** (1913) is distinguished by banded leaded-glass windows, urns, a wide overhanging roofline, and Maher's signature flattened-arch entrance. Maher's 1909 **Grace Brackebush House [G]** (*no. 839*) marks the integration of

145

picturesque period revival elements with the horizontal emphasis of the Prairie school. The **John C. Scales House [H]** *(no. 840)* resembles a Queen Anne home replete with shingles and round turrets. In fact, it is an 1894 Maher design that experiments with volumes in a manner similar to that of contemporary architect Frank Lloyd Wright.

■ Devon Avenue

Located on the city's Far North Side, Devon (pronounced duh-vonne) Avenue (6400N) runs right through the hearts of Chicago's Indian and Jewish communities. West of Sacramento Avenue, several stores on the 2700W block—including the Russian American Book Store *(2746 W. Devon Ave.* ☎ *773-761-3233)*—feature signs written in Cyrillic and cater to Russian immigrants. The Croatian Cultural Center of Chicago *(2845 W. Devon Ave.* ☎ *773-338-3834)* is located on the next block. Farther along the street, signs in Hebrew adorn dozens of businesses. Hundreds of books, journals, magazines and gifts are available at Rosenblum's World of Judaica *(2906 W. Devon Ave.* ☎ *773-262-1700)* and across the street, Hashalom Restaurant *(2905 W. Devon Ave.* ☎ *773-465-5675)* serves up kebabs and other Israeli dishes. The Kol-Tov Kosher Foods deli *(2938 W. Devon Ave.* ☎ *773-764-4663)* offers Jewish specialties prepared under the supervision of the Chicago Rabbinical Council.

Walk east on Devon toward Oakley Street to admire beautiful silk and hand-embroidered fabrics hanging in the window of Regal Sarees *(2616 W. Devon Ave.* ☎ *773-973-1368)*. Although dozens of restaurants mingle with jewelry stores, video-rental shops and markets, three stand out from the crowd: Viceroy of India *(2516 W. Devon Ave.* ☎ *773-743-4100)*, renowned for its hearty buffet, Moti Mahal *(2525 W. Devon Ave.* ☎ *773-262-2080)*, which serves the best *nan* bread in town, and Woodland of Madras *(2340 W. Devon Ave.* ☎ *773-338-8550)*, offering great vegetarian fare.

Additional Sights

Uptown – Recalling the Roaring Twenties, the intersection of Lawrence Avenue and Broadway still features numerous large theaters and terra-cotta buildings from the era. The restored **Uptown National Bank** (1924, Marshall & Fox), at 4753 N. Broadway, uses white terra-cotta in a stately Neoclassical composition with a curving corner entrance. Erected in 1925 by Rapp & Rapp, the once majestic **Uptown Theatre** *(4814 N. Broadway)* awaits renovation of its interior, seating almost 4,400. The 1926 Moorish-style **Aragon Ballroom** *(1106 W. Lawrence Ave.)*, once the hot spot for ballroom dancing under a "starry sky" (the blue dome was adorned with stellar ornament), regularly hosts major rock-and-roll acts, as does the **Riviera Theatre** (1918, Rapp & Rapp) at 4746 N. Broadway.

Ravenswood – Several structures along Hermitage Avenue are worth the trip to Ravenswood, a newly rediscovered residential area stretching to the west of Uptown. Erected in 1883, the distinctive **All Saints Episcopal Church [J]** *(no. 4550)* is a rare Chicago example of Stick-style architecture. Across the intersection, the grand Victorian **Wallace C. Abbott House [K]** *(no. 4605)* was built by the founders of Abbott Laboratories. At no. 4646 stands the **Carl Sandburg House [L]**, a nondescript 3-flat where the famous author composed his *Chicago Poems* in 1916.

 The Green Mill
4802 N. Broadway.
☎ 773-878-5552.
Al Capone's crew used to hang out in this charming jazz club. The interior looks much as it did back in the 1920s and 30s. Owner Dave Jemilo books jazz acts seven nights a week, and the music plays until 4am (5am Saturdays). On Sunday evening, thick-skinned poets read their works to the rowdy-yet-discerning crowds who attend the infamous Uptown Poetry Slam competitions.

 Architectural Artifacts
4325 N. Ravenswood Ave.
☎ 773-348-0622.
Baptismal fonts from crumbled churches and portraits of secret-society leaders are among the treasures (both architectural and decorative) that the store's owners have rescued from demolished buildings. The first floor features large furniture (antique sideboards, tables, mantles), tiles and smaller terra-cotta, iron and concrete pieces. A mishmash of signs, paintings and chairs can be found upstairs.

NEAR WEST SIDE

Time: 2 hours
Map p 149

Located west and south of the Loop, this neighborhood is bounded by the Chicago River on the east, 16th Street on the south, Ogden Avenue on the west and Kinzie Street on the north. Largely unscathed by the 1871 Fire, it has faced other agents of change throughout its history. Encroaching immigrant communities eventually supplanted the "West Side Gold Coast" above Harrison Street, while the ethnic neighborhoods to the south have been neutralized over the years by various urban-renewal projects. However, through the layers of progress and blight peek the remnants of Chicago's old West Side.

Historical Notes

A Study in Contrasts – Bordering the South Branch of the Chicago River, the Near West Side attracted early settlers and was included, to Wood Street, in the incorporation of Chicago in 1837. The Irish arrived in the 1840s and 50s to work in the lumber mills, railroad yards and other riverside industries. Their frame cottages and barns crowded west to Halsted Street and south to Roosevelt Road, establishing the area as a port of entry for immigrants until well into the 20C. Meanwhile, mere blocks to the north and west, the city's merchant class built elegant homes along Washington and Ashland Boulevards. In true suburban fashion, developers widened and paved the streets, installed sewers and planted trees; horsecar lines provided transport to the central city. A multitude of churches and pretty Union Park, at Randolph Street and Ogden Avenue, added to the appeal of the neighborhood.

Such was the profile of the Near West Side, when, in 1871, a fire ignited in Mrs. O'Leary's barn on DeKoven Street in the heart of the Irish district. The blaze spread rapidly, consuming hundreds of wooden shanties along Clinton and Canal Streets, but jumped the river and headed northeast without damaging more of the West Side. Spared the flames, the neighborhood provided refuge for thousands of fire victims; the population soared to 200,000 and construction boomed. The wealthy continued to build fine homes along the northern boulevards, and to the south, new waves of immigrants settled in closely knit enclaves.

Land of Opportunity – By the end of the century, however, congestion, traffic and the spreading industrial city had emptied the exclusive residential sections of the West Side. In addition, violent labor protests frightened many well-to-do homeowners away. Events at Haymarket Square at Randolph and Desplaines Streets on May 4, 1886, hastened the process and changed forever the course of American labor history *(p 12)*. Still the immigrants came, settling up and down Halsted Street into multiple communities, each anchored by churches, synagogues and other ethnic institutions. By the 1890s, thousands of Russian and Polish Jews had come to escape the intensifying pogroms in Europe. They lived around Maxwell and Halsted Streets as they had in the Old World shtetls, abiding strictly by Orthodox ways. Many worked in the garment district along Jackson Boulevard; many were peddlers. The legendary **Maxwell Street Market**, crowded with kosher meat shops, bakeries and vendors of everything imaginable, resembled the open-air bazaars of European villages.

Just north, Italians teemed around Halsted and Taylor Streets in the largest Italian community in Chicago. The Delta near Halsted and Harrison Streets became the most populous Greek enclave in the US by 1930. In the midst of it all, Hull-House, Chicago's first settlement house, established by Jane Addams in 1889, provided a refuge from the slums where immigrants could learn American ways, celebrate their own national pride and participate in finding solutions to industrial problems. The renowned settlement house served the community until the 1960s when the social service programs were relocated to other parts of the city to make way for the University of Illinois at Chicago Campus.

Urban Renewal or Upheaval? – The controversial campus was but one of many redevelopment projects to transform the Near West Side landscape in the last several decades. Beginning in 1938, a frenzy of construction resulted in the largest concentration of public housing in the city. In 1941, the state legislature established the Medical Center District just east of Ogden Avenue, recognizing a cluster of facilities that had been operating there since 1884 and opening the way for more.

The Eisenhower Expressway, begun in 1954, cut a swath down the center of the Near West Side, and perpendicular to it, the Dan Ryan and the Kennedy Expressways devastated the neighborhoods in their paths.

Still, remnants remain. Graystones along Jackson Boulevard echo the street's elegant era. Loft conversions in the garment district preserve the old warehouses. Although disrupted and diminished by the university, Little Italy *(p150)* prevails, complete with trendy trattorias along Taylor Street. Greektown *(p151)* thrives in the restaurants along Halsted Street north of Van Buren Street.

Most recently, African Americans and Mexicans have come to live on the Near West Side, replacing the Jews who moved west and establishing their own ethnic enclaves. The Maxwell Street Market *(p 243)* was kept bustling—offering everything from hubcaps to hot dogs—until it too was relocated in 1994.

SIGHTS

The far-flung sights on the Near West Side do not lend themselves to a walking tour. The area is best seen by car.

Certain pockets around the Near West Side have survived the hand of change. Many of them seem incongruous in their settings now—the isolated mansion surrounded by vacant lots, the grand church hard by the expressway, the prep school in the tough neighborhood—but the vigilant visitor will be rewarded by these unexpected glimpses into the neighborhood's past. East of the Kennedy Expressway, for instance, stands **St. Patrick's Roman Catholic Church** *(140 S. Desplaines St.)*, Chicago's oldest extant church building, erected between 1852 and 1856. The asymmetrical steeples were added in 1885: the onion dome represents the Eastern Church, while the spire symbolizes the Roman Church in the west.

To the south, at 558 W. DeKoven Street, the **Chicago Fire Academy** fittingly occupies the site of the O'Leary barn *(p 147)*. In front, the tripartite **Pillar of Fire [1]**, sculpted in bronze by Egon Weiner in 1961, commemorates the event. A small exhibit in the academy's lobby traces the history of the Chicago Fire Department, covering the Great Fire in particularly interesting detail from the fire-fighting standpoint *(open year-round Mon–Fri 8am–4pm; closed major holidays;* ☎ *312-747-7238)*.

★ **Holy Family Church and St. Ignatius College Prep** – *1076-1080 W. Roosevelt Rd.* This interesting pair of buildings creates an enduring West Side silhouette that transcends the gritty city blocks around it. The church was the cornerstone of the Irish community when it was built by the Jesuits in 1857. Rescued from demolition by fund-raising parishioners in 1990, the church today is undergoing meticulous restoration. Next door, the elaborate Second Empire facade of the prep school has been beautifully preserved *(open year-round Mon–Fri 7am–8pm, Sat 9am–2pm; closed major holidays; 2hr guided tour last Sat Mar–May, Sept–Oct, $5; rest of the year by request;* 🅿 ☎ *312-421-5900)*. Built in 1870, the school offered students from all over the city the quality of a Jesuit education. Today, more than 1,200 students come from every background and neighborhood to take advantage of its rigorous curriculum.

Across Roosevelt Road stands the **Illinois Regional Library for the Blind and Physically Handicapped** *(1055 W. Roosevelt Rd.)*, whose primary purpose is as the state's distribution center for Braille books and books on tape. The building, sheathed in boldly colored metal, sports a wonderful wavelike window incised along its Blue Island Avenue side. The work of Stanley Tigerman & Assocs., the structure (1975) is designed for ease of access and use while displaying Tigerman's signature whimsy.

University of Illinois at Chicago (East Campus) – *The core of the campus is located between Halsted, Taylor, Morgan and Harrison Sts. Refer to the detailed campus map in the lobby at University Hall, 601 S. Morgan St.* This inner-city campus has generated much controversy since it was first conceived as a commuter school to serve the throngs of students poised to enter college in the mid-1960s. This location was proposed after a survey of 83 possible sites, and despite considerable protest by the mostly Italian residents of the densely populated area, construction began in 1963. The university's radical plan, devised by architect Walter A. Netsch, Jr. of Skidmore, Owings & Merrill, has long been debated. Netsch attempted to create a campus appropriate to its city setting and able to accommodate up to 32,000 students. But what seemed like a fitting, if dramatic, direction for this prototypical urban university in the 1960s has today been acknowledged as cold, unmanageable and at times downright inhuman. Inspired by the movement known as

Brutalism, the hulking concrete and brick exoskeletons of the buildings are punctuated by slit-like vertical windows. Netsch included a layer of "express" walkways above those at grade level, all converging at the campus' center, where an outdoor amphitheater ringed by six lecture halls with a common roof-deck formed an "intellectual agora" for outdoor classes and socializing. This Great Court proved to be inhospitably hot in summer and windswept in winter. Disintegrating concrete, water seepage and security fears contributed to the 1992 decision to reconfigure it.

As a result, the amphitheater and elevated walkways have been demolished, and the lecture halls reroofed. Greenery, colored stone and wooden benches soften the open plaza of the new **Great Court**, which offers a pleasing visual break from the hard lines of the surrounding buildings. The **Science & Engineering Laboratories [A]** lie to the south, the **University Library [B]** to the west and the **Chicago Circle Center [C]** (the work of C.F. Murphy Assocs., the only original structure not designed by SOM) to the east. To the northwest stands the campus' only "skyscraper": **University Hall**, the 28-story administrative center. Due north, the brick **Architecture & Art Laboratories [D]** represent Netsch's "field theory," an experiment in rotated squares. Another major change on campus was the addition of dormitories at the corner of Halsted and Harrison Streets in 1988. Some 1,350 of the one-time commuter school's 25,000 students reside here. The 4- to 6-story dorms designed by Solomon Cordwell Buenz & Assocs. are the visual antithesis of the rest of the campus, built of warm, buff-colored brick sparsely decorated with delicate geometric designs.

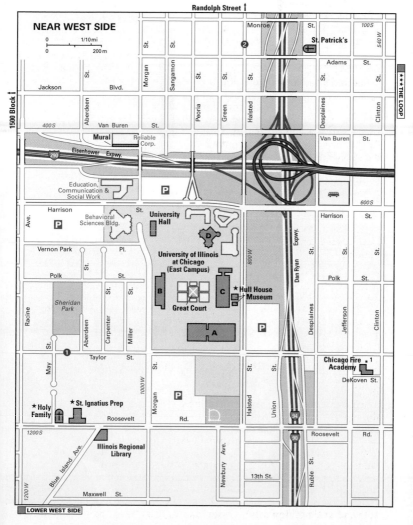

The north side of campus offers a good view of Richard Haas' trompe l'oeil **supermural** across the Eisenhower Expressway. Ten tons of paint cover two city blocks along the west and south sides of the Reliable Corporation Building at 1001 W. Van Buren Street. The colossal work depicts the Civic Center of Daniel Burnham's 1909 Plan of Chicago, which would have been located close to that spot, along with the city's modern skyline and medallions commemorating its historic role as a transportation hub.

★ **Jane Addams' Hull-House Museum** – *800 S. Halsted St. Open year-round Mon–Fri 10am–4pm, Sun noon–5pm. Closed major holidays. Guided tours (45min) available.* ☎312-413-5354. Dwarfed by the surrounding campus buildings, the Hull-House Museum offers a glimpse into an important chapter in the history of American social welfare and reform. Founded in 1889 by pioneering social workers Jane Addams and Ellen Gates Starr, this settlement house became a focal point for citywide and national movements to improve living and working conditions of the nation's poor and disadvantaged.

A Life of Service – Jane Addams was born in 1860 near Rockford, Illinois, the youngest child of Sarah and John Addams. Among the first generation of American women to receive a college education, Addams was determined to find meaningful work and make a contribution to society. Inspired by a trip to London in 1886 and a visit to Toynbee Hall, the world's first social settlement

1 Little Italy

The restaurants lining Taylor Street (1000S) between Halsted and Ashland Streets bear witness to Chicago's original Italian settlement in the area. **Tuscany** *(1014 W. Taylor St. ☎ 312-829-1990)*, with its fresh, light decor, yummy designer pizzas and unorthodox pasta dishes, attracts trendy upscale crowds. Try **Mario's** Italian lemonade and ice sidewalk stand *(1066 W. Taylor St.; open May–Sept)* for a refreshing taste of the old neighborhood. Cannoli and other fresh-made Italian pastries are available from the **Pompeii Bakery** *(1455 W. Taylor St. ☎ 312-421-5179)*, which also serves lunch and dinner in its casual dining area. The king of Taylor Street restaurants is the popular **Rosebud Cafe** *(1500 W. Taylor St. ☎ 312-942-1117)*, renowned for its excellent food served in mammoth portions. Walk 3 blocks north to **Tufano's**—called the Vernon Park Tap by regulars *(1073 W. Vernon Park. ☎ 312-733-3393)*—a cozy dining room tucked in back of a well-worn barroom offering wonderful homemade pastas served family style from large platters.

Hull-House, 1912

dedicated to helping the poor through activity, culture and education, Addams returned to Chicago to launch a similar program with her college friend Ellen Gates Starr. Her success at Hull-House came in part from her willingness to "settle" among the immigrant poor on the Near West Side. Her method was to work with her neighbors to share experiences and find solutions to social and industrial problems. She became famous worldwide as a social reformer, suffragist, writer and pacifist, winning the Nobel Peace Prize in 1931. Hull-House achieved fame internationally as the birthplace of social work. Addams lived at Hull-House until her death in 1935.

In the Heart of the Immigrant City – Real estate developer and philanthropist Charles J. Hull built his home in 1856 on the western outskirts of the city. Addams and Starr moved into the house in 1889, at which point it was surrounded by diverse immigrant communities, industry, crowded tenements and sweatshops. Hull-House eventually grew to a complex of 13 buildings, among them Chicago's first public gymnasium, art and music schools and a cooperative residence for working women. In this spacious setting, Hull-House residents carried out their aggressive agenda of education, social service and reform. In 1963 a part of the Near West Side neighborhood was torn down to make way for the University of Illinois at Chicago. Of the original 13 buildings, the university retained the mansion and the Residents' Dining Hall, renovating and converting them into a museum. Hull-House's social services were dispersed to locations around the city where the work is carried on today.

Visit – Today, both museum buildings are open to visitors. The dining hall, built in the Arts and Crafts style in 1905, features a 15min slide show *(2nd floor)* providing information about Jane Addams and the philosophy behind the Hull-House settlement. Photographs of life at the settlement in the 1920s and 30s by Wallace Kirkland and a model of the original buildings are displayed here. The first floor has been restored to its 1905 appearance as a dining hall. Documents, photographs and other materials interpret the significance of this room and the influence of individuals who gathered here to shape US social policy during the first half of the 20C.

An attempt has been made to return the mansion, much remodeled over the years, to its earliest appearance. The 2-story, brick Italianate exterior is topped by a cupola and surrounded by a white-columned veranda. The four rooms on the first floor are furnished and decorated in the Victorian style with many original pieces, including **Jane Addams' desk**, and they exude the homelike atmosphere that Addams herself cultivated. The setting belies the activity that once enlivened this space, always the business and social center of the settlement. News clippings, photographs, quotations and descriptive labeling convey a feeling for the daily life here. The resident settlement workers lived in rooms upstairs, which today house administrative offices.

North of the Eisenhower Expressway, two east-west streets several blocks apart epitomize the historic double image of the Near West Side. A panoply of Italianate, Queen Anne, Second Empire and Richardsonian Romanesque homes line the landmark 1500 block of **West Jackson Boulevard** (between Ashland and Laflin Streets). Built between 1871 and 1900,

2 Greektown

Although the area first settled by Greek immigrants was destroyed by the construction of the Eisenhower Expressway and the University of Illinois at Chicago, many Greek restaurants, clubs, diners and shops remain along the stretch of S. Halsted Street (800W) between Van Buren and Monroe Streets. The oldest restaurant, **The Parthenon** (314 S. Halsted St. ☎ 312-726-2407), boasts a huge menu with appetizer- and entree-size portions of stuffed grape leaves, gyros, cheese-and-spinach pies, and other Greek favorites.

Religious statuettes, incense, candles and medicinal herbs and oils imported from the old country line the shelves of the **Athenian Candle Company** (300 S. Halsted St. ☎ 312-332-6988). For live Greek music and belly dancing, duck into the **Neon Greek Village** (310 S. Halsted St. ☎ 312-648-9800). **Roditys** (222 S. Halsted St. ☎ 312-454-0800) is the spot for a boisterous evening of dining and drinking. At the north end of the strip, you'll find **Santorini** (800 W. Adams St. ☎ 312-829-8820), an upscale seafood restaurant.

these residences recall the neighborhood's gilded era. Five blocks north, along **Randolph Street**, wholesale merchants supply fruits and vegetables, meat and poultry, flowers and other goods much as they have since the market opened in 1852. Trendy restaurants have also discovered the street, appreciating the huge spaces of its warehouses and loft buildings. To the east, the intersection of Randolph and Desplaines Streets marks Haymarket Square, scene of the 1886 labor disturbance.

Museum of Holography – *1134 W. Washington Blvd. Open Wed–Sun 12:30–5pm. Closed major holidays. $2.50.* ☎*312-226-1007.* Founded in 1976 to advance the science and art of holography, this museum encompasses four exhibit galleries that display items from the extensive permanent collection as well as changing exhibits of holograms by artists from the world over. Holograms are created through a complicated photographic process that records light waves reflected from an object illuminated with laser light on a light-sensitive medium. The three-dimensional effects can be dazzling since the process reproduces every blemish and nuance with molecular exactness. Although any subject is fair holographic game, human and animal portraits are particularly fascinating.

■ United Center
The Near West Side is home to United Center, a sports venue for Chicago's basketball team, the Bulls, and hockey team, the Blackhawks. Erected at a cost of $175 million, the 1,000,000sq ft structure replaced the 1929 Chicago Stadium, which was torn down in 1994. The old Chicago Stadium gained fame for hosting the first football game to be played indoors in 1932, when a snowstorm forced the players inside. For more information on performances and sporting events at United Center, see p 236 and p 245.

LOWER WEST SIDE

Time: 2 hours. **CTA** Blue line to 18th St.
Map below

This industrial, working-class community of modest homes and grand churches is bordered on the south and east by the Chicago River, on the north by railroad tracks near 16th Street and on the west by Pulaski Road. Encompassing four neighborhoods—Pilsen, Heart of Chicago, Little Village and Lawndale—the Lower West Side is today the center of Mexican culture in Chicago.

Historical Notes – The industrial district along the South Branch of the Chicago River was settled by immigrant Bohemians after the Fire of 1871 and named Pilsen in honor of their homeland's second largest city. Between long hours of stacking lumber on the river edge and brewing Pilsener beer, the immigrants erected churches and social halls reminiscent of their native Bohemia. The already crowded district experienced a rapid expansion after the construction in 1854 of Blue Island Avenue, known as Black Road from the soot of the surrounding factories. Blue Island Avenue led to the McCormick Reaper Works at Western Avenue, where 35 percent of the nation's harvesters were built in the early 1900s. The neighborhood made headline news in the late 19C as labor strife rocked the area in

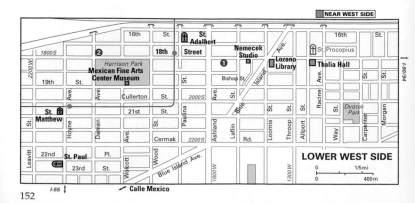

1877 and 1886. The Battle of the Viaduct, where 30 workers were killed and 200 injured near 16th and Halsted Streets, took place here during the Great Railroad Strike of 1877 (p 11). West of Damen Avenue, the district known as "Heart of Chicago" developed around the McCormick (later International Harvester) plant at 27th Street and Western Avenue. Here, enclaves of Germans and Poles, and later Italians and Jews, settled and worked in McCormick's factory. As the Bohemian immigrants prospered, they moved to the Lawndale community west of California Avenue, called "Czech California" by the early 20C, when Chicago had the third largest population of Czechs in the world after Prague and Vienna. The neighborhood produced **Mayor Anton Cermak**, and 22nd Street was renamed Cermak Road nine days after his 1933 assassination (p 13).

In the 1950s Pilsen became the entrepot for Mexican immigrants in Chicago. In the ensuing decades they followed their Bohemian predecessors, moving west along the river, and by the 1970s, Czech California had been renamed *Pueblo Pequeño*, or "Little Village." The area continues to harbor Mexican and South American immigrants, who today make up 20 percent of the city's population.

SIGHTS

Drive south on I-90/94 and exit at 18th St. Continue west along 18th St.

The main thoroughfare in Pilsen, **18th Street** (between Morgan Street and Ashland Avenue) is lined with 1870s and 1880s Second Empire commercial buildings distinguished by mansard roofs and elaborate window moldings. The limestone St. Procopius Church (1883), at Allport Street, faces the massive, Romanesque-style **Thalia Hall**, one of numerous community centers erected by Bohemians in the late 19C. At the intersection of 18th and Loomis Streets and Blue Island Avenue (southeast corner), immortalized in the Carl Sandburg poem "Blue Island Intersection," the **Rudy Lozano Branch Library** stands out with its lively frieze of decorative tile recalling pre-Columbian monuments in Mitla, Oaxaca. At Bishop Street, note the **Francis D. Nemecek Studio** (1439 W. 18th St.) with its corner tower and sloped skylight. Twin towers rising 185ft flank the Renaissance Revival facade of **St. Adalbert Catholic Church** (1656 W. 17th St.), designed in 1914 by Henry J. Schlacks.

West of Damen Avenue, the Heart of Chicago neighborhood was settled by Germans who erected **St. Matthew Lutheran Church** (2100 W. 21st St.) in 1888, and **St. Paul Catholic Church** (2234 S. Hoyne Ave.) nine years later. Extending south from 23rd Street, Oakley Avenue boasts a small Italian district—called Heart of Italy—that draws its multiethnic neighbors to a variety of small restaurants and cafes. West of California Avenue, 22nd and 26th Streets form the busy commercial spines of the Hispanic Little Village neighborhood. Colorful flags and banners flutter above 26th Street, known as **Calle Mexico**. Note the pink stucco arch (1987, Adrian Lozano), topped by a red-tiled roof, spanning the street between Albany and Troy Streets.

Mexican Fine Arts Center Museum – *1852 W. 19th St. in Harrison Park. Open Tue–Sun 10am–5pm. Closed major holidays. Guided tours (1hr) available.* ♿ ☎*312-738-1503.* The largest institution of its kind in the US, this respected ethnic center is best known for its Day of the Dead (November 1) exhibitions featuring visiting Mexican artists at work. Two large galleries host activities ranging from fine arts exhibits to performances and community meetings. A $4 million expansion (*scheduled completion: 1998*) will triple the size of the museum.

1 Nuevo Leon

1515 W. 18th St. ☎*312-421-1517.* Named for the area of Mexico where the owners grew up, this tile-decorated restaurant is known for serving some of the best food in Pilsen. The menu ranges from tacos, burritos and nachos to less well-known Mexican delicacies like *cesos* (beef brains) and *menudo* (tripe soup). Be sure to try one of the dishes prepared with mole sauce, which is flavored with the surprisingly delicious combination of chocolate and hot peppers.

2 Bishop's Chili

1958 W. 18th St. ☎*312-829-6345.* This faded corner diner attracts chili-lovers from across the city and often ranks at the top of local critics' "Best Chili" lists. The famed beef-and-bean stew is nice and spicy; a bowl of it will warm you up on a cold, windy day.

NEAR SOUTH SIDE

Time: 1/2 day
Maps p 157 and p 161

One of Chicago's oldest areas extends from 16th Street south to Washington Park along the lakefront. Primarily African-American today, the area encompasses grand mansions on Prairie Avenue and King Drive as well as poverty-stricken high rises lining the Dan Ryan Expressway. Marked by large swaths of urban renewal and pockets of gentrified historic homes, the Near South Side is full of the contradictions and color of a mature urban environment.

Historical Notes

From Prairie to Prairie Avenue – In 1835, New York merchant Henry Clarke acquired 20 acres of prairie land in the Near South Side and built a lakefront home at Michigan Avenue between 16th and 17th Streets, not far from the site it occupies today *(p 155)*. However, the area remained sparsely settled for several decades. In 1852, politician Stephen A. Douglas developed a 70-acre lakefront tract north of 35th Street, which included the first University of Chicago, opened in 1856 (and closed five years later). Douglas' famed 1858 debates with Abraham Lincoln led to his election as senator. During the Civil War, his widow donated land for Camp Douglas, which held prisoners of war. Douglas lies buried near his homesite in a massive stone tomb *(636 E. 35th St.)*.

When the 1871 Fire destroyed the central city, Chicago's most prominent families moved south to develop a "Millionaire's Row" along Prairie Avenue between 16th and 20th Streets. On "the sunny street of the sifted few" lived industrial and commercial leaders like Marshall Field and George Pullman in mansions designed by architects such as Richard Morris Hunt, Burnham & Root and H. H. Richardson. From 1872 to 1900, Prairie Avenue was the city's most fashionable address. In contrast, State Street between 16th and 22nd Streets became the notorious Levee, an area of saloons and brothels. A small African-American community occupied a thin belt of land on Federal Street south of 22nd Street (later called the black belt), while Irish Catholic and German Jewish immigrants developed prosperous middle-class communities along Grand and Drexel Boulevards.

Bootleg and Boogie – The establishment of four of Chicago's six major railroad terminals on the south side of the Loop after 1885 benefited the saloons, gaming dens and brothels of the Levee and drove many respectable families away from Prairie Avenue. The wealthy movers and shakers gravitated north to the GOLD COAST, following Potter Palmer's lead. Finally, the Levee grew too outrageous even for the city, which shut it down in 1915. Throughout the Near South Side, residential uses gave way to warehousing and industry that pushed south from the train stations all the way to 22nd Street.

The 1920s witnessed the rise of bootlegging mobster **Al Capone** (1899-1947), headquartered in the Lexington Hotel, and the rapid expansion of the black belt, as the Great Migration of 1914-1930 brought thousands of blacks traveling north from the American South in search of jobs. By the late 1920s, a Black Metropolis thrived around 35th and State Streets, as African-American entrepreneurs built retail and service industries and black entertainers like Louis Armstrong and Jelly Roll Morton turned Chicago into a renowned center for jazz and blues. As the Irish and German Jews settled farther south, middle-class blacks moved in and occupied the mansions and row houses of Grand Boulevard, while their poorer brethren filled the Federal Street slums, stretching from 22nd to 54th Streets.

Rebuilding – If decline hit the South Side first, so did renewal. Arriving in 1938, German refugee **Ludwig Mies van der Rohe** *(p 35)* instituted a new campus plan for the Illinois Institute of Technology (IIT) that eliminated a half-mile stretch of slums along State Street, Wabash and Michigan Avenues south of 30th Street. By the 1940s, Michael Reese Hospital and IIT began an urban renewal plan, which would replace acres of derelict housing with modern town houses and high rises. The redevelopment continued into the 1960s as middle-class apartments were erected along the lakefront north of 35th Street, and several public-housing high rises replaced the Federal Street slum. By 1966, industrial growth had caused the demolition of most of Prairie Avenue's once-proud mansions. Following a public outcry that year, the Glessner House was saved from the wrecking ball by the fledgling CHICAGO ARCHITECTURE FOUNDATION, and a Chicago Landmark District was created in 1979, preserving the remaining mansions. A pocket of homes untouched by urban renewal and known as The Gap has been restored by middle-class blacks, who are also maintaining the mansions along King Drive (former Grand Boulevard) and promoting the Black Metropolis Historic District in an effort to preserve the region's cultural and architectural heritage.

SIGHTS

It is best to tour the Near South Side by car. The Black Metropolis driving tour travels through a great variety of neighborhoods, not all of which will feel welcoming to the visitor. Travel on foot should only be undertaken by those familiar with the area. In addition to the driving tour, the Near South Side encompasses the Prairie Avenue Historic District and the Illinois Institute of Technology. Directions for each area are given from the Loop.

★ Prairie Avenue Historic District

Drive south from the Loop on Michigan Ave., turn left at 18th St. and continue two blocks to Prairie Ave. (no through traffic).

Caught between the industrial wasteland south of the Loop and the expanding McCormick Place Convention Center, the Prairie Avenue Historic District between 18th and 20th Streets preserves a sampling of Chicago's prestigious homes from the late 19C, highlighted by the city's two most historically significant house museums *(visit by guided tour only, 1hr each house; tours depart from Glessner House Coach House year-round Wed–Sun noon–4pm; closed major holidays; $5 one house or $8 both houses; & ☎312-326-1480).*

★ **Henry B. Clarke House** – *1855 S. Indiana Ave.* Designed in 1836, this white clapboard home is considered Chicago's oldest structure. The spacious, 2-story residence has a Doric temple entrance characteristic of the Greek Revival style. Grand, 9ft-high triple-sash windows, tiny "frieze windows" and a central hall plan further illustrate the style. An 1850s Italianate cupola surmounts the hipped roof. Although Chicago pioneered "balloon frame" architecture *(p 32)* in the 1830s, the Clarkes used the sturdier mortise-and-tenon timber frame construction, which has allowed the house to be moved twice—in 1872 and 1977.

The interior represents the Clarkes' occupation of the home from 1836 to 1872 through period furnishings, artifacts and faithful reproductions of floor, wall and window coverings. The southern parlors, completed in the 1850s, exemplify the Italianate style with brilliant ceiling medallions, pocket doors and a Chickering piano. The upstairs bedrooms feature a marvelous sleigh bed and coal stove along with period toys, china and samplers. The basement contains a reconstructed kitchen and an exhibition gallery displaying photographs, artifacts and models that document the building's history and restoration.

John Jacob Glessner House

155

★★ **John Jacob Glessner House** – *1800 S. Prairie Ave.* Designed by **Henry Hobson Richardson** in 1886, the Glessner House revolutionized domestic American architecture with its open floor plan and unadorned Romanesque facades. Richardson, whose work influenced that of both Louis Sullivan and Frank Lloyd Wright, combined Medieval, Renaissance and American colonial elements in designing the exterior. The fortress-like house turned its back on the street to focus on an inner courtyard, making it the first modern urban home. At the time, its spare exterior shocked many Prairie Avenue inhabitants. The house was commissioned by Glessner, a manufacturer of farm implements who lived on the tony NEAR WEST SIDE until the Haymarket Riot occurred there in 1886, spreading fear of labor anarchy and spurring Glessner to move to Prairie Avenue.

The **interior★** is organized in an L-shape around a sunny southern courtyard, carrying through the medieval motif with heavy beamed ceilings (Richardson purposely bowed the beams to create an antique appearance) and a wealth of Arts and Crafts details, including wall and tile patterns by William Morris and furniture by local artist Isaac Scott. Over 80 percent of the items displayed were originally owned by the Glessners, and restoration has been guided by their profuse documentation and period photos of each room. Focal point of the house, the **library** contains a large sampling of the Glessners' extensive book, print and ceramics collections. In the Music Room, note the Steinway piano in a Francis Bacon case. The second-floor hall features a walnut Isaac Scott bookcase with Gothic arches and buttresses. The main bedroom has been exactingly restored down to the William Morris tiles, draperies, upholstery and carpet.

Across Prairie Avenue stand the **Kimball House** *(no. 1801)* and **Coleman-Ames House** *(no. 1811)*, both now headquarters of the US Soccer Federation. In 1896, George Pullman *(p 187)*, wary of any more "modern" houses on Prairie Avenue, convinced piano and organ manufacturer W.W. Kimball to hire his architect, Solon Beman. The result is a highly ornate French chateauesque house with crested turrets and elaborate carvings in limestone. The more restrained Coleman-Ames House was designed in 1886 by Cobb & Frost in the Romanesque Revival style. To the south, the street leads past plaques depicting homes demolished before the Chicago Landmark District was created in 1979. Within the park surrounding the Clarke House stands an 1893 statue **[1]** commemorating the 1812 Fort Dearborn Massacre *(p 10)*. Also open to the public is the first floor of the 1870 **Elbridge Keith House** *(no. 1900; open by appointment only* ☎*312-842-4523)*, where the Prairie Avenue Gallery exhibits contemporary art. The derelict **Marshall Field Jr. House** *(no. 1919)* still awaits restoration of its 44-room grandeur.

Farther west on Michigan Avenue, **Second Presbyterian Church** (1874) was designed by James Renwick and features superb Tiffany stained-glass windows.

Black Metropolis Driving Tour   *distance: 8.1mi*

> *Drive south from the Loop on Michigan Ave. to 21st St.*

This tour cuts a path through various South Chicago neighborhoods documenting black history in the city, and ends at a museum that pays tribute to African-American culture.

The former **Chess Records Studio** *(2120 S. Michigan Ave., between 21st and 22nd Sts.)* is an unassuming building (1911) sporting a 1957 storefront. Chuck Berry recorded "Johnny B. Goode" in this studio that helped define rhythm and blues with legends such as Howlin' Wolf, Bo Diddley and the Flamingos.

> *Continue south on Michigan Ave.*

Known as "Automobile Row," a series of early automobile showrooms (1910-1930) are now primarily warehouses. Colorful terra-cotta facades reveal the logos of one-time brands such as Packard, Premier and Hupmobile, as well as survivors like Chevrolet. The Mediterranean-style **Chicago Defender Building** *(southwest corner of Michigan Ave. and 24th St.)* originally housed the Illinois Automobile Club.

> *Turn right on 24th St.*

1 **The Velvet Lounge**
2128 1/2 S. Indiana Ave.
☎ *312-791-9050.* Blink and you'll miss this wonderful little club which offers excellent jazz on Saturday and Sunday nights. Acclaimed saxophonist Fred Anderson owns the place and plays in the legendary Sunday night jam sessions. During the annual jazz festival *(p 220)*, players from around the world gather here for impromptu concerts.

SOUTH LOOP

★ GRANT PARK

18th St.

200 W

1800 S

★★ Glessner House

Kimball House

★ Clarke House

1

Coleman-Ames House

Second Presbyterian

Keith House

★ PRAIRIE AVENUE HISTORIC DISTRICT

Field House

Avenue

Cullerton

St.

21st St.

China Pl.

Archer

Federal

Street

P

Chinatown

Chess Records

❶

Michigan

Prairie

Ave.

Lakeside Press

Burnham Park Harbor

Meigs Field

Cermak

Rd.

McCormick

Place

23rd

Ave.

State

St.

24th

Wentworth

Ave.

★ Quinn Chapel

❷

Indiana

Chicago Defender Bldg.

Stevenson Expwy.

Mercy Medical Center

26th

St.

Prairie Shores

55

27th St.

Ave.

Street

Avenue

Prairie

Calumet

Ave.

Martin Luther King, Jr. Dr.

St.

Reese Hospital

Lake Shore

Ave.

29th

St.

LaSalle

Wabash

St.

Dunbar Park

Vernon

Lake Park Ave.

Drive

41

Prairie

G

31st St.

★ ILLINOIS INSTITUTE OF TECHNOLOGY

F

3144-48

3141

Michigan

Ave.

Olivet Baptist ★

Rhodes

31st St.

Wells

H

2

E

★ Roloson Houses

Lake Meadows

B

★ Pilgrim Baptist

33rd St.

Knight House

A

33rd St.

P

33rd

Pl.

Indiana

★ CALUMET-GILES-PRAIRIE DISTRICT

C

35th St.

D

3435

35th

St.

Comiskey Park

Dan Ryan Expwy.

Victory Monument

Eighth Regiment Armory

Lake Park Ave.

Cottage Grove

Ellis

Ave.

Street

★ Wells House

Nichols House

★ Hammer House

37th St.

37th St.

Wentworth

Ave.

Michigan

Avenue

Ave.

Giles

St.

Martin Luther King, Jr. Dr.

Pershing

Rd.

Pershing

Rd.

State

St.

Federal

St.

LaSalle

St.

Root

St.

200 W

Michigan

Ave.

Ave.

Metropolitan Community

Oakwood

Blvd.

41st

St.

Bowen

Ave.

Ave.

Vincennes

Ave.

Ave.

43rd

Wabash

Indiana

Prairie

Calumet

Ave.

Ave.

43rd

St.

❸

St. Lawrence

Langley

Cottage

4300 S

45th

St.

800 E

BRIDGEPORT/CANARYVILLE

NEAR SOUTH SIDE

0   1/5 mi
0   400 m

Continued on following map

★ **Quinn Chapel African Methodist Episcopal Church** – *2401 S. Wabash Ave. Open year-round Mon–Fri 10am–4pm, Sat by appointment only. Guided tour (20min) available, advance notice requested.* ♿ ▣ ☎*312-791-1846*. This lovely limestone chapel (1892, Henry Starbuck) was built by blacks before they constituted a significant portion of the population. The site, at the time located in a middle-class white neighborhood, was purchased by a fair-skinned member of the congregation who could "pass" for white, thereby avoiding community opposition!

Continue west on 24th St., turn left on State St. and then left again on 26th St.

26th Street passes underneath the Jackson Park elevated train line, the oldest in Chicago. Opened in 1893 to link the Loop with the World's Columbian Exposition, it was known as the "Alley L" since its right-of-way was carved through back alleys. Located east of Michigan Avenue are the Mercy Hospital and Medical Center and Michael Reese Hospital, institutions created a century ago by the Irish Catholic and German Jewish communities respectively.

Turn right on Martin Luther King Dr.

This boulevard is dominated on the east by the **Prairie Shores** and **Lake Meadows** developments extending south to 35th Street. These tall, white and blue-green pastel buildings, set at an angle to the street, were planned as integrated middle-class housing in a massive, and largely successful, urban-renewal effort. To the east at 31st Street, note the **Olivet Baptist Church★**, built as First Baptist Church in 1873 by Wilcox & Miller. Now home to one of Chicago's oldest African-American congregations, this edifice dates back to 1853.

Turn right on 31st St. and left immediately on Calumet Ave.

> **2** **The Clique**
> *2347 S. Michigan Ave.* ☎ *312-326-0274.*
> This 3-story nightclub caters to Chicago's upscale African Americans. Stand-up comics, jazz combos and singers entertain in the posh, first-floor lounge. Girate to house music upstairs on the club's spacious dance floor. Keep an eye on the surrounding balcony for celebrities watching the action from the exclusive VIP area. Dress sharp, especially on weekends when the bouncers pick and choose who gets in and who stays on the sidewalk.

The cluster of Victorian houses south of 31st Street was named The Gap because it was untouched by urban renewal efforts to the north, west and east. In the 1980s, the restored homes earned landmark status as the **Calumet-Giles-Prairie District★**. Of note on Calumet Avenue are several lovely Romanesque Revival graystones on the left, a Victorian-style building (1887) by Adler & Sullivan at **no. 3141** , as well as limestone row houses on the right, such as **nos. 3144-48**. South of 32nd Street on the left, stand the only row houses designed by Frank Lloyd Wright, the landmark **Robert Roloson Houses★** *(nos. 3213-19)*, built in 1894 just after Wright left the office of Adler & Sullivan. Sullivan's influence is seen in the

" Then there was the fabulous city in which Bigger lived,
an indescribable city, huge, roaring, dirty, noisy, raw, stark, brutal;
a city of extremes; torrid summers and subzero winters, white people
and black people, the English language and strange tongues,
foreign born and native born, scabby poverty and gaudy luxury,
high idealism and hard cynicism! A city so young that, in thinking of
its short history, one's mind, as it travels backwards in time,
is stopped abruptly by the barren stretches of wind-swept prairie!
But a city old enough to have caught within the homes of its long,
straight streets the symbols and images of man's age-old destiny,
of truths as old as the mountains and seasons, of dramas
as abiding as the soul of man itself."

Richard Wright, *How Bigger Was Born* (1939)

large, foliate, terra-cotta panels that enliven the center of the uncharacteristically tall and narrow gabled facades. At no. 3322, the **Clarence Knight House** (1891) is a unique composition by Flanders & Zimmerman in orange stone and Roman brick.

> *Continue south on Calumet Ave., turn right on 35th St. and then right again on Indiana Ave.*

Seven buildings located on or near 35th Street comprise the recently created **Black Metropolis Historic District**, which commemorates the cultural flowering during the Great Migration *(p 154)*. As the community grew, it developed its own commerce, industry and culture, isolated by racism from the rest of the city. These buildings are unique because many were not inherited from other ethnic groups, but financed and built by African-American capital.

One of the seven buildings is located at **3435 S. Indiana Avenue**, a 3-story buff brick structure that served as headquarters of *The Chicago Defender* from 1921 to 1960 and today houses the Second Ward Regular Democratic Organization. Founded in 1905, the influential African-American newspaper is credited with starting the Great Migration; its rousing editorials, written by Robert Sengstacke Abbott, extolled Chicago's opportunities, calling for a "New Exodus."

The **Pilgrim Baptist Church★** has existed at the southeast corner of 33rd Street and Indiana Avenue since 1926, but the present landmark edifice was designed 36 years earlier by Adler & Sullivan for Chicago's oldest Jewish congregation, K.A.M., founded in 1846.

Adler's skill at designing auditoriums and Sullivan's irrepressible decorative talents combined—as they had in the AUDITORIUM BUILDING—to create a stunning assembly space *(open during services only)*.

To the west lies the campus of the ILLINOIS INSTITUTE OF TECHNOLOGY.

> *Turn right on 33rd St. and right on Giles St.*

Giles Street was named after Lt. George Giles of the "Fighting Eighth," a black regiment formed from the community at the turn of the century. The **Eighth Regiment Armory** (1915) stretches on the left side of Giles Avenue south of 35th Street and is a landmark of the Black Metropolis.

> *Turn left at 35th St. and continue to King Dr.*

Pilgrim Baptist Church, Interior

Grand Boulevard was developed in the 19C as an elite residential area, part of a 28mi ring of city boulevards. Known later as South Parkway, it was renamed in 1968 for the late Dr. Martin Luther King, Jr. **Victory Monument** (1928, Leonard Crunelle), the first dedicated to African-American soldiers, honors those of the "Fighting Eighth" who fought in World War I.

> *Turn right on King Dr., staying to the right to drive along the frontage road of the boulevard.*

At no. 3624, the **Ida B. Wells House★** was named a National Historic Landmark in 1973 in honor of the civil rights leader who lived here from 1919 to 1929. Wells, one of the first to document lynching in the US, moved to Chicago in 1893 to continue a lifelong crusade against racism and sexism. The 1889 Romanesque Revival home features a pressed-metal corner turret. Built in 1886, the **Charles H. Nichols House** *(no. 3630)* is distinguished by rough-faced Romanesque arches enlivened by Queen Anne oriels. The orange brick and brownstone **D. Harry Hammer**

159

House★ *(no. 3656)* pounds the corner of 37th Street with massive ostentation. Exuberant detailing in terra-cotta, copper and stained glass enlivens this 1885 design by William W. Clay.

Continue south on the main roadway of King Dr.

At the southwest corner of 41st Street stands the **Metropolitan Community Church** (1891, John T. Long), originally 41st Street Presbyterian Church, a Romanesque Revival edifice featuring a large corner tower and gabled facade. 43rd Street bears the honorary name of legendary blues artist Muddy Waters, who lived to the east on Lake Park Avenue.

Just south of 46th Street, the **Mt. Pisgah Missionary Baptist Church★** occupies the large Sinai Temple designed by Alfred Alschuler in 1910. At 49th Street, note the Renaissance-style towers of **Corpus Christi Church** (1916), noted for its high-quality stained glass by the F. X. Zettler company of Munich.

At 51st Street, a large equestrian statue of **George Washington** (1904, Daniel Chester French and Edward Clark Potter) marks the entrance to Washington Park.

Turn left on 51st St. and continue to Cottage Grove Ave.

> **❸ Checkerboard Lounge**
> *423 E. 43rd St. (secure valet parking available).*
> ☎ *773-624-3240.* In the 1950s, 43rd Street was lined with nightclubs; today, only this popular joint remains. The South Side's preeminent blues club presents live music four nights a week.
> A wall of memorabilia honors Muddy Waters—who brought the Mississippi Delta Blues to Chicago—and other local blues legends.

Provident Hospital of Cook County, to the left, one of the first founded by and for blacks, was established in 1891 by Dr. Daniel Hale Williams, who on July 9, 1893, became the first physician to perform successful open-heart surgery.

Turn right on Cottage Grove Ave. and right again immediately on Payne Dr., which enters Washington Park.

Designed in 1871 by Frederick Law Olmsted and Calvert Vaux, **Washington Park** is connected to its southern neighbor, JACKSON PARK, by the MIDWAY PLAISANCE. The vast, 100-acre meadow covering the park's northern section was originally mown by sheep, kept in the park for this purpose.

Bear to the left at the fork at 55th St. to access the DuSable Museum.

DuSable Museum of African-American History – *740 E. 56th Pl. Open Apr–Sept Mon–Sat 10am–5pm (Thu 6pm), Sun noon–5pm. Rest of the year Mon–Sat 10am–4pm, Sun noon–4pm. Closed major holidays. $3. Guided tours (90min) available.* & 🅿 ☎773-947-0600. Founded in 1961 by Dr. Margaret Goss Burroughs in her home, this cultural and historical center now occupies a former park administration building (1910, D. H. Burnham & Co.). The modern Harold Washington wing, added to the structure's south side in 1992, houses educational and cultural programs that supplement permanent and traveling exhibits on African-American life and history.

On the first floor of the old wing, to the right, a small room is dedicated to boxer Joe Louis (1914-1981), nicknamed the "Brown Bomber," who remained the unde-feated world heavyweight champ from 1937 to 1949. Another room presents a timeline of African-American history from the slave trade to the civil rights move-ment through exhibits that rotate every six months. To the left, an exhibit of art and artifacts, assembled from the museum's permanent collection, includes works by 20C painter Archibald Motley and 20C sculptor Joseph Kersey. The second floor hosts major traveling exhibits. The museum maintains an active theater and cultural agenda *(call ☎773-947-0600 for schedule and tickets).*

★ Illinois Institute of Technology (IIT)

Drive south from the Loop on State St. to 33rd St., turn left and park in the IIT Visitors Parking Lot.

Unique in both design and curriculum, IIT fills a campus that largely realizes the plan of master Modernist **Ludwig Mies van der Rohe** (1886-1969), who came to direct the institute's architecture school in 1938 after fleeing Nazi Germany. The institute, formed in 1940 by the merger of the Armour and Lewis Institutes, has garnered an international reputation for excellence in the fields of technology and design. Its 120-acre campus is bounded by 30th Street on the north, the Dan Ryan Expressway on the west, Michigan Avenue on the east and 35th Street on the south.

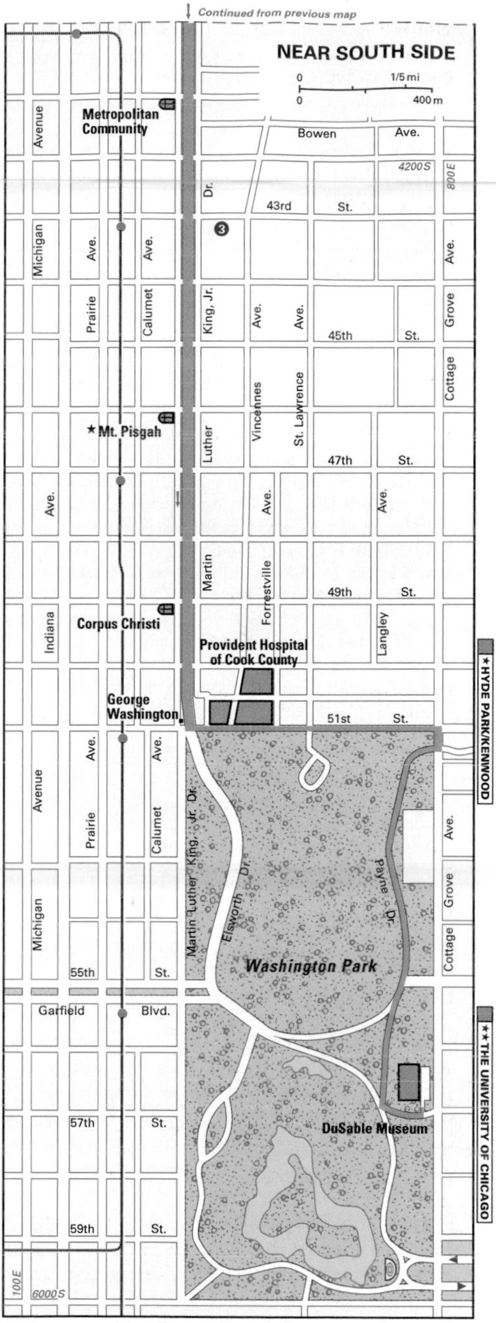

Visit – *Stop at the Information Center in Hermann Hall (3241 S. Federal St.) for brochures and a self-guided tour map (open mid-Aug–late May Mon–Fri 7am–midnight, Sat 9am–midnight, Sun noon–10pm; rest of the year Mon–Thu 7am–8pm, Fri–Sat 8am–5pm; closed during academic holidays;* ☎312-567-3075). *Guided tours (1hr) depart from Perlstein Hall (10 W. 33rd St.) year-round Mon–Fri 11am & 2pm. Advance reservations requested.* ☎312-567-3025. Located at Federal and 33rd Streets, the **Main Building★ [A]** (1891; Patton, Fisher & Miller) epitomizes the Romanesque Revival style; note in particular the lower stories faced in rough brownstone, the red-brick upper floors, the windows framed with round arches and the gabled dormers punctuating the roof. Across 33rd Street stands the simpler **Machinery Hall [B]**, erected ten years later by the same firm.

Mies' first construction for the institute, the 1943 **IIT Research Institute Materials Technology Building [C]**, illustrates the central principle behind his campus design: a "module" of 24x24x12ft

NEAR SOUTH SIDE

"blocks" that comprise both the buildings and the spaces between them. This concept has been thoroughly carried out—almost all the campus buildings employ the module in structures of steel, concrete, glass and pale yellow brick. There is said to be only one curving wall on the entire campus!

Headquarters of IIT's architecture school, **S. R. Crown Hall★★ [D]** is the capital achievement of both the campus and Mies van der Rohe, eloquently expressing his philosophy of design, materials, purpose and proportion. Calling it a "representational building" on campus, Mies here abandoned his "module" to create a simple glass-walled pavilion housing a singular space 220ft wide, 120ft deep and 18ft high. The 1956 structure appears to hover above the ground, its flat roof suspended from four huge I beams that wrap around the building. Entered on

161

floating travertine steps, the building defines space by its structure, stripping away ornament without losing the humanizing effects of proportion and enclosure *(not open to the public).*

The 3-story concrete and brick **Wishnick Hall [E]** (1946, Mies van der Rohe) became the standard for academic buildings on campus. Just north of this hall, note the George Segal statue, *Man on a Bench* **[2]**. Farther north stands **Alumni Memorial Hall [F]** (1946, Mies van der Rohe), framed in steel with large glass windows. Here, as in many other Miesian campus buildings, the yellow bricks form a skin over the frame, but pull back at the corners to hint at the building's true skeleton.

At Wabash Avenue, the **Keating Sports Center [G]** (1966, Skidmore, Owings & Merrill) seems set upon an invisible podium, but its walls are sheer glass, hiding the structural steel beneath. **Carr Memorial Chapel [H]** is the only church designed by Mies. Known as the "God box," this nondenominational chapel features a glass facade on the east and west and brick walls on the remaining sides.

■ Chinatown

Every major city in the US seems to have a Chinatown. Located at the intersection of 22nd and Wentworth Streets, Chicago's dates from the 1910s, when Chinese immigrants filled in a tiny neighborhood between the black belt on the east, Irish and Italian communities to the south and an industrial area to the north and east along the South Branch of the Chicago River. By the 1920s, Chinese architectural forms appeared in the district, which has become a popular dinner destination for Chicagoans and tourists alike.

The entrance arch spanning Wentworth Avenue was erected in the 1970s and features giant ideograms, dragons and other traditional designs sheltered by red-tile rooftops. Buildings of interest along Wentworth include the **Pui Tak Center**, formerly known as the On Leong Merchants' Association Building, at no. 2216, with its prominent corner "pagodas," balconies and colorful terra-cotta tile decoration. **Woks 'n Things** *(no. 2234)* sells its namesake pans and a wide variety of cookware and kitchen utensils, as well as a fascinating assemblage of intricate vegetable- and cookie-cutters. The **Emperor's Choice Restaurant** *(no. 2238;* ☎ *312-225-8800)*, with its green and white terra-cotta facade enlivened by twisted snake columns, serves everything from egg rolls to spicy ducks' feet, while **The Mandar Inn** *(no. 2249;* ☎ *312-842-4014)* specializes in Mandarin cuisine.

BRIDGEPORT/CANARYVILLE

Time: 2 hours. `cta` Red line to 35th St.
Map p 164

Dotted with churches, this small neighborhood of quiet streets and modest bungalows is flanked to the west and south by large industrial concentrations occupying the site of the former Union Stock Yards district. Settled by Irish canal workers in the 1830s, the community became the focal point of Chicago politics in the 20C.

Historical Notes

From Canal Town to Cow Town – In the 1830s, the small trading post of Hardscrabble, located at the South Fork of the South Branch of the Chicago River, mushroomed with construction of the ILLINOIS & MICHIGAN CANAL, which connected the Great Lakes to the Mississippi River. Irish workers settled the town north of 31st Street and renamed it for the port area around the Ashland Avenue Bridge. Grain elevators and lumberyards developed on the river edge as thousands of immigrants harvested the prairies of Illinois and the forests of Michigan. In 1853, Bridgeport was annexed to the City of Chicago.

Slaughterhouses, which had sprung up in the 1840s along the South Fork of the river, were consolidated in 1865 into the great Union Stock Yards, which supplied meat to the world for

"… men and women and children bending over whirling machines and sawing bits of bone into all sorts of shapes, breathing their lungs full of fine dust, and doomed to die, every one of them, within a certain definite time."

Upton Sinclair, *The Jungle* (1906)

over a century. Gustavus Swift, Philip Armour, Arthur and Charles Libby and other meat barons pioneered the refrigerated railcar, and made their fortunes in the industry that earned Chicago the nickname of "hog butcher of the world": in 1892 alone, 2.5 million cattle and 5 million hogs were slaughtered in Chicago, and some 30,000 people worked in the stockyards. The districts of Canaryville, south of Bridgeport, and Back of the Yards, to the west, filled with insalubrious, crowded tenements, while the South Fork of the river became known as "Bubbly Creek" for the gases released by the decomposing animal carcasses floating along it. The area literally stank, drawing the attention of urban reformers such as **Upton Sinclair**, whose 1906 book *The Jungle* exposed the horrors of the industry and led to the adoption of the Pure Food and Drug Act. In 1905, the nation's first industrial park, the Central Manufacturing District (East District), was created at 35th Street between Morgan Street and Ashland Avenue, adding more manufacturers to the sooty environs.

Rise of the Political Machine – Italian, German, Polish, Lithuanian and Slovakian immigrants piled into the neighborhood as the century progressed, but the clannish Irish remained dominant through their rapid integration into the public service, which they parlayed into an effective political organization in the early 20C. In 1933, Bridgeport native Ed Kelly was appointed mayor following the assassination of Anton Cermak *(p 13)*. A Bridgeport politician would hold the office until 1979, providing employment for and preserving the isolation and segregation of the community. Mayor for 21 years, political "Boss" **Richard J. Daley** *(p 20)* lived his entire life on Lowe Street. His son Richard M. Daley is the fifth mayor hailing from Bridgeport, although he has resided at the CENTRAL STATION development since 1993. The community's power has gradually declined with the dismantling of the political "machine" *(p 19)*. Chinese Americans, spilling over from neighboring Chinatown, and Mexican Americans, who moved in after World War II, now comprise a large portion of increasingly polyglot Bridgeport, which retains a quiet, small-town ambiance.

SIGHTS

To visit sights in Bridgeport, drive south on I-90/94 and exit at 31st St. Continue west to the intersection with Halsted St.

Busy, urban **Halsted Street** forms the commercial heart of the community. The more prosperous section of Bridgeport lies to the east along streets such as Emerald and Lowe, lined with early-20C brick homes, bungalows and newer ranch houses. The oldest section occupies the northern triangle, anchored by Archer Avenue, while the area west of Halsted boasts numerous churches and narrow houses inhabited today mainly by Hispanics, Poles and some Lithuanians along Lituanica Avenue.

1 Healthy Food

3236 S. Halsted St.

☎ 312-326-2724

Traditional folk art decorates the walls of this pleasant restaurant. The menu offers a mix of Lithuanian specialties, vegetarian entrees and good, old-fashioned American home cooking. Try the *kugelis* (potato dumplings filled with meat) or *blynais* (pancakes served with sour cream), then finish your meal with a slice of delicious, fresh pie.

One of Chicago's oldest roads, **Archer Avenue** was built in 1836 by Col. William Archer to supply the Illinois & Michigan Canal. Italianate storefronts at **nos. 2727** and **2731** and a pre-Fire cottage at **no. 2815** suggest the canal era. The old canal was replaced by the Sanitary & Ship Canal in 1900, and in 1964, the city erected the Stevenson Expressway (I-55) over the former waterway. The giant trailer-truck warehouses and barges on the modern canal are modeled on the narrow canal boats that first made Chicago a commercial power.

Burnham & Root designed the **Immanuel Presbyterian Church** *(1035 W. 31st St.)* in 1892; today it houses a Buddhist school. To the west, on Aberdeen Street, stands the **Monastery of the Holy Cross** *(3109 S. Aberdeen St.)*, formerly Immaculate Conception Church and Rectory, built in 1909 for German Catholics. One of the finest of Bridgeport's numerous Catholic churches is **St. Mary of Perpetual Help★** (1892, Henry Englebert), distinguished by its massive copper dome towering over the neighborhood. Located at 1035 W. 32nd Street, the church occupies most of the block.

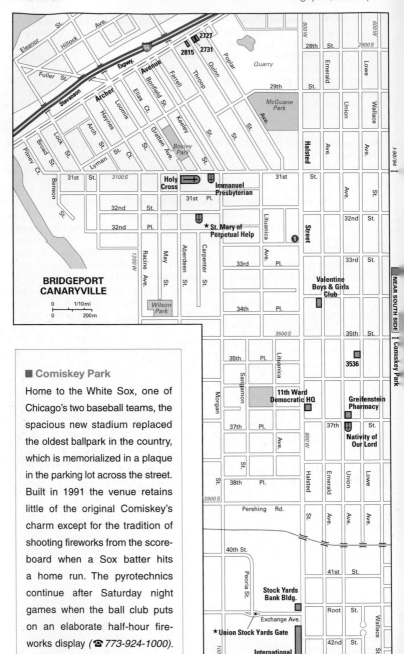

■ Comiskey Park

Home to the White Sox, one of Chicago's two baseball teams, the spacious new stadium replaced the oldest ballpark in the country, which is memorialized in a plaque in the parking lot across the street. Built in 1991 the venue retains little of the original Comiskey's charm except for the tradition of shooting fireworks from the scoreboard when a Sox batter hits a home run. The pyrotechnics continue after Saturday night games when the ball club puts on an elaborate half-hour fireworks display (☎ 773-924-1000).

The Art Moderne **Valentine Boys & Girls Club** (*3400 S. Emerald Ave.*) was designed in 1938 by Childs & Smith. The terra-cotta entrance flanked by totem poles combines Pacific Coast Indian motifs with the sleek fluted chevrons and glass block of the International style.

Visible to the east are the bright blue rafters of the new **Comiskey Park** (1991, Hellmuth, Obata & Kassabaum). At **3536 S. Lowe Street** stands the home of Mayor Richard J. Daley (1902-1976); a police car still stands guard in front of the large but unassuming red brick bungalow (1939).

The intersection of Union Avenue and 37th Street boasts two structures of merit. At the southeast corner stands the recently restored **Nativity of Our Lord Church** (1868), where Daley's funeral was held in 1976. The **Greifenstein Pharmacy** (*north-*

east corner) has been in the same family for a century. Its classic drugstore paraphernalia includes large stoppered flasks, carved wooden screens and a myriad
advertising knickknacks. Schaller's Pump (*3714 S. Halsted St.*) is an old-time
Chicago tavern (1881) sited across the street from the **11th Ward Regular
Democratic Headquarters**, the heart of the machine that ran Chicago politics for
most of the century. Popular legend states that political decisions were made in
the smoky back rooms of Schaller's.

Drive south on Halsted St., past Pershing Ave. to visit sights in Canaryville.

At the corner of Exchange Avenue and Halsted Street note the **Stock Yards Bank
Building** (1924, A. Epstein), patterned after Philadelphia's Independence Hall. At
850 W. Exchange Avenue, the **Union Stock Yards Gate★** (1879, Burnham & Root) is
the sole reminder of the once flourishing industry. A cattle head surmounts the
large central arch, which marked the entrance to the livestock pens. The stock-

Union Stock Yards, c.1905

Barnes-Crosby/Chicago Historical Society (ICHi-19106)

yards closed in 1971 and the site is now an industrial park. Farther south at 4220 S.
Halsted Street, the **International Amphitheater**, one of Chicago's premier conven-
tion halls for 40 years, hosted the infamous 1968 Democratic National Convention.
Since the development of MCCORMICK PLACE, it has fallen into decline.

Located at 4501 S. Lowe Avenue, **St. Gabriel Church★** (1887, Burnham & Root), a
masterful red brick and stone Romanesque Revival design, features a square corner tower with lancet windows and massive triangular gables that seem to reach
from earth to spire. The Canaryville parish has remained Irish Catholic since its
founding in 1880 by Father Maurice J. Dorney, known as "King of the Yards" for
ministering to packinghouse workers.

*Consult the legend on the inside front cover for an explanation of symbols
and colors appearing on maps throughout this guide.*

THE UNIVERSITY OF CHICAGO★★

Time: 1/2 day. CTA bus no. 6 (Jeffrey Express).
Map p 168

A bastion of scholarship, the University of Chicago (U of C) has spent its first century as a world leader in research and education. Called "the teacher of teachers," one in seven alumni works in education and a great number of them serve as college or university presidents or provosts. The 3,500 undergraduates and 7,500 graduate and professional students live in a world apart from the hustle and bustle of Chicago, a division reinforced by a unique physical setting covering 190 acres of HYDE PARK, 8mi south of the Loop.

Historical Notes

Instant Tradition: Rockefeller Builds the U of C – Built on land donated by Marshall Field, the University of Chicago was founded in 1890 by the American Baptist Educational Society and oil magnate **John D. Rockefeller**, whose initial $600,000 drew $1 million from Chicago business leaders. Armed with a strong academic vision and Rockefeller's ample purse, President William Rainey Harper gathered scholars from leading schools, creating a first-rate faculty that included eight former university presidents.

University of Chicago from Midway Plaisance

Rockefeller continued to contribute—$35 million over 25 years—and pronounced the university "the best investment I ever made in my life." U of C opened on October 1, 1892, not with ceremony or celebration, but by starting classes at 8:30am. Within ten years, it was one of the nation's leading research universities. The architecture was steeped in academic history. The trustees insisted that architect **Henry Ives Cobb**, famous for Romanesque Revival buildings such as the NEWBERRY LIBRARY, use a late-English Gothic style, which they considered ennobling. Cobb designed 18 buildings, then passed the baton to the architectural firm of Shepley, Rutan & Coolidge. Gothic remained the style used by the U of C architects until 1940. Borrowing liberally from Oxford and Cambridge, Cobb's cloistered quadrangular plan (one of the first by an American university) guided subsequent development: four city blocks form the main campus, which is divided into six small quads grouped around a seventh central quadrangle.

The Life of the Mind – Despite its Baptist roots, the university was quite progressive, admitting women and minorities from the start. It was also rigorous: Harper established a 2-year "common core curriculum," mandating that each undergraduate complete course work in physical sciences, social sciences, biology and the humanities, a program still firmly in place. Within two decades of the university's birth, U of C physicists had measured the speed of light and made other important breakthroughs in physics. By the 1920s, the university's social scientists had invented modern sociology and developed the first community colleges.

From Football to Physics – The university also became known for its Big Ten football team coached by Amos Alonzo Stagg, whose record of victories was surpassed only recently. The "Monsters of the Midway" dominated in the 1920s and premiered the huddle, the forward pass and the "T" formation. The first Heisman Trophy was awarded in 1935 to U of C running back Jay Berwanger. Charismatic Robert Maynard Hutchins became president in 1929 at age 30 and instituted numerous reforms during his 22-year tenure. He and Mortimer Adler created a system of teaching based on "Great Books" that is still a national model. Hutchins abolished football because he felt it detracted from scholarship. In 1942, the unused football stands concealed the Manhattan Project laboratory of physicist **Enrico Fermi**, whose team of physicists achieved the first self-sustaining, controlled nuclear reaction. The top secret project was the most significant step in the development of the atomic bomb and nuclear energy.

Maintaining Tradition – The university underwent a brief period in the 1930s as a hotbed of radicalism and was engaged in urban-renewal programs in the 1940s and 1960s. In 1969 football returned (NCAA Division III) to the U of C, and radical students occupied the Administration Building, but none of these events changed the rigorous curriculum. During the 1970s and 1980s President Hanna Gray avoided the overspending trend and maintained faculty and academic standards despite an endowment one-third the size of Harvard's. In the 1970s, the university began its dominance in economics, while maintaining its leadership roles in physics, sociology and Near Eastern studies. The tradition of interdisciplinary inquiry established by Harper continues today with Law School professors borrowing concepts from the university's Nobel laureate economists. The Medical School remains in the forefront of research while developing important medical techniques, especially in cancer and brain research.

> ### Nobels at the U of C
>
> ■ Sixty-five Nobel prize winners have been faculty, students or researchers at the U of C, more than any other university. Twenty-three of the prizes have been in physics, 18 in economics, 11 in chemistry, 11 in physiology or medicine and 2 in literature, including novelist Saul Bellow.
>
> ■ The first American Nobel laureate in science was the university's Albert A. Michaelson, who received the award in 1907 for measuring the speed of light. Physicists Robert Millikan and Arthur Compton won in 1923 and 1927 for their pioneering work in quantum mechanics. James Dewey Watson, a 1962 winner, codiscovered the structure of DNA.
>
> ■ The school is best known for its economists, eight of whom have brought home the famed prize, beginning with Milton Friedman who won in 1976. The most recent awards went to Merton Miller, Ronald Coase, Gary Becker, Robert Fogel and Robert Lucas, who won in 1990, 1991, 1992, 1993 and 1995.
>
> ■ U of C may boast, but its Nobelists would rather study than bask in glory. When physicist James Cronin won the Nobel Prize in 1980, he was asked to hold a 10am press conference. "I can't do it then," he said, "I've got a 10 o'clock class." Impressed by his dedication, the U of C spokesman asked what class he was teaching. "No, no," Cronin protested, "I'm not teaching a course. I'm taking Chandrasekhar's graduate course on the theory of relativity." Subrahmanyan Chandrasekhar won the Nobel three years later.

WALKING TOUR   *distance: 2mi*

Begin the tour at Ida Noyes Hall, at 59th St. and Woodlawn Ave.

While walking through campus, watch for the innumerable gargoyles and bas-reliefs that adorn the buildings, depicting everything from invertebrate fossils to American presidents.

Ida Noyes Hall [A] – Built in 1915 (Shepley, Rutan & Coolidge) as a women's center in a Tudor Revival style, the hall is noteworthy for its finely detailed interior, in particular the beamed ceilings, wood-paneled parlors, original furnishings and a dramatic central staircase with carved monkeys on the handrails. The mural in the third-floor theater depicts "The Masque of Youth" enacted at the building's dedication. DOC Films, the oldest college film society in the US, shows films daily in the Max Palevsky Cinema. Several student organizations share the building with a pub, pool and dance studio.

Cross Woodlawn Ave. to Rockefeller Chapel.

The mile-long MIDWAY PLAISANCE, designed by Frederick Law Olmsted in 1869, connects Washington and Jackson Parks and was the site of commercial side-shows during the 1893 World's Fair. Legend has it that the gargoyles on campus were designed to deter Midway patrons from frequenting the university.

★ **Rockefeller Chapel** – *Open year-round daily 8am–4pm. Closed major holidays and for special events; it is recommended to call before visiting.* ✆773-702-2100. Completed in 1928, the chapel was designed by Bertram G. Goodhue Assocs. and named for its donor in 1937. At 207ft, the structure remains the tallest building on campus. Using true Gothic principles, the brick and limestone edifice has little structural steel. The arches carry the weight of the vaulting, while the buttresses help withstand the outward thrust of the walls. Foundations 80ft deep support 32,000 tons of wall, tower and roof.

The 43ft-high nave windows composed of tracery glass in muted tones contrast with the bright cinquefoil window above the altar, added in 1979. Tall proportions draw the eye heavenward to the colored, glazed Guastavino tile ceiling, revealed in a 1988 restoration. The elaborate chancel with its organ pipes, pulpit and carved oak choir seats creates a sense of pomp for the four annual graduation ceremonies. Outdoor summer concerts feature the tower's 72-bell carillon (*mid-Jun–mid-Aug Sun 6pm*), while other productions showcase the 103-stop E.M. Skinner organ.

Continue north on Woodlawn Ave. to 58th St.

North of Ida Noyes Hall stands **Woodward Court [B]** (1958, Eero Saarinen), a modern, U-shaped dormitory with a 2-story dining hall.

★★ **Robie House** – *Northeast corner of Woodlawn Ave. and 58th St. See description p 173.*

Walk west on 58th St. toward University Ave.

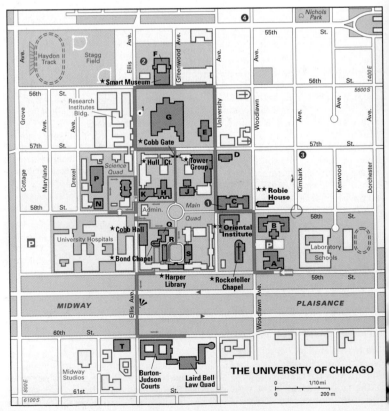

THE UNIVERSITY OF CHICAGO

Chicago Theological Seminary [C] – Dating from 1857, this is the oldest of a cluster of seminaries in Hyde Park. The 1926 edifice (Riddle & Riddle) is composed of two wings connected by a skywalk. Visit the lovely **Hilton Memorial Chapel** *(1st floor; open Sept–May Mon–Fri 8:30am–4:30pm; rest of the year Mon–Thu 8am–5pm; ☎773-752-5757)* and the cloisters beneath the Lawson Tower. Scholars prize the Seminary Co-op Bookstore for its outstanding selection in the humanities and social sciences.

① Seminary Co-op
In Chicago Theological Seminary, lower level. ☎ *773-752-4381.* This huge, underground bookstore offering close to 100,000 volumes caters to more highbrow tastes than its sister store, 57th Street Books *(p 173).* The staff is renowned for tracking down obscure and out-of-print books: in the unlikely event that they cannot locate something for you, they will happily search for it and ship it to you.

★ **Oriental Institute** – *Southeast corner of 58th St. and University Ave. The institute is undergoing an extensive restoration and closed its doors to the public in Jan. 1996. The renovation is scheduled to last 2 years. Call* ☎773-702-9521 *for information concerning temporary exhibits, which will be mounted at the Smart Museum (p 170).* Dedicated to the study of languages, history and cultures of the Ancient Near East, this research institution is the premier authority in the dating and identification of archaeological artifacts. Its museum contains one of the world's choicest collections of Near Eastern art and antiquities. The majority of the items in the collection have been uncovered by the institute's own archaeological excavations. Since its inception, the university has been a center for Near Eastern studies. Its first president, William Rainey Harper, taught Semitic languages and in 1896 set up an Ancient Near East museum close to his offices in Haskell Hall *(p 172).* **James Henry Breasted**, the first American to earn a PhD in Egyptology, led the university's first field expedition to Iraq in 1904 and began excavating Egyptian and Nubian temples a year later. In 1919 he created the Oriental Institute, funded by John D. Rockefeller, Jr. Breasted was the expert sought by archaeologists in 1922 to positively identify the tomb of Tutankhamen. In 1931, the museum/research institution moved into its permanent home, designed by Mayers, Murray & Phillip in the Art Deco style. Researchers from the institute continue to excavate numerous sites and publish the definitive dictionaries of Assyrian, Demotic (Egyptian) and Hittite languages.

Collections – With more than 75,000 registered artifacts, the institute boasts extensive collections covering the Egyptian, Assyrian, Mesopotamian, Anatolian, Palestinian and Persian cultures, featuring not only tomb treasures but also domestic items such as tools, cookware and sculptor's models. Items of interest in the Egyptian collection include a complete burial from 3600 BC, a model of a home excavated by the institute, early papyrus scrolls, a bed and headrest from 3000 BC and an 18ft statue of King Tutankhamen. The colorfully glazed and molded brick gates of Babylon (which guarded Nebuchadnezzar II's city in the 6C BC) highlight the Mesopotamian collection, along with insightful exhibits on the development of cuneiform and modern writing, displays on temple construction techniques and figurative sculpture. A black bull head from the palace of Xerxes at Persepolis, carved in the early 5C BC, forms part of the institute's fine Persian collection. A highlight of the newly installed galleries will be a re-creation of a palace courtyard of an Assyrian king dating back to 700 BC, including the 40-ton sculpture of a winged, human-headed bull which once stood before the gateway. The institute will also feature a model of an ancient Nubian tomb as well as special exhibits devoted to the land of the Bible, illustrated by objects from the institute's excavation of Megiddo, ancient Armageddon.

At University Avenue, look south to the pointed Gothic spires of Foster, Kelly, Green and Beecher Halls, completed as women's dormitories in 1893, and now housing the Psychology Department. The 1971 Albert Pick Hall for International Studies suggests Gothic verticality with stone-like facing and lancet windows.

Walk north on University Ave.

★ **The Tower Group** – *West side of University Ave.* Located north of Eckhart Hall (1930, Charles Z. Klauder), the Tower Group (1903, Shepley, Rutan & Coolidge) anchors the northeast corner of the main quadrangle. **Leon Mandel Hall**, a theater and assembly hall, imitates a campus cathedral with its arched windows and tracery. Mitchell Tower, modeled on Oxford's Magdalen College bell tower, contains the Alice Palmer bells used for the Medieval art of "change ringing." Below the tower is Reynolds Club, a student center inspired by Oxford's St. John's College. Hutchinson Hall's design came from Oxford's Christ Church Hall and is noted for its grand dining hall featuring a hammer-beam ceiling, paneled walls, massive stone fireplaces and portraits of benefactors, including Rockefeller, Harper and Martin A. Ryerson.

The distinguished, red brick **Quadrangle Club [D]** *(southeast corner of University Ave. and 57th St.)*, designed in 1922 by Howard Van Doren Shaw, serves the university faculty and their guests.

Cross 57th St. and continue north on University Ave.

Bartlett Gymnasium – *Northwest corner of 57th St. and University Ave. Lobby accessible year-round Mon–Fri 9am–5pm. Closed major holidays.* This 1904 structure (Shepley, Rutan & Coolidge) features a striking, romantic mural by the donor's son, Frederic Clay Bartlett *(p 62)*, and a stained-glass window depicting Ivanhoe winning a tournament. The pool and gym were supplemented by the newer Henry Crown Field House in 1932.

Continue north to 56th St. and turn left; walk west to Greenwood Ave.

The **Cochrane-Woods Arts Center** (1974) contains the Art History Department and the Smart Museum. Sculptures by Richard Hunt, Henry Moore and Pomodoro frame the garden outside the entrance to the 1-story, box-like museum designed by Edward Larrabee Barnes.

② Court Theatre
5535 S. Ellis Ave.
☎ *773-753-4472.* Renowned for its excellent productions of Shakespeare's and Molière's works, the Court ranks with the Goodman *(p 113)* and Steppenwolf *(p 127)* as one of the best theaters in the city. Its artistic board corrals Chicago's top caliber actors, production designers and directors for its five or six annual productions (season runs fall to spring).

★ **David and Alfred Smart Museum of Art** – *5550 S. Greenwood Ave. Open year-round Tue–Fri 10am–4pm, weekends noon–6pm. Guided tours available.* ♿ 🅿 ☎*773-702-0200.* Opened in 1974 and named for the founders of *Esquire* magazine, this small jewel of a museum holds 7,000 pieces donated to the university. Its surprisingly diverse collection is richest in late-19C and 20C paintings, sculpture and decorative arts. Eight temporary exhibits a year supplement the permanent collection.

Visit – The exhibits, organized chronologically in 12 galleries, begin with the Classical world and include a Euphronios fragment and other Attic vases, small bronzes, fragmentary late-Roman sculpture, and a fine 6C Syrian mosaic.

Shang Dynasty cast-bronze vessels highlight the Asian gallery along with Neolithic ceramics, Tang terra-cotta funerary figures and ink paintings from China and Japan. The Early Renaissance gallery contains works by Lorenzetti and Bramantino and a 2-panel *Apollo and Daphne Legend* by an anonymous Florentine master (c.1500). A lovely silver reliquary commissioned by Pope Paul III leads into the High Renaissance and Baroque room, with paintings and sculpture from Italy, Germany and the Low Countries. The gallery is dominated by Pordenone's *Milo of Croton Attacked by Wild Beasts* (c.1535).

The Neoclassical gallery features Dutch and Austrian genre painters, including Jan Steen's *A Game of Skittles* and decorative arts in glass and ceramic. The adjacent 19C gallery is anchored by Auguste Rodin's *The Thinker, Titan* (model) and *Cathedral* (model). Pieces range from portraiture to allegory and are often interpreted by different versions of a work, as in Antoine Chapu's *Joan of Arc*.

The two 20C galleries introduce turbulent modernity through works by Arthur Davies, Rodin, Jean Arp, Henry Moore and Russian Suprematists Seligman and Rybchenkov. Alfonso Ianelli's *John L. Lewis* glares ferociously above three sculptures by Lipchitz. Bronzes by Matisse and Degas and paintings by du Bois, Dove and Rothko complete the exhibit.

The prize of the Decorative Arts gallery, the ROBIE HOUSE dining-room set by Frank Lloyd Wright, illustrates his attempt to create a "room within a room" by the use of high-backed chairs and corner posts with lanterns. Displayed in nearby cases, ceramics and glass by Tiffany, Mackintosh, Rookwood and the Wiener Werkstätte give a good sense of the design revolution of the early 20C. Works by Chicago Imagists *(p 27)* of the 1980s, including Karl Wirsum, Ed Paschke and Jim Nutt, dominate the Contemporary gallery. The Mellon gallery offers rotating exhibits for comparative study.

Continue west on 56th St., turn left at Ellis Ave. and walk south.

The 3-ton bronze massiveness of **Nuclear Energy [1]**, a 1967 sculpture by Henry Moore, marks the site where Enrico Fermi's team of 41 scientists split the atom on December 2, 1942.

On the right, the Research Institutes Building connects to the Science Quadrangle by a skywalk across 57th Street.

Turn left on 57th St.

Hitchcock Hall *(southeast corner of 57th St. and Ellis Ave.)* was listed on the National Register of Historic Houses for its 1902 "Prairie Gothic" design by Dwight Perkins, who meshed the horizontal Prairie style with the vertical Gothic. Hitchcock and adjacent Snell Hall are the only dormitories still on the Main Quadrangle.

Continue east on 57th St.

Joseph Regenstein Library [G] – This massive structure holds most of the university's 5.7 million texts and 7 million other volumes. Two of its seven stories of open book stacks are below ground. The 1970 design by Walter A. Netsch, Jr. (also responsible for the UNIVERSITY OF ILLINOIS AT CHICAGO) used irregular massing, vertical emphasis and setback to relate to the campus.

Continue east on 57th St. to Cobb Gate, on the right.

A gift to the university from the architect Henry Ives Cobb, the ornate **Cobb Gate★** (1900) leads into the main quadrangles. Tradition holds that the climbing gargoyles represent students struggling from their first year of college to eventual fourth-year triumph at the apex.

Gargoyles at Cobb Gate

★ Hull Court – This courtyard designed in 1897 by Henry Ives Cobb consists of the botany, anatomy, zoology and physiology buildings, joined by pleasant arcades. John C. Olmsted designed the romantic Botany Pond—allegedly the preferred site for marriage proposals—and Hutchinson Court.

Walk south through the quad.

The **Kent Chemical [H]** and **Ryerson Physical Laboratories [J]** (1894, Henry Ives Cobb) exhibit full-blown Gothic ornament, peaked dormers, crocheted finials and crenellated towers. West of Kent Hall is the **Jones Laboratory [K]** (1929, Coolidge &

Hodgdon). A first-floor exhibit documents the weighing of plutonium in Room 405 on September 10, 1942, by Dr. Glenn T. Seaborg *(open year-round Mon–Fri 8am–5pm; closed major holidays)*. To the left is the Administration Building (1948).

Walk west and return to Ellis Ave.

The University of Chicago Hospitals occupy 18 buildings covering 14 acres between 58th and 59th Streets. The largest teaching hospital in the nation is also the largest provider of indigent care in Chicago. At 58th Street is the University Bookstore (1902, Shepley, Rutan & Coolidge), distinguished by its red brick and arched windows.

Walk west on 58th St., past the bookstore, and turn right into the Science Quadrangle.

I. W. Colburn's 1969 **Henry Hinds Laboratory for the Geophysical Sciences [I.]** and 1973 **Cummings Life Science Center [N]** play with Gothic ideas in limestone and red brick. The 40 red brick chimneys of Cummings ventilate laboratories requiring 20 fume hoods per floor. At the center of the quad, the 4-story **John Crerar Library [P]** (1984, Hugh Stubbins Assocs.) holds thousands of scientific and medical texts. Step inside to view *Crystara*, an aluminum and Waterford crystal sculpture by John David Mooney, which refracts light into the atrium. The terraced glass walls of the Samuel Kersten, Jr. Physics Teaching Center (1985; Holabird & Root, Harold T. Hellman) facing the Science Quadrangle contrast with the more traditional limestone facade on Ellis Avenue.

Return to Ellis Ave., walk south to the Administration Building and reenter the main quadrangles.

★ **Cobb Hall** – Classes began October 1, 1892, in this building (1892, Henry Ives Cobb) named after Silas Cobb (no relation). Freshmen still take their "common core" courses here. The top floor of the oldest campus building houses the **Renaissance Society** contemporary art gallery, well regarded for its progressive exhibits *(open Jan–Jun, Oct–Dec Tue–Fri 10am–4pm, weekends noon–4pm; guided tours available;* ♿ ☎*773-702-8670).*

Continue east toward the center of the quadrangle.

On the right is **Swift Hall [Q]** (1926, Coolidge & Hodgdon), home to the Divinity School, sited here to represent the centrality of religion to all fields of study.

Walk south toward Harper Memorial Library.

U of C students are known for their bookish nature. The university recently banned "Sleep Out," a spring ritual that saw hundreds of students camping here overnight in order to secure places in popular classes.

Haskell Hall [R] (1896, Henry Ives Cobb), on the right, housed the ORIENTAL INSTITUTE until 1931. A simple roofline accommodated gallery skylights. Today it is the Department of Anthropology. On the left, **Stuart Hall [S]** (1904, Shepley, Rutan & Coolidge), modeled on King's College in Cambridge, houses parts of the Business School. Note the eclectic array of carved animals protruding from the facade.

★ **Harper Memorial Library** – *Open year-round Mon–Thu 8:30am–11:30pm, Fri 8:30am–5pm, Sat 10:30am–5pm, Sun 1–11:30pm. Closed major holidays.* Distinguished by two massive, square towers, the library (1912, Shepley, Rutan & Coolidge) anchors the south end of the quadrangle and presents an impressive facade to the Midway. Bridges connect the library to reading rooms in Haskell and Stuart Halls. Visit the main reading room on the third floor to admire the vaulted ceilings, huge chandeliers and stone screens carved with the insignia of universities from both hemispheres. To the east stands the Social Sciences Research Building (1929, Coolidge & Hodgdon).

Walk through the archway in Haskell Hall and head north.

★ **Bond Chapel** – *Open year-round Mon–Fri 8:30am–4pm. Closed major holidays.* ♿. This delicate gem (1926, Coolidge & Hodgdon), covered with ivy and sculpture, is connected by a covered cloister to Swift Hall. Its intimate interior is noted for its Charles Connick stained glass, elaborate wood carvings and a hammer-beamed ceiling with polychrome angels. The frieze of beatitudes ringing the space conceals heating grates to warm the body as well as the soul. The chancel window facing the entrance represents the entire New Testament.

Walk south to the Classics Quadrangle.

Gates, Blake and Goodspeed Halls (1892, Henry Ives Cobb), originally men's dormitories, are now classrooms. The Classics Building (1915, Shepley, Rutan & Coolidge) and Wieboldt Hall (1928, Coolidge & Hodgdon) complete the serene ambience of the quadrangle.

Walk through the arch and continue south across the Midway.

From 1906 to 1936, sculptor **Lorado Taft** *(p 27)* lived and worked with students in the Midway Studios located one block east of here at 60th Street and Ingleside Avenue. Taft, the most prominent Midwestern sculptor at the turn of the century, developed the rambling studios as a Renaissance-style *bottega*, or informal arts school. Taft completed his greatest works here, including the *Fountain of the Great Lakes*, gracing the Art Institute's South Wing, and the nearby *Fountain of Time (p 179)*. The studio, a National Historic Landmark, is still used by university artists.

Look back across the Midway for an expansive **view★** of the main quadrangles. The **School of Social Service Administration [T]** *(southwest corner of Ellis Ave. and 60th St.)* was designed by master Modernist Ludwig Mies van der Rohe in 1965, in his familiar, rectangular, glass-and-steel style.

Located just east, across Ellis Avenue, the **Burton-Judson Courts** (1931, Zantzinger, Borie and Medary) were the first university buildings erected south of the Midway. These dormitories feature a square tower, an interior quadrangle and simplified Gothic styling.

Walk east on 60th St. to the Law School.

Four buildings compose the **Laird Bell Law Quadrangle**, designed by Eero Saarinen & Assocs. in 1959 as part of his master plan for the campus. The 6-story D'Angelo Law Library is flanked by two long and low buildings holding classrooms and offices, organized around a large reflecting pool. A circular assembly hall and courtroom mark the eastern end.

★★ ROBIE HOUSE

5757 S. Woodlawn Ave. Visit by guided tour (1hr) only, year-round daily at noon. Closed major holidays and for occasional university functions. $3. ☎773-702-8374.

Seemingly floating on the corner of 58th Street and Woodlawn Avenue, this quintessential Prairie school home by Frank Lloyd Wright is the one that made him world famous and helped "break the box" of traditional architecture. Built as a private residence, it was saved from the wrecking ball at the eleventh hour and today houses the University of Chicago Alumni Association.

Robie and Wright – The house was commissioned by Frederick Robie, a rich, young inventor and heir to a bicycle and automobile firm. Robie's ideas for his home caused architects to mutter that he wanted "one of those damned Wright houses"—so he hired the iconoclastic Wright! The Robies only lived in the house from 1910 to 1911, when the firm went bust and the marriage dissolved. It was sold to the Taylor family, who occupied the house for 11 months, and then the Wilber Marshall family. In 1926 it was taken over by the Chicago Theological Seminary as a dormitory and dining hall, accelerating its deterioration. Saved from demolition in 1957, it was donated to the university in 1963 and designated a National Historic Landmark that same year. In 1995, the university entered into

3 57th Street Books

1301 E. 57th St. ☎ *773-684-1300.* Help yourself to a cup of complimentary coffee and wander through this well-stocked bookshop. Though the store is part of the huge Seminary Co-op *(p 169)*, 57th Street Books features a selection geared toward general interest rather than academic pursuits. The intelligent, helpful staff encourages browsing, and kids can play with toys set out for them in the children's section.

4 Jimmy's Woodlawn Tap

1172 E. 55th St. ☎ *773-643-5516.* Known as Jimmy's after the owner, this dimly lit tavern is *the* off-campus hangout for U of C students. Frazzled graduate students unwind at the Woodlawn Tap talking theory and university politics into the wee hours. Jimmy's prices are low, beer selection good and the bartenders are friendly, so drop by and drink in the relaxed academic atmosphere.

an agreement with the Frank Lloyd Wright Home & Studio Foundation *(p 192)* to renovate Robie House into a house museum, a process expected to cost some $2.5 million and last several years.

Visit – Viewed from the exterior, the house is composed of intersecting rectangular volumes that alternately lead and fool the eye, dissolving the borders between interior and exterior and creating fluid spaces. Horizontal emphasis is found not only in the roofs, dramatic balconies and banded windows, but also in Wright's trademark long Roman bricks.

Although Robie House is three stories high, the cantilevered eaves and roofline make it appear shorter. Wright violated the block's 35ft setback by setting the house back, but extending the porch—and thus the living area—into the front yard. Robie's desire for both natural light and privacy is evidenced by the windows, which conceal the interior by stained, leaded patterns while admitting

Robie House Living Room

natural light. The unusual designs are said to represent geometrized versions of Midwestern foliage. Wright preferred casement windows that hinge on the side since the act of pushing them open created interaction with nature.

As in most Wright homes, the entrance is hidden under a deep overhang. Wright challenged the idea that a facade should be designed around an entrance, preferring a "pathway of discovery." The foyer is deliberately cramped, forcing the visitor to proceed immediately to one of the living spaces.

The guided tour only takes in the main living area upstairs—a **living room** and **dining room** separated and united by a grand hearth. The space is striking, lit by sidewalls of art glass and a rectangularly coved ceiling studded with a series of sphere-in-square "moonlights," another characteristic Wright motif. Wood trim reinforces the dramatic horizontal flow of the space.

By designing furniture and built-ins and leaving little empty wall space, Wright limited the ability of owners to change his design. Apocryphal stories have the architect reappearing at the house to ensure that the furniture was not rearranged. The finest furniture in the Robie House, the dining-room set, is preserved at the SMART MUSEUM.

Until the renovation is completed, the rest of the house will not be accessible. The six bedrooms, servant's wing, and ground-floor billiards and play rooms have until recently been occupied by the offices of the University of Chicago Alumni Association.

Cross-references to sights described in this guide are indicated by SMALL CAPITALS. *Consult the index (p 246) for the appropriate page number.*

HYDE PARK/KENWOOD★

Time: 1/2 day
Map p 176

An island of stability on Chicago's impoverished and embattled South Side, this racially integrated, middle-class community is closely identified with the cerebral UNIVERSITY OF CHICAGO and the popular MUSEUM OF SCIENCE AND INDUSTRY. Bordered by Lake Michigan on the east, WASHINGTON PARK on the west, 47th Street on the north and 61st Street on the south, Hyde Park/Kenwood also encompasses renowned architectural landmarks, sweeping greenswards and an array of shops and eateries. Once the site of the gleaming "White City" of World's Fair fame, Hyde Park/Kenwood remains a cosmopolitan and sophisticated neighborhood, well worth exploring.

Historical Notes

Suburbs "in Horto" – Paul Cornell envisioned a quiet residential suburb when he purchased 300 lakefront acres south of Chicago in 1852 and named the area Hyde Park. He lured the Illinois Central commuter train in 1856, barred industry in 1861 and helped create the South Parks Commission in 1869, which hired renowned landscape architect Frederick Law Olmsted to design Jackson and Washington Parks. To the north, dentist John Kennicott had purchased eight acres near 43rd Street in 1856 and named his suburb Kenwood, subdividing it into large, 50ft-wide lots. By 1874 it was hailed as the "LAKE FOREST of the South Side" for its large Italianate and Shingle-style mansions. Both communities were conservative and exclusive. They soon established the separate township of Hyde Park and began fighting annexation to the City of Chicago.

As public transportation improved in the 1880s, apartment buildings and commercial strips began to transform Hyde Park into an urban neighborhood. New residents in favor of annexation to the city outvoted their tony neighbors in 1889 as the entire town from 39th Street to 138th Street became part of Chicago. In 1891, Hyde Park was chosen as the site of the **World's Columbian Exposition** *(p 181)*, fostering the completion of Jackson and Washington Parks and ending the neighborhood's exclusivity.

Simultaneously, the University of Chicago was built just north of the Midway Plaisance. The two events forever changed the destiny of the community.

The World's Fair brought an avalanche of real estate development as hotels,

View from Promontory Point

apartment buildings and shops sprang up to cater to the 27 million visitors during the summer of 1893. The University of Chicago grew just as quickly, and Hyde Park became a bustling area comprised of a large university, fashionable residential hotels and vibrant commercial strips on 47th, 53rd and 55th Streets. The 1910 opening of the Kenwood "L" train increased Kenwood's density, and a streetcar line on 47th Street created a split between North and South Kenwood. By the 1920s the crowded black belt *(p 154)* pushed toward Kenwood, setting off racial conflicts that continued for twenty years and divided largely black North Kenwood from mainly white South Kenwood. While it declined economically,

175

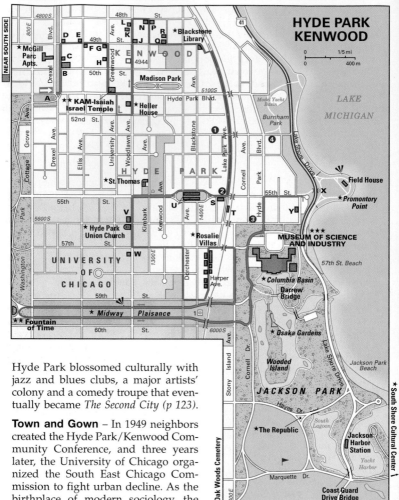

Hyde Park blossomed culturally with jazz and blues clubs, a major artists' colony and a comedy troupe that eventually became *The Second City (p 123)*.

Town and Gown – In 1949 neighbors created the Hyde Park/Kenwood Community Conference, and three years later, the University of Chicago organized the South East Chicago Commission to fight urban decline. As the birthplace of modern sociology, the university held a critical role: U of C scholars studied their declining neighborhood and developed guidelines for urban renewal. These studies were formalized into the Federal Housing Act of 1954, and when federal funds were released in 1955, it was no surprise that Hyde Park/Kenwood qualified for the largest urban-renewal project in the nation. Over 900 acres of buildings were demolished over the next decade, including almost every bar and nightclub on 55th Street. The south side of 47th Street was stripped of retail, so it could act as a buffer against the deteriorating North Kenwood community. Shopping centers replaced mansions on Lake Park Avenue and apartments on 53rd Street. Cottages with porches gave way to town houses oriented around interior courtyards. The radical surgery worked: the University of Chicago abandoned thoughts of leaving the city, the neighborhood maintained its integrated middle-class character and the economic decline sweeping the South Side leapfrogged over Hyde Park/Kenwood. Today one of the nation's most successful models for integration, the community remains a part and parcel of the university, which has helped shape its destiny.

DRIVING TOUR *distance: 9.3mi*

Begin at the intersection of Drexel Blvd. and 51st St. (Hyde Park Blvd.).

Drexel Square's restored **Drexel Fountain [A]** is the oldest monument in the boulevard system, dedicated in 1883 by the sons of financier Martin Drexel. To the west lies Washington Park, designed in 1869 by Frederick Law Olmsted.

Drive north on Drexel Blvd.

Drexel Boulevard separates Kenwood from Washington Park and was one of Chicago's most fashionable streets from 1880 to 1930. Today large courtyard apartment buildings share the street with mansions from the horse-and-carriage era. On the east side, the Classical Greek temple facade of **Operation PUSH [B]** *(950 E. 50th St.)*, founded by the Reverend Jesse Jackson in 1971, was built in 1923 by the K.A.M. congregation, which later merged with the Isaiah Israel congregation and now owns one of the city's most magnificent houses of worship *(below)*. The **John H. Nolan House★ [C]** *(no. 4941)*, an 1887 work by John W. Root of Burnham & Root, exemplifies the Romanesque Revival style. Across the street the **McGill Parc Apartments★** *(no. 4938)*, created in 1982, occupy the massive, Chateau-style John McGill mansion (1890, Henry Ives Cobb). At 49th Street note the **Martin A. Ryerson House [D]** *(no. 4851)*, erected in 1887 in the Richardsonian Romanesque style, with its large stone veranda and coach house.

Turn right on 49th St. and continue east to Ellis Ave.

To the left at 4848 S. Ellis Avenue stands the **Gustavus Swift House [E]** (1898, Flanders & Zimmerman), an exuberant Renaissance palace befitting the meat packer's imperial wealth. Across Ellis Avenue, on the southeast corner, the large, 42-room **Julius Rosenwald House [F]** *(4901 S. Ellis Ave.)* was built for the Sears, Roebuck & Co. chairman in 1903 by Nimmons & Fellows.

Continue to Greenwood Ave. and turn right.

On the southwest corner of 49th Street and Greenwood Avenue *(no. 4900)*, note the **Henry Veeder House★ [G]** (1907, Howard Van Doren Shaw), a free interpretation of Neoclassical architecture. The variety of grand mansions along Greenwood Avenue recalls the elegance of the GOLD COAST in the more expansive setting of Kenwood. Respect for the past disappears in the design of the **Ernest J. Magerstadt House★ [H]** *(no. 4930)*, an important 1908 work by Prairie school architect George W. Maher. A wide, flat roofline, banded windows and a wide porch display the Prairie style, while columns adorned with poppies provide a motif that Maher repeats in the leaded-glass windows.

The Byzantine dome of **K.A.M.–Isaiah Israel Temple★★**, a masterful 1923 work by Alfred S. Alschuler, rises on the northeast corner of Hyde Park Boulevard. The synagogue's minaret (which actually disguises a smokestack) and the multicolored brick walls are based on a Palestinian precedent from AD 2C. The interior is renowned for its acoustics and features a Guastavino tile dome *(open year-round Mon–Thu 9am–5pm, Fri 9am–4pm, Sun 9am–noon; closed major and Jewish holidays; 30min guided tour available; ♿ 🅿 ☎773-924-1234)*.

Turn left on Hyde Park Blvd., the dividing line between Hyde Park and Kenwood, and then right on Woodlawn Ave.

The **Isidore Heller House★** *(5132 S. Woodlawn Ave.)* is an 1897 work by Frank Lloyd Wright that illustrates the emergence of his distinctive Prairie style. Wright achieved a horizontal effect on the vertical home by aligning windows under lowslung eaves and using brick banding and a frieze by sculptor Richard W. Bock. Like all of Wright's Prairie homes, the house has an open interior plan and eschews a front door for a "pathway of discovery."

Continue on Woodlawn to 52nd St. and turn right. Turn right on University Ave., right again on Hyde Park Blvd. and left on Woodlawn Ave.

To the right is **Madison Park**, an exclusive residential area set around a private boulevard, laid out in 1883 by John Dunham but not fully developed until the apartment-building boom of the 1920s. Past 50th Street, on the left, note the 1916 brick mansion at no. 4944, once inhabited by heavyweight boxer Muhammad Ali. On the northeast corner of 49th and Woodlawn stands the **Elijah Muhammad House [J]** *(no. 4855)*, erected in 1971 in a Mediterranean Modern style for the Nation of Islam leader. The home, which faces four smaller versions built for his sons on the west side of the street, features huge doors, stained-glass windows and a red tiled roof. The mansion is now occupied by controversial Nation minister Louis Farrakhan. To the north, on the west side, is the **James Douglas House [K]** *(no. 4830)*, a 1907 Howard Van Doren Shaw design that helped establish the Georgian Revival style in Kenwood. The neighborhood's oldest home is the **Christopher B. Bouton House★ [L]** (1873), a large, wooden, Italianate mansion located at no. 4812.

Turn right on 48th St. and right again on Kimbark Ave.

This block is unique in Chicago for its adoption of the Shingle style, although stone and brick are also used in deference to Chicago's climate. The **George Miller House [N]** *(no. 4800)*, an 1888 design by George Garnsey, was copied from an 1874 H. H. Richardson house in Newport, Rhode Island. Across the street at no. 4801, the **Joseph H. Howard House [P]** (1891, Patton & Fisher) uses pink slate shingles in a picturesque composition of turrets and dormers.

Turn left on 49th St. and continue to the intersection with Kenwood Ave.

On the northwest side of the intersection stand two of Frank Lloyd Wright's secret commissions, built in 1892 while he still worked for Adler & Sullivan: the **George W. Blossom House [Q]** *(4858 Kenwood Ave.)* and the **Warren McArthur House [R]** *(4852 Kenwood Ave.)*. Like his Oak Park "bootlegs" *(p 193)*, these homes are traditional in style, but Wright's restless creativity is visible in windows that sit below wide eaves and open interior plans.

Continue on 49th St. toward Lake Park Ave.

The **Blackstone Branch, Chicago Public Library★** (1902, Solon S. Beman) typifies the Neoclassical style inspired by the 1893 World's Columbian Exposition, with its dome, acanthus leaves and pedimented temple entrance. In fact, Beman's design is a copy of his own Merchant Tailors Building at the Fair.

Drive south on Lake Park Ave. and turn right on 55th St.

55th Street forms the heart of the Hyde Park/Kenwood Urban Renewal plan, which transformed the street from a jazzy nightlife district to a modern residential strip and shopping mall. The **University National Bank★ [S]** (1929, M. Louis Kroman), on the southwest corner of 55th Street and Lake Park Avenue, was built as an automobile showroom, its facade enlivened with playful terra-cotta roadsters, dashboards, engines and wheels. Farther south at 5529 Lake Park Avenue is the **Hyde Park Historical Society [T]**, located in a tiny cable-car station *(open year-round weekends 2–4pm; ☎773-493-1893)*.

Looming ahead on 55th Street are the twin 10-story towers of I.M. Pei's **University Apartments [U]**, built in 1961 and known locally as "Monoxide Island" because the roadway circumscribes the high rises. Modern 2- and 3-story town houses face the island and line adjacent streets.

Continue west on 55th St.

At the northwest corner of 55th Street and Kimbark Avenue, **St. Thomas the Apostle Catholic Church★** *(visit by 1hr guided tour only, year-round Mon–Fri 9am–8pm; reservations required; ♿ 🅿 ☎773-324-2626)* is a revolutionary 1924 design by Barry Byrne, an apprentice of Frank Lloyd Wright and the first American to design a European cathedral (The Church of Christ the King in Cork, Ireland). Byrne used unusual massing, narrow windows and scalloped terra-cotta ornament by Alfonso Ianelli to obliquely reference Gothic forms. The interior features a column-free sanctuary

1 Valois

1518 E. 53rd St.
☎ 773-667-0647. The sign outside this cafeteria-style diner reads "See Your Food." If you eat at Valois (pronounced "vuh-loys"), you'll see plenty more than the roast beef, baked chicken, greens and casserole on your tray. Here factory workers rub elbows with professors and professionals, and the resulting conversations make for great eavesdropping. When the restaurant is crowded, customers sit wherever there's room, so prepare to dine—and converse— with strangers.

2 Hyde Park Co-op

1526 E. 55th St.
☎ 773-667-1444. Founded in 1932, this is one of the oldest cooperative grocery stores operating in the US. The co-op moved into a building designed by I.M. Pei in 1959 and is now open to the public. Its deli and bakery counters are good places to grab a quick snack or to stock up for a picnic on one of the university quads or Promontory Point *(p 180)*.

measuring 95ft by 125ft, with the altar pushed into the nave—anticipating
Vatican II reforms four decades later. Stations of the cross by Alfeo Faggi complete
this modern interpretation of a traditional building.

Continue west on 55th St. and turn left on Woodlawn Ave.

Many of the large homes on Woodlawn are owned by the University of Chicago,
fraternal associations or theological schools that have clustered in Hyde Park. The
massive, Queen Anne **Theodore Rice House★ [V]** (1892, Mifflin E. Bell) at the
northwest corner of Woodlawn Avenue and 56th Street has colorful pink and gray
tiles and a wide porch. Across 56th Street, the Romanesque Revival-style **Hyde
Park Union Church★** (1906, James Gamble Rogers) features orange sandstone and
stunning Tiffany and Connick stained glass. South of 57th Street on the west side
stands the **Edgar Johnson Goodspeed House [W]** *(5706 Woodlawn Ave.)*, a 1906 Arts
and Crafts-style home by Howard Van Doren Shaw.

*Turn left on 57th St. and pass a small commercial area. Turn right on Dorchester Ave.,
left on 59th St., then left on Harper Ave. at the Illinois Central railroad viaduct.*

This quaint street provides insight into Hyde Park's early development, its small
lots filled with Queen Anne and Shingle-style homes. The street was a planned
community called **Rosalie Villas★**, designed in 1883 by Solon Beman, who was the
architect for nos. 5832-34 and no. 5759. Other architects followed the same vocabulary of wood clapboard siding, shingles and cutout ornament.

*Turn right on 57th St., and right again on Stony Island Ave., heading south to
the Midway Plaisance. Follow the Midway Plaisance west, then double back at the*
Fountain of Time *and follow it eastbound until it intersects with Cornell Dr.*

The open, grassy expanse of the **Midway Plaisance★** belies the raucous carnival
atmosphere of the 1893 World's Columbian Exposition *(p 181)*. While the term
"midway" is still applied to carnival sideshows, its namesake now serves as the
city's broadest boulevard and a foreground for the university. Designed in 1869 by

Fountain of Time by Lorado Taft

Frederick Law Olmsted and Calvert Vaux as the connecting link between
Washington and Jackson Parks, the Midway was intended to have a central canal
linking the lagoons of the two parks. Although the center of the Midway is
depressed below grade level, the water link was never implemented. The **Fountain
of Time★★**, a monumental 1922 sculpture by Lorado Taft anchors the western
end of the Midway at Washington Park. A curving wave of humanity rises and
falls as a solitary hooded figure of Time watches in passive solemnity. Inspired
by these lines from Austin Dobson, "Time goes, you say? Ah, no!/ Alas, Time
stays, we go...," the sculpture took 14 years and a 4,500-piece mold to complete.

179

③ Piccolo Mondo
1642 E. 56th St.
☎ *773-643-1106.*
The wide, arched windows of
this Italian restaurant afford a
pleasant view of Jackson
Park and the facade of the
Museum of Science and
Industry *(p 182)*. Spool
spaghetti and sip Chianti in
the candlelit dining room, or
grab a sandwich and salad
at the gourmet deli counter.

④ Hyde Park Art Center
5307 S. Hyde Park Blvd.
☎ *773-324-5520.*
A spacious corner of the
Del Prado apartment building
houses a good-size gallery
and a handful of studios for
ceramics, painting and crafts
classes. The gallery mounts
about three shows a year
often featuring prominent
Chicago artists.

Taft designed a complementary *Fountain of Creation* for the other end of the Midway, but it was never built. Instead, an equestrian sculpture **[1]** of a black knight, St. Wenceslaus, sculpted by Albin Polasek and dedicated to Czechoslovakian nationalist Tomas Masaryk, occupies the intended site. The drive around the Midway offers some of the best **views★** of the Gothic facades of the University of Chicago.

Turn left and head north on Cornell Ave., as it curves eastward in front of the Museum of Science and Industry, and turn left on S. Hyde Park Blvd. Continue to 55th St. and turn right. Park in the parking lot at the eastern end of 55th St. Promontory Point is accessed by a pedestrian tunnel under Lake Shore Dr.

Jutting into the lake, the small **Promontory Point★** was designed in 1937 by Alfred Caldwell, a student of Jens Jensen. Caldwell even supervised a restoration in 1987. The entrance is marked by the **David Wallach Fountain [X]**, a drinking fountain designed for people and their pets, topped by a bronze of a resting doe. At the far end of "The Point," a stone **Field House** (1937) takes the appearance of a lighthouse with its circular tower. The **view★★** *(illustration p 175)* north to the Loop is spectacular. At 5530 S. Shore Drive are the **Promontory Apartments [Y]**, the first high rise by Ludwig Mies van der Rohe. Completed in 1949 in concrete and glass, these prefigured Mies' steel-and-glass apartment towers built on North Lake Shore Drive four years later *(p 87)*.

JACKSON PARK
E. 56th to 67th Sts., Stony Island Ave. to Lake Michigan.
Renowned landscape architect Frederick Law Olmsted's 1870 plan for the park was only partially implemented when he redesigned and completed it for the World's Columbian Exposition in 1893, using Lake Michigan and a series of lagoons and formal ponds as the organizing principle. Following the Fair's demolition, Olmsted's sons redesigned it again in 1895. Despite the ravages of time, several Olmsted landscapes and turn-of-the-century structures survive today.
A highlight of the park is the gleaming, 24ft-high statue **The Republic★**, by Daniel Chester French, cast in 1918 from a scale model of the original 65ft sculpture that stood in the Court of Honor during the 1893 Fair. The only sculpture in Jackson Park, it was regilded in 1992 and stands on the site of the Fair's Administration Building.
Wooded Island, one of the original features of Jackson Park, was designed as a natural area and rookery by Olmsted and is known today as the Paul H. Douglas Nature Sanctuary. More than 300 bird species have been spotted here, with some two dozen varieties nesting on small islands Olmsted designed for that purpose in the east and west lagoons. At the north end of Wooded Island lie the **Osaka Gardens★**, a modern replica of a landscape created during the 1893 Fair by Japan, which replicated the *Ho-o-den* or "Phoenix Temple" at Uji, near Kyoto. In the traditional Japanese garden style, rocks, flowers, shrubs, decorative lanterns and pavilions are arranged to provide a succession of contemplative views and vistas *(to access: turn right toward Jackson Park at far eastern end of the Museum of Science and Industry parking lot; continue to small parking area overlooking Columbia Basin)*. North of Wooded Island is the **Columbia Basin★**, designed by Olmsted as a romantic, reflecting pond for the Palace of Fine Arts, now the Museum of Science and Industry. Wooded Island, the east and west lagoons and Columbia Basin are the only landscapes that survive from the 1893 Fair. To the east, the **Clarence Darrow Bridge** is named for the famous attorney who defended the Pullman strik-

The 1893 World's Columbian Exposition

Following on the heels of the successful centennial exhibit in Philadelphia in 1876, the 1893 World's Columbian Exposition heralded another American city's debut on the world stage. In a spirited battle to host the fair, Chicago outbid three other cities—New York, Washington and St. Louis—claiming the best amenities and the largest funds (over $10 million were pledged by 1890). That same year, President Harrison signed a bill that provided for "celebrating the 400th anniversary of the discovery of America by Christopher Columbus, by holding an International Exhibition of the arts, industries, manufactures and the products of the soil, mine and sea, in the City of Chicago."

Covering over 650 acres along present-day Jackson Park and the Midway Plaisance, the grounds encompassed some 200 buildings erected at a cost of $30 million by such esteemed architects as John W. Root, Daniel Burnham, Charles Atwood and Louis Sullivan. Under the masterful hand of landscape artist Frederick Law Olmsted, several lagoons, three miles of canals and elaborate gardens appeared, lending the fair a Venetian look. From its opening day on May 1, 1893, to its close in October, the Fair attracted some 27 million visitors and awed them with its architecture (the Fair's largest structure, the Manufactures and Liberal Arts Building, encompassed 40 acres of gallery space and its 380ft-long roof was pierced by 11 acres of skylights) and attractions—including the world's first Ferris Wheel towering above the spires of the University of Chicago and the infamous "Little Egypt" dancing the hootchie kootchie in the "Street of Cairo" exhibit. Fair officials quipped that it would take more than three weeks of walking some 150mi to take in all exhibits.

Uniform in design, the Fair's structures reflected the grandiose Neoclassical style. At night, enormous floodlights—a first at the time—illuminated the buildings, creating a sparkling, white, fairy-like atmosphere, and the complex was soon dubbed the "White City." The Fair had an enormous impact on American architecture, spawning the "City Beautiful" movement and marking a return to monumental Classical architecture. Several cities, including Washington, DC, and Cleveland, OH, later called on Daniel Burnham's skills to create grand, spacious downtown areas.

Within a few years, most buildings—erected on iron and wood frames and clad with "staff," an amalgam of plaster, cement and fiber that had the appearance of white stucco—had been destroyed by fire and vandalism. The only structure remaining today is the MUSEUM OF SCIENCE AND INDUSTRY, formerly the Palace of Fine Arts.

ers in the 1890s and the teaching of evolution in the 1924 Scopes Trial. The **Coast Guard Drive Bridge** at Marquette Drive is a rough-faced stone bridge (1904), ornamented with gargoyle-like sculptures of hippopotamuses, alligators and other water creatures. The former **Jackson Harbor Coast Guard Station**, a quaint 1906 Shingle-style boat house, was restored in 1992 as the South Pier restaurant.

A half-mile south of the park stands the **South Shore Cultural Center★** (*71st St. and South Shore Dr.; open Mon–Sat 10am–6pm;* & 🄿 ☎312-747-2536), an elegant former country club (1916, Marshall & Fox) that is now part of the Chicago Park District. A broad entrance colonnade leads to a Mediterranean structure framed by square towers topped by red tile roofs. The blue and white Renaissance interior boasts massive ballrooms, oak-paneled meeting rooms and a dazzling solarium that host classes, community events and private functions.

OAK WOODS CEMETERY

Enter off of 67th St. at Greenwood Ave. The office will provide a free map and listing of some of the more notable grave sites and monuments. Open year-round Mon–Fri 8:30am–4:30pm, Sat 9am–3pm. Guided tours available, reservations required. & ☎773-288-3800.

Designed in the monumental and picturesque 19C tradition by Adolph Strauch, the cemetery hosts a diversity of occupants ranging from Confederate soldiers to mayors, governors and industrialists. Rows of tiny white tombstones, cannons and a statue of a Civil War soldier mark the Soldier's Home Lot, while a sculpture of Abraham Lincoln stands at the Grand Army of the Republic Lot. Neither Union burial equals the grandeur of the **Confederate Mound★** at the southern end of the cemetery, where some 6,000 Confederate prisoners of war are buried in concentric trenches under a massive obelisk surmounted by a statue of a defeated rebel. Four cannons guard the corners, while marble tombstones number the nameless Union guards who also died at Chicago's Camp Douglas (*p 154*), where the greatest killers were smallpox and cholera. More than 4,000 of the deceased are named on the monument erected in May 1895 with elaborate ceremony and 100,000 in attendance.

Distinguished by a red granite marker, the **Jesse Owens monument**, adjacent to the Lake of Memories, is one of the most impressive tombstones; note the stylized Olympic urns flanking the monument. The gray granite **Mayor Harold Washington grave** commemorates the long political career of the city's first black mayor. Among the others buried here are Hyde Park founder Paul Cornell, University of Chicago founding president William Rainey Harper, baseball pioneer Cap Anson and nuclear physicist Enrico Fermi.

MUSEUM OF SCIENCE AND INDUSTRY★★★

Time: 1 day. 57th St. at S. Lake Shore Dr. **CTA** bus no. 6 (Jeffrey Express).
Map p 176

Part amusement park, part trade show and part museum, this cacophonous hall of wonders and widgets is Chicago's most popular attraction. Located since 1933 in the only building left standing after the World's Columbian Exposition of 1893, its more than 2,000 exhibits cover 14 acres spread over three floors. Dedicated to presenting science, industry and technology to the public in an entertaining way, the museum's hands-on displays invite visitors to push, pull, compute and enjoy.

Historical Notes

The Building – Perhaps the grandest structure at the World's Fair of 1893, the Palace of Fine Arts represented the essence of that great Beaux-Arts extravaganza. Designer **Charles B. Atwood** of D. H. Burnham & Co. left no Neoclassical reference unmade by combining elements from the Parthenon and other temples on the Acropolis along with ancient Roman forms. (The versatile Atwood would later design the strikingly modern RELIANCE BUILDING in the Loop.) The sprawling edifice, encircled by 276 columns, extends 1,145ft across the front and contains 650,000sq ft of exhibit space. Its two wings, east and west, echo the central pavilion in a rigorous Ionic symmetry. At its rear, the Columbia Basin (North Pond), traversed by gondolas during the Fair, laps at the building's south steps.

Born Again – Much has happened to the palace since its glory days at the Fair when it housed works of art from around the world. In its second life as the home of the FIELD MUSEUM, it slipped into such disrepair as to be dubbed a "scaly, wormy pile." Its condition resulted not from poor maintenance, but rather from the ephemeral materials of its construction, which were never intended to outlive the Fair. By 1920, when the Field moved to its new Grant Park facility (*p 89*), the palace's walls, made of brick covered with "staff," a flimsy compound of plaster and hemp, had seriously decayed. It stood forlornly empty in Jackson Park for several years, until a marriage of ideas and resources came to pass. Public sentiment to save the building was strong, since it was a remnant of the beloved Fair and an unexcelled example of American Neoclassicism. At the same time, philanthropist **Julius Rosenwald**, who had made millions as chairman of Sears, Roebuck and Co., felt Chicago could benefit from a "hands-on" industrial museum like the Deutsches Museum he had seen in Munich, Germany. He would eventually contribute over $7 million to the project.

In 1926, the idea of using the old **Palace of Fine Arts** took root and plans for the complicated renovation got under way. After stripping the moldering plaster skin away from the building's brick and iron skeleton, crews fortified the walls using limestone on the outside and marble on the inside. Fragile skylights were eliminated; 200,000lbs of copper sheathed the domes. Sturdy stone columns and caryatids replaced their deteriorating predecessors around the facade. Architects gave the interior an Art Moderne look, a most appropriate backdrop for the march of modern technology and science and an acknowledgment of the Century of Progress International Exposition planned to open in 1933 along the lakefront. A portion of the new Museum of Science and Industry (MSI) debuted simultaneously: the revered Palace of Fine Arts would see another World's Fair.

E.R. Walker/Chicago Historical Society (ICHi-02226)

Palace of Fine Arts, South Facade
World's Columbian Exposition, 1893

An Invitation to Industry – Times were hard for the museum during the Great Depression. Support was difficult to come by; exhibits remained sparse and restoration incomplete until 1940. The main attraction of those years was the "Coal Mine," its actual bituminous walls so convincing that visitors often wondered where they might place their orders for coal. The Century of Progress Exposition left the museum with two legacies: many of its exhibits made their way into the collection, and the man who had masterminded the successful two-year pageant, **Major Lenox Lohr**, was hired on as president. In 1940, Lohr, a practiced promoter and showman, left the presidency of the National Broadcasting Company to energize the struggling museum. Injecting life, color and controversy into the serious business of science and technology, Lohr began to shape the modern institution. He invited industries to underwrite, develop and maintain exhibits; he hired architects to enliven the halls; he startled visitors with displays on pregnancy and the human body and he added entertainment to the museum's agenda.

A Continuing Challenge – Lohr remained in charge until his death in 1968. During those years, the museum amassed an amazing array of oddities and wonders, including the U-505 Submarine, Colleen Moore's miniature Fairy Castle, the world's largest model railroad and the world's fastest car. At the same time, the corporate presence grew ever stronger as more and more exhibits carried company logos and transmitted overt and subliminal messages to thousands of daily visitors. That legacy has bequeathed the museum a continuing challenge: how to weave these disparate parts into a meaningful and evenhanded whole. The **MSI 2000** master plan introduced in 1990 addresses that concern. The most immediate effect of the plan was to establish an admission fee in 1991. (Entrance to the museum had always been free.) Reassessing everything from parking to programs, the plan includes a consolidation of the museum's exhibits from a random medley into six thematic "zones"—human body, transportation, communication, energy and environment, space and defense, manufacturing—to make visiting easier and understanding clearer. Also proposed is a redesign and expansion of the Henry Crown Space Center, constructed in 1986 to house the popular Omnimax Theater and exhibits about space exploration. In addition, most of the exhibit planning and development will pass from corporate sponsors to museum staff in an effort to present a more balanced vision of today's complicated technological, industrial and scientific issues.

How to Visit the Museum – In the throes of its physical and thematic reorganization, the MSI remains a difficult space to negotiate efficiently. Because of the throngs (especially on Thursdays when admission is free and on weekends), timing is everything here. Be sure to pick up a map at the information desk, as the vast maze of exhibits in little logical order can be confounding. The visitor's best bet is to decide whether to attend a viewing of the 40min Omnimax Theater film and then build the day around that. If you are interested, plan to visit the "Coal Mine" and the "U-505 Submarine" early in the day; waits in excess of an hour are not unusual for these attractions. The flight simulators in "Navy: Technology at Sea" can also attract a crowd.

The most interesting exhibits are presented here floor by floor. Consult the map for changing exhibits and other areas of interest.

VISIT

Open Memorial Day–Labor Day daily 9:30am–5:30pm (Fri 7pm). Rest of the year Mon–Fri 9:30am–4pm, weekends & holidays 9:30am–5:30pm. Closed Dec 25. $6 (free admission on Thu), $10 museum admission & Omnimax Theater. ✗ ♿ ▯ ⅲⅲ ☎773-684-1414. *The museum is currently building an underground parking garage to be completed in 1997 (there will be a parking fee).*

Stairways – The three floors of the museum are connected by four symmetrical stairways that flank the central rotunda. Each has been painted a different color to help orient visitors. Elevators are located in the red stairwell. Powered by sunlight, a **solar fountain** in the yellow stairwell measures the intensity of the day's sunshine. A huge sculpture bearing the **periodic table of elements** hangs in the green stairwell. Below the second landing of the blue stairwell, a **Foucault's pendulum** swings through its unceasing rounds with comforting regularity, a sure sign that the earth continues to rotate. Among the enduring curiosities of the MSI are the **slices of the human body** on display in the upper level of this stairwell. A mainstay of the museum since 1943, the cross-sectional slivers sandwiched between pieces of glass can be both intriguing and somewhat disquieting at the same time. The display includes horizontal slices of a man and head-to-toe vertical slices of a woman. The bodies were frozen after death, cut with a power saw and preserved in solution.

Ground Floor – The **Omnimax Theater**, located in the Henry Crown Space Center, offers a truly sensational experience: its 76ft-high screen nearly engulfs the audience, absorbing them into the **film★★**, while the throb of the sound track makes the action nearly palpable. Story lines transport viewers to the Grand Canyon, Antarctica and other spectacular settings in new films introduced about three times a year. The theater repeats its presentation throughout the day *(40min; year-round daily 30min after opening until 1hr before closing; $10 Museum/Omnimax combination ticket, Thu $6; reservations suggested; special features, 90min, May–Sept Thu–Sun evenings)*. In addition to the theater, the 36,000sq ft hall contains displays on space exploration and travel, including the **Apollo 8 command module★**, the first vessel ever to circle the moon in 1968. An open hatch reveals the cramped interior, but perhaps most evocative is the pockmarked surface of the pod, which is covered with the burns and scars of space travel. Also on display are a moon rock from the Apollo 17 mission, a lunar module training unit and a **"space shuttle"** which enables visitors to experience the sensations of liftoff and space travel.

An icon of the museum, the **U-505 Submarine★** seems as popular now as when it arrived in 1954. Captured off the coast of French West Africa in 1944, this German reconnaissance vessel was the first enemy warship apprehended by the US Navy since 1815. Cipher books found aboard enabled American cryptographers to crack a code used to track ships. Tour guides take 15 people into the ship every 15min; browse through a brief history of the war in the Atlantic and objects removed from the sub while you wait. An amazingly complicated array of switches, controls, tubes and hardware crowds every inch inside the sub, punctuated by tiny and efficient living and working quarters and bunks made up with gingham sheets. Indeed, the interior of the 252ft-long sub is as much a testament to the human spirit as it is a wonder of science and industry. Enduring months at

> **■ U-Boat Facts:**
>
> Designed to house 56 enlisted men and 4 officers, the U-505 is 252ft long, 37ft high at the conning tower, 22ft wide at the widest point, and weighs 1,120 tons when loaded on the surface (1,232 tons when submerged). It travels underwater at 4.5mph (7.5 knots); on the surface, the speed can reach 13.8mph (19 knots). The means of communication used on board include telephone, speaking tubes, public-address system, crash-dive alarm bell and engine order telegraph.

sea here must have been quite a feat. So small are the spaces that sailors were required to be no taller than 5ft 7in in height. When leaving the submarine, take a look through the periscope for a view of Jackson Park. An exhibit at the exit describes the vessel's capture and eventual move to Chicago.

The MSI excels in its collections of **vehicles**, most of which are displayed around the ground floor in chronological sequence. In random corners and corridors are found groupings of wagons and carriages (all in beautiful repair), classic and racing cars, ships and firefighting equipment. Also of note on this floor, the "Business Hall of Fame," sponsored by Junior Achievement to honor American entrepreneurs, offers an intriguing **computer challenge★** of your business acumen. By answering questions about production, management, finance and marketing, visitors have a chance to rack up the day's high score and to learn something about economics as well. In the **Energy Lab** Kids, simple and colorful hands-on experiments demonstrate the ways various forms of energy are produced and converted thermally, mechanically, electromagnetically and also chemically.

An exhibit of a very different stripe is the quirky **Fairy Castle★** Kids, whose place at the museum is largely a sentimental one. The gift of silent-movie actress Colleen Moore in 1949, the miniature castle and its jewel-encrusted furnishings took seven years to complete when they were fashioned to her specifications in the mid-1930s. Measuring 9sq ft, the castle contains some 200 pieces of furniture and over 1,000 miniatures; it is even equipped with electricity and running water (although finding a plumber to work on the small scale has proven problematic).

> ■ **A Bite to Eat:**
>
> MSI offers five restaurants to its hordes of hungry and weary visitors: the self-service cafeteria Century Room *(ground floor)*, Cafe Spectrum *(ground floor)*, Pizza Hut *(main floor)*, Finnigan's Ice Cream Parlor *(main floor)* and Astro Cafe *(Henry Crown Space Center)*. All eateries are generally open from 11am to about 4pm. In addition, vending machines are located at the Miner's Stop.

Main Floor – The **Coal Mine★★** Kids *(allow 20min for the tour, not including any wait)* has thrilled visitors since the museum opened in 1933. From the top of the 60ft "headframe" (which visitors must climb to access the mine), an elevator operated by a guide plunges in semidarkness to what seems like a great depth, but which is actually only to the ground floor. (The experience can be frightening so some children.) The "mine" itself has walls composed of bituminous coal excavated in southern Illinois, and the guide demonstrates the grind and groan of the authentic mining equipment on display. A ride in the rattling caged car of a mine train moves the tour along and the final stop is the "safety room," where the guide describes the use of safety lamps to detect methane gas in the mine, creating a contained explosion to illustrate the point. Not unlike the submarine experience, a trip into this subterranean world inspires some awe over the difficult life of the coal miner.

An interesting exhibit in the far-flung east pavilion is worth investigating. **Navy: Technology at Sea★** gives visitors a chance to "tour" three different types of modern Navy vessels by reconstructing the aircraft elevator of the carrier USS *George Washington*, the bridge of the fast-attack sub USS *Chicago* and the control center of the destroyer USS *Arleigh Burke*. For many, the highlight of the galleries is a ride in one of two authentic F-14 Tomcat **flight simulators★**, complete with visuals of a mock bombing run and radio chatter. Taking off, evasive maneuvering, banking and other in-flight drills are so realistic that one is advised to hold on. And landing on the aircraft carrier is certainly exciting.

Food for Life is a handsome exhibit. Opened in its present form in 1976, it has worn well over the years. Designed to resemble an open-air market, its glass cases contain scads of nicely crafted wax foods: a cornucopia of fruits, breads, vegetables, entrees and desserts all arranged in various combinations to convey the fundamentals of good nutrition. Such didactic information is supplemented by historical and poetic tidbits regarding food preparation and consumption. At computer terminals, visitors learn the nutritional value of menus they concoct or discover their personal nutritional needs based on their height, weight, gender and age. At the very back of the gallery, a chick hatchery quietly incubates eggs and houses the downy new babies. The hatchery is the only element remaining from the original "Food for Life" exhibit installed by Swift & Co. in 1954; since then, over 50,000 chicks have hatched here. The chicks are given to the FARM IN THE ZOO at Lincoln Park.

The **Transportation Zone**★—the first-completed thematic zone in the new museum exhibit scheme—takes up the eastern portion of the large East Court Hall as well as the second-floor balcony and is easily recognized by the mammoth railcars and the breathtaking Boeing 727 that looms only 10ft overhead. This is an exhibit of juggernauts and superlatives. A steam engine called Buchanan's 999, for instance, broke the record in 1893 by achieving a speed of 112.5mph. The *Spirit of America*, a specially designed jet-powered automobile, was driven by Craig Breedlove to smash the 500mph land speed barrier in 1964. A minutely detailed **O-gauge model railroad**★ 🧒 (7mm = 1ft) takes up 3,000sq ft in the middle of the hall. It is the largest in the world, built in 1941 and revamped in 1988 to reflect Santa Fe Railroad's departure from the passenger business. Visitors can watch state-of-the-art computerized railroad traffic-controlling from the booth at the far end. The star of the exhibit is undoubtedly the United Airlines **Boeing 727**★ that is suspended from the second-story balcony. It is a thrill to stand beneath its highly polished underbelly and the impressive starboard wing that stretches for 50ft overhead. At designated times throughout the day the gleaming craft becomes the center of a **light and sound show** intended to evoke a fantasy of movement and flight. Wing flaps, rudder and wheels respond as if in takeoff and landing modes as the plane makes an imaginary seven-minute flight between San Francisco and Chicago *(Memorial Day–Labor Day daily 10, 11:30am, 1, 2:30, 3:30, 4:30pm, Fri additional 6pm show; rest of the year Mon–Fri 10, 11am, 1, 2:30, 3:30pm, weekends additional 4:30pm show; the best place to view the spectacle is from the balcony opposite the huge bird on the second floor)*.

For a brief respite, stroll down **Yesterday's Main Street**, a nostalgic re-creation of 1910 Chicago. At the very end of the street, a nickelodean theater shows silent films, while Finnigan's Ice Cream Parlor serves snacks and desserts in an old-fashioned decor.

On the west side of the main floor, **Earth Trek**, sponsored by Amoco Oil Co., creates a journey through the geologic and fossil record and into the business of oil drilling. Take a ride on the **Augernaut**, a kind of Jules Verne flight simulator that embarks on a trip through and around the earth in a search for oil *(Memorial Day–Labor Day daily 9:30am–5:15pm; rest of the year Mon–Fri 9:30am–3:45pm, weekends & holidays 9:30am–5:15pm)*. Toward the end of the exhibit, at a replica of a **drilling-rig floor**, an interactive computer invites visitors to try their hand at drilling. The setting even simulates an oily smell for further authenticity.

Beyond the "Communications" exhibit at the front of the main floor, the classic **Whispering Gallery** 🧒 still astonishes visitors as it has for years by demonstrating the peculiar ability of sound waves to bounce between two widely spaced parabolic shells. Visitors delight in throwing whispers across this room.

The fascinating exhibit **Imaging: The Tools of Science**★★ explores another, more modern phenomenon. "Imaging" refers to the very high-tech science of gathering, processing and displaying data in visual forms, and the computer is its primary tool. It enables us to picture the far reaches of space, the inner reaches of the microworld, the body's interior and climatic changes, even on other planets. Computers throughout the exhibit invite visitors to manipulate images of their faces, investigate how MRI and CT scans work, and create computer "art" by image enhancement and modeling. Indeed, part of the wonder of this exhibit is the overlap it reveals between science and art, technology and creativity. A "Mystery Lab" at the end goes further in describing the practical forensic applications of this technology to age faces by computer, match fingerprints and enhance microscopic analyses. A small section on virtual reality gives visitors a taste of the virtual world.

Balcony – The second-floor balcony encircles the entire perimeter of the building and houses a variety of exhibits pertaining largely to the basic sciences: chemistry, astronomy, geology, biology, physics, health and so on. Live demonstrations in the Grainger Hall of Basic Science animate fundamental physical theories with discussions and experiments in chemistry and physics *(30min, Memorial Day–Labor Day daily 11am–4:30pm; rest of the year Mon–Fri 11am–3pm, weekends & holidays 11am–4:30pm)*. Exhibits on the heart, brain, sickle-cell anemia and AIDS—all part of the thematic **Human Body Zone**★—address not only basic issues of anatomy but

Don Jiskra/Museum of Science and Industry

"Take Flight" Exhibit

timely health concerns as well. The museum's classic "walk-through" heart, a perennial favorite since 1952, has been incorporated into an updated exhibit on cardiac health called **Your Heart**. Computer exercises in concentration, memory, reasoning and other brain functions highlight **Learning and Learning Disabilities**, which explores the human mind in the context of how we learn. A brightly illustrated explanation of the origins and effects of different types of virus introduces the museum's most recent exhibit, **AIDS – The War Within**, the first major permanent museum exhibit on AIDS. By means of easy-to-understand explanations, graphics and hands-on activities, the younger visitor learns the characteristics of the HIV virus, how it spreads, how it affects the human immune system and what effective protection is available.

In the eastern portion of the balcony, the 133ft cutaway Boeing 727 that visitors marveled at from below makes a dandy exhibit space, enticing the visitor to wander up and down the aisle and learn about thrust, drag, lift and other aerodynamics as part of an exhibit entitled **Take Flight**. The aircraft, donated by United Airlines, was the seventeenth 727 ever built and remained in service between 1964 and 1991. In its journey to the museum it became the largest plane ever to land at Meigs Field, Chicago's lakefront commuter airport. Floated by barge south to the museum, the huge craft then stopped traffic as it was rolled across Lake Shore Drive. Along the balcony outside the craft, more interactive experiments demonstrate how planes fly, and cutaway aircraft parts reveal the complexity of modern flight mechanics.

PULLMAN HISTORIC DISTRICT ★

Time: 2 hours
Map p 3

Located in an industrial district on the Far South Side, this fascinating enclave was created by railroad-car magnate George Pullman in 1881 as an experimental company town. After years of neglect, the community was lovingly restored and today offers an architectural unity and unique history best sampled by a stroll down the 19C streets.

Historical Notes

George Pullman: Entrepreneur – George Mortimer Pullman (1831-1897) was an inventor who embodied both the American dream and Chicago's "I Will" spirit. He made his first fortune in the 1850s when Chicago raised the street grade to construct sewers in the perennially muddy town. Downtown hotels and banks with elegant lobbies were faced with the prospect of rebuilding or losing a clientele who would not descend into luxury. Pullman figured out a way of elevating the buildings by placing hundreds of jackscrews around the foundation, and having workers turn them in unison. He bragged that he could raise a hotel "without disturbing a guest or cracking a cup." For his next venture, George Pullman developed luxurious train coaches—dining cars, club cars, rolling barbershops and his famous sleeping cars—to cater to the tastes of America's wealthy. At first, railroads did not want the weighty, oversized cars that would require alterations to platforms and new tracks. However, when Abraham Lincoln was assassinated in 1865, Pullman offered his "Pioneer" sleeping car to transport the slain President back to Illinois, and the railroads finally complied for the fallen national hero. Pullman incorporated the Pullman Palace Car Company in 1867, with a starting capital of one million dollars.

Pullman's Vision: Peace, Planning and Profits – The 1877 railroad strike shocked the nation and many expected open conflict between capital and labor. Wishing to isolate his workers from the strike- and strife-prone city, Pullman built a new factory town 13mi south of Chicago at Lake Calumet. By creating a clean, orderly environment far from the city's evils, Pullman hoped to live at peace with his employees. In 1880 he hired architect **Solon Spencer Beman** and landscaper **Nathan F. Barrett** to design not only the factories of the Pullman Palace Car Company, but also a comprehensive town plan. He sent them to Europe to study the planned industrial towns of Krupp in Germany and Saltaire in England. For the next 14 years Beman created rows and rows of red brick Queen Anne homes for the workers, along with a livery, church, hotel, shops and library set in formal, French-inspired landscapes. The result was a stunning, unified architectural vision, soon called the most perfect town in the world.

From the start, the community was a business for Pullman. The factory was to provide an eight percent profit, the town, six. He collected rents from the workers for their homes, for the shops, even for the library and the church. In turn, Pullman provided conveniences like daily garbage pickup, paved alleys, water and sewer and fire protection. Sewage water was used to irrigate fields that produced vegetables for the town, and the huge Corliss engine that ran the factories provided heat to all the homes. The only thing lacking in Pullman were taverns, since Pullman thought they would detract from his workers' productivity. Only visiting businessmen could be served alcohol at the Hotel Florence, which was off-limits to workers. One consequence of the policy was the construction by the Schlitz brewing company of a huge public saloon just outside Pullman's border!

"The Best Laid Schemes..." – Pullman's paternalism was tempered by his capitalism. Just as he retained ownership of all of his railroad cars, which were only leased to the railroads, he maintained ownership of the entire Pullman community, setting rents, controlling food prices and refusing to let anyone own individual houses. The town grew to 11,000 persons, half of whom toiled in the factories, which produced not only Pullman cars at costs of up to $25,000, but railroad cars of every type.

Many visitors to the 1893 World's Columbian Exposition went to see the model town. Shortly after, the severe depression that struck the American economy that year would turn Pullman's dream into his nightmare. By 1894, Pullman was forced to fire workers and cut wages to maintain the profits from his factories. To keep the town profitable, rents and food prices stayed high. Workers caught in the bind revolted, joining Eugene V. Debs' American Railway Union and striking in May 1894. The union asked its workers nationwide to stop handling Pullman cars, and the strike became national. Pullman refused to negotiate, assembling a group of railroad magnates who convinced President Grover Cleveland to send federal troops, since the strike was interfering with the US Mail. Bloody conflicts led to a victory for Pullman and loss for the strikers, but the "perfect town" was exposed as a fraud.

Pullman died bitter in 1897, leaving the company to Robert Todd Lincoln. In 1898, the company was ordered by the Illinois Supreme Court to sell its nonindustrial property, and by 1908 the residential sections had been purchased by former renters. The community declined and its population dwindled, but the factory continued to turn out Pullman cars until 1981. In 1971 Pullman was listed on the National Register of Historic Places, and restoration efforts began under the leadership of the Historic Pullman Foundation, which bought the Hotel Florence in 1975. In 1988 the State of Illinois drew up plans for a Pullman Railroad Museum for the site, purchasing the Clocktower Building and the Hotel Florence in 1991 (not to be completed until the 21C).

Visiting Pullman

Access – Pullman is located about 13mi south of the Loop. Drive south on I-94 and exit at 111th St. westbound (Exit 66A). The Pullman Historic District is four blocks west of the Expressway. The Metra Electric District Line services the Pullman area; exit at 111th St. stop; ☎ 312-836-7000.

Tours – A self-guided walking tour brochure is available at the reception desk of Hotel Florence ☎ 773-785-8181. Guided walking tours (1hr 45min) are offered May through October, the first Sunday of each month, and depart from the Visitor Center *(p 190)*, $4. The CHICAGO ARCHITECTURE FOUNDATION also conducts tours of the district; contact ☎ 312-922-3432 for information.

Dining – Pullman's historic district does not encompass a dining area, so schedule your trip to Pullman for a Sunday, when the Hotel Florence hosts a well-known and copious brunch. Served in a lovely, old-fashioned setting, the all-you-can-eat buffet features traditional breakfast items as well as sandwiches and hearty soups and casseroles.

WALKING TOUR   *distance: .6mi*

A variety of Victorian homes make up the **South Pullman** residential district. The larger homes of managers face 111th Street, while smaller row houses and double houses of craftsmen and workers line the streets south to 115th Street. The homes, all designed by architect Solon Beman in the Queen Anne and Shingle styles, sport varied and picturesque rooflines despite their modest scale. Beman also platted and designed **North Pullman** between 103rd and 107th Streets, but the area was segregated from South Pullman in the 20C. South Pullman, largely white, became a landmark in the 1970s, while predominantly African-American North Pullman was only designated in the 1990s. An active community organization is restoring many of the North Pullman homes, which are similar in design, but often simpler in detailing. The most picturesque stretch is along Cottage Grove at 107th Street where the houses are staggered along the angling thoroughfare.

Begin at the Hotel Florence.

★**Hotel Florence** – *11111 S. Forrestville Ave. Open Apr–Oct Mon–Fri 11am–2pm, Sat 8am–12:30pm, Sun 10am–3pm. Rest of the year Mon–Fri 11am–2pm, Sun 10am–3pm.* ✗ & ☎ *773-785-8900.* This grandiose structure (1881) exhibits a picturesque roofline with dormers above red brick walls, a wide Eastlake-style veranda and a Joliet limestone foundation.

Wooden trim is painted in the color scheme seen throughout Pullman, which combines maroon and two shades of green to set off the red brick and gray roofs. The interior contains an elegant lobby with several small displays, the hotel bar and a restaurant ornamented with wood and stained glass and original furnishings. The second floor includes several restored hotel rooms and numerous items from Pullman's demolished home on Prairie Avenue *(p 156)*. The Hotel functioned until 1975, when it was purchased by the Historic Pullman Foundation. It was acquired by the State of Illinois in 1991.

Walk south through Arcade Park.

Hotel Florence

Robert Holmes

The pleasant **Arcade Park**, restored in 1977, is embellished with 19C gaslight-style lanterns and three formal planting beds. A series of double houses built for factory foremen flanks the park to the east on St. Lawrence Avenue. Most of these feature a central shared porch and a roofline punctuated by three dormers, although the compositions are varied and subsequent alterations have created very individual homes.

To the south on 112th Street stands the **Livery/Stables Building★**, now an automotive repair facility. Like the other structures, the Livery has a picturesque roofline studded with dormers as well as two carved horses' heads between the central arches. Across 112th Street the gray, modern **Historic Pullman Foundation Visitor Center** occupies the former site of the Arcade Building, a massive structure that contained the library, post office, theater and shops until it was demolished in the 1920s (*open Apr–Oct Sat 11am–2pm, Sun noon–3pm; rest of the year Sun noon–3pm; closed major holidays; $3* �609 🅿 ☎*773-785-8181*).

Walk east on 112th St. to St. Lawrence Ave.

At the southeast corner of 112th Street and St. Lawrence Avenue is the **Greenstone Church★** (Pullman United Methodist Church), a lovely structure dominated by a rich roofline of dormers and monitors and a square corner tower. The Romanesque-style walls are faced with unusual green stone, and trimmed with black stone. The church was intended to service all denominations and was available for rent. Pullman wanted every element of his community to turn a profit, including religious edifices! During the 1894 strike, Rev. William H. Carwardine preached a "social gospel" against Pullman's policies here, and his book *The Pullman Strike* gained public support for the strikers.

Designed for skilled craftsmen, the homes to the south on St. Lawrence Avenue included marble fireplaces and plaster walls.

Continue east on 112th St. to Champlain St.

Today in need of restoration, the **Market Hall** was originally three stories high. The first floor housed a market, which sold the commodities of life to Pullman workers, while the second floor contained an assembly hall and gymnasium; the third floor consisted of meeting rooms. The building is flanked on all four corners by the curved **Colonnade Apartments and Town Houses★**, creating a unique and attractive streetscape. Both the hall and apartments were built in 1892 for the Columbian Exposition.

Continue east on 112th St. to Langley St.

The block houses north of 112th Street on the east side of Langley Street were the meanest in Pullman, designed for unskilled labor. Similar blocks are found in North Pullman.

Return to Champlain St. and walk north to 111th St.

This block comprises simple workers' homes—2-story double houses in brick with minimal detailing. Many have been restored with new porches and trim work painted in the Pullman colors. The homes are small, but the backyards and alleys are ample, rare amenities in the 1880s. The larger structures at the north end of the block were reserved for company managers and officers. At 111th Street look north to the **Pullman Firehouse**, recognizable by its distinctive Tuscan tower originally used for drying fire hoses.

Walk west on 111th St.

The homes on 111th Street, created for company executives, were the finest in Pullman. The home of Pullman Company doctor John McLean, at no. 623, has been exquisitely restored. The Chief Superintendent's residence at no. 605 now houses The Retreat restaurant, known for its French-American cuisine.

Walk north on Cottage Grove Ave.

A stroll north along Cottage Grove Avenue affords a view of the **Clocktower Building and Erection Shops★**, currently under restoration to house a state museum. The central tower, which contained administrative offices, is flanked by well-proportioned bays marked by round arches and large window openings used for assembly of the Pullman cars. Various other factory buildings surround the landmark, which once faced an artificial lake to the west.

OAK PARK ★★★

Population 54,217. Time: 1/2 day.
Map pp 194-195

A prosperous integrated suburb bordering Chicago on the west, **Oak Park** is known worldwide as the birthplace of Prairie school architecture and the modern American home. Attracting hordes of architecture buffs as well as lay folk, the town boasts the highest concentration of houses designed by American icon of architecture **Frank Lloyd Wright**. True to his vision of creating a style of architecture that could embody America's frontier spirit, Wright designed hundreds of unique homes distinguished by horizontal lines, ribbons of stained-glass windows and low, projecting profiles. The adjacent town of **River Forest** encompasses additional Prairie designs, including six by Wright.

Historical Notes

Frank Lloyd Wright: "Truth Against the World" – Born in Richland Center, Wisconsin in 1867, Frank Lloyd Wright credited the educational Froebel blocks, given to him by his mother and his musician father, as his earliest influences toward the design of form and space. After briefly attending the University of Wisconsin, Wright came to Chicago in 1887 and was hired as a draftsman by the firm of Adler & Sullivan. He worked on the AUDITORIUM BUILDING, becoming "a good pencil in the Master's hand" to Louis Sullivan, the only architect whose influence he ever acknowledged. In 1889 he married Catherine Tobin and moved to Oak Park, where he built a home and fathered six children.

Frank Lloyd Wright at Taliesin East, 1958

The restless Wright began designing on his own and left the employ of Adler & Sullivan in 1893 at the age of 25, developing his distinctive Prairie style of architecture over the next decade. In 1909, Wright left his wife and six children for the wife of an Oak Park client, effectively ending his practice in the socially conservative community. His architecture became more expressionistic in the 1910s and 20s, and in 1931 he established Taliesin in his home state of Wisconsin to train architects. Following construction of the stunning 1936 Fallingwater House in Pennsylvania, Wright opened Taliesin West in Arizona and remained in the limelight, refining his iconoclastic image until his death in 1959 at age 93.

His own home and studio, now restored to their 1909 appearance, trace the evolution of Wright's horizontal, organic architecture, introduced to the world in the 1911 Wasmuth folio printed in Berlin. Wright apprentices William Drummond, Marion Mahony, Walter Burley Griffin, Barry Byrne and John Van Bergen became prominent in their own right, and contemporaries George W. Maher, Robert C. Spencer and E. E. Roberts also designed many Prairie-style buildings in Oak Park and throughout the region.

191

Oak Park: A Suburb Evolves – Oak Park was settled in the years after the Fire of 1871 by a prosperous Puritan population that kept the tiny suburb free of alcohol, immigrants and other harbingers of moral decay. After supporting the annexation of neighboring Austin by the City of Chicago in 1899, Oak Park preserved its independence by seceding from the township of Cicero and becoming an independent village in 1902. The population grew rapidly, from 5,000 in 1890 to almost 20,000 by 1910. Novelist **Ernest Hemingway** was born on Oak Park Avenue in 1899. Like Wright, his progressive ideas led him to abandon Oak Park for a world of adventure in 1918, later deriding the conservative suburb for its "wide lawns and narrow minds." Author Edgar Rice Burroughs also dwelled here until called to Hollywood to supervise the filming of the *Tarzan* movies starring Chicago native Johnny Weissmuller.

Linked to the city by two rapid-transit lines and commuter rail, Oak Park's convenience made it a suburb of choice for progressive suburbanites in this century, swelling its population to 50,000 by mid-century. As racial change swept across Austin in the 1960s and 70s, Oak Park resolved to become an integrated, middle-class community, setting up a housing center to mix arriving African Americans into its increasingly diverse population, while buttressing its border against the city. In 1973, the Frank Lloyd Wright and Prairie School of Architecture Historic District was listed on the National Register of Historic Places, marking the beginning of restoration efforts in the community. Today Oak Park is known as an economically stable, socially progressive, well-educated community that easily accommodates lifestyles and ideas more radical than those of Wright and Hemingway three generations ago.

Visiting Oak Park

Access – Oak Park lies 8mi west of Chicago's Loop along the Eisenhower Expwy. between Austin Blvd. and Harlem Ave. The ▣ Green line and Blue line serve the suburb, as does the Metra West commuter rail line. Exit all train lines at Oak Park Ave. or Harlem Ave. stops.

Tours – Audio cassette and map for self-guided tours of the historic district are available at the Gingko Tree Bookshop (at the Frank Lloyd Wright Home and Studio) year-round daily 10am–3:30pm. $6 ($9 combination ticket available if also visiting Home and Studio). Guided walking tours conducted by the CHICAGO ARCHITECTURE FOUNDATION begin from the Home and Studio on Sundays (Mar–Oct 10:30am, noon & 2pm; rest of the year noon & 2pm; $9, $6 CAF members). Ten privately owned homes are opened to the public the 3rd Saturday in May for the "Wright Plus" tour ($30). Advance tickets required (tickets go on sale Mar 1).

Shopping and dining – A variety of specialty shops and restaurants are clustered on Lake St., Chicago Ave. and Oak Park Ave.

SIGHTS

Oak Park is best experienced by leisurely strolling the pleasant, tree-lined streets. While feasting your eyes on the architectural marvels, keep in mind that the homes are not open to the public, and that visitors should respect owners' privacy.

Begin at the **Oak Park Visitor Center** (*158 Forest Ave.*), which offers informative maps and brochures and sells tickets to various Oak Park attractions (*open year-round daily 10am–5pm; ♿ ▣ ☎708-848-1500*). The following descriptions cover Oak Park's highlights.

★★ **Frank Lloyd Wright Home and Studio** – *951 W. Chicago Ave. Visit by guided tour (45min) only, year-round Mon–Fri 11am, 1 & 3pm; weekends 11am–4pm; every 15min. Closed Jan 1, Thanksgiving Day, Dec 25. $6. ☎708-848-1976.* Opened to the public in 1974, this National Historic Landmark helped usher in Oak Park's era

" The prairie has a beauty of its own. A building on the prairie should recognize the features of its quiet level and accentuate them harmoniously. It should be quiet, broad, inclusive, a welcome associate of trees and flowers, not a nervous, fussy interloper, and should be 'married' to the ground. Hence, broad, sheltering eaves over determined masses, gentle roofs, spreading base and outreaching walls."

Frank Lloyd Wright

as an essential architectural pilgrimage. Wright first built the home in 1889, and continued to remodel and add to it over time, offering visitors the opportunity to view his architectural growth. The home has been restored to its 1909 appearance, when Wright last lived there and the studio was fully operational.

The tour begins with the 1889 Forest Avenue home that resembles a Shingle-style Victorian but for its horizontal bands of windows and low, earth-hugging profile. The **living room** is centered on the rectilinear hearth and inglenook that would characterize the later Prairie houses. The 1895 **dining room** reveals the emerging Prairie style in elegant, if uncomfortable, high-backed chairs and table beneath a false skylight. The tour continues to the modified second floor, where Wright's first office became a bedroom for his growing family. Wall murals in the master bedroom evoke Native American themes also seen in the 1895 **children's playroom★**, a marvelous barrel-vaulted space with balconies that distort perspective, banded windows and sphere-in-square lanterns. Returning to the main floor, visitors pass a tree that grows through the house—Wright endeavored to keep natural elements as part of his designs. The 2-story **studio★** addition of 1898 affords a glimpse into the

Frank Lloyd Wright Home and Studio, Living Room

Balthazar Korab

busy, creative world where Prairie architects apprenticed to the master. The octagonal library and low office entrance include intricate leaded-glass patterns that mimic the environment and intersecting volumes that defy and define interior space. A forest of columns and sculpture by Richard Bock ornament the Chicago Avenue entrance. The basement contains archives, while the Gingko Tree Bookshop occupies the former garage *(open year-round daily 10am–5pm; closed Jan 1, Thanksgiving Day, Dec 25;* ☎*708-848-1606).*

Farther west on Chicago Avenue stand the **Robert P. Parker [A]**, **Thomas H. Gale [B]** and **Walter H. Gale [C] Houses** *(nos. 1019, 1027 and 1031)*, "bootleg" homes Wright designed in violation of his exclusive contract with Adler & Sullivan. These 1892-93 Queen Anne structures betray the emerging sensibilities of the 25-year-old Wright with their horizontal clapboards and banded windows.

★ **Nathan G. Moore House** – *333 N. Forest Ave. Visit by guided tour (45min) only, Fri–Sat 10am–5pm, Sun noon–5pm. Purchase tickets at the Oak Park Visitor Center.* ☎*708-524-7473.* With its steep roofline, Sullivanesque balustrade fence and Tudor Revival style, the 1895 Moore House presents a dramatic contrast to Wright's later horizontal compositions. The house was a remodeling of an earlier structure that all but disappeared under the busy hand of Wright. The architect rebuilt the home after a 1922 fire, providing Oak Park visitors a rare glimpse of his 1920s experimentation with Japanese themes in encrusted ornament.

★ **Arthur Heurtley House** – *318 N. Forest Ave.* Wright's admired 1902 design prefigures many of the elements of his 1909 ROBIE HOUSE, including a raised living space curtained by ornate stained glass, a wide roof that hovers above a band of windows, and horizontally textured brick walls. The front door is hidden by a wall but revealed by a rounded arch, suggesting a serene and organic fortress.

Wright moved and remodeled the 1883 Stick-style **Hills-DeCaro House★** *(313 N. Forest Ave.)* in 1900, adding horizontal shingling and flattening the roof.

★ **Laura Gale House** – *6 Elizabeth Ct.* Anticipating Europe's International style of the 1920s, the broad cantilevered planes of this 1909 home also prefigure Wright's 1936 Fallingwater. The porches both anchor and expand the living spaces, "breaking the box" of architecture and shifting it into the landscape.

The **Joseph D. Everett House [D]** *(228 N. Forest Ave.)*, an 1888 Queen Anne Victorian, represents the dominant residential style in the years that Frank Lloyd Wright wreaked his revolution on the serene side streets of Oak Park.

★ **Frank W. Thomas House** – *210 N. Forest Ave.* Considered the first true Prairie-style house by Wright, this 1901 commission abandons all elements and ornaments of Victorian design. The entrance arch below the main floor leads not to a door but a staircase proceeding to the hidden entry. Bands of art-glass windows are squeezed and sheltered between flattened roofs and high stucco walls. Immediately south, Victorian row houses from 1892 illustrate the architectural shift Wright led at the turn of the century.

★★ **Unity Temple** – *875 W. Lake St. Self-guided audio cassette tours Memorial Day–Labor Day Mon–Fri noon–4pm. Rest of the year Mon–Fri 1–4pm. $3. Weekends year-round visit by guided tour (45min) only, 1–3pm. $5. Closed Jan 1, Thanksgiving Day, Dec 25.* ☎*708-383-8873.* In 1905, Frank Lloyd Wright took a small site and limited budget and created one of his great works of architecture. Called "my little jewel" by Wright, Unity Temple is an endlessly intriguing succession of form and space inside and out. The small budget ($45,000) dictated the use of unadorned reinforced concrete for the interlocking rectangular forms of the worship space and social hall. The two are joined with a low lobby shielded from busy Lake Street by a "pathway of discovery" leading from Kenilworth Avenue onto a raised entrance behind a high wall. Entered from behind the lectern, the worship space seems at once massive and intimate. Framed by rectilinear balconies, three levels allow 400 persons to sit no more than 45ft from the pulpit. Bathed by a grid of square sky-lights and clerestory windows, the room is framed with wood trim in a deceptively simple series of borders and inset rectangles and hung with sphere-in-square chandeliers. The clamor outside is forgotten behind high concrete walls as the eye travels along forms that simultaneously embrace and overreach the room itself, suggesting the spiritual quest at the heart of Unitarian-Universalism. The smaller social hall is filled with familiar Prairie forms and centers on a hearth, as in Wright's homes, reinforcing the human scale and purpose of this space.

Additional Sights

East of Forest Avenue, Kenilworth Avenue offers a wealth of large-scale Victorian mansions and early modern homes. On the southwest corner of Oak Park Avenue and Lake Street, **Scoville Square** (1908, E. E. Roberts) exhibits the influence of the Prairie school on commercial architecture with its broad rooflines. Euclid Avenue near the Oak Park and River Forest High School hosts an array of expansive man-

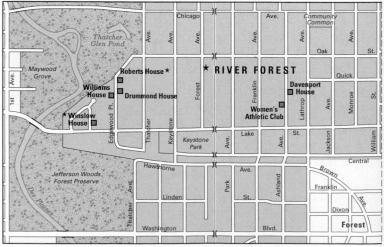

sions, including early works by Wright, Maher, and the **Edward W. McCready House** at no. 231 (1907, Spencer & Powers), with its stately entrance and elegant integration into the landscape.

Ernest Hemingway Birthplace – *339 N. Oak Park Ave. Open year-round Fri 1–5pm, Sat 10am–5pm, Sun 1–5pm. $3 Birthplace or Museum only, $5 combination ticket.* 🅿 ☎*708-848-2222*. This partially restored Victorian home (1890, Wesley A. Arnold) re-creates the novelist's comfortable family upbringing, providing a glimpse of the suburb's social order in the early 20C. Two blocks south at 200 N. Oak Park Avenue, the **Hemingway Museum** *(hours same as above)* offers exhibits about the high school writing of the Nobel Prize winning author.

★ **"Pleasant Home" (Farson-Mills House)** – *217 S. Home Ave. Visit by guided tour (1hr) only, year-round Thu–Sun 1–4pm. Closed major holidays. $3 (Thu free).* ☎*708-383-2654*. George Washington Maher (1864-1926) is unique among Prairie school architects, both for his symmetrical, straightforward facades and his motif-rhythm theory of design, where ornamental elements and local flora are repeated throughout the composition. Owned by the Park District of Oak Park since 1939, the Pleasant Home is set in Mills Park, originally the mansion's grounds. This 1897 house was the first in Maher's modern (or Prairie) style, with its broad facade, hipped roof and use of four repeated motifs—the honeysuckle, Roman tray or shield, lion's head and segmented arch—in exterior decoration, art glass and light fixtures, interior furnishings and trim. The main hall features exquisitely detailed quartersawn oak trim studded with lights. Adjacent sunny parlors are being restored to reflect their original Arts and Crafts design, and the dining room contains the table and chairs intended for the space by Maher. Tours also include upstairs bedrooms and the second-floor collections of the Oak Park and River Forest Historical Society.

★ RIVER FOREST   Population 11,896

The more exclusive town of River Forest encompasses several notable Prairie school designs. Frank Lloyd Wright's 1893 **William Winslow House**★ *(515 Auvergne Pl.)* was his first significant independent commission. Centered on a square, Sullivanesque arch, the flat and symmetrical facade begins to reach for prairie-like horizontality in its Roman brick, low-pitched roof and shaded second story. On nearby Edgewood Place, an elm tree grows through the parlor of Wright's 1908 split-level **Isabel Roberts House**★ *(no. 603)*. The home was restored by Wright in 1955. Next door at no. 559, the **William Drummond House** (1910, William Drummond) exemplifies the work of Wright's student with its broad porch and flat roof, while the **Chauncey Williams House** at no. 530 (1895, Frank Lloyd Wright) is a rare high-roofed Wright design with Japanese influence. Ashland Avenue features Wright's 1901 **Arthur Davenport House** at no. 559, and the elegantly scaled **Women's Athletic Club** at no. 526 (1911, Drummond and Guenzel).

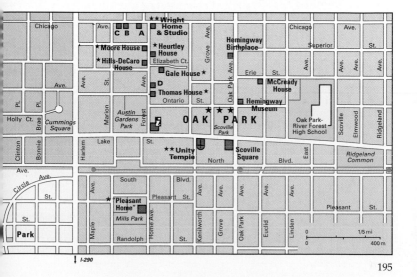

Time: 1 day
Map p 197

Chicago's northern suburbs: historian Michael H. Ebner pictures them "strung like pearls" along Lake Michigan. Each with its own personality, collectively they conjure a vision of elegant living called the North Shore. The lovely—and unusual—geography of ravines, bluffs, beaches and woodlands, and the area's architecture and history combine to make a drive up the shore a pleasant one-day excursion.

All of the North Shore communities considered here were established in the mid- to late 19C. Prosperous city folk, drawn by the beauty of the lakeshore and tired of life in an increasingly crowded, industrial Chicago, moved north with the help of the railroad (operating by 1855) and the development of Sheridan Road. The Chicago Fire in 1871 and the Haymarket Riot in 1886 hastened the exodus; the sylvan glades to the north seemed far removed from such urban cataclysms. As a result, an array of building styles crafted largely by prominent architects spread from Evanston to Lake Forest. Today, Sheridan Road twists, turns and dips up the lakeshore, revealing grand vistas of homes and landscape. Visitors with the time have ample opportunities to stop and admire architecture and nature on foot, shop and dine or acquire picnic makings for lunch in a lakefront park.

Visiting the North Shore

Access – The excursion is a 62mi round-trip; leave Chicago on Lake Shore Dr., which turns into Sheridan Rd. and continue through Rogers Park toward Evanston. To return to Chicago, take Rte. 41 to I-94. The ▒▒ Purple line reaches Evanston; the Metra North Line (☎312-322-6777) accesses each suburb's downtown and is particularly convenient for visiting Ravinia Park and Market Square in Lake Forest. Note that parking may be difficult along this itinerary.

Public Parks & Beaches – **Evanston** beaches are open for swimming from mid-Jun–Labor Day; lifeguards on duty daily 10:30am–7:30 or 8pm; $4 daily fee payable at beach entrances *(mid-Jun–Labor Day only)*. Gillson Park in **Wilmette** is open for swimming Memorial Day–Labor Day 9am–8pm; lifeguard services provided; $5 nonresident fee required to enter park year-round. Public parks in **Kenilworth** are open to nonresidents year-round at no charge; a $5 nonresident fee is charged at Kenilworth Beach payable at entrance; lifeguards on duty from Memorial Day–Labor Day daily 9am–6pm. **Winnetka** beaches are open mid-Jun–Labor Day; lifeguards on duty daily 10am–6pm; $8 daily fee, plus $5 parking fee payable at beach entrances *(mid-Jun–Labor Day only)*. Beaches in **Glencoe** are open Jun–Aug; lifeguards on duty Mon–Fri 10am–6pm, weekends & holidays 10am–8pm; $4 daily fee Mon–Fri, $5 weekends.

Shopping and dining – **Evanston's** main shopping and dining areas cluster along Main, Dempster, Davis and Central Sts. Many art galleries are located on Sherman St. **Highland Park** also boasts a small gallery district on Central Ave.; specialty shops and restaurants can be found along St. John's Ave. In **Wilmette**, several boutiques, restaurants and gourmet food shops crowd the Plaza del Lago mall *(p 200)* on Sheridan Rd. **Lake Forest** draws avid shoppers to its Market Square neighborhood *(p 203)*.

★EVANSTON   Population 74,188

A cosmopolitan community, Evanston makes a good segue from city to suburbs. First settled in the 1830s, Evanston blossomed in the 1850s around a new Methodist university later to be known as Northwestern. Four bursts of growth characterized the town's development, and many of its homes date from the 1870s, 1890s, 1920s (marked by a flurry of apartment building) and 1950s.

At the city line, Sheridan Road *(which briefly turns into Burnham Pl. and then Forest Ave.)* enters the **Evanston Lakeshore Historic District★**, listed on the National Register since 1980. Begin a walking tour at the **Charles Gates Dawes House★** *(225 Greenwood St.)*, home of the Evanston Historical Society. One of the few area houses open to the public, it offers a rare glimpse into opulent 19C North Shore life. Perhaps the finest example of the Chateauesque style in the region, the mansion was designed in 1894 by Henry Edwards-Ficken for Northwestern University treasurer Robert Sheppard. The house has been beautifully restored to the residency of Charles Gates Dawes, who purchased it in 1909. Dawes won the Nobel

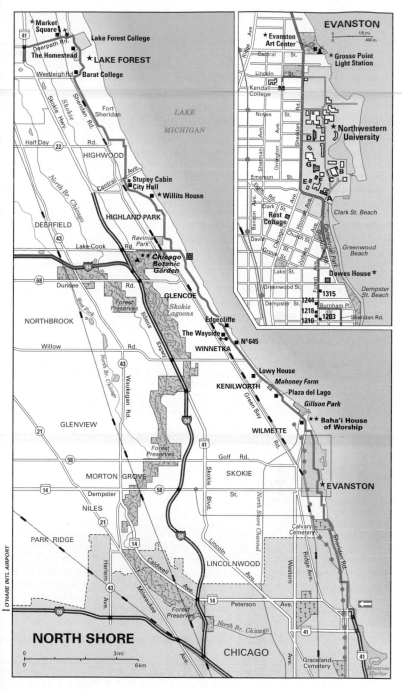

Prize for his part in developing an economic recovery plan for Europe following World War I. He also served as vice-president under Calvin Coolidge and composed popular music in his spare time. The home comprises 28 rooms (not all on view) and 14 fireplaces; among the restored and furnished rooms on display are the elegantly wood-paneled library and second-floor nursery (*visit by 1hr guided tour only, year-round Wed–Sun 1–5pm; closed for two weeks in Sept or Oct, call for specific dates; $5;* ☎ *847-475-3410*).

Houses in the surrounding blocks span years of development and many styles, from the post-Chicago Fire cottages planned by Luther Greenleaf in the 1870s—**1218** and **1244 Forest Avenue**—to the imposing Tudor structures of Ernest Mayo dating from the 1910s, as seen at **nos. 1210** and **1203 Forest Avenue**, and the Prairie school work of Tallmadge and Watson. Note also the lovely windows at **1315 Forest Avenue**, built in 1907. Now subdivided, the block bounded by Burnham Place, Forest Avenue, Dempster Street and Lake Michigan was once the estate of renowned city planner and architect **Daniel Burnham** who moved there in 1887. The circuitous course of Sheridan Road (actually Burnham Place to Forest Avenue) undoubtedly reflects the influence of Burnham and his neighbors.

Continue north on Forest Ave., which merges with Sheridan Rd. To tour Northwestern University, park along Sheridan Rd. at Centennial Park just south of campus.

★ **Northwestern University** – *The academic campus extends east of Sheridan Rd. to Lake Michigan, between Lincoln St. and Clark St.* This prestigious Big Ten university originated as the dream of a group of devout Methodists in 1850, who selected a swampy parcel of land along Lake Michigan about 14mi from downtown Chicago as the place to plant their college. By 1855, with one building (since demolished) and 10 students, the school was already the nucleus of a growing town. Responsible for the platting of Evanston (named for Dr. John Evans, a founder of Northwestern), the university founders also set forth the temperate moral tone that would come to influence the sweep of the North Shore. The university's charter established the notorious "4mi limit" that prohibited the sale of alcohol within that radius of the campus. Architecturally, Northwestern never developed along a master plan and seems today a random collection of buildings that bridges two centuries. Past **Fisk Hall [A]** (1899, Daniel Burnham & Co.), which fronts on Sheridan Road and houses the renowned Medill School of Journalism, lies the Arts Circle, a cluster of buildings devoted to the fine and performing arts. The **Mary & Leigh Block Gallery [B]** *(1967 South Campus Dr.)* presents a wide-ranging schedule of fine arts exhibitions throughout the year *(open year-round Tue–Thu noon–5pm, Fri–Sun noon–8pm; closed major holidays and between exhibitions;* ⅆ 🅿 ☎847-491-4000*)*. An outdoor **sculpture garden★ [C]** surrounding the gallery includes works by Jean Arp, Jacques Lipchitz, Joan Miró and Henry Moore. For an extended walk providing fine views, take the path around the man-made lagoon behind the Arts Circle. This portion of campus was landfilled in the early 1960s. The tower of **Garrett-Evangelical Theological Seminary [D]** (not affiliated with the university) rises above the monochromatic assembly of lecture halls, laboratories and offices that form the core of the campus and date mostly to the early 1970s. At the heart of the old campus west of the Arts Circle stands its most venerable building, the Gothic-style **University Hall [E]** (1869, Gordon P. Randall), surrounded by lush greenery. **Annie May Swift Hall [F]** (1895, Charles Robert Ayars) contrasts with its warm red decorative brickwork and Arts and Crafts styling. The classically collegiate **Deering Library [G]** (1932, James Gamble Rogers) was augmented in 1971 with three connecting pavilions (Skidmore, Owings & Merrill).

From the corner of campus at Sheridan Road and Chicago Avenue, it is a short walk to **Rest Cottage** *(1730 Chicago Ave.)*, the home of Frances E. Willard, well-known educator, suffragist and national president of the Women's Christian Temperance Union from 1879 to her death in 1898. Run as a museum by the WCTU, the home is furnished with period pieces and Miss Willard's personal belongings. It was built in 1865, a lovely example of residential Gothic style *(visit by 1hr guided tour year-round Mon–Fri 10am–2:30pm; closed mid–late Dec; contribution requested; reservations suggested;* ☎847-864-1397*)*.

Continue north on Sheridan Rd. Turn left on Lincoln St. and left again on Orrington St. to reach the Kendall College campus.

Mitchell Indian Museum – *On Kendall College campus, at 2408 Orrington Ave. Open Sept–Jul Tue–Fri 9am–4:30pm, weekends 1–4pm; Aug by appointment only. Closed major & academic holidays. $1. Guided tours available.* 🅿 ☎847-866-1395. This small museum presents the history of Native American cultures and plays an active role as advocate for Chicago's modern Indian population. A permanent exhibit about the changing lives of Midwestern Indians is particularly nice for children, as are the "touch tables" in the main gallery 🄺🄸🄳🅂. Displays of beadwork, pottery, weaving, clothing, dolls, basketry, kachinas and other artifacts demonstrate the rich artfulness and practicality of Native American crafts. A second gallery is devoted to temporary exhibits of historic and contemporary Indian arts. The museum shares space with Kendall College's culinary school, where, on weekdays, a reasonably priced lunch can be had in the cafeteria-style dining room.

Return to Sheridan Rd. and continue north.

★ **Evanston Art Center** – *2603 Sheridan Rd. Open year-round Mon–Thu 10am–4pm & 7–10pm, Fri–Sat 10am–4pm, Sun 2–5pm. Closed major holidays. Contribution requested.* ▱ ☎*847-475-5300.* Beautifully situated at the edge of the lake, the art center occupies a one-time private home built in 1926 by Richard Powers and presents changing exhibitions of contemporary Midwestern artists. Outside, the naturalistic landscaping of Jens Jensen makes a lovely buffer between house and beach. Jensen, who designed several Chicago parks, was a leading proponent of Prairie school principles as they applied to landscape architecture. He advocated a return to natural prairie where possible and used native plants extensively. His influence pervades the parks of the North Shore. The beach has been restored as a small **dune ecosystem** to convey a sense of the primordial Lake Michigan shoreline.

Built in 1873, the adjacent **Grosse Point Light Station**★ *(2601 Sheridan Rd.)* comprises a 90ft tower, two structures (1880) to house steam-powered fog sirens (removed in 1922) and the lighthouse keeper's cottage. On summer weekends, visitors can climb 141 stairs to the top of the tower for a wonderful view. The lighthouse is a stunning reminder of the time when thousands of ships plied the hazardous waters of Lake Michigan. The collision of the paddle wheeler *Lady Elgin* with a lumber schooner off of Wilmette in 1860, resulting in the loss of nearly 300 lives, provided considerable impetus for a landmark at this location. The lighthouse structure was restored in 1980 and still serves as a beacon to mariners *(open Jun–Sept weekends 2–5pm; $2; 45min guided tours available; children under 5 not permitted;* ▱ ☎*847-328-6961).*

Continue north on Sheridan Rd.

WILMETTE   Population 27,116

Early developers envisioned Wilmette (so named for its first settler, fur trader Antoine Ouilmette) as a true railroad suburb and successfully lobbied for a train stop there by 1871. One year later, Wilmette's population swelled to 300 and the village became incorporated. In contrast to booming Evanston, however, Wilmette remained a sleepy rural community until well into the 1880s when suburban amenities—sewers, library, schools, telephone service and so on—began to take root. The question of consolidation with Evanston hindered Wilmette's independence until voters finally rejected the possibility in 1897.

★★ **Baha'i House of Worship** – *100 Linden Ave. Open May–Sept daily 10am–10pm. Rest of the year daily 10am–5pm. Guided tours available.* ♿ ▱ ☎*847-853-2300.* The lacy, opalescent dome of the Baha'i temple startles motorists on Sheridan Road passing from Evanston into Wilmette. The mammoth, 9-sided structure, rising 191ft to its pinnacle and set about with beautifully landscaped gardens, cuts an exotic profile against the low suburban skyline. This is the North American seat of the Baha'i faith, which maintains six other equally monumental houses of worship around the world. Its presence in the Chicago area dates to the religion's introduction here at the World's Columbian Exposition in 1893. Baha'is, who follow the teachings of the 19C Persian prophet Baha'u'llah, believe in the "oneness" of religion and of

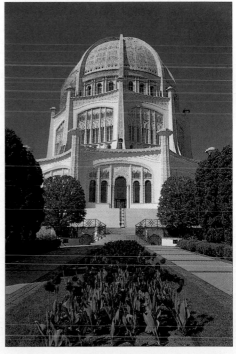

Baha'i House of Worship

David Frazier

humankind, and hopefully anticipate complete equality among people and the evolution of a global civilization. They draw inspiration from all of the world's great faiths and consider Buddha, Christ, Mohammed and the other major prophets to have been messengers from a single God.

Although the origins of the Baha'i faith are Persian, and the temple itself bears a distinctly Eastern look, in fact its design elements are eclectic and intended to represent unity in their blend. A close inspection of the intricate interlocking patterns that inscribe most surfaces of the building reveals the influence of the organic ornamentation of Louis Sullivan. Icons of the world's great religions decorate the outside columns. Other aspects of the temple carry symbolic significance for the Baha'i, such as the circular plan and the nine entryways, each surmounted by an inscription.

The temple is the work of French-Canadian architect Louis Bourgeois, who began its planning in 1909. Construction did not start until 1920, however, and proceeded slowly until completion in 1953, beset by funding and technical problems. The elaborate lacework on the dome posed the biggest challenge; crafted of quartz and white cement, the panels were shipped by rail from Washington, DC and hung on the temple's framework of steel.

The interior space, infused with natural light, soars elegantly to the apex of the dome where the invocation "O Thou the Glory of the Most Glorious" appears in Arabic calligraphy. The auditorium seats 1,191. An exhibit with a distinctly missionary tone in the Visitor Center on the lower level explains the faith through the sayings of Baha'u'llah and other Baha'i writings.

Continue north on Sheridan Rd.

Just around the bend from the temple is the 59-acre lakefront **Gillson Park**, a nice spot for a picnic lunch. Farther along, **Plaza del Lago** shopping center offers several restaurants as well as a trendy food shop and bistro (Convito Italiano) where fixings for a gourmet picnic can be purchased or a sit-down lunch can be enjoyed. The center itself is of some historic interest. Built in 1928, the stores and apartments along the north side of the plaza comprised one of the nation's first shopping centers. Located in a "no-man's-land" outside of Wilmette proper, the complex included a speakeasy known as Miralago, a popular destination among Chicago's Prohibition-era drinking crowd. When the notorious roadhouse caught fire in 1932, adjacent villages refused to send fire fighters and cut off the water supply, ensuring its destruction. Wilmette annexed the area in 1942, and the shopping center filled with hot-dog and ice-cream stands befitting its lakefront location. In 1968, after high-rise apartment buildings blocked the beach, Plaza del Lago opened in its present form. Its bell tower is original to the 1920s.

KENILWORTH Population 2,432

Incorporated in 1896, the town of Kenilworth, named after Sir Walter Scott's romantic novel, is the youngest North Shore community. Inspired by the English countryside, businessman Joseph Sears envisioned a genteel village that would attract a certain caliber of residents. In 1889, he purchased the land and developed the amenities that would entice property buyers, platting the village with such care as to insure that its houses would enjoy so many hours of daily sunlight. He spared nothing on public works and even laid the first stretch of macadam road on the North Shore.

Contemporary of Frank Lloyd Wright, renowned Midwestern architect **George W. Maher** designed more than 40 buildings in the community, his work chronicling the transition in architectural styles from late Victorian to Prairie. Today, Kenilworth retains an air of exclusivity.

Just north of the southern gates of Kenilworth lies **Mahoney Farm**, which straddles Sheridan Road. This land was deeded to Kenilworth for use as a park, and in 1933 the village asked Jens Jensen to design a sanctuary for birds and flowers there. In addition to native plantings, Jensen included seven **"council rings"**—stone seating areas meant for quiet contemplation that grace many of his landscapes. The park was restored and added to the National Register in 1985. *To visit this sanctuary, park at Plaza del Lago (above) and walk north.*

East of the intersection of Sheridan Road and Kenilworth Avenue, note the two adjacent houses closest to the lake. Both built in the early 1890s, they typify the elegance that characterized the village's early homes.

Continue north on Sheridan Rd.

WINNETKA Population 12,493

Although it grew slowly, Winnetka (from an Indian word for "beautiful land") developed a political and cultural milieu apart from its neighbors, largely due to the influence of Henry Demarest Lloyd who made his home there in 1878. Lloyd, essayist and social reformer with a strong belief in direct democracy, viewed family and community as the linchpins of society and eschewed the power of corporations and monopolies. As a leading citizen of Winnetka, he succeeded in applying his theories of government on a practical level, striving to involve the people in municipal decision making. Around Lloyd grew something of a cultural and political salon; he often entertained the likes of Jane Addams *(p 150)* and Eugene Debs *(p 188)*.

At 140 Sheridan Road, the **Felix Lowy House** (1925, Mayo & Mayo) is a fine example of the Tudor style popular in the 1920s. The lakefront home at **no. 645** was built in 1902, and the grounds and lovely cemetery at **Christ Church** (*784 Sheridan Rd.*) date to 1876. At no. 830 stands Henry Lloyd's home, **The Wayside**, some parts of which date to the 1850s. It was listed on the National Register in 1966. At no. 915, the twin gatehouses of **Edgecliffe**, designed in 1930 by Samuel Marx for businessman Max Epstein, signal the elegant formality of the mansion beyond.

Continue north on Sheridan Rd.

GLENCOE Population 8,720

After a poorly planned scheme to develop Glencoe fell apart in the 1870s, the village lagged behind its growing neighbors. Its lovely ravines and woods continued to attract excursionists and picnickers and the village gradually blossomed. Poet Archibald MacLeish was born here in 1892.

At 1185 Sheridan Road stands **North Shore Congregation Israel**. The curvilinear, organic lines of the temple to the north (1963, Minoru Yamasaki) contrast sharply with the geometric post-Modern cylinder of the smaller sanctuary created by Hammond, Beeby & Babka in 1983.

Continue north on Sheridan Rd. until it turns westward as Lake-Cook Rd. (a half-mile west, Sheridan Rd. continues north). Follow Lake-Cook Rd. straight ahead for 1mi to reach the Chicago Botanic Garden.

★ **Chicago Botanic Garden** – *1000 Lake-Cook Rd. Open year-round daily 8am–sunset. Closed Dec 25. $4/car.* ✗ ♿ 🅿 ☎ *847-835-5440*. This 385-acre preserve makes a lovely stop at any time of year. With 20 garden areas, over a million individual plants of 7,000 different varieties and a plethora of bird life, the site attracts half a million people annually. Established in 1965 under the auspices of the venerable Chicago Horticultural Society, the Garden considers itself a "Noah's Ark for

Japanese Garden, Chicago Botanic Garden

plants" devoted to collection, education, research and plant testing and conservation. Begin at the **Gateway Center** for a film orientation. The **tram tour**, which provides a general overview of the grounds, is a good way to see the far-flung 11-acre **prairie**. The excursion might also yield a glimpse of the rare trumpeter swans that have recently made their home among the hundreds of resident Canada geese (*departs from Gateway Center Apr–Oct Mon–Fri 10am–3:30pm, weekends 10:30am–4:30pm; rest of the year Mon–Fri by appt only, weekends 11am–2pm; round-trip 30-45min; commentary; reservations recommended Apr–Oct weekends; $3.50; &.*).

Changing exhibits in the **Education Center** explore botanical topics, while greenhouses feature exotics, succulents and topiary. The heart of the Garden occupies the largest of nine islands in the 60-acre man-made lagoon, and each garden setting rivals the next. In the formal **Rose Garden★**, 5,000 plants include 100 varieties of the fragrant blossoms; the **English Walled Garden★** encompasses a charming collection of six "rooms" representing various English gardening styles. The tactile and fragrant plantings of the **Sensory Garden** encourage visitors to use every sense to enjoy them. Across the lagoon, note the **Carillon**, whose 48 bells chime on the hour and play evening concerts in the summer. The **Regenstein Fruit and Vegetable Garden** demonstrates the variety of ways local gardeners can succeed in small balcony planters or extensive backyard plots. The **Japanese Garden★**, *Sansho-En* ("The Garden of Three Islands"), offers a peaceful and contemplative refuge. A bridge connects two of the islands; the third is to be observed from afar. In Japanese style, shape and form create serene spaces, a concept that works beautifully in the quiet "dry garden" of sand, rocks and carefully placed vegetation.

Return to Sheridan Rd. and continue north to Highland Park. Follow the signs carefully as the route takes some unexpected turns.

HIGHLAND PARK   Population 30,468

One of the larger North Shore communities, Highland Park was incorporated in 1869 and grew through several annexations, including that of Ravinia in 1899. The Highland Park Building Company shaped its early development, selling lots and building homes from pattern books. The natural beauty of the ravines and the extensive hardwood forests of the area attracted year-round and summer residents alike, and made the perfect setting for the work of Jens Jensen (who lived in Ravinia) and other naturalistic landscape architects.

Highlighting this town is 36-acre Ravinia Park, home to the world-renowned **Ravinia Music Festival** (*p 220*). Originally intended as an amusement park to attract riders to the adjacent interurban railroad, the grounds were converted in 1911 to a venue for opera and symphony performances. Wildly successful over the years, Ravinia has hosted Arthur Rubinstein, George Gershwin, Ella Fitzgerald, Placido Domingo and hundreds of other internationally acclaimed performers. The summer home of the Chicago Symphony Orchestra since 1936, Ravinia today also offers everything from jazz, popular and chamber music to folk, dance and children's programs. The complex includes restaurants, covered seating in the Pavilion, and two indoor theaters. Most fun, however, is to enjoy performances with a picnic dinner on the expansive lawn.

At 1445 Sheridan Road stands Frank Lloyd Wright's masterpiece, the **Ward W. Willits House★**, familiar to students of architecture as an archetype of the Prairie school. This 1902 commission—six years before Wright's ROBIE HOUSE—gave the architect his first full-blown opportunity to apply his theories of "organic simplicity." The house exhibits beautifully the hallmarks of Prairie school design: strong horizontal lines, a symbiosis with its natural surroundings and the influence of Japanese domestic architecture. Beyond the Willits House, circuitous Sheridan Road passes through Highland Park's business district as St. John's Avenue. Note the stately **City Hall** (*1707 St. John's Ave.*), built in 1930, and the adjacent **Stupey Cabin**, which dates from 1847, the oldest building in town. Moved to this site in 1969, it has been restored and furnished to 1850.

Continue north on Sheridan Rd. Follow signs as the itinerary makes a short detour on Central Ave. and then Oak St. before returning to Sheridan Rd.

Fort Sheridan was established in 1887 following the Haymarket Riot and deactivated in 1993, a victim of cuts in defense spending. The military base is unusual in that most of it was designed by the private architectural firm of Holabird and Roche. The 167ft stone water tower (1890) can be seen in the distance.

Continue north on Sheridan Rd. through Highwood to Lake Forest.

★LAKE FOREST   Population 18,477

Lake Forest has long cultivated a reputation as Chicago's most elite suburb, though its creation was inspired by a group of Presbyterians who chose that locale to build a college in the 1850s. They hired a St. Louis landscape architect named Hotchkiss to lay out the town in 1857, and he designed picturesque streets to curve along the natural contours of the ravines and hills and wind through the verdurous forest with calculated leisure. The spacious lots offered privacy for the most gracious homes. Lake Forest's high society grew more so as wealthy summer visitors took up residence year-round, bringing with them the entertainments and trappings of Chicago's aristocracy. F. Scott Fitzgerald later equated Lake Forest with Newport and South Hampton, and that sense lingers today.

As Sheridan Road passes into Lake Forest, note **Barat College**, founded in 1858. The middle campus of **Lake Forest College**, established by Presbyterians as Lind University in 1857, occupies the intersection of Sheridan and College Roads. Its buildings date to several eras. Immediately on the right, the handsome **Reid Memorial Library** (1899, Frost & Granger) blends Gothic, Norman and English-abbey elements into a suitably collegiate whole. Farther ahead, one of the earlier buildings, **Young Hall** (1878), comprises three stories of yellow brick topped with a mansard roof. Hidden in the trees to the east, stout **Hotchkiss Hall** (once the Gymnasium) is worthy of note for its solid Romanesque lines and massive red-stone construction. It was designed by Henry Ives Cobb in 1890.

On a small rise immediately across from the campus sits **The Homestead** (*570 N. Sheridan Rd.*) built in 1860 for Devillo R. Holt, a Chicago lumberman and a founder of Lake Forest. The house's exterior remains unaltered today and features lovely Italianate details. Its construction is of brick sheathed in clapboard.

Continue north on Sheridan Rd. to Deerpath Rd.

The massive Shingle-style **First Presbyterian Church** (1887, Charles Frost) at the corner of Sheridan and Deerpath Roads is a testament to the Presbyterians who founded Lake Forest. Unusual on the North Shore, this Shingle church, though elegant, exudes the summer-resort ambience that once characterized the town. Across the street, on the north campus of Lake Forest College, note the **Durand Art Institute** (1891), another of Henry Ives Cobb's Richardsonian Romanesque edifices. A frieze above the main entryway spells out the building's name in elaborate foliate ornament.

Turn left on Deerpath Rd.

Just west of the train tracks at 700 N. Western Avenue, **Market Square★** has defined the character of downtown Lake Forest since 1916. Designed by Howard Van Doren Shaw to resemble an English town market, the square includes elements derived from several European traditions. Among America's earliest planned suburban shopping centers, Market Square today houses boutiques and restaurants but has changed little in appearance over the years.

Return to Chicago by proceeding west on Deerpath Rd. to Rte. 41 South, which merges with the Edens Expwy. (I-94). Head south on I-94 toward Chicago.

Prairie Flowers

MORTON ARBORETUM★

Sprawling over 1,700 acres bisected by Route 53, this preserve is both a serious scientific laboratory of woody plants from around the world and a very pleasant place to spend the day. Visitors who wander by car and on foot among 35,000 individual plants and 3,000 species may not realize the contributions to horticulture, botany and ecology that this arboreal microcosm makes possible. Open year-round, the arboretum attracts professional landscapers and gardeners, horticultural hobbyists, bird-watchers and inexhaustible hikers.

Historical Notes – Joy Morton, founder of the arboretum in 1922, came by his love of trees naturally. His father, J. Sterling, had been Secretary of Agriculture under Grover Cleveland and is well remembered as the instigator of Arbor Day. Joy, his fortune made at the helm of the Morton Salt Company, established the arboretum on 400 acres at Thornhill, his DuPage County estate, and proceeded to carry out the family motto to "Plant Trees." From the beginning, Morton intended the arboretum as a place to preserve and study trees suitable for growing in Illinois' temperate climate—a veritable "museum of woody plants."

Today, the arboretum's far-flung collection is divided into four general categories: botanical groups (plants in the same genus or family, such as the *Quercus*, or oaks), landscape groups (plants with a similar use, such as the ground-cover garden), geographic groups (plants from the same region, such as the Japanese collection) and special habitat groups (plants that live in "amended" soil or in special sites, such as those in the sand beds). The grounds also support native landscapes—oak groves, wetlands and prairie. Particularly strong among the arboretum's collections are its Rosaceae (rose family), its elms and its sugar maples (especially beautiful in the fall).

Visiting Morton Arboretum

Access – The arboretum is located on Rte. 53, 25mi west of the city, just north of I-88 and west of I-355. From the Loop, take I-290 West and then continue west on the I-88 tollway. At Rte. 53, turn north toward the arboretum.

Hours & Fees – The arboretum is open Apr–Oct daily 7am–7pm. Rest of the year daily 7am–5pm. $6/car ($3/car on Wed). ♿ ☎630-719-2400.

Tours – Open-air bus tours depart from the visitor center: May Mon–Fri noon–1:15pm, weekends 10:45am–2:30pm. Jun–Sept Wed & weekends noon–1:15pm. Oct Mon–Fri noon–1:15pm, weekends 10:45am–2:30pm. Round-trip 1hr. $2. ♿. Other specialized tours available, contact Visitor Center for details, ☎630-719-2467.

Amenities – Food services available at the Coffee Shop daily 9am–5pm and the Ginkgo Restaurant daily 11am–3pm, both located in the visitor center. Public restrooms and telephones located in visitor center and across from the Thornhill Education Center by parking lot 19.

VISIT

Begin at the **visitor center** on the East Side to gather information about the grounds, pick up trail maps and find out what is in bloom. Several gardens can be reached on foot from here including ground covers, roses, dwarf shrubs and the sand beds. The elegant **hedge garden★** displays formal rows of woody plants extending into a stately pinetum, or plantation of pine trees. The four columns at its east end represent Joy Morton and his three brothers, Carl, Paul and Mark. It is an easy stroll from here around Meadow Lake, one of several man-made lakes on the grounds, along the first loop of the **Illinois trees trail★**. Interpretive labeling identifies local trees along this paved path. For more hiking, follow the second and third loops past the azaleas and rhododendrons and deeper into the forest to view wildflowers, woodlands, meadows and marshes.

To see the rest of the arboretum, take the hour-long narrated open **tram tour★**, an excellent nonstop excursion that follows the main route from the east to the west side and affords a complete overview of the grounds. Visitors can also drive the 12mi one-way route in their car *(a driving map is provided at the entry gate)*. Twenty-six parking areas along the way make it possible to stop and hike any of the 10 major trails or explore the ancillary tracks and paths. In all, 25mi of trails wind through the grounds and visitors have virtually unlimited access to the woods, glades and meadows (*a compass is recommended on the lesser paths as there is little signage*). A particularly interesting walk winds through the **geographic collections★** of specimens from Asia, the Balkans, Appalachia and the eastern US wetlands. Located on the west side, the **Thornhill Education Center** is the site of the original Morton estate. An exhibit in the Founder's Room, the only remaining wing of the home, provides a brief history of the arboretum and the family. Outside, in the lovely **fragrance garden★**, the aromas of peonies, mock oranges and mint combine enticingly. The nearby daffodil glade planted with 130,000 bulbs makes an incredible springtime sight.

On the far perimeter of the west side, at parking lot 25, a narrow trail makes a circuit through a reconstructed **prairie landscape★**, which blooms beautifully during the summer. The prairies of Illinois have been largely eliminated since the settlement of the area, and restorations such as this one are important keys to understanding the native ecology of the Midwest. Over 90 varieties of grasses and plants blanket the prairie's 100 acres.

The arboretum is a haven for at least 20 varieties of mammals including racoons, red foxes and coyotes. Birds abound as well, and 70 nesting boxes provide homes for eastern bluebirds.

BROOKFIELD ZOO★★

Time: 1/2 day
Map p 206

Covering 216 acres in west suburban Chicago, this expansive zoo in a garden is home to 2,900 animals inhabiting carefully re-created rain forests, seascapes, savannas and deserts both indoors and out. For its human denizens, 15mi of footpaths wind through the lovely grounds, and shady stretches of lawn invite picnicking. Formal flower beds complement the patchwork of animal habitats. Nearly 2 million people each year enjoy this animal haven, leaving with a heightened respect for our fragile environment.

Historical Notes – Brookfield Zoo's meticulous attention to habitat continues a long tradition of cageless homes for its animals. The idea behind Brookfield was to create a zoo big enough to accommodate natural outdoor habitats, thereby eliminating the use of small, spartan enclosures, and emulating conditions in the wild to provide more realistic study and breeding opportunities. Such was the trend in European zoos, and the Bronx Zoo in New York had incorporated naturalistic settings into its plan when it debuted in 1899. Built on land donated to the Forest Preserve District of Cook County by Edith Rockefeller McCormick in 1919, Brookfield, modeled largely after the Hagenbeck Zoo in Hamburg, Germany, would finally open in 1934 after years of controversy over taxes and public funding. The "barless" Bear Grottos, Goat Mountain and Monkey Island were among the first habitats completed, along with the Small Mammal House, the Reptile House and the Pachyderm House. In the last several decades, the trend toward cageless habitats has moved indoors with the construction of Tropic World: A Primate's Journey (among the world's largest zoo exhibits) and Fragile Kingdom.

Visiting Brookfield Zoo

Access – The zoo is located 14mi from the Loop at 8400 W. 31st St., in Brookfield. From the Loop, drive west on I-290 to the 1st Ave. Exit, then continue south on 1st Ave. to 31st St. Follow signs to the zoo. The Burlington Northern Metra Train line runs from Union Station in the Loop. Get off at the zoo stop at Hollywood Station, and walk north for four blocks.

Hours and fees – The zoo is open Memorial Day–Labor Day daily 9:30am–5:30pm. Rest of the year daily 10am–4:30pm. $4.50; Apr–Sept Tue & Thu $2.50, Oct–Mar Tue & Thu free (some activities in the zoo have additional fees). ✗ ⅙ ▣ ($4) ☎ 708-485-0263. Check at entrances or information kiosks located throughout the park for schedule of special shows and demonstrations.

Amenities – Restaurants offering varied cuisine are located primarily in the eastern and southwestern sections of the park. Restrooms can be found near dining facilities. Public telephones are available at the Discovery Center and both zoo entrances.

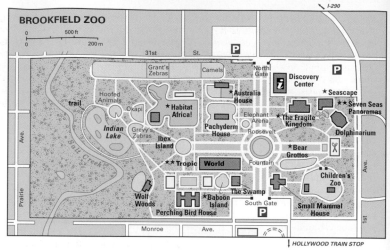

VISIT

Begin your visit at the **Discovery Center** on the north side of the zoo for a 12min orientation film and information about the day's activities, talks and demonstrations. Departing just west of the gates, the **Motor Safari** tour offers a narrated overview of the zoo. The tram can also be used to shuttle to the various areas of interest as passengers can disembark and re-board at any of four tram stops throughout the day *(operates, weather permitting, Apr–Oct daily; round-trip 45min; commentary; $2)*. During the winter months, ride the Snowball Express for free.

Wet and Wild – The park fans out from Roosevelt Fountain, the formally landscaped heart of the grounds approached from four directions by grassy esplanades and pathways. To the northeast, **The Fragile Kingdom★**, a large 3-part exhibit opened in 1990, explores the complex webs of life and survival in an African desert and an Asian rain forest. In these naturalistic habitats, species commingle as they would in the wild, and the experience envelops the visitor as each setting extends to the public areas of the space. Linger a moment to spot and identify each creature: a flash of orange gives the rain forest's Prevost's squirrels away, but the camouflage of the elegant clouded leopard makes finding him more of a challenge. Also in the rain forest, watch for the web-footed Southeast Asian fishing cat catching minnows as it would in the wild. The Fragile Desert tells a story of survival in a seemingly inhospitable climate and how such animals as meerkats

Dolphin Show

make a home there. Tiny windows reveal a subterranean world of burrowing creatures, including the fascinating naked mole-rats, hairless mammals that live in colonies like bees and feed on underground plant parts. Outside, the big cats are displayed as part of the Fragile Kingdom in the context of their increasingly difficult struggle to survive as hunters in their vanishing ecosystems.

Seven Seas Panoramas★★, likely the most popular attraction at the zoo, consists of two parts. The **Seascape**★ features a series of outdoor pools designed to resemble the Pacific Northwest shoreline environment of the pinnipeds—walruses, seals and sea lions—that this exhibit houses. An underwater viewing area beneath the pool allows visitors to enjoy the animals at their most graceful. Next door, the **Dolphin Show**★ **Kids** *(several 20min performances daily; $2)* has been a perpetual favorite since its inception in 1961 as the first inland dolphin exhibition. Spectators generally jam the 2,000-seat **Dolphinarium** at several shows each day to view the antics of Atlantic bottle-nosed dolphins. The zoo uses the performance to reinforce its conservation message, and trainers are careful to explain the significance of dolphin behaviors in the wild. Natural dolphin feeding strategies, for instance, include smashing prey with its heavy tail,

■ The zoo's animal collection started with the gift of 143 mammals, 123 birds and 4 reptiles from a private zoo in Holland, Michigan. In the ensuing years, Brookfield has had its share of famous inhabitants, including the first giant pandas in an American zoo, Su-lin (arrived in 1937), Mei-mei (1938) and Mei-lan (1939). Museka, the first okapi in America, arrived in 1955. Temperamental Asian bull elephant Ziggy (named for his original owner Florenz Ziegfield) lived to a ripe old age of 55, and the popular Olga died in 1988 at 27, the oldest walrus in captivity.

known to scientists as "fish-whacking." To demonstrate, trainers cue dolphins and audience to volley beach balls back and forth, the animals' powerful tails often catapulting the balls high into the stands. Trainers elicit vocalizations (which dolphins make through their blowholes), demonstrate the animals' tendency to mimic, and even swim with them in an aquatic pas de deux.

Please Touch – The large **Children's Zoo** **Kids** takes up most of the quadrant southeast of the fountain. This is a busy place that provides ample opportunities for kids to interact with barnyard and other gentle animals *(opens at 10am year-round; $1, free Nov–Apr)*. The beguiling Nubian and pygmy goats are particularly popular, along with the llamas and reindeer. Demonstrations of "Animals in Action," cow and goat milking, and other activities take place daily, weather permitting.

Monkey Business – Primates and birds dominate southwest of the fountain. The exhibit **The Swamp: Wonders of our Wetlands** (in the former Primate House) offers insight into a North American cypress swamp populated by alligators, snakes and a variety of birds, as well as an Illinois wetland alive with otters, fish and alligator snapping turtles. **Baboon Island**★ (the zoo's original Monkey Island, refurbished) houses a large colony of rambunctious Guinea baboons whose interactions are fascinating to watch.

Opened in the 1980s, the ground-breaking **Tropic World: A Primate's Journey**★★ comprises three indoor rain-forest habitats: Asia, Africa and South America. One of the first exhibits to group compatible species together as they might live in nature, Tropic World offers visitors a dramatic treetop perspective on life in these tropical realms. Realistic trees, foliage, waterfalls, rockwork and pools combine in a breathtaking and cavernous environment bustling with activity. The exhibit guides visitors through all three regions explaining the daily lives of primates and what choices they must make to survive. Most intriguing of all are the animals themselves, from the tiny Brazilian golden lion tamarin to the lordly western lowland gorillas that reside on their own island in Tropic World-Africa. *Visit Tropic World early in the day to avoid the long lines.*

Of Kangaroos and Klipspringers – The greatest expanse of zoo lies to the north and west of Tropic World. **Ibex Island**, a prominent landmark due west of the fountain, is the artificial mountain home of a herd of surefooted ibex, where Tubbs, the eldest male, sports the curliest horns and claims the summit as his own. In **Australia House**★, audio stations guide visitors through a nocturnal "walkabout" past wombats and into a space alive with free-flying fruit bats. In spite of the strong odor, the proximity of the bats makes this a compelling experience. Kookaburras, echidnas (with the platypus, the only mammal that lays eggs), kangaroos, cassowaries and ostriches can be found outdoors.

Phase one of an ambitious undertaking that will transform 30 acres of the zoo's northwest section into various African immersion exhibits, the 5-acre **Habitat Africa!**★ comprises a multipart exhibit of life around that continent. Giraffes, wild dogs and other inhabitants of the African savanna populate the dusty plain, while a variety of hoofed animals slack their thirst at the **water hole**. A reconstructed **kopje** (KAH-pee), a kind of grassland oasis surrounded by granite outcroppings, shelters a complex ecosystem that includes the delicate klipspringer (a tiny rock-climbing antelope) and the rock hyrax, a small mammal that judges the width of its rockbound hideaways with its whiskers.

At the western edge of the zoo lies man-made **Indian Lake**, surrounded by a restored wild area teeming with local plant, bird and animal life. A cedar-chip **trail** (.25mi) circles the far side of the lake and to walk it provides a restful break from the zoo crowds. Guideposts along the way identify resident wildlife.

A Random Bestiary – Other favorite sights around the zoo include **Wolf Woods**, home to a pack of gray wolves, and the **Bear Grottos**★, where polar, brown, sloth and spectacled bears cavort. Chinchillas, lemurs and other nocturnal creatures in the **Small Mammal House** go about their nightly business under special lights that induce them to remain awake during the daytime. The Art Deco **Pachyderm House** and outdoor enclosures are home to black rhinos, Nile hippopotamuses and African elephants. In the **Perching Bird House**, iridescent avian gems reside behind "jewel-box" window enclosures, and Cookie, a Mitchell's cockatoo, lays claim to the longest zoo residence: this pink Australian has lived at Brookfield since 1934.

ILLINOIS & MICHIGAN CANAL NATIONAL HERITAGE CORRIDOR★

Time: 1 day (Northern Section)
Maps p 209 and pp 210-211

The Illinois & Michigan (I&M) Canal, running 96mi from BRIDGEPORT to LaSalle/Peru, first linked the Great Lakes to the Mississippi and helped Chicago build its reputation as an industrial powerhouse. Today a popular recreational area hosting over five million visitors yearly, the National Heritage Corridor encompasses historic canal towns offering a glimpse into bygone days, as well as native prairies and state parks laced with miles of pleasant hiking and biking trails.

Historical Notes

Between 20,000 and 10,000 years ago, meltwaters from retreating glaciers (p 8) carved a wide valley southwest of Chicago to the Mississippi River. As the glacial lake drained, a low, 12ft-high ridge rose slowly between the Des Plaines and Chicago Rivers, separating the watershed of the Mississippi from the Great Lakes. Native Americans traveled by canoe through this corridor, and guided the first Europeans, explorer Louis Jolliet and missionary Jacques Marquette, to the Chicago Portage between the two rivers in 1673. As the French continued to explore Illinois and establish a lucrative fur trade, they realized that a canal through this low divide would open the continent to commerce.

After the area became part of the US in 1782, a canal was proposed and by the 1820s, a federal commission was established to create the channel connecting Lake Michigan to the Illinois River. Along with the Erie Canal, the I&M Canal would provide an inland link from New York to New Orleans. The towns of Chicago and OTTAWA were platted in 1830, and canal construction began at Bridgeport on July 4, 1836. Despite a three-year hiatus caused by Illinois' unstable financial condition, the canal was completed in 1848. Chicago's population boomed from 4,000 to over 20,000 during construction, and other canal towns blossomed as well. As the narrow, 60ft-wide channel brought grains and livestock from Illinois' rich prairie soils to eastern markets, Chicago more than quadrupled its population to over 112,000 by 1860. Stone quarrying, steel production, and coal, zinc and sand mining thrived throughout the corridor in the 19C.

Horses towed passenger boats and mules pulled boats laden with lumber, stone and grains. Although railroads made their appearance in the corridor by 1854, the canal continued to carry freight, reaching its apogee in 1882 when steam-powered boats had replaced the mule teams. Unlike most canals, the I&M paid off its debt by 1871, and was deepened that year from 6 to 8ft in an attempt to reverse the flow of the Chicago River *(p 9)*. The effort was not entirely successful, and after cholera and typhoid epidemics decimated the city in the 1880s, Chicago created a Metropolitan Sanitary District to dig a much larger drainage canal from Chicago to Lockport; completed in 1900, it permanently reversed the Chicago River. By 1914, the northern section of the I&M Canal was replaced as a shipping channel by the new Sanitary & Ship Canal.

In 1933, the Illinois River was made navigable, and the obsolete I&M began to be developed for recreational use. In the 1950s, the section of the canal in Chicago was filled in for construction of the Stevenson Expressway (I-55). In 1963, the I&M Canal was designated a National Historic Landmark, and nine years later, the southern section became a state park. Efforts to develop the canal's recreational and historic potential culminated in the designation by Congress of the entire canal route (120mi) as a National Heritage Corridor in 1984. Today, numerous historic buildings have been preserved and new trails and wayside exhibits promote the region's historic, recreational and economic resources.

Visiting the I&M Canal

Access – Northern section driving tour: follow itinerary directions *(p 211)*. Southern section: drive south on I-55 for 46mi to Rte. 6 West for Channahon; for other sights in southern section, drive south on I-55 and then west on I-80, exiting at Rte. 47 for Morris, Rte. 23 for Ottawa, Rte. 178 for Utica and Starved Rock State Park, and Rte. 351 for LaSalle.

Visitor Information – The I&M Canal is best visited on summer weekends when most activities occur. The route can be difficult to follow as signs bearing the canal logo *(map below)* are sometimes hard to locate. The following agencies provide maps and information about accommodations and recreation: **Illinois & Michigan Canal Heritage Corridor Commission**, 15701 S. Independence Blvd., Lockport IL 60441 ☎815-740-2047 (contact for location and hours of visitor centers along the Canal); **Heritage Corridor Visitors Bureau**, 81 N. Chicago St., Joliet IL 60431 ☎815-467-4271 or 800-926-2262 (US & Canada only); the **Forest Preserve District of Cook County**, 536 N. Harlem Ave., River Forest IL 60305 ☎708-261-8400.

Tours – National Heritage Corridor Cruises of the northernmost section of the I&M Canal are conducted September weekends *(depart from Mercury dock at Michigan Ave. & Wacker Dr., map p 221, at 9am; round-trip 7hrs; $45; commentary; reservations required; Mercury ☎312-332-1366)*.

Recreation – Hiking: I&M Canal State Trail (61mi) from Channahon to Peru; other trails found in state parks and forest preserves along the Canal. **Cross-country skiing** permitted on most hiking trails. **Canoe trails**: Des Plaines River from Lyons to Lockport (23mi); I&M Canal from Channahon to Morris (15mi).

Dining & Accommodations – Hotels and restaurants can be found in the major commercial areas of Joliet, Morris, Ottawa and LaSalle. **Campsites** at Starved Rock, Illini and Channahon State Parks and designated sites along the I&M Canal State Trail.

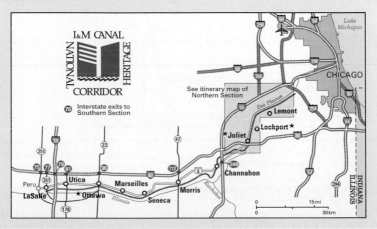

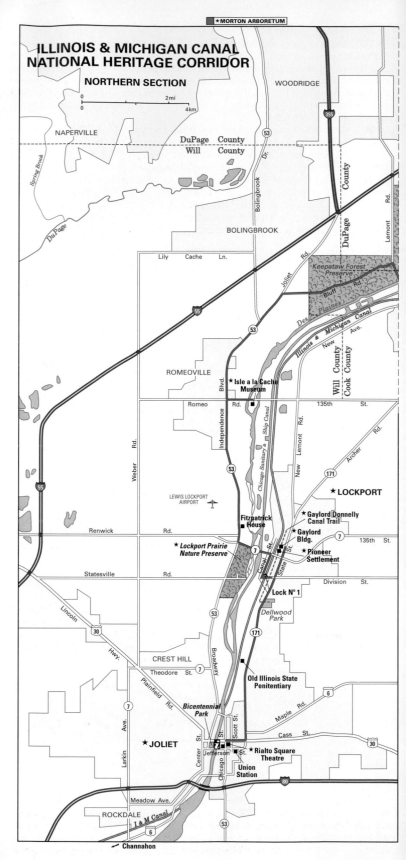

★ MORTON ARBORETUM

ILLINOIS & MICHIGAN CANAL
NATIONAL HERITAGE CORRIDOR

NORTHERN SECTION

0   2mi
0   4km

WOODRIDGE

355

NAPERVILLE

53

Spring Brook

DuPage County
Will County

DuPage

Bolingbrook Dr.

BOLINGBROOK

Lily Cache Ln.

Des Plaines

Joliet Rd.

Keepataw Forest Preserve

Bluff Rd.

Illinois & Michigan Canal

New Ave.

Will County
Cook County

Lemont Rd.

55

53

ROMEOVILLE

★ Isle a la Cache Museum

Romeo Rd.

Independence Blvd.

Chicago Sanitary & Ship Canal

135th St.

New Lemont Rd.

Archer Rd.

Weber Rd.

53

LEWIS LOCKPORT AIRPORT

171

★ LOCKPORT

Renwick Rd.

■ Fitzpatrick House

★ Gaylord Donnelly Canal Trail

★ Lockport Prairie Nature Preserve

7

Canal St.

State St.

★ Gaylord Bldg.

★ Pioneer Settlement

7

135th St.

Statesville Rd.

Division St.

■ Lock N° 1

Dellwood Park

53

171

Lincoln Hwy.

30

CREST HILL

Theodore St.

7

Broadway

■ Old Illinois State Penitentiary

6

Plainfield Rd.

Maple Rd.

Bicentennial Park

Larkin Ave.

Cass St.

30

★ JOLIET

Center St.

Chicago St.

Scott St.

Jefferson St.

★ Rialto Square Theatre

Union Station

80

Meadow Ave.

ROCKDALE

I & M Canal

6

53

← Channahon

210

NORTHERN SECTION DRIVING TOUR – Chicago to Joliet
distance: about 90mi round-trip

The highly industrialized northern section of the canal borders Chicago and includes several evocative historic sites as well as recreational and natural areas. Note that several sections of the drive are highly commercialized or wind through ordinary suburban landscapes, offering few vistas of the canal. However, quaint canal towns and various museums make this a worthwhile day trip from Chicago. Follow the map and the directions carefully, as this stretch is sometimes difficult to navigate.

> *Leave Chicago on I-55 (Stevenson Expwy.) and take the LaGrange Rd./Rte. 45 exit (279A); bear right and follow the signs to Rte. 171 (Archer Ave.) south.*

Archer Avenue, built in 1836 as a construction route for the canal, leads through the suburb of Willow Springs, where a 9mi-loop bicycle trail follows the canal towpath, and into the 14,000-acre Palos Forest Preserves. After about 5mi, to the left before Route 83, stands the historic **St. James at Sag Bridge★** (1833), the oldest church and cemetery complex in Cook County. The simple local limestone church sits on a hill surrounded by graves dating back to 1846, containing the remains of hundreds of canal workers, including a large number of Irish immigrants.

> *Continue on Rte. 171 as it turns left at Rte. 83.*

The road crosses the Calumet-Sag Channel, built in 1911 to link the Sanitary & Ship Canal with Chicago's southern port at Lake Calumet.

> *Keep right to follow Rte. 171; turn right after about 3mi at McCarthy Rd., which becomes Stephen St., and drive into Lemont.*

Lemont – Pop 8,439. Known in the 19C for its dolomite-limestone quarries, Lemont is a well-preserved historic canal town set on a bluff in the Des Plaines River valley. The **Lemont Area Historical Society Museum** *(306 Lemont St.)*, located in an 1861 limestone church, offers exhibits and research facilities; pick up a self-guided brochure to the downtown area here *(open May–Sept Tue–Fri 10am–2pm, weekends 1–4pm; rest of the year Thu–Fri 10am–2pm, weekends 1–4pm; closed major* *holidays; $1; 45min guided tour available;* ☎708-257-2972). The downtown shopping area *(on Main and Stephen Sts.)* is dominated by 19C Italianate buildings constructed of Lemont stone, including the 1870 Norton Building *(101 Stephens St.),* today home to the Strand Antique Emporium, and the highly ornate 1870s Friedley Building *(311 Canal St.).* A 3mi canal trail begins at General Fry Landing, located on Stephens Street west of the canal.

From downtown, backtrack on Stephen St. to Illinois St. and turn right. Continue to State St. and turn right, following State St. over the bridge west of town. Turn left at Bluff Rd. on the other side of the valley and continue for 3mi. At Joliet Rd. (Rte. 53), turn left and continue south 3mi to Romeo Rd. (135th St.). Turn left and drive .5mi.

★ **Isle a la Cache Museum** – *501 E. Romeo Rd. Open year-round Tue–Sun 10am–4pm. Closed Jan 1, Dec 25. Guided tours available.* ⚐ ▣ ☎815-727-8700. This small island in the Des Plaines River was named by the French *coureurs de bois* who used the 80-acre haven to hide their trade goods. The museum presents historical exhibits highlighting daily life during the French-Indian fur-trade era, including a reconstructed wigwam. Occasionally, interpreters in Native American and 18C French costume demonstrate how to build a fire, portage a canoe and fire a musket. The modern building imitates a typical French Colonial structure with its steeply pitched roof overhanging a pavilion.

Return to Rte. 53 (Independence Blvd.) and continue south 2.5mi.

Just before the intersection with Route 7, on the left, stands the **Fitzpatrick House**, headquarters of the Illinois & Michigan Canal National Heritage Corridor Commission. The restored 1850s limestone farmhouse once anchored a 1,000-acre farm.

Continue south to Rte. 7 and turn left.

Immediately south of Route 7, on the right, extends the 269-acre **Lockport Prairie Nature Preserve★**, designated in 1983 as the largest presettlement prairie in Northern Illinois *(access from Division St., .5mi south of Rte. 7 off Rte. 53; open Apr– Oct daily 8am–8pm; rest of the year daily 8am–5pm; closed Dec 25;* ▣ ☎815-727-8700). An easy .5mi trail winds through native prairie grass and a profusion of wildflowers.
The Route 7 bridge crosses over the meandering Des Plaines River and then the Sanitary & Ship Canal, flanked by large grain elevators, before entering Lockport.

Turn right on Canal St. before the I&M Canal and continue .5mi to view Lock no. 1. Then turn left at Division St. just past the lock, and left again on State St. (Rte. 171) to enter downtown Lockport. Turn left on 8th St. one block after the intersection with Rte. 7 and park in the lot for the Gaylord Building.

★ **Lockport** – Pop 9,814. Founded in 1836 as the canal headquarters, this picturesque canal town features a lovely downtown listed on the National Register of Historic Places. A short drive along the canal leads to **Lock no. 1**, a featured sight on the 2.5mi **Gaylord Donnelley Canal Trail★** that follows the canal through Lockport and includes several wayside exhibits. This was the first of 15 locks used to raise and lower the boats and barges plying the canal.
The **Gaylord Building★** *(200 E. 8th St.)* was restored in the 1980s to its 1860s appearance. The 2-story western section of the local limestone building, completed in 1838 as a warehouse for canal construction, now contains the Public Landing restaurant. The 3-story 1859 Italianate addition served as the store and offices of the grain companies who occupied the building from 1848 to 1890. Today, the structure houses the **I&M Canal Visitor Center** on the lower levels, featuring exhibits and films about the history of the building, the canal and the Heritage Corridor *(open year-round Wed–Sun 10am–5pm; closed Dec 24–1st Wed in Jan; 45min guided tours available;* ⚐ ▣ ☎815-838-4830). On the upper levels, the Illinois State Museum–Lockport Gallery offers rotating art exhibits and special programs *(open year-round Tue–Sat 10am–5pm, Sun noon–5pm; may be closed in between exhibits; 45min guided tours available;* ⚐ ▣ ☎815-838-7400).
Extending south from the Gaylord Building, **Pioneer Settlement★**, a collection of 19C historic buildings—including schoolhouse, blacksmith shop, jail and log cabins—comes alive the second Saturday of each summer month *(10am–noon),* when volunteers adopt the characters of early settlers in a "living history" tableau *(open May–Sept daily 1–4:30pm; closed major holidays;* ⚐ ▣ ☎815-838-5080). South of the parking lot on State Street stands the **Will County Historical Society Museum** *(803 S. State St.),* located in an 1837 white clapboard structure. Costumed docents con

duct tours of this former canal-headquarters building, today crammed with arti-facts documenting the canal era *(visit by 45min guided tour only, year-round daily 1–4:30pm; closed major holidays; ₺ 🅿 ☎815-838-5080).*

Continue south on State St. (Rte. 171) into Joliet. Turn right on Cass St. (Rte. 6).

★ **Joliet** – Pop 78,917. The entrance to Joliet is marked by the **Old Illinois State Penitentiary** (1857, William W. Boyington) resembling the architect's CHICAGO WATER TOWER with its castle-like limestone walls and towers.

Cass Street leads into downtown Joliet and toward the riverboat casinos that boosted its economy in the early 1990s. Historic highlights include the restored **Union Station** *(Scott and Jefferson Sts.)* from 1907, and **Rialto Square Theatre★** *(Chicago and Van Buren Sts.),* erected in 1926 by Rapp & Rapp. An opulent mirror-lined lobby leads into the rotunda dominated by an enormous, hand-cut crystal chandelier, claimed to be the largest in the US *(visit by 45min guided tour only year-round Tue 12:45pm; closed major holidays; $3; 🅿 ☎815-726-6600).* Also of interest is **Bicentennial Park** *(Cass and Bluff Sts.; open year-round Mon–Thu 8am–4:30pm, Fri 8am–noon, weekends for scheduled events only; closed weeks prior to and following Christmas; 30min guided tours available;₺ 🅿 ☎815-740-2216)* with its waterside walk, mosaic mural and boulders commemorating important events in a city defined in the 19C by limestone quarrying and the steel industry.

Return to Chicago via Rte. 30 and I-55 (about 40mi).

SOUTHERN SECTION – Channahon to LaSalle/Peru

Though industrialized, the southern section of the Heritage Corridor boasts numerous recreational opportunities in the wide Illinois River Valley. Fishing afi-cionados will find a wealth of choice spots, while hiking and biking enthusiasts can follow the canal for miles along the rambling trails. *The following sights are not part of a driving tour. The visitor may choose to spend an entire day at one of the state parks, hike or bike along the 61mi canal trail, or rent a canoe and paddle down the canal (p 209). Access to each sight has been given from I-80. If you wish to drive through the var-ious towns, follow Rte. 6 West until Ottawa, then continue on Dee Bennett Rd. to Utica, returning to Rte. 6 for LaSalle.*

Channahon – Pop 4,784. *From I-55 (exit 248), follow Rte. 6 for 2mi through the town and turn left at Canal St. onto I&M Canal State Trail.* The scenic 61mi **I&M Canal State Trail★** (from Rockdale to LaSalle) provides a historic route for hiking, bicy-cling, canoeing and snowmobiling. Offering access to the trail, a lovely park at Channahon includes **Locks no. 6 and 7**, a weir where the DuPage River crosses the canal, and an original 1840s **Locktender's House**.

Balthazar Korab

I & M Canal at Channahon

Morris – Pop 10,888 *From I-80 (exit 112), follow Rte. 47.* Downtown Morris retains the feel of a canal town and county seat. Just outside town, the **Aux Sable Aqueduct,** near the Locktender's House and Lock no. 8, carries the canal over a creek. **Gebhard Woods State Park★** *(401 Ottawa St.)* includes a visitor center and the Nettle Creek Aqueduct. Picnic tables scattered under oak and maple trees make this a pleasant lunchtime spot *(open year-round daily 10am–4pm;* & ▣ ☎*815-942-0796).*

Farther west along Route 6 lie the old canal towns of Seneca and Marseilles, as well as Locks no. 9 and no. 10. In **Seneca**, note the 65ft-tall, 70,000-bushel capacity **grain elevator** erected in 1861; a rare survivor from the canal's heyday, it towers over the canal, today nothing more than an overgrown ditch. **Marseilles** comprises a quaint downtown of pubs and antique shops.

★ **Ottawa** – *From I-80 (exit 90), follow Rte. 23.* Here the visitor will find a wealth of history, including Washington Park, where Abraham Lincoln and Stephen A. Douglas held the first of their famous 1858 debates, an event reenacted each August. The park is surrounded by historic buildings, most notably the large Italianate **Reddick Mansion★** from 1856 *(Lafayette and Columbus Sts.; open year-round Mon–Fri 9am–5pm, other times by appointment; closed major holidays;* ▣ *).* The canal itself is dry in Ottawa, but the 100ft **Fox River Aqueduct**, which carried the canal over the intersecting stream, still stands at the eastern edge of the community, while the famous Ottawa silica sand quarries lie to the west.

Several historic sites are located on Dee Bennett Road *(access off Rte. 23)* along the Illinois River between Ottawa and Utica. At **Buffalo Rock State Park★** take the River Bluff trail down to two overlooks affording fine **vistas★** of the Illinois River *(open year-round daily 8am–4pm; 30min guided tours available, reservations required;* & ▣ ☎*815-433-2224).* At the western end of the parking lot, a wooden platform provides views of the **Effigy Tumuli**, giant earth sculptures in the form of indigenous aquatic animals completed as part of a strip-mine reclamation by artist Michael Heizer in 1985 *(trail access from platform).*

Farther west is the modern **Illinois Waterway Visitor Center★** erected by the US Army Corps of Engineers *(open Memorial Day–Labor Day daily 9am–8pm; rest of the year daily 9am–5pm; closed Jan 1, Thanksgiving Day, Dec 25; 45min guided tours available;* & ▣ ☎*815-667-4054).* Exhibits describe the workings of the modern waterway connection between the Great Lakes and the Mississippi River that superseded the I&M Canal in 1933. From the observation deck, visitors can watch the lock in operation as barges enter the lock chamber and are slowly raised or lowered. Near Utica, the 4-story sandstone **Sulphur Springs Hotel** (1852) marks the halfway point on the old stagecoach trail between Chicago and Peoria. West of the hotel is the Grand Village of the Illinois, an archaeological site where 10,000 Illinois Indians and members of related tribes lived in the late 17C.

Utica – Pop 1,526. *From I-80 (exit 81), follow Rte. 178.* The **LaSalle County Historical Society Museum** *(Rte. 178 and Canal St.),* located in an 1838 canal warehouse, features an eclectic collection of artifacts related to the county's history, including furnishings, clothing, tools and even a carriage used by Abraham Lincoln in 1858 *(open mid-Apr–Nov Wed–Fri 10am–4pm, weekends noon–4pm; rest of the year weekends noon–4pm; $1; 1hr 30min guided tours available;* & ▣ ☎*815-667-4861).*
The canal can be canoed from Utica to LaSalle, and bicycles can be rented here to visit Split Rock, a dramatic limestone outcrop through which the canal was carved. Utica is also the gateway to the popular **Starved Rock State Park★**, 2,600 acres of forested bluffs. Some 15mi of trails lead down canyons to lovely waterfalls and pools along the Illinois River *(open daily year-round; 1hr 30min guided tours available;* ✕ & ▣ ☎*815-667-4726).* The rustic **lodge** was first built by the Civilian Conservation Corps in the 1930s. Step inside to view the massive fireplace dominating the Great Room.

LaSalle – *From I-80 (exit 77), follow Rte. 351.* The twin towns of LaSalle and Peru mark the end of the canal and the Heritage Corridor. Located in downtown LaSalle, **Lock no. 14★** is the only restored lock on the canal. The 15-lock system allowed barges to conquer the 160ft difference in water level between Chicago and the Illinois River.
Adjacent Peru contains the remnants of a historic waterfront district along **Water Street**.

Return to Chicago via Rte. 351 and I-80 (about 100mi).

Time: 1 day
Map p 3

A sliver of pristine land lining the southern edge of Lake Michigan, the Indiana Dunes National Lakeshore encompasses 14,000 acres of windswept beaches, dunes, marshes and forests containing a great diversity of species. Over the years, much of the area around the dunes was industrialized, and today parklands are interrupted by steel and power plants. This, however, has not thwarted the mass of urban dwellers who crowd the trails and beaches in their ubiquitous search for unspoiled land.

Historical Notes

Glaciers that carved the Great Lakes sculpted the first chapter in the history of the dunes some 15,000 years ago. As the glaciers retreated to the north, they left moraines—ridges formed from glacial till—south of present-day Lake Michigan. Glacial meltwaters created further ridges as the shoreline shrank to the north by stages. As the Ice Age drew to a close about 11,000 years ago, various ecosystems developed between the various ridges. Ice Age plants such as bearberry and jack pine persisted, while cacti and other southern plants began to thrive in the warmer climate.

Prevailing northwesterly winds and lake waves continue to create new sand dunes at the lake shore, while older dunes beyond the shoreline gradually evolve from sparse grasslands and marshes into dense forests. When University of Chicago ecologist **Henry Chandler Cowles** (1869-1939) began to study the dunes in the 1890s, he was fascinated not only by the evidence of glacial action, but also by

Visiting Indiana Dunes

Access – By **car**: south on I-94/I-90 (Dan Ryan Expwy.) to Chicago Skyway toll-road (I-90). After Hammond and Gary in Indiana, exit at I-65/Hwy. 20/Hwy. 12 Dunes Hwy. and continue eastbound. Stay on Hwy. 12, forking left as I-65 forks right, and forking left again as Hwy. 20 forks right. All Dunes sights can be accessed from Hwy. 12. From Chicago Loop to West Beach entrance: 37mi; to Buell Visitor Center: 49mi; to Mt. Baldy: 54mi. By **train**: the South Shore Railroad departs daily year-round from the Randolph St. Metra station (☎219-926-5744).

Visitor Information – Encompassing two park sections separated by an industrialized area, this popular venue measures about 20mi in length and is accessible in all seasons. Contact the following agencies for maps and additional information about camping and recreation: **Indiana Dunes National Lakeshore**, 1100 N. Mineral Springs Rd., Porter IN 46304 ☎219-926-7561 (ext. 668 for trails, skiing or beach conditions); **Indiana Dunes State Park**, 1600 North 25 East, Chesterton IN 46304 ☎219-926-1952.

Camping & Recreation – **Campsites** are available mid-Mar–mid-Nov at Dunewood Campground ($8-$10), and year-round at Indiana Dunes State Park ($7-11). Pleasant **hiking trails** crisscross the area. Most trails have a detailed trail map and brochure placed in boxes at trail head. Trail maps are also available at visitor centers. The Calumet **bike trail** (9mi) begins at Mt. Baldy and ends near the park headquarters. **Cross-country skiing** allowed on most park trails. **Swimming** recommended only at the following beaches (*manned by lifeguards Memorial Day–Labor Day*): Central, Kemil, West, and in the state park.

Water Safety – Swimmers may find rip currents, commonly called **undertow** (strong, narrow, lakeward flows) all along the shore during periods of high wind and waves. If caught in an undertow, swim parallel to the shoreline until out of the current. Strong winter currents coupled with continual freezing temperatures create **shelf ice** along the shore. Deceptively thin, this ice is unstable and dangerous.

Amenities – Bathhouses containing rest rooms, information desks and first-aid stations are located at West and Porter Beaches (*open Memorial Day–Labor Day*). Comfort stations in the state park are open Apr–Oct. Snack bars at Marquette Park, West Beach, Porter Beach and Mt. Baldy (*Memorial Day–Labor Day*). Motels, restaurants and service stations are located in nearby towns.

the fact that the plant forms on each ridge continue to change over time. Cowles discovered that plants alter their environment, providing fertile ground for new species that will crowd out the originals. Marram grasses become established on sand dunes, gradually collecting water and humus until a pine or cottonwood forest takes root, eventually to be succeeded by oak-hickory and then beech-maple forests.

The effort to preserve the Indiana Dunes began in 1911 when landscape architect Jens Jensen and other Chicago conservationists formed the Prairie Club, leading train excursions to the then-unbroken 25mi stretch of dunes between Gary and Michigan City, Indiana. In 1913, Dr. Cowles led ten European botanists on a trip to the dunes, which they determined to be one of the four most important natur-al sites in America, along with Yellowstone, Yosemite and the Grand Canyon. Chicago-based efforts to preserve the dunes met great resistance in rural Indiana, but a small state park was established in 1923, comprising 2,000 acres by 1927.

As industry grew again after World War II, Bethlehem Steel bought large tracts of the Central Dunes for a steel plant, harbor and sand mine. A new effort to save the dunes as a national park was led by Illinois Senator Paul Douglas. Legislation was passed in 1966 to preserve a 6,400-acre area split in two by the Bethlehem complex, designated the Indiana Dunes National Lakeshore. Park expansion continued into the 1980s even as lakefront industry mushroomed. Today the region presents a fascinating array of flora, encompassing within its small confines arctic wild-flowers as well as prickly pear cacti. Indeed, vistas unfolding along the numerous trails take in swirling dunes, lowland marshes and dense forests in the space of a few hundred yards.

VISIT

★ **West Beach Area** – *Turn left on County Line Rd. shortly after entering the park. Open May–Sept 9am–sunset. Rest of the year 8am–sunset. Closed Jan 1, Thanksgiving Day, Dec 25. $3/car (May–Sept). Pets are prohibited. ☒ (May–Sept) ♿ ⛽ . Note: trails through sand dunes can be more strenuous due to the sandy soil and rapid elevation changes.* Known primarily for its splendid beach, this large section of the park also includes several pleasant hiking trails. Behind the visitor center, "blowout" dunes that have eroded to a great degree slowly evolve as water collects in the center and forms interdunal ponds, stabilizing the dune and allowing it to mutate into the next ecosystem—a cottonwood or conifer stand, to be succeeded by oak savanna and oak-hickory forest.

Constantly changing between seasons and over the years, a walk along the **Dune Succession Trail**★ offers a look at the park's surprising biological diversity. The 1mi boardwalk trail runs from the beach near the bathhouse to the parking lot near the visitor center and provides one of the best views of rapid ecosystem change. Beginning with sand dunes and marram grasses located on the waterfront, the trail leads past a blowout dune and then abruptly comes upon a conifer forest thick with evergreens and vines. At another interdunal pond, the conifer forest ends just as suddenly and is succeeded by oaks and hardwoods. The short trail offers several excellent **viewpoints**★.

Inland Marsh – *Access to the right off Hwy. 12, about 1.5mi past West Beach.* The 4mi trail *(1.5hrs)* follows the Tolleston Beach ridge, formed 10,000 years ago by melt-ing glacial waters. Sand dunes form the basis of the soil-supporting cottonwood, wildflowers and prickly pear cacti around a large marsh. New plants appear around each bend, delicately layered from ground to sky, springing from sand ridge and wetland marsh.

★ **Bailly-Chellberg Visitor Center and Trail** – *Drive 6mi east of Inland Marsh, passing through a heavy industrialized area before reentering the park. Turn right on Mineral Springs Rd. and continue for about 1mi. Open Memorial Day–Labor Day daily 10am–4:30pm. Rest of the year weekends 10am–4:30pm. Closed Jan 1, Thanksgiving Day, Dec 25. ♿ ⛽ .* This stop provides a historic counterpoint to the natural won-ders of the dunes. A 1.7mi trail burrowing through a lush forest of basswood, beech and sugar maple, leads to an 1820s homestead consisting of several log structures (1822) and a 2.5-story main house *(open Memorial Day–Oct Sun 1–4pm)*, illustrating early European settlement of the region. The trail follows an old Indian path before reaching a French-Canadian cemetery noteworthy for the elaborate raised stone structures, and then loops back to a preserved 1870s Swedish farm and outbuildings.

Dorothy Buell Memorial Visitor Center – *Access to the right off Hwy. 12, about 4.5mi east of Mineral Springs Rd. Open Memorial Day–Labor Day daily 8am–6pm. Rest of the year daily 8am–5pm. Closed Jan 1, Thanksgiving Day, Dec 25.* ⅃ ▣ . Named for the woman who founded the Save the Dunes Council in 1952, the visitor center presents a 10min audio-visual introduction to the park, its glacial formation and its continuing evolution by the forces of the wind and lake. A boulder in front of the center commemorates the work of Jens Jensen, Stephen Mather and Henry Cowles in preserving the dunes. Informative exhibits explain the ecosystems, plant and animal life, including examinations of specific native and "foreign" species. Regular guided nature walks are listed in the activity schedule, and a bookshop sells useful field guides.

Kemil Beach Area – *Cross Hwy. 12 from the visitor center and continue on Kemil Rd. to Kemil Beach. The parking area for the beach is on the right, 1/4mi before the beach. The 1mi Dune Ridge Trail is accessed from the parking area.* In summer, the long stretch of sandy beach welcomes visitors as well as nearby homeowners in Beverly Shores. The 4mi drive to **Central Beach**, another popular swimming area, affords spectacular **views★** of the vast blue expanse of Lake Michigan.

★ **Mount Baldy** – *To the left off Hwy. 12, about 6mi east of Kemil Beach. Mt. Baldy is located 54mi from Chicago.* The largest (123ft) remaining dune in the park is constantly shifting by a process called saltation, in which the lake winds whip the sand inland across the surface of the dune to the forests behind. Mt. Baldy is moving inland at a rate of 4 to 5ft a year, killing the trees behind its crest. The effect of wind also creates the "singing sands" that seem to whistle when walked upon. The walk up and around the dune to the beach is short *(.5mi)* and very steep *(use caution)*. A great bowl of sand leads down to the beach from the summit, which provides a grand **panorama** of the lake and the dunes, unfortunately disrupted by the massive cooling tower of a power plant to the east.

Indiana Dunes National Lakeshore

Practical Information

Calendar of Events

Listed below is a selection of Chicago's most popular annual events; some dates may vary each year. A detailed listing of art fairs can be found on p 238, and neighborhood festivals on p 223. For more information about events in Chicago consult the periodicals listed on p 231 or contact the Chicago Office of Tourism ☎312-744-2400.

Date	Event /*Location*	☎
Spring & Summer		
Mar 17	**St. Patrick's Day Parade** *Dearborn St. from Wacker Dr. to Van Buren St.*	312-942-9188
early Apr	**Chicago Park District Spring Flower Show**	
	Garfield Park Conservatory	312-746-5100
	Lincoln Park Conservatory	312-742-7736
Memorial Day weekend	**Viva Chicago!** *Petrillo Music Shell*	312-744-3315
1st weekend in Jun	**57th St. Art Fair** *S. Kimbark Ave. & E. 57th St.*	773-493-3247
	Chicago Blues Festival *Petrillo Music Shell*	312-744-3315
	Printer's Row Book Fair *S. Dearborn St.*	312-987-1980
2nd weekend in Jun	**Chicago Gospel Festival** *Petrillo Music Shell*	312-744-3315
	Old Town Art Fair *Lincoln Park West*	312-337-1938
mid-Jun–late Aug	**Grant Park Music Festival** *Petrillo Music Shell*	312-819-0614
late Jun–Jul 4	**Taste of Chicago** *Grant Park*	312-744-3315
late Jun–Labor Day	**Ravinia Festival** *Highland Park (North Shore)*	773-728-4642
last weekend in Jun	**Chicago Country Music Festival** *Petrillo Music Shell*	312-744-3315
Jul 3	**Independence Day Concert & Fireworks** *Petrillo Music Shell*	312-294-2420
mid–late Jul	**Chicago to Mackinac Island Yacht Race** *starts at Monroe Harbor*	312-861-7777
2nd Sat in Aug	**Bud Billiken Parade & Picnic** *39th St. & Martin Luther King, Jr. Dr. to 55th St. (Washington Park)*	312-225-2400
mid-Aug	**Venetian Night** *Monroe Harbor*	312-744-3315
late Aug	**Chicago Air & Water Show** *North Ave. Beach*	312-744-3370
Labor Day weekend	**Chicago Jazz Festival** *Petrillo Music Shell*	312-744-3315
Fall & Winter		
2nd weekend in Sept	**Around the Coyote** *N. Damen & Milwaukee Aves. (Wicker Park)*	312-342-6777
2nd Sun in Oct	**Windy City International Marathon** *Loyola University*	312-915-6226
mid–late Oct	**Chicago International Film Festival** *Various theaters*	312-644-3400
Nov 1	**Day of the Dead Celebration** *Mexican Fine Arts Center Museum*	312-738-1503
mid-Nov	**Magnificent Mile Festival of Lights**	312-642-3570
Thanksgiving Day	**City of Chicago Tree-Lighting Ceremony** *Daley Center Plaza*	312-744-3315
late Nov	**Ringling Brothers Barnum & Bailey Circus** *United Center*	312-455-4650
1st Sun in Dec	**Caroling to the Animals** *Lincoln Park Zoo*	773-935-6700
mid-Dec	**Kwanza Festival** *location varies*	312-744-2400
	Chicago Park District Christmas Flower Show	
	Garfield Park Conservatory	312-746-5100
	Lincoln Park Conservatory	312-742-7736
late Jan–Feb	**Chinese New Year Parade** *Wentworth Ave. from Cermak Rd. to 24th St.*	312-225-6198
early–mid-Feb	**WinterBreak Chicago Festival** *various locations*	312-744-3315
mid-Feb	**Chicago Auto Show** *McCormick Place*	630-954-0600

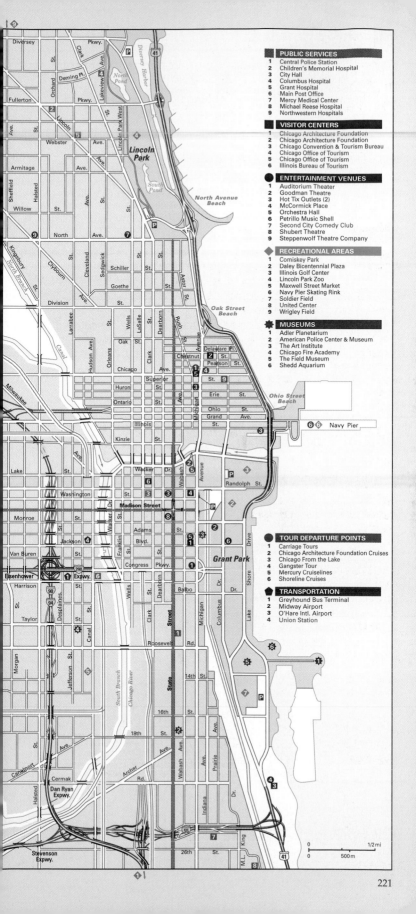

PUBLIC SERVICES

1 Central Police Station
2 Children's Memorial Hospital
3 City Hall
4 Columbus Hospital
5 Grant Hospital
6 Main Post Office
7 Mercy Medical Center
8 Michael Reese Hospital
9 Northwestern Hospitals

VISITOR CENTERS

1 Chicago Architecture Foundation
2 Chicago Architecture Foundation
3 Chicago Convention & Tourism Bureau
4 Chicago Office of Tourism
5 Chicago Office of Tourism
6 Illinois Bureau of Tourism

ENTERTAINMENT VENUES

1 Auditorium Theater
2 Goodman Theatre
3 Hot Tix Outlets (2)
4 McCormick Place
5 Orchestra Hall
6 Petrillo Music Shell
7 Second City Comedy Club
8 Shubert Theatre
9 Steppenwolf Theatre Company

RECREATIONAL AREAS

1 Comiskey Park
2 Daley Bicentennial Plaza
3 Illinois Golf Center
4 Lincoln Park Zoo
5 Maxwell Street Market
6 Navy Pier Skating Rink
7 Soldier Field
8 United Center
9 Wrigley Field

MUSEUMS

1 Adler Planetarium
2 American Police Center & Museum
3 The Art Institute
4 Chicago Fire Academy
5 The Field Museum
6 Shedd Aquarium

TOUR DEPARTURE POINTS

1 Carriage Tours
2 Chicago Architecture Foundation Cruises
3 Chicago From the Lake
4 Gangster Tour
5 Mercury Cruiselines
6 Shoreline Cruises

TRANSPORTATION

1 Greyhound Bus Terminal
2 Midway Airport
3 O'Hare Intl. Airport
4 Union Station

0   1/2 mi
0   500 m

Neighborhoods

Over the years, Chicago has managed to capture and preserve the essence of myriad ethnic groups in its quaint and diverse neighborhoods. Other areas have developed distinct characteristics as artists' meccas or shopping havens. Together the districts weave a colorful quilt and combine to form "the city of neighborhoods."

Downtown

Center of the city, the **Loop** (*p 42*) offers a lesson in American architecture—bar none. Lined with department stores, State Street is the city's original shopping thoroughfare. Since the 1960s, it has been eclipsed by the **Magnificent Mile** (*p 77*), a boulevard of glitzy shops of international renown. Trendy and upscale **River North** (*p 97*) has garnered a reputation for its art-gallery district and charming bistros and boutiques; the neighborhood has also become a favorite of tourists who flock to its celebrity-owned and thematic restaurants. Recently rehabilitated **Printer's Row** (*p 106*), in the South Loop, caters to a young crowd drawn to its coffee shops and bookstores.

North Side

The affluent **Gold Coast** (*p 114*), most of it preserved as a landmark historic district, provides a restful retreat from bustling Michigan Avenue. One of the city's oldest neighborhoods, **Old Town** (*p 120*) includes an offbeat assortment of comedy clubs,

shops and restaurants. Just west of Lincoln Park, gentrified **Lincoln Park/DePaul** *(p 126)* encompasses the bulk of the city's theaters, jazz and blues clubs, as well as a wide range of eateries. Considered the artistic area of Chicago, **Wicker Park** *(p 139)* and **Bucktown,** both found along Milwaukee Avenue, propose quaint coffeehouses, alternative performance venues and unique bookshops to a motley crew of yuppies and Hispanic immigrants. Just south of Milwaukee Avenue, **Ukrainian Village** *(p 138)* forms the core of a small but lively Ukrainian community, distinguished by cozy ethnic shops and eateries. A large number of Chicagoans of Polish origin reside north of Logan Square in **Avondale.** Located in the N. Clark Street area, the Swedish community of **Andersonville** offers Scandinavian crafts and foods. Center of the city's gay population, **Lakeview/Wrigleyville** *(p 142)* is a diverse area boasting funky nightclubs, vintage clothing stores and inexpensive restaurants. **Argyle Street** *(p 143)*, just north of Uptown, is home to a large community of recent Asian immigrants, who have set up Vietnamese and Korean shops and restaurants along the colorful street. Farther north lies **Devon Avenue** *(p 146)*, lined with a variety of ethnic restaurants reflecting the different waves of settlement in the area: Pakistani, Indian, Jewish and Thai.

West Side

Located in the Near West Side, **Little Italy** *(p 150)* offers a choice concentration of Italian restaurants and markets; just north, the delicious aromas of Greek fare imbue the streets of **Greektown** *(p 151)*. Heart of the Hispanic community, **Little Village** and **Pilsen** *(p 152)* in the Lower West Side offer stores selling imported goods as well as a variety of Mexican restaurants. Also in the Lower West Side is **Heart of Italy**, one of Chicago's original Italian neighborhoods with restaurants offering traditional Italian meals. Along Western Avenue and 47th Street, the **Brighton Park** neighborhood is home to Lithuanian immigrants.

South Side

The predominantly African-American **Near South Side** *(p 154)* features renowned blues and jazz clubs and some of the city's oldest religious edifices. Nearby, **Chinatown** *(p 162)* boasts numerous restaurants and markets offering authentic oriental goods. **Bridgeport**'s main claim to fame are its Irish mayors, including Richard J. Daley, who have for years presided over Chicago politics. A liberal and eclectic area surrounding the University of Chicago campus, **Hyde Park** *(p 175)* is best known for its well-stocked bookshops and student hangouts.

Neighborhood Festivals

Date	Event/Location	☎
1st weekend in May	**Cinco De Mayo** *Douglas Park*	312-744-2400
1st weekend in Jun	**Taste of the Heart of Italy** *Oakley Ave.*	773-254-6168
2nd weekend in Jun	**Old Town & Wells St. Art Fairs** *Lincoln Park West & N. Wells St.*	312-337-1938 312-951-6106
1st Sat in Jun	**Calumet/Giles/Prairie Historical Festival** *S. Calumet Ave. (Near South Side)*	312-225-2257
1st Sat in Jul	**Kwanza Summer Festival** *Soweto Center, 19 W. 103rd St. (Near South Side)*	773-264-1298
2nd weekend in Jul	**Rock Around the Block** *Lincoln Ave. (Lakeview/Wrigleyville)*	773-472-7171
3rd weekend in Jul	**Brighton Park Lithuanian Fair** *S. Western Ave.*	773-847-0664
late Jul	**Chinatown Summer Fair** *S. Wentworth Ave. at Cermak Rd.*	312-326-5320
last weekend in Jul	**Taste of Lincoln Avenue**	773-472-9046
2nd weekend in Aug	**Taste of River North** *Superior St.*	312-645-1047
Mid-Aug	**Northalsted Market Days** *Halsted St. & Belmont Ave. (Lakeview/Wrigleyville)*	773-868-3010
	Wicker Park Greening Festival, *Wicker Park*	773-868-3010
late Aug	**Bucktown Arts Fest** *N. Oakley Blvd.*	773-489-4662
	Argyle Festival *Argyle St.*	773-784-2900
Labor Day weekend	**Ukrainian Fest** *Smith Park*	312-357-1750
Mid-Sept	**Feast of San Gennaro** *Morgan & Taylor Sts. (Little Italy)*	773-775-3459

Planning the Trip

Visitors can contact the following agencies before their trip to obtain maps and information on points of interest, accommodations and seasonal events.

Chicago Office of Tourism – Chicago Cultural Center, 78 E. Washington St., Chicago IL 60602 ☎ 312-744-2400 or 800-487-2446 (North America only). *Chicago Mosaic* provides information about the city on the World Wide Web, address: http://www.ci.chi.il.us.

Chicago Convention and Tourism Bureau – McCormick Place on the Lake, 2301 S. Lake Shore Dr., Chicago IL 60616 ☎ 312-567-8500.

CHICAGO'S SEASONS

Chicago's temperatures can drop as low as -20°F during the winter and soar up to 100°F in the summer months. The city averages 33" of rain and 40" of snow each year. Lake Michigan has a noticeable effect on the city's weather: temperatures near the lake are markedly cooler in summer and warmer in winter. Most tourists visit Chicago between Memorial Day and Labor Day.

Spring – A brief and generally unpredictable season, spring begins in late March and lasts through the end of May. Daytime highs usually reach the 50s (10-15°C) and nighttime lows rarely dip below 35°F (2°C). Snow remains a possibility well into April.

Summer – From Memorial Day to Labor Day, Chicagoans flock to parks and beaches to take their fill of sun and warmth in preparation for the long months of winter. Daytime temperatures are hot, averaging in the 80s (26-31°C). The relative humidity can be uncomfortably high, and a haze often settles over the city. In the evenings, a light jacket or sweater may be necessary, especially if strolling along the lakefront (temperatures normally in the 60s, 15-20°C).

Autumn – Lasting from mid-September through October, autumn may be the mos[t] pleasant time to visit Chicago. Crisp, clear days with temperatures in the 50s and 60 (10-20°C) give way to cool nights, usually dropping into the 40s (4-8°C). Hints of th[e] impending winter may appear with the occasional frost and freeze warning.

Winter – This is Chicago's longest season and is a part of the city's culture. It ca[n] extend from mid-October through April. Brutal winds sweep through tunnels creat[ed] by the towering buildings, and windchills are known to fall to a dangerous 60[°] below zero (-51°C). Daytime temperatures average between 20-40°F (-7°C to 4°C) nights drop to 15-20°F (-9°C to -7°C). **Lake-effect snow** occurs throughout the season These small storm systems often reach several miles inland and bring with the[m] large amounts of snow (12-24in/30-60cm) in short periods. Protective clothing (coat[s,] boots, gloves, hats) is essential when venturing outside. Note that the abundant[ly] used road salt will leave a white residue on shoes and boots.

Temperature Chart		
	avg. high	avg. low	precipitation
Jan	29°F (-2°C)	14°F (-10°C)	1.6in (4.1cm)
Apr	59°F (15°C)	39°F (4°C)	3.7in (9.5cm)
Jul	83°F (28°C)	63°F (17°C)	3.6in (9.3cm)
Oct	64°F (18°C)	43°F (6°C)	2.3in (5.8cm)

Getting There

PLANES

O'Hare International Airport – ☎ *773-686-2200. 14mi northwest of the Loop.* Most international flights arrive and depart from O'Hare, "the world's busiest airport." Airport information booths *(open daily 9am–8pm)* are located on the lower level of terminals 1-3, as well as the upper and lower levels of terminal 5 (there is no terminal 4). Departing passengers should allow themselves the maximum amount of time recommended by their airline. Restaurants with sit-down service are located in terminal 1, Gate C; between terminals 2 and 3, upper level; terminal 3, Gate K; and terminal 5, upper level. Most modes of public transportation depart from the lower level of each terminal; departure points are clearly signed. An Airport Transit System provides free transportation between the terminals and long-term parking lots.

Taxis – The Starter taxi system is in effect at O'Hare Airport. Passengers are obligated to wait in line and allow a Starter to hail the next available cab for them. Taxi service to the Loop takes approximately 50min in rush hour ($23-$30). All cab companies that offer airport service participate in the **Shared-Ride** discount program wherein individual riders willing to share a cab to downtown pay a flat rate of $15. Inform the Starter or driver if you wish to participate; wait is limited to 10min, maximum four passengers (discounted rate applies even if there are no additional riders). The program is designed for individual riders; groups pay regular posted fares.

Shuttles – **Airport Express** offers transport between O'Hare, downtown hotels and North Shore suburbs year-round. Shuttles run between the airport and downtown hotels daily, 5am–11:30pm (transit time: 45-60min); $14.75 one-way/$25.50 round-trip. Shuttles between O'Hare and the North Shore suburbs run daily 5am–8:30pm; transit time and fares vary. ☎ 312-454-7800 or 800-654-7871 (US only).

Rental Cars – *p 228.* Most major rental car agencies have shuttle buses offering transportation to their lots. Conduct all rental car business in the terminal before boarding a shuttle.

Trains – CTA Blue Line trains *(p 227)* operate between O'Hare and Downtown daily, 24hrs/day (transit time: 40-45min); departures every 5-15min (1–4am every 30-60min). The O'Hare station is located under the Hilton Hotel, in terminal 2.

Chicago Midway Airport – ☎ *773-767-0500. 10mi southwest of the Loop.* Many travelers find this smaller airport easier to navigate. Flights are limited to domestic carriers. Information booths *(open daily 6am–10pm)* offering airline and transport information are located between concourses A and B.

Taxis and Shuttles – Taxis are located outside exits M10 through M12 (service to downtown area 30min, $16-$20). Operators participate in the **Shared-Ride** discount program *($10, see above).* **Airport Express** offers transport between Midway and Downtown. Shuttles are located across from the Southwest Airlines ticket counter and run daily year-round 5:15am–10:30pm (transit time: 30-45min); $10.75 one-way/$19 round-trip. ☎ 312-454-7800 or 800-654-7871 (US only).

Rental Cars – *p 228.* Rental-car-agency shuttle buses depart near taxi stands *(above).* Conduct all rental car business in the terminal before boarding a shuttle.

Trains – CTA Orange Line trains *(p 227)* operate between Midway and Downtown Monday through Saturday 5am–11:30pm, Sunday & holidays 7:30am–11:30pm (transit time: 25-30min); departures every 6-10min. The Midway station is located across Cicero Ave. (a covered walkway can be found on level 2 of concourse A).

TRAINS

The **Amtrak** rail network offers a relaxing alternative for the traveler with time to spare. Advance reservations are recommended to ensure reduced fares and availability of desired accommodations. Passengers can choose from first class, coach, sleeping accommodations and glass-domed cars that allow a panoramic view. Fares are comparable to air travel. Major long-distance routes to Chicago are: *Lake Shore Limited* from Boston and New York along the Great Lakes (21hrs); *Capital Limited* from Washington, DC (18hrs); *City of New Orleans* from New Orleans (18hrs); *Texas Eagle* from Houston and San Antonio (30hrs); *Southwest Chief* from Los Angeles along the Santa Fe Trail (39hrs); *California Zephyr* from San Francisco (49hrs); *Empire Builder* from Seattle (43hrs). Travelers from Canada should inquire with their local travel agents about Amtrak/VIARail connections. **All-Aboard Pass** allows travel over any distance within 45 days (limited to three stops). **USARailPass** (not available to US or Canadian citizens or legal residents) offers unlimited travel within Amtrak-designated regions at discounted rates; 15- and 30-day passes are available. Chicago's **Amtrak** station is located at Union Station, 225 S. Canal St. Schedule and route information: ☎ 800-872-7245 (North America only; outside North America, contact your local travel agent).

BUSES

Greyhound, the largest bus company in the US, offers access to Chicago at a leisurely pace. Overall, fares are lower than other forms of public transportation. **Ameripass** allows unlimited travel for 7, 14 or 21 days. Some travelers may find long-distance bus travel uncomfortable due to the lack of sleeping accommodations. Advance reservations are suggested. The main Greyhound station in Chicago is located at 630 W. Harrison St. Schedule and route information: ☎ 402-341-1900 or 800-231-2222 (US only).

CARS

Travelers driving to Chicago will find it easily accessible by major interstate highways. The Dan Ryan Expressway (I-90/94), Chicago Skyway (toll road) and I-57 serve the South Side while the Stevenson Expressway (I-55) offers access to the Southwest Side. The Eisenhower Expressway (I-290), called Congress Parkway within downtown Chicago, provides the quickest route to reach the western suburbs. The Kennedy (I-90) and Edens (I-94) Expressways service the Northwest and North Sides respectively. Lake Shore Drive (Route 41) follows the lakefront through the city.

Getting Around

LAY OF THE LAND

Bordered on the east by Lake Michigan, Chicago is divided into North, West and South Sides by the Y-shaped Chicago River. The Loop, bounded by the lake and the Main Channel and South Branch of the Chicago River, forms the heart of the metropolis. Chicago's most fashionable neighborhoods lie on the North Side of the city. The South Side is home to the city's large African-American population, while the West Side attracts immigrants to its myriad ethnic neighborhoods *(p 222)*.

How to find an address – Chicago's street system makes it easy to locate any address based on its north and south coordinates. The intersection of State and Madison Streets is the zero-mile point. Running north to south, State Street serves as the east/west baseline, while Madison Street, running east to west, functions as the north/south baseline. Every address north of Madison is preceded by "North," every address east or west of State is designated "East" or "West," and so forth. In addition, address numbers originate from this point, usually in increments of 100 for each block (400 equals .5mi).

PUBLIC TRANSPORTATION

The **Chicago Transit Authority** (CTA) runs an extensive network of urban trains (elevated and underground) and buses that serve the city and some adjacent suburbs. Other suburbs are served by the **Pace** bus line *(Pace buses run every 30-60min; CTA tokens and transfers may be used)* and **Metra** commuter trains *(Metra's $5 weekend pass offers unlimited rides for one adult and three children under 12, ☎312-836-7000)*. The Transit Information Center offers route and fare information for all systems in the Metro Chicago area, ☎312-836-7000 *(daily 5–1am)*.

Chicago Transit Authority

System maps and the publication *Downtown TransIt Sightseeing Guide* are available *(free)* at train stations, downtown hotels and visitor information centers around the city. Detailed system timetables are available from the CTA main office *(located at the Merchandise Mart, 7th floor; 350 N. Wells St., Chicago IL 60654; open Mon–Fri 8am–4:30pm)*. In this guide, rapid transit and bus stops are indicated with the 🚇 symbol.

Rapid Transit System – *Map p 4*. Originally all routes for the city's rapid transit trains ran on elevated tracks. Although today the city operates elevated and underground trains, the nickname "L" (short for elevated) still designates lines circling the Loop. Train entrances are indicated by blue "Rapid Transit" signs. Access stairwells to the above-ground (elevated, or "L," lines) and below-ground trains may look a bit foreboding, but stations and waiting areas are generally clean and well lit. Many trains are accessible to riders with disabilities, and some stations are equipped with elevators. Trains run every 3-12min in weekday rush hours, 6-20min at most other times (every 30min overnight). The seven different lines are referred to by color; however, signs on trains and stations still refer to the routes by their names (note that route names do not necessarily indicate destination or end points). Transfers are not needed for changes within the rapid transit system.

CTA LINES		Service Hours
■ RED	(Howard-Dan Ryan)	24hrs, daily
■ BLUE	(O'Hare-Congress-Douglas)	24hrs, daily
■ PURPLE	(Evanston)	24hrs, daily between Linden & Howard; peak period service only between Howard and the Loop
■ GREEN	(Lake-Englewood/Jackson Park)	Mon–Sat 5am–11pm; Sun & holidays 7:30am–11pm
■ ORANGE	(Midway)	Mon–Sat 5am–11:30pm; Sun & holidays 7:30am–11:30pm
■ BROWN	(Ravenswood)	Mon–Fri 5am–10pm, Sat 5am–8pm; additional late evening, Sun & holidays hours between Kimball & Belmont stations
YELLOW	(Skokie Swift)	Mon–Fri 5:15am–10pm

Times given are approximate; contact CTA for more specific information.

Buses – CTA buses generally operate daily 6am–midnight; some routes run 24hrs/day. During the weekday rush hour, most buses run every 5-15min, and every 8-20min at other times. Stops (clearly marked by blue and white signs) are customarily made at posted locations only, one to two blocks apart. If unsure about the route, verify desired stop with driver. Oversized street signs are helpful in identifying upcoming stops. Many routes are accessible to riders with disabilities. *Times given are approximate; contact CTA for more specific information.*

Fares – All system fares are $1.50 one-way (exact fare is required for buses; $1 bills accepted). Full-fare tokens (10/$13.50) are valid for one ride on trains or buses and are available at banks, currency exchange offices, Jewel and Dominick's grocery stores. Transfers are $.30. A surcharge ($.25) is added from Downtown on certain Express bus routes.

TAXIS

Chicago taxis are metered. All Chicago cab companies share the same rate schedule: $1.50 for the first mile, $1.20 for each additional mile, $.50 for each additional passenger. There are no extra fees for baggage handling or assistance for passengers with physical disabilities. Cabs are easily hailed in the downtown area. Taxi stands are located at most hotels and major attractions (in other areas, call for service). To report lost property ☎312-744-2900; be sure to give taxi identification number.
The main cab companies in Chicago are: **Checker Taxi Co.** ☎312-829-4222 and **Yellow Cab Co.** ☎312-225-7440.

DRIVING IN CHICAGO   *Chicago Road Conditions:* ☎*847-705-4650*

Given the efficiency of the public transportation system, and the ease with which many sights can be reached on foot, a car is not necessary to visit downtown Chicago. However, a car is recommended for visiting other areas. Keep in mind that roads are often congested, street parking can be difficult to find and public parking lots are expensive. **Rush hour**, the peak transit time for business commuters, is weekdays between 7:30–9:30am and 4:30–6:30pm. Visitors are encouraged to avoid driving during these times.

Road Regulations – The maximum speed limit on major expressways is 55mph (90km/h). Speed limits within the city range from 25mph (40km/h) in residential areas to 35mph (56km/h) on major streets. Use of seat belts is mandatory for passengers in the front seat of the car, and children 4-6 years in the back seat. Child-safety seats are required for children under 4 years (seats available from most rental car agencies). Illinois school-bus law requires motorists to bring vehicles to a full stop when warning signals on a school bus are flashing. Unless otherwise posted, drivers may turn right on a red traffic light after coming to a complete stop. Parking spaces identified with ♿ are reserved for people with disabilities only. Anyone parking in these spaces without proper identification is subject to a heavy fine.

Parking – Metered street parking is available on most downtown and arterial streets; note that vehicles will be towed if left overnight. Many streets are designated Snow Routes (indicated by red, white and blue signs); parking is not allowed on either side of these streets overnight during winter or when there are two or more inches of snow on the ground. No parking is allowed on many streets during specific street cleaning days; note signs. Major parking facilities are indicated on maps in this guide with the ⓟ symbol. Parking in some residential areas is by permit only (restricted to area residents).

Rentals – Major automobile rental companies have offices downtown and at both O'Hare and Midway Airports. Rental cars are available for persons at least 25 years old, but some rental car agencies will rent to drivers under 25 for a daily surcharge. Rentals are subject to the agency checking the renter's driving record for violations. A major credit card and valid driver's license are required for rental (some agencies also require proof of insurance). The average daily rate for a compact car, when renting for 5-7 days, ranges from $30-$65. Note that rental cars are taxed 18%.

Rental Company	Reservation ☎	Rental Company	Reservation ☎
Alamo	800-327-9633	Hertz	800-654-3131
Avis	800-331-1212	National	800-328-4567
Budget	800-527-0700	Thrifty	800-331-4200
Enterprise	800-325-8007		

(toll-free numbers valid worldwide)

International Visitors

PLANNING THE TRIP

Visitors from outside the US can obtain information from the tourism agencies listed on p 224, or from the US embassy or consulate in their country of residence.

Entry Requirements – Citizens of countries participating in the Visa Waiver Pilot Program (VWPP) are not required to obtain a visa to enter the US for visits of less than 90 days. For a list of countries participating in the VWPP, contact the US consulate in your country of residence. Citizens of nonparticipating countries must have a visitor's visa. Upon entry, nonresident foreign visitors must present a valid passport and round-trip transportation ticket. Canadian citizens are not required to present a passport or visa to enter the US, although identification and proof of citizenship may be requested (the best proof of citizenship is a passport, but a Canadian birth certificate and photo identification are usually acceptable). Naturalized Canadian citizens should carry their citizenship papers. Inoculations are generally not required (contingent upon country of residence and countries recently visited). Check with the US embassy or consulate before departing.

For futher information of interest to international travelers, see pp 231-232.

Health Insurance – The United States does not have a national health program. Before departing, visitors from abroad should check with their insurance company to determine if their medical insurance covers doctor's visits, medication and hospitalization in the US. Prescription drugs should be properly identified, and accompanied by a copy of the prescription.

US Customs – All articles brought into the US must be declared at the time of entry. **Exempt** from customs regulations: personal effects; one liter of alcoholic beverages (providing visitor is at least 21 years old); either 200 cigarettes, 50 cigars or 2 kilograms of smoking tobacco; and gifts (to persons in the US) that do not exceed $100 in value. **Prohibited items**: any plant material; firearms and ammunition (if not intended for legitimate sporting purposes); meat or poultry products; and items from restricted countries. For further information about US customs, contact the US embassy or consulate, or the Chicago District Office, US Customs Service, 610 S. Canal St., Chicago IL 60607 ☎312-353-6100. It is also recommended that visitors contact their country's customs service to determine reentry regulations.

Foreign Consulates – In Chicago, international visitors can contact the consulate of their country of origin.

Country	Address	☎
Brazil	401 N. Michigan Ave, Suite 3050	312-464-0244
Canada	180 N. Stetson Ave., Suite 2400	312-616-1860
France	737 N. Michigan Ave., Suite 2020	312-787-5359
Germany	676 N. Michigan Ave., 32nd Floor	312-580-1199
India	150 N. Michigan Ave., Suite 1100	312-781-6273
Japan	737 N. Michigan Ave., Suite 1100	312-280-0400
Mexico	300 N. Michigan Ave., 2nd Floor	312-855-1380
United Kingdom	33 N. Dearborn St., 9th Floor	312-346-1810

Getting Around by Car – Foreign visitors are not required to obtain an International Driver's License to drive in the US. A valid license issued by the country of residence is sufficient. Drivers must carry vehicle registration and/or rental contract, and proof of automobile insurance at all times. Rental cars *(p 228)* in the US are usually equipped with automatic transmission, and rental rates tend to be less expensive than overseas. Gasoline is sold by the gallon (1 gal = 3.8l) and is considerably more affordable than in other countries. Gas stations are found in clusters near expressway entrances. In rural areas, they are usually located on the major roads. Self-service gas stations do not offer car repair, although many sell standard maintenance items. Road regulations in the US require that vehicles be driven on the right side of the road. Traffic lights are usually mounted above the middle of the intersection; drivers should stop well before the pedestrian crosswalk.

BASIC INFORMATION

Electricity – Voltage in the US is 120 volts AC, 60 HZ. Foreign-made appliances may need AC adapters (available at specialty travel and electronics stores) and North American flat-blade plugs.

Telephone – *See also p 232*. **Emergencies** (police, fire, ambulance): **911**. To call other area codes, dial 1+area code+number. To place an international call, dial 011+country code+area code+number. A list of country codes can be found in the Yellow Pages. Telephone numbers preceded by **800** or **888** are toll-free (no charge) in the US. The charge for numbers preceded by **900** can range anywhere from $.50-$15/minute. Most hotels add a surcharge for local and long-distance calls. For further information dial "0" for operator assistance.

Money

Credit Cards & Travelers Checks – Most banks are members of the network of Automatic Teller Machines (ATMs) allowing visitors from around the world access to cash withdrawals using bank cards and major credit cards. Most network names (Cirrus, Honor, Plus) are displayed on the ATMs. Visitors should check with their bank before departing for transaction fees. MasterCard/Eurocard offers its members emergency aid service at all Thomas Cook offices. Banks and almost all stores accept travelers checks with proper identification. **American Express Company Travel Service** offices are located at: 625 N. Michigan Ave. ☎312-435-2570, 122 S. Michigan Ave. ☎312-435-2595 and in Marshall Field's at 111 N. State St. ☎312-781-4477.

Currency Exchange – Many banks located in the Loop offer foreign currency exchange including: **American National Bank & Trust,** 1 N. LaSalle St. ☎312-661-5000 and **Northern Trust Bank,** 50 S. LaSalle St. ☎312-630-6000. The banks charge a small fee for this service. Private companies generally charge higher fees: **Thomas Cook,** 11 W. Washington St. ☎312-236-0583 and **World Money Exchange,** 6 E. Randolph St., Suite 204 ☎312-641-2151. Currency exchange offices can also be found at O'Hare in the International Terminal, upper and lower levels and in terminal 3, Gate K: **O'Hare International Airport Currency Exchange** ☎773-686-7965.

Taxes & Tips – *See also p 232.* Prices displayed or quoted in the US do not generally include sales tax. Note that in the US sales tax is not reimbursable.

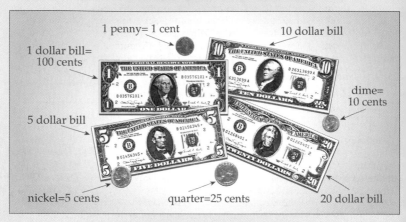

1 penny= 1 cent
10 dollar bill
1 dollar bill= 100 cents
dime= 10 cents
5 dollar bill
nickel=5 cents
quarter=25 cents
20 dollar bill

Accommodations

The Chicago area offers a wide range of accommodations from elegant hotels ($125-$200/day) located in the Loop and around N. Michigan Ave. to more moderately priced motels ($70-$95/day) found throughout the city. Rates tend to be lower in suburban areas (including O'Hare Airport) and on weekends. Amenities include television, restaurant and smoking/nonsmoking rooms. The more elegant hotels also offer room dining and valet service. Some hotels located near Lake Shore Dr. may be within walking distance of a public beach. Inquire when making reservation. *All rates quoted are average prices for a double room.*

Hotels/Motels – The *Metro Chicago Hotel Guide* and *Hotel/Motel Illinois Directory* are available *(free)* from the tourism offices listed on p 224. Major hotel chains with locations in Chicago include:

☎		☎	
Best Western	800-528-1234	Howard Johnson	800-446-4656
Comfort Inn	800-228-5150	Marriott	800-228-9290
Days Inn	800-325-2525	Omni	800-843-6664
Hampton Inn	800-426-7866	Radisson	800-333-3333
Hilton	800-445-8667	Ramada Inn	800-272-6232
Holiday Inn	800-465-4329	Westin Hotels	800-228-3000

Reservation services	☎
Accommodations Express	800-444-7666
Discount Hotel Reservations Network	800-964-6835
Hot Rooms	773-468-7666
	or (North America only) 800-468-3500
Illinois Reservation Service	800-491-1800
Quikbook	800-789-9887
RMC Travel Centre	212-754-6560
	or (US only) 800-782-2674

(toll-free numbers valid worldwide except where indicated)

Bed and Breakfasts – Most of the B&Bs in Chicago are located Downtown and in the Gold Coast, Old Town and Lincoln Park areas. Many B&Bs are privately owned historic homes ($85-$125/day). Continental breakfast is customarily included. Private baths are not always available. Smoking indoors is usually not allowed. **Bed and Breakfast Chicago** offers reservation service for most of the B&Bs in the area; PO Box 14088, Chicago IL 60614 ☎312-951-0085.

Hostels, apartments and dormitory rooms – A no-frills, economical alternative, **hostels** average $13-$45/day. Amenities include community living room, showers, laundry facilities, full-service kitchen and dining room, dormitory-style and private rooms (guests are required to bring their own towels). The **Chicago International Hostel** is located at 6318 N. Winthrop Ave., Chicago IL 60660 ☎773-262-1011. American Youth Hostel operates the **International House of the University of Chicago** (1414 E. 59th St., Chicago IL 60637 ☎773-753-2270), offering year-round rentals of dormitory rooms ($33/day), and the Hostelling International Chicago Summer Hostel at **Columbia College** (731 S. Plymouth Ct., Chicago IL 60605 ☎312-327-5350), providing room rentals from the first week in June through the first week in September ($18-$20/day). Linens are provided; private baths are not available. Advance reservations (7 days) are recommended. Furnished apartment rentals ($95-$125/day) are available through **Bed and Breakfast Chicago** *(above)*.

The Basics

Business Hours – In general most businesses operate Monday to Saturday 9am–6pm. Banks are customarily open Monday to Friday 9am–5:30pm although some may have later hours. Shopping centers operate Monday to Saturday 10am–7 or 9pm, Sunday noon–6pm, and offer extended hours between Thanksgiving and Christmas.

Liquor Law – The legal age for purchase and consumption of alcoholic beverages is 21. Proof of age is normally required. Most bars and taverns are open until 2am and some have extended weekend hours until 4 or 5am. Almost all package-goods stores sell beer, wine and liquor.

Lottery – The Illinois Lottery consists of several number-matching games (prize amounts are determined by total sales for each drawing and the number of prize winners), and a multitude of instant "scratch-and-win" games. Lottery tickets are sold at convenience stores, gas stations and supermarkets; prices range from $.50 to $5. Depending on the game, drawings are held Monday through Saturday. Players must be at least 18 years old. Prize amounts and winning numbers: ☎217-524-5155 or 800-252-1775 (Illinois only).

Major Holidays – Most banks and government offices in the Chicago area are closed on the following legal holidays *(many retail stores and restaurants remain open on days shown with*)*:

New Year's Day	January 1
Martin Luther King, Jr.'s Birthday*	3rd Monday in January
Presidents' Day*	3rd Monday in February
Pulaski Day*	1st Monday in March
Memorial Day*	Last Monday in May or May 30
Independence Day*	July 4
Labor Day*	1st Monday in September
Columbus Day*	2nd Monday in October
Veterans Day*	November 10 or 11
Thanksgiving Day	4th Thursday in November
Christmas Day	December 25

Newspapers & Magazines – Chicago's two main daily newspapers, the *Chicago Tribune* and the *Chicago Sun-Times*, are distributed in the morning. The arts & entertainment sections appear in the *Tribune* on Sunday and in the *Sun-Times* on Friday. Another popular newspaper, the *Chicago Defender* caters to the African-American population. Weekly alternative publications available at bookstores and restaurants around town include *New City* and the *Chicago Reader*.

Safety Tips – Chicago is a relatively safe city. Visitors should remember these common sense tips to ensure a safe and enjoyable visit:

■ Do not carry large sums of money, and don't let strangers see *how much* money you are carrying.

■ Keep a firm hold on purses and knapsacks, carry your wallet in your front pocket and avoid wearing expensive jewelry.

■ Stay awake when riding public transportation, and keep packages close by. CTA buses and trains are equipped with devices that enable riders to notify personnel of emergencies.

■ Always park your car in a well-lit area. Close windows, lock doors and place valuables in the trunk. Exercise caution when visiting areas in the South and West Sides of Chicago.

Taxes & Tips – In Chicago, the sales tax is 8.75%. Taxation of food items in grocery stores is 2%; magazine and newspapers are exempt. The tax rate for rental cars is 18%. The hotel occupancy tax in the city of Chicago is 14.9%; tax percentages vary in outlying suburbs. Since hotel and car rental rates do not reflect the taxes, travelers should be aware of these added charges. It is customary in restaurants to tip the server 15-20% of the bill. At hotels, porters should be given $1 per suitcase and hotel maids $1 per day of occupancy. Taxi drivers are usually tipped 15% of the fare.

Telephone – Instructions for using public telephones are listed on or near the phone. The cost for a local call from a pay phone is $.35 to $.80, depending on the number being called (any combination of nickels, dimes or quarters is accepted). Long-distance calling cards can be used at all public phones (contact the operator if assistance is needed). Most hotels will add a surcharge for local and long-distance calls. Telephone numbers listed in this guide that start with "800" or "888" are toll-free.

Area Codes – Throughout 1996, new area codes are being introduced in the Greater Chicago region. In this guidebook, all phone numbers are preceded by these latest area codes. Note that numbers preceded by the 773 area code should be dialed with the 312 area code until October 1996.

Chicago (*downtown*)	312	**Western suburbs**	630
Chicago (*other areas*)	773	**Southern suburbs**	708
Northern suburbs	847		

Important Numbers

Police/Ambulance/Fire (*24hrs*)	**911**
Police (nonemergency, *24hrs*)	312-746-6000
Medical Society Referrals (*Mon–Fri 8:30am–4:30pm*)	312-670-2550
Dental Association Referrals (*Mon–Fri 9am–5pm*)	312-836-7300
24-hour pharmacy Walgreens	(US only) 800-925-4733

(over 30 locations in Greater Chicago area, call for closest store)

Time Zone – Chicago is on Central Standard Time (CST), 1 hour behind Eastern Standard Time (EST), 6 hours behind Greenwich Mean Time (GMT). Therefore, when it is 9am in Chicago, it is 10am in New York City and 3pm in London. Daylight Saving Time (clocks advanced 1hr) is in effect for most of the US from the first Sunday in April until the last Sunday in October.

TV & Radio – In Chicago, many network television programs run an hour earlier than in other US time zones.

MAJOR TV NETWORKS			
ABC	Channel 7	NBC	Channel 5
CBS	Channel 2	FOX	Channel 32

MAJOR AM RADIO STATIONS		MAJOR FM RADIO STATIONS			
670	News/talk	88.1	Blues	98.3	Country
720	News/talk	91.5	NPR	98.7	Classical
820	Sport	93.1	Rock	100.3	Contemporary
1000	Sports/talk	97.1	Classical/Jazz	101.1	Alternative rock
1480	Contemporary	97.9	Rock	103.5	Rock

Sightseeing

VISITOR INFORMATION CENTERS

Two free publications, *Key This Week* and *Where Chicago* (monthly), offer information on events, attractions, shopping and dining. Both are available at hotels and visitor information kiosks.

Chicago Office of Tourism

Chicago Cultural Center:	78 E. Washington St. *(open year-round Mon–Fri 10am–6pm, Thu 7pm; Sat 10am–5pm, Sun noon–5pm; closed major holidays; &.)*
Chicago Water Tower:	806 N. Michigan Ave. *(open Memorial Day–Labor Day Mon–Fri 9:30am–7pm, Sat 10am–7pm, Sun 11am–6pm; rest of the year Mon–Fri 9:30am–6pm, Sat 10am–6pm, Sun 11am–5pm; closed Jan 1, Dec 25).*

TOURS *Map p 221*

A variety of guided tours are available to the visitor. Below you will find a selection of the principal tours.

Chicago Architecture Foundation (CAF) – *224 S. Michigan Ave., Chicago IL 60604* ☎*312-922-3432; recorded tour information 312-922-8687.* The CAF was founded in 1966 to preserve and increase public appreciation of Chicago's architecture. Today, the organization conducts over 50 tours of Chicago's neighborhoods by foot, bus, boat and bicycle. Cost of tours is discounted for CAF members.

CAF River Cruise – In-depth study of the architecture of the Loop as seen from the Chicago River *(1hr 30min; departs from southwest corner of Michigan Ave. Bridge May–early Jun Mon–Fri noon, weekends noon & 2pm; early Jun–Sept daily 9:30am, noon, 2pm; Oct Mon–Fri noon, weekends noon & 2pm; $17; & reservations ☎312-902-1500).*

Tour Boats, Chicago River

Carol Mallory/DPA

Loop Walking Tours – "Early Skyscrapers" examines the beginnings of the Chicago school of architecture through study of structures built between 1880 and 1940 *(2hrs; departs from CAF Shop & Tour Center Mar–Nov Mon–Fri 10am, Sat 10am & 2:30pm, Sun 1:30pm; Dec–Feb Mon–Sat 10am, Sun 1:30pm; $10).*
"Modern and Beyond" looks at International, Modern and post-Modern works *(2hrs; departs from CAF Shop & Tour Center Mar–Nov Mon–Fri 1:30pm, Sat 11am & 1:30pm, Sun 1:30pm; Dec–Feb daily 1:30pm; $10).*

Chicago Architecture Highlights by Bus – This tour of Downtown, the Gold Coast and Hyde Park emphasizes the diversity and significance of the city's buildings *(3hrs 30min; departs from CAF Shop & Tour Center Mar–Nov Sat 9:30am; rest of the year 1st & 3rd Sat 9:30am; $25; reservations ☎312-922-3432 ext. 140).*

Shoreline Sightseeing – Narrated tours (in 12 languages) on Lake Michigan offer a panoramic view of the entire skyline *(30min; departs from: Navy Pier Memorial Day–Oct daily 11am–9pm; Buckingham Fountain Jun–Aug daily 7:15–11:15pm; Shedd Aquarium May–Sept daily 11:15am–6:15pm; $6; Shoreline ☎312-222-9328).*

Summer Sunset Cruise – This narrated tour highlights the city's history and architecture from the Chicago River and Lake Michigan *(2hrs; departs from southwest corner of Michigan Ave. Bridge May–Oct daily 7:30pm; arrive 45min prior to departure for best seating; $12; Mercury ☎312-332-1368).*

Chicago Trolley & Chicago Motor Coach – Tours of Chicago aboard trolleys and double-decker buses are offered daily year-round. Visitors can board every 10-15min at any of the 12 stops located at major attractions. The itinerary lasts about 1hr 30min; the same ticket allows free reboarding for the entire day. Tickets $10 (non-stop), $13 or $15 (on/off). **Chicago Trolley Co.** *(year-round daily Mon–Fri 9:30am–5pm, weekends 9am–5:30pm; ☎312-738-0900);* **Chicago Motor Coach Co.** *(Memorial Day–Labor Day daily 9:30am–6pm; rest of the year daily 9:30am–5pm; ☎312-922-8919).*

Carriage – Several companies offer tours that originate from the Chicago Water Tower area. In general, carriages hold 4-6 passengers. Tour route depends on passenger preference, and the tour can last from 30min–1hr 30min *(year-round Mon–Fri 10:30am–3:30pm & 6:30pm–midnight, weekends 10am–2-3am; $30-$90 depending on tour length; tours not offered if daytime temperatures exceed 90°F).*

Gangster – A lighthearted and often silly look at Prohibition-era Chicago and the gangsters that ruled this city *(2hrs; departs mornings from Pumping Station, evenings from Capone's Chicago year-round daily, hours determined by demand; not offered Jan 1, Easter Sunday and Dec 25; reservations recommended; $20; Untouchable Gangster Tours ☎773-881-1195).*

Historical – Narrated cruise of the Chicago River and Lake Michigan providing in-depth information about Chicago's checkered past *(1hr 30min; departures on the Marquette from North Pier May–Sept Mon–Fri 11am, 1 & 3pm, weekends 9 & 11am, 1 & 3pm; board 15min before departure; reservations recommended; $16; Chicago From the Lake Historical Tour ☎312-527-1977).*

Self-guided Literary Tour *(consult the index for descriptions)*

Location/Fame	Area
Fine Arts Building	Loop
Site of the "Little Room" 1890s literary gatherings Founding of Harriet Monroe's *Poetry* magazine in 1911 Founding of Margaret Anderson's *Little Review* in 1914	
Chicago Board of Trade	Loop
Setting (previous building) for *The Titan* by Theodore Dreiser and *The Pit* by Frank Norris	
Tribune Tower	Magnificent Mile
Columnist Mike Royko's place of employment	
1340 N. State Pkwy.	Gold Coast
Former *Playboy* Mansion	
4646 N. Hermitage Ave. (Ravenswood)	Uptown
Dwelling (2nd floor) of Carl Sandburg when writing *Chicago Poems*	
1958 W. Evergreen Ave. (Wicker Park)	Milwaukee Avenue
Dwelling (3rd floor) of Nelson Algren, 1959-1975	
Printer's Row	South Loop
Setting for Sara Paretsky novels	
47th Street, Drexel Blvd. to M.L. King, Jr. Dr.	Near South Side
Setting for *Native Son* by Richard Wright, and *A Street in Bronzeville* by Gwendolyn Brooks	
Union Stock Yards	Bridgeport/Canaryville
Setting for Upton Sinclair's *The Jungle*	
University of Chicago	University of Chicago
Setting for novels by Saul Bellow, Pearl S. Buck, Phillip Roth, Robert Pirsig, Robert Herrick	
339 and 600 N. Oak Park Ave.	Oak Park
Birthplace and boyhood home of Ernest Hemingway	

Outdoor sculpture in and around the Loop
Sculptures described in this guide are indicated with a page reference.

Sculptor / *Works*	Location

From Congress Pkwy. to Monroe St.

Ivan Mestrovic
The Bowman and The Spearman .... Grant Park, Grand Entrance *(p 110)*

Alexander Calder
Flamingo .... Federal Center plaza *(p 52)*

Augustus Saint-Gaudens
The Seated Lincoln .... Grant Park, *Court of Presidents (p 110)*

Lorado Taft
The Fountain of the Great Lakes .... Art Institute of Chicago, South Wing

Edward Kemeys
Lions .... Art Institute of Chicago, main entrance *(p 60)*

Dankmar Adler and Louis Sullivan
Chicago Stock Exchange Arch .... Art Institute of Chicago, Columbus Drive entrance

From Monroe St. to Washington St.

Marc Chagall
Four Seasons .... First National Bank plaza *(p 51)*

Louise Nevelson
Dawn Shadows .... Madison Plaza *(p 55)*

Joan Miró
Miró's Chicago .... Washington St., next to Chicago Temple *(p 55)*

From Washington St. to Wacker Dr.

Pablo Picasso
Untitled .... Daley Center plaza *(p 56)*

Virginio Ferrari
Being Born .... Corner of State and Washington Sts. *(p 50)*

Jean Dubuffet
Monument with Standing Beast .... James R. Thompson Center plaza *(p 56)*

Jerry Peart
Splash .... Corner of S. Michigan Ave. and Lake St.

TIPS FOR SPECIAL VISITORS

Chicago for Children – *Chicago Parent*, a free monthly magazine, includes articles of interest to parents as well as an extensive calendar of family-oriented events, and is available at major attractions and libraries throughout the area. Copies by mail: 141 S. Oak Park Ave., Oak Park IL 60302 ☎708-386-5555. The popular Chicago Children's Museum *(p 88)* features interactive exhibits designed for children under age 12. Most attractions in Chicago offer discounted, if not free, admission to visitors under 18 years of age. In addition, many hotels boast special family discount packages, and restaurants can provide a special children's menu. Two annual events, the **Oz Festival** near the Lincoln Park Zoo *(mid-Jul ☎773-929-8686)* and the **57th Street Children's Book Fair** *(mid-Sept ☎773-702-6421)* are conceived especially for children. **The Children's Bookstore** carries a large selection of books and educational toys for children and young adults *(2465 N. Lincoln Ave. ☎773-248-2665)*. Sights of particular interest to children and students in this guide are indicated with [Kids] symbol. Many of these attractions offer special children's programs.

Disabled Travelers – *Wheelchair access to the sights described in this guide is indicated in admission information accompanying the sight description by ⅀ symbol.* Recent federal law requires that existing businesses (including hotels and restaurants) increase accessibility and provide specially designed accommodations for the disabled. It also requires that wheelchair access, devices for the hearing impaired, and designated parking spaces be available at newly constructed hotels and restaurants. The front seats of CTA transportation are reserved for persons with disabilities.

Senior Citizens – Most attractions, hotels and restaurants offer discounts to visitors age 62 and older (proof of age may be required). The **American Association of Retired Persons** (AARP) offers additional discounts to members. 601 E St. NW, Washington DC 20049 ☎202-434-2277.

Entertainment

USEFUL NUMBERS

(prerecorded information)

Mayor's Office of Special Events
☎312-744-3370

Dance Hotline
☎312-419-8383

Fine Arts Hotline
☎312-346-3278

Jam Concert Line
☎312-666-6667

Jazz Hotline
☎312-427-3300

Kevin O Mooney /Odyssey

PERFORMING ARTS

Chicago provides a variety of music and entertainment year-round. Close to 100 theaters host a variety of dramas and musicals, ranging from traveling Broadway productions to performances by highly acclaimed local companies. Dance, symphony and opera productions are performed at venues throughout the city. Small clubs specializing in jazz, blues, rock and country offer first-class music in an intimate setting. Popular rock and alternative performers play in stadiums or convention centers in outlying areas. Summer brings the suburban Ravinia Festival *(p 220)* as well as outdoor performances at parks and downtown plazas. For a detailed listing of events, call the Mayor's Office of Special Events *(above)* or consult the arts and entertainment sections listed on p 231.

Music & Dance

Classical Music	Venue	☎
Chicago Symphony Orchestra	Orchestra Hall 220 S. Michigan Ave. (Loop)	312-435-6666
Chicago Sinfonietta	Orchestra Hall 220 S. Michigan Ave. (Loop)	312-857-1062
Chicago Opera Theater	Merle Reskin Theatre 60 E. Balbo Ave. (South Loop)	773-292-7578
Concerts Under the Dome	Ascension Church 815 S. East Ave., Oak Park	708-383-6456
Grant Park Symphony Orchestra *(mid-Jun–late Aug)*	Petrillo Music Shell (Loop/Grant Park)	312-819-0614
Lyric Opera	20 N. Wacker Dr. (Loop)	312-332-2244
Old Town School of Folk Music	909 W. Armitage Ave. (Lincoln Park/DePaul)	773-525-7793

Rock/Pop		
Aragon Ballroom	1106 W. Lawrence Ave. (Uptown)	312-559-1212
Double Door	1572 N. Milwaukee Ave. (Wicker Park)	773-489-3160
Metro	3730 N. Clark St. (Lakeview/Wrigleyville)	312-549-0203
Rosemont Horizon	5400 N. River Rd., Rosemont	312-559-1212
Skyline Stage	Navy Pier (Streeterville)	312-791-7437
Star Plaza Theater	I-65 and US 30, Merrillville IN	773-734-7266
United Center	1901 W. Madison St. (Near West Side)	312-559-1212

Dance		
Ballet Chicago	22 W. Monroe St. (Loop)	312-251-8838
Hubbard Street Dance Chicago	218 S. Wabash Ave. (Loop)	312-663-0853
Joffrey Ballet of Chicago	22 W. Monroe St. (Loop)	312-739-0120

Theaters & Performances

Theater in Chicago Guide, a free bimonthly publication available at major hotels and visitor information centers, provides descriptions and schedules of plays currently being performed.

Theaters	Address	☎
Apollo Theater	2540 N. Lincoln Ave. (Lincoln Park/DePaul)	773-935-6100
Athenaeum Theatre	2936 N. Southport Ave. (Lakeview/Wrigleyville)	773-935-6860
Auditorium Theatre	50 E. Congress Pkwy. (Loop)	312-431-2357
Body Politic/ Victory Gardens Theatre	2257-61 N. Lincoln Ave. (Lincoln Park/DePaul)	773-871-3000
Briar Street Theatre	3133 N. Halsted St. (Lakeview/Wrigleyville)	773-348-4000
Chicago Theatre	175 N. State St. (Loop)	312-902-1500
Lincolnshire Theatre	10 Marriott Dr., Lincolnshire	847-634-0200
Goodman Theatre	200 S. Columbus Dr. (Loop/Grant Park)	312-443-3800
Mayfair Theatre *(Shear Madness)*	636 S. Michigan Ave. (Loop)	312-786-9120
Organic Theatre	3319 N. Clark St. (Lakeview/Wrigleyville)	773-327-5588
Puppet Parlor	1922 W. Montrose Ave.	773-774-2919
Royal George Theatre	1641 N. Halsted St. (Lincoln Park/DePaul)	312-988-9000
Shakespeare Repertory *(mid-Oct–mid-May)* *(Aug, free)*	Ruth Page Theater 1016 N. Dearborn St. (River North) Petrillo Music Shell (Loop/Grant Park)	312-642-2273
Shubert Theatre	22 W. Monroe St. (Loop)	312-977-1710
Steppenwolf Theatre Company	1650 N. Halsted St. (Lincoln Park/DePaul)	312-335-1650
Theatre Building	1225 W. Belmont Ave. (Lakeview/Wrigleyville)	773-327-5252
Touchstone Theatre	2851 N. Halsted St. (Lakeview/Wrigleyville)	773-404-4700

Tickets

As some of the more popular events sell out months in advance, it is recommended to buy tickets early. Full-price tickets can be purchased directly from the venue's box office or from one of the companies listed below; major credit cards are accepted (a service charge of $1-$5 may be added to the ticket price). Licensed ticket agencies sometimes have tickets available when the box office is sold-out but expect to pay a substantial service fee (up to 35%). The hotel concierge may be able to help secure tickets for a performance.

Hot Tix offers half-price tickets for selected events on the day of the show. Purchases must be made in person *(two locations in Chicago: 108 N. State St. and 700 N. Michigan Ave. in Chicago Place; open year-round Mon–Fri 10am–7pm, Sat 10am–6pm, Sun noon–5pm; ☎312-977-1755)*. **Ticketmaster** *(☎312-559-1212)* outlets are found at most locations of Carson Pirie Scott, Tower Records, Blockbuster Music and Hot Tix.

NIGHTLIFE

Nightlife in Chicago ranges from quiet, elegant hotel lounges to lively rock bars along Rush and Division Streets or sultry blues and jazz clubs on the North and South sides. The city has also garnered an excellent reputation for its numerous comedy clubs, which have hosted the likes of John Belushi, Dan Aykroyd and Bonnie Hunt. Consult the arts and entertainment sections of the alternative publications listed on p 231 for a detailed listing of events. Some establishments have a "cover charge." Many bars and clubs serve food (menu may be scaled down to light appetizers after 10 or 11pm). As alcoholic beverages are served, proof of age is required to enter clubs.

Nightclubs

Blues

Blues	Address	☎
Blue Chicago	736 N. Clark St. (River North)	312-642-6261
Blue Chicago on Clark	536 N. Clark St. (River North)	312-661-0100
B.L.U.E.S.	2519 N. Halsted St. (Lincoln Park/DePaul)	773-528-1012
B.L.U.E.S. Etcetera	1124 W. Belmont Ave. (Lakeview/Wrigleyville)	773-525-8989
Buddy Guy's Legends	754 S. Wabash Ave. (South Loop)	312-427-0333
Checkerboard Lounge	423 E. 43rd St. (Near South Side)	773-624-3240
Kingston Mines	2548 N. Halsted St. (Lincoln Park/DePaul)	773-477-4646
Koko Taylor's Chicago Blues	7 W. Division St. (Gold Coast)	312-337-2583

Comedy

Comedy		
The Chicago Improv	504 N. Wells St. (River North)	312-782-6387
The Second City	1616 N. Wells St. (Old Town)	312-337-3992
Zanies Comedy Night Club	1548 N. Wells St. (Old Town)	312-337-4027

Dinner Theater

Dinner Theater		
Tommy Gun's Garage	1239 S. State St. (South Loop)	773-728-2828
Tony n' Tina's Wedding	230 W. North Ave. (Old Town)	312-664-8844

Jazz

Jazz		
Andy's	11 E. Hubbard St. (River North)	312-642-6805
Cotton Club	1710 S. Michigan Ave. (South Loop)	312-341-9787
Dick's Last Resort	435 E. Illinois St. (Streeterville)	312-836-7870
Gold Star Sardine Bar	680 N. Lake Shore Pl. (Streeterville)	312-664-4215
The Green Mill	4802 N. Broadway (Uptown)	773-878-5552
Pops for Champagne	2934 N. Sheffield Ave. (Lakeview/Wrigleyville)	773-472-1000
Underground Wonder Bar	10 E. Walton Pl. (Magnificent Mile)	312-266-7761

Clubs

Clubs		
Excalibur Entertainment Complex	632 N. Dearborn St. (River North)	312-266-1944
Red Dog	1958 W. North Ave. (Wicker Park)	773-278-1009
Wild Hare & Singing Armadillo Frog Sanctuary	3530 N. Clark St. (Lakeview/Wrigleyville)	773-327-4273

GALLERIES & ART FAIRS

Art Galleries

In general, most galleries are open Tuesday through Saturday from 9-11am to 5-6pm; many close between exhibits. The *chicago gallery news*, published quarterly, provides a comprehensive listing of exhibits and their locations (free, available at galleries and visitor centers). Chicago's main gallery districts are:

River North .... between N. Wells, N. Orleans, W. Superior and W. Huron Sts.
Michigan Avenue .... between E. Oak and E. Ontario Sts.

Clusters of galleries can also be found in:
West Side .... along N. Milwaukee Ave. between N. Damen Ave. and N. Wood St.
North Side .... off N. Lincoln Ave. between W. School and W. Division Sts.
Evanston *(p 196)* .... along Sherman Ave. and Grove St.

Chicago Art Fairs

Featuring a variety of unique handcrafted items, including ceramics, wood carvings, paintings and photography, art fairs offer a lively forum for local artisans to sell their wares. Festivals held in the summer may include musicians and other entertainment. Most of the events listed below have food and beverages for sale. Note that many vendors will reduce the prices of their wares on the last day of sale.

Fairs and Festivals	Date
Body Politic Street Festival (Lincoln Park/DePaul) 2200 N. block of Lincoln Ave.	last weekend in May ☎773-868-3010
57th Street Art Fair (Hyde Park/Kenwood) E. 57th St. at Kenwood Ave.	1st weekend in Jun ☎773-493-3247
Park West Antiques Fair (Lincoln Park/DePaul) W. Fullerton Pkwy. and N. Orchard St.	1st weekend in Jun ☎773-477-5100

Fairs and Festivals (*continued*)   **Date**

Wells Street Art Festival (Old Town)   2nd weekend in Jun
1543 N. Wells St.   ☎ 312-951-6106

Old Town Art Fair (Old Town)   2nd weekend in Jun
W. Menomonee & N. Orleans Sts.   ☎ 312-337-1938

"Celebrate on State" Festival (Loop)   3rd Wed–Fri in Jun
State St., between Wacker Dr. & Van Buren St.   ☎ 708-325-8080

Lakeview Central Festival (Lakeview/Wrigleyville)   3rd weekend in Jun
W. Belmont & N. Sheffield Aves.   ☎ 773-868-3010

Water Tower Art & Craft Festival (Magnificent Mile)   last weekend in Jun
E. Chicago Ave. between N. Michigan Ave. & Lake Shore Dr. ☎ 312-751-2500

Gold Coast Art Fair (Gold Coast)   2nd weekend in Aug
N. Dearborn to N. Wells Sts.   ☎ 312-744-2400

Northalsted Market Days   2nd weekend in Aug
N. Halsted St. between W. Belmont Ave. & Addison St.   ☎ 773-868-3010

New East Side Artworks (Loop)   3rd weekend in Aug
E. Lake St. east of S. Michigan Ave.   ☎ 312-551-9290

African Festival of the Arts (Field Museum)   Labor Day weekend
Roosevelt Rd. at Lake Shore Dr.   ☎ 773-955-7742

RESTAURANTS

Chicago's cuisine is as varied as its population. A unique dining experience can be
found on almost every city block. The list below represents a sampling of some of
the city's more popular and well-frequented establishments and does not constitute
a recommendation. Most restaurants are open daily and accept major credit cards.
The $ symbol under the Price category represents: $=inexpensive; $$=moderate;
$$$= expensive. *Reservations are highly recommended for $$$ restaurants.*

Restaurant/Address	*Area*/☎	Price
AMERICAN		
Ed Debevic's 640 N. Wells St.	*River North* ☎ 312-664-1707	$
Goose Island Brewing Co. 1800 N. Clybourn Ave.	*Lincoln Park/DePaul* ☎ 312-915-0071	$
Hard Rock Cafe 63 W. Ontario St.	*River North* ☎ 312-943-2252	$
Kinzie Street Chophouse 400 N. Wells St.	*River North* ☎ 312-822-0191	$$
Lou Mitchell's 565 W. Jackson Blvd.	*Loop* ☎ 312-939-3111	$
Michael Jordan's Restaurant 500 N. LaSalle St.	*River North* ☎ 312-644-3865	$$
Planet Hollywood 633 N. Wells St.	*River North* ☎ 312-266-7827	$$
Prairie 500 S. Dearborn St.	*South Loop* ☎ 312-663-1143	$$$
Pump Room 1301 N. State Pkwy.	*Gold Coast* ☎ 312-266-0360	$$$
CHINESE		
Emperor's Choice 2238 S. Wentworth Ave.	*Chinatown (Near South Side)* ☎ 312-225-8800	$
Hong Min Restaurant 221 W. Cermak Rd.	*Chinatown (Near South Side)* ☎ 312-842-5026	$
House of Hunan 535 N. Michigan Ave.	*Magnificent Mile* ☎ 312-329-9494	$$
DELI		
Manny's Coffee Shop 1141 S. Jefferson St.	*South Loop/Near South Side* ☎ 312-939-2855	$

Restaurant/Address	Area/☎	Price
FRENCH		
Ambria 2300 N. Lincoln Park West	*Lincoln Park/DePaul* ☎ 773-472-5959	$$$
Bistro 110 110 E. Pearson St.	*Magnificent Mile* ☎ 312-266-3110	$$
Charlie Trotter's 816 W. Armitage Ave.	*Lincoln Park/DePaul* ☎ 773-248-6228	$$$
Chez Paul 660 N. Rush St.	*River North* ☎ 312-944-6680	$$$
Everest 440 S. LaSalle St., 40th Fl.	*Loop* ☎ 312-663-8920	$$$
St. Germain Bakery & Cafe 1210 N. State Pkwy.	*Gold Coast* ☎ 312-266-9900	$$
Un Grand Café 2300 N. Lincoln Park West	*Lincoln Park/DePaul* ☎ 773-348-8886	$$
GERMAN		
Berghoff Restaurant 17 W. Adams St.	*Loop* ☎ 312-427-3170	$
Chicago Brauhaus 4732 N. Lincoln Ave.	*Lincoln Square* ☎ 773-784-4444	$
GREEK		
Greek Islands 200 S. Halsted St.	*Near West Side* ☎ 312-782-9855	$
Papagus 600 N. State St.	*River North* ☎ 312-642-8450	$$
Santorini's Restaurant 138 S. Halsted St.	*Near West Side* ☎ 312-829-8820	$$
INDIAN		
Bukhara 2 E. Ontario St.	*River North* ☎ 312-943-0188	$$
Klay Oven 414 N. Orleans St.	*River North* ☎ 312-527-3999	$$$
ITALIAN		
Bice Ristorante 158 E. Ontario St.	*Magnificent Mile* ☎ 312-664-1474	$$$
Cafe Spiaggia 980 N. Michigan Ave.	*Magnificent Mile* ☎ 312-280-2764	$$
Carlucci 2215 N. Halsted St.	*Lincoln Park/DePaul* ☎ 773-281-1220	$$$
Harry Caray's Restaurant 33 W. Kinzie St.	*River North* ☎ 312-828-0966	$$$
Italian Village 71 W. Monroe St.	*Loop* ☎ 312-332-7005	$$
La Locanda 745 N. LaSalle St.	*River North* ☎ 312-335-9550	$$$
New Rosebud Cafe 1500 W. Taylor St.	*Little Italy (Near West Side)* ☎ 312-942-1117	$$$
Salvatore's Ristorante 525 W. Arlington Pl.	*Lincoln Park/DePaul* ☎ 773-528-1200	$$
Scoozi! 410 W. Huron St.	*River North* ☎ 312-943-5900	$$
Spiaggia Restaurant 980 N. Michigan Ave.	*Magnificent Mile* ☎ 312-280-2750	$$$
Trattoria No. 10 10 N. Dearborn St.	*Loop* ☎ 312-984-1718	$$

Restaurant/Address	Area/☎	Price
JAPANESE		
Benkay 320 N. Dearborn St.	*River North* ☎ 312-836-5490	$$$
Ron of Japan 230 E. Ontario St.	*Magnificent Mile* ☎ 312-644-6500	$$$
LATIN AMERICAN		
Cafe Ba-Ba-Reeba! 2024 N. Halsted St.	*Lincoln Park/DePaul* ☎ 773-935-5000	$$$
Frontera Grill 445 N. Clark St.	*River North* ☎ 312-661-1434	$$
Hat Dance Restaurant 325 W. Huron St.	*River North* ☎ 312-649-0066	$$
Tania's 2659 N. Milwaukee Ave.	*Logan Square* ☎ 773-235-7120	$$
Topolobampo 445 N. Clark St.	*River North* ☎ 312-661-1434	$$$
PIZZA		
Edwardo's Natural Pizza 1212 N. Dearborn St.	*Gold Coast* ☎ 312-337-4490	$
Gino's East 160 E. Superior St.	*Magnificent Mile* ☎ 312-943-1124	$
Pizzeria Due 619 N. Wabash Ave.	*River North* ☎ 312-943-2400	$
Pizzeria Uno 29 E. Ohio St.	*River North* ☎ 312-321-1000	$
RUSSIAN		
Russian Tea Time 77 E. Adams St.	*Loop* ☎ 312-360-0000	$$
SEAFOOD		
Cape Cod Room 140 E. Walton Pl.	*Magnificent Mile* ☎ 312-787-2200	$$$
Catch 35 35 W. Wacker Dr.	*Loop* ☎ 312-346-3500	$$
The Crabhouse 745 N. Wells St.	*River North* ☎ 312-664-2722	$$
Nick's Fishmarket W. Monroe St. at Dearborn St.	*Loop* ☎ 312-621-0200	$$$
Palmer's Steak & Seafood House 17 E. Monroe St.	*Loop* ☎ 312-726-7500	$$
Shaw's Crab House 21 E. Hubbard St.	*River North* ☎ 312-527-2722	$$$
STEAKHOUSE		
Chicago Chop House 60 W. Ontario St.	*River North* ☎ 312-787-7100	$$$
Club Gene & Georgetti 500 N. Franklin St.	*River North* ☎ 312-527-3718	$$$
Eli's, The Place For Steak 215 E. Chicago Ave.	*Magnificent Mile* ☎ 312-642-1393	$$$
Lawry's The Prime Rib 100 E. Ontario St.	*River North* ☎ 312-787-5000	$$$
Morton's of Chicago 1050 N. State St.	*Gold Coast* ☎ 312-266-4820	$$$
That Steak Joynt 1610 N. Wells St.	*Old Town* ☎ 312-943-5091	$$$

Shopping

A world-class shopping mecca, Chicago attracts residents and tourists alike to its famous department stores, designer boutiques and trendy second-hand shops, not to mention its large flea market featuring live blues. The main shopping areas are clustered around Downtown, but the various neighborhoods offer their fill of tiny stores stocked with used books, unusual crafts or ethnic fare. Most stores accept major credit cards and travelers checks, but are reluctant to take out-of-state checks. Many shops extend their hours during the Christmas season (typically starting in mid-November). The *Chicago Official Visitors Guide*, published by the Chicago Convention and Tourism Bureau *(p 224)*, offers detailed information on the types of shops, their locations and hours of operation.

Main Shopping Areas

The Loop – Chicago's two largest department stores, **Carson Pirie Scott & Co.** *(1 S. State St.; Mon–Fri 9:45am–7pm, Sat 9:45am–6pm, Sun noon–5pm;* ☎*312-641-7000)* and **Marshall Field & Co.** *(111 N. State St.; Mon–Sat 9:45am–7pm, Sun noon–5pm;* ☎*312-781-1000)* anchor the main shopping area along State St. **Jewelers Row** *(Wabash Ave. between Madison & Washington Sts.),* the center of Chicago's jewelry business, includes **Wabash Jewelers Mall** *(21 N. Wabash Ave.; Mon–Wed 10am–5:30pm, Thu 10am–6:30pm, Sat 10am–5pm;* ☎*312-263-1757)* and the **Mallers Building** *(5 S. Wabash Ave.; Mon–Fri 9:30am–4:30pm, Sat 9am–3pm;* ☎*312-853-2057).* **Booksellers Row** *(408 S. Michigan Ave.; Mon–Thu 11:30am–9:30pm, Fri–Sat 11:30am–10:30pm, Sun noon–8pm;* ☎*312-427-4242)* offers a vast selection of used books in excellent condition. The **Atrium Mall** *(100 W. Randolph St., Level 2 of the James R. Thompson Center; Mon–Fri 8am–6pm, Sat 11am–4pm;* ☎*312-346-0777)* includes over 30 stores and restaurants.

River North – Best known for its art galleries *(p 103)* and boutiques, River North also includes the **Jazz Record Mart** *(444 N. Wabash Ave.; Mon–Sat 10am–8pm, Sun noon–5pm;* ☎*312-222-1467),* reportedly the world's largest jazz and blues record store. **Jay Robert's Antique Warehouse** *(149 W. Kinzie St.; Mon–Sat 10am–5pm;* ☎*312-222-0167)*

North Michigan Avenue Shopping

- Jil Sander
- Sonia Rykiel
- Hermès
- Ultimo
- Oak St. — 1000N
- ▲ Barneys New York
- Ann Taylor
- Giorgio Armani
- Shops of One Magnificent Mile ■
- Walton St. — 932N
- 900 N. Michigan Shops ■
- ● Bally Mark Shale
- ● Bulgari
- Delaware Pl. — 900N
- Rush St.
- Michigan Avenue
- Chestnut St. — 860N
- FAO Schwarz
- Water Tower Place ■
- Borders Books & Music
- Filene's Basement ●
- Pearson St. — 830N
- Chicago Ave. — 800N
- THE MAGNIFICENT MILE
- Banana Republic
- Neiman Marcus ▲
- Superior St. — 732N
- ● Joan & David
- ● Tiffany & Co.
- Chicago Place ■
- ● Brooks Bros.
- Huron St. — 700N
- ● The Gap
- ● Cole-Haan
- Express ●
- ● Nike Town
- Erie St. — 658N
- Crate & Barrel ●
- Waterford Wedgwood ●
- Cartier Inc. ●
- Ontario St. — 628N
- 600 N. Michigan ■ (opens late 1996)
- Ohio St. — 600N
- Rush St.
- Michigan Avenue
- ● Timberland Co.
- Grand Ave. — 530N
- 65 E
- 100 E
- Illinois St. — 500N
- ● Hammacher Schlemmer & Co.
- ● Retail Store ▲ Department Store ■ Shopping Mall

houses 54,000sq ft of antique furniture and housewares on three floors. Also in this area, the collection of stores at the Merchandise Mart, **Shops at the Mart** *(300 N. Wells St.; hours vary;* ☎*312-527-7615)*, incorporates over 50 food, specialty and apparel shops including **Carson Pirie Scott**, **Crabtree & Evelyn** and the **Coach Store**.

Lincoln Park/DePaul – This district offers an eclectic assortment of second-hand shops, funky boutiques and a branch of the Hollywood landmark music store, **Tower Records** *(2301 N. Clark St.; daily 9am–midnight;* ☎*773-477-5994)*. Several used book-stores line Lincoln Ave. north of Fullerton Ave.

Hyde Park – This neighborhood is a bookworm's delight, offering a slew of book-stores, grouped around the University of Chicago and along E. 57th and E. 55th Sts., featuring new, used and hard-to-find books. **Harper Court** *(5210-25 S. Harper Ave.; hours vary;* ☎*773-363-8282)* is an open-air mall consisting of close to 20 specialty shops and restaurants.

Devon Avenue – *Between Western & California Aves.* The "Midwest capital of gold dealers" contains close to 20 jewelers selling mostly 22- and 24-karat gold jewelry. The heart of Chicago's Indian community, Devon also features Indian restaurants, sari shops and electronics dealers.

Magnificent Mile – CTA *bus no. 15, $.50, makes a loop from W. Harrison & S. State Sts. to Walton St. & N. Michigan Ave. weekdays 11am–2pm.* This section of N. Michigan Ave. between Illinois and Oak Sts. is *the* prime shopping area of Chicago. It includes expansive malls *(below)*, department stores and some of the world's finest designer boutiques (located primarily on Oak St. between N. Michigan Ave. and Rush St.).

Malls

For locations, see map facing page.

Chicago Place .... ☎312-642-4811
*Over 50 shops, including **Saks Fifth Avenue** and the **Body Shop**, as well as restaurants and a gourmet supermarket.*

900 N. Michigan Shops .... ☎312-915-3916
*Over 60 shops, including **Bloomingdale's**, **Jessica McClintock** and **Henri Bendel**.*

Water Tower Place .... ☎312-440-3165
*125 shops and restaurants on 7 levels including **Marshall Field's**, **Lord & Taylor**, **Eddie Bauer** and **Laura Ashley**.*

Shops of One Magnificent Mile .... ☎312-664-7777
*Several upscale shops including **Chanel** and **Ralph Lauren**.*

Other Shops

Banana Republic	☎312-642-0020
Barneys New York	☎312-587-1700
FAO Schwarz	☎312-587-5000
Giorgio Armani	☎312-751-2244
Neiman Marcus	☎312-642-5900
Sonia Rykiel	☎312-951-0800
Tiffany & Co.	☎312-944-7500

Maxwell Street Market

Canal St. between Roosevelt Rd. and 15th St. Open year-round Sun 7am–3pm. ☎*312-922-3100*. This colorful, open-air flea market offers a mixture of antiques, collectibles, new and used merchandise, a live blues band and close to 30 food vendors. Arrive early for the largest selection.

Sports & Recreation

Chicago's primary recreation area is along its 30-plus miles of lakefront forming an almost continuous span of public parks, including Lincoln *(p 130)*, Grant *(p 108)*, Burnham *(p 109)* and Jackson *(p 180)*. The **Chicago Park District** maintains these parks, and well over 500 other recreational areas offering a wide range of facilities including swimming, archery and bocci ball (information and maps, 425 E. McFetridge Dr., Chicago IL 60605 ☎312-742-7529). The **Forest Preserve District of Cook County** offers information about natural areas and activities outside the city boundaries (536 N. Harlem Ave., River Forest IL 60305 ☎708-261-8400).

The Lake

Swimming – There are over 30 public beaches scattered along Lake Michigan. Lifeguards are on duty from mid-Jun–Labor Day, 9am–9:30pm. Many beaches have refreshment stands and changing facilities; no alcoholic beverages are allowed ☎312-747-0832. The beaches listed below are presented from north to south according to block numbers on Lake Shore Drive.

Beaches	Block #	Beaches	Block #
Howard St. Beach	7500N	Foster Ave. Beach	5200N
Fargo Ave. Beach	7432N	Montrose Beach	4400N
Jarvis Ave. Beach	7400N	North Ave. Beach *(p 131)*	1600N-2400N
Loyola Beach	7100N	Oak St. Beach *(p 115)*	1000N-1400N
Rogers Park	6700N	49th St. Beach	3100S
Berger Park	6200N	57th St. Beach	5700S
Lane Beach	5900N	South Shore Cultural Center	7100S

Fishing – Lake Michigan abounds with many species of fish, including coho and Chinook salmon (prime season May–Jun); brown, rainbow and lake trout (prime season Jul–Aug); and yellow perch. Most charter boats depart from Burnham Harbor. A fishing license is required; one-day nonresident licenses are available in fishing supply stores (some also offer rental equipment). **Smelt fishing** runs from early April until mid-May (after 6pm) all along the lake. **Ice fishing** is permitted on area lakes when the ice is at least 4in thick; contact the Forest Preserve District of Cook County for more information *(above)*. **Onshore fishing** (prohibited from May 15 to Oct 15) is allowed at Burnham and Montrose Harbors and Jackson Park.

Boating – The lake also offers wonderful sailing and power boating year-round. Contact the Harbor Division of the Chicago Park District for temporary docking facilities ☎312-747-0737. **Sailboat rentals** (1-4 persons) are available through the Chicago Park District's *Rainbow Fleet* at Burnham Park and North Shore Beach *(late Jun–Labor Day daily; $15-$25/hr; sailing proficiency is necessary, instruction provided;* ☎312-747-0737). Contact the **Chicagoland Canoe Base** (4019 N. Narragansett Ave., ☎773-779-1489) for rentals and information about places to canoe or kayak.

Biking, hiking and jogging – Bike Way is a paved 18.5mi lakefront path that extends along the Chicago shoreline. The path is also open to pedestrians and in-line skaters. In addition, 15 Chicago parks offer dedicated bicycle paths (contact the Chicago Park District for information, *above*). For additional information and map of bike routes in the area, contact the **Chicagoland Bicycle Federation**, 417 S. Dearborn St., Chicago IL 60604 ☎312-427-3325. Bike and in-line skate rentals are available from **Bike Chicago** *(May–mid-Oct, protective gear provided;* ☎312-944-2337). The **Chicago Area Runners Association** provides maps and information about races and routes (59 E. Van Buren St., Chicago IL 60605 ☎312-666-9836).

Where to get a work-out

The following clubs allow nonmembers to utilize their facilities (weight rooms, aerobics classes and pools) for a small daily fee *($5-$15)*:

Illinois Center Athletic Club, 211 N. Stetson Ave. (Loop) ☎312-616-1234

Chicago Fitness Center, 3131 N. Lincoln Ave. (Lincoln Park/DePaul) ☎773-549-8181

Chicago Hilton & Towers Athletic Club, 720 S. Michigan Ave. (S. Loop) ☎312-294-6800

Lakeshore Athletic Club, 441 N. Wabash Ave. (River North) ☎312-644-4880 and 1320 W. Fullerton Ave. (Lincoln Park/DePaul) ☎773-477-9888

Lehmann Sports Club, 2700 N. Lehmann Ct. (Lincoln Park/DePaul) ☎773-871-8300

O'Hare Health & Racquet Club, 6100 N. River Rd. (O'Hare Airport) ☎847-698-1366

Many private fitness centers are available to guests of major hotels; check with the concierge. **YMCA** memberships are valid worldwide; call for closest recreation center and available facilities ☎312-977-0031.

Winter Activities

Cross-Country Skiing – The Chicago Park District has extensive cross-country facilities throughout the city *(open Mon–Fri 2–9pm, weekends noon–5pm, weather permitting; rentals available at some facilities;* ☎*312-294-2200).*

Ice Skating – Enjoy skating (weather permitting) among the skyscrapers at Daley Bicentennial Plaza *(337 E. Randolph St.; Nov–Mar Mon–Fri 10am–10pm, weekends 10am–5pm; closed Thanksgiving Day, Dec 25; $1.50; rentals available;* ☎*312-294-4790)* and Skate on State *(State & Randolph Sts.; Nov–Mar daily 9am–7:15pm; closed Thanksgiving Day, Dec 25; rentals available;* ☎*312-744-3315);* or take in superb views of the lake and city while gliding at Navy Pier *(600 E. Grand Ave.; Nov–mid-Apr daily 10am–8pm; rentals available;* ☎*312-595-7437).*

Snowmobiling & Tobogganing – The Forest Preserve District of Cook County *(p 244)* maintains five snowmobiling areas; courses are open when snow depth is over 4in *(open daily 10am–10pm).* Snowmobiles must be registered with the Forest Preserve. Also contact the Forest Preserve for information about toboggan runs in the Dan Ryan Woods and other locations (many offer rentals).

SPECTATOR SPORTS

Tickets can be purchased at the venue or through Ticketmaster *(p 237).*

Sport/Team	Season	Home Stadium	☎ Information
Major League Baseball	**Apr–Oct**		
Cubs (NL)		**Wrigley Field** *(p 144)*	**773-404-2827**
White Sox (AL)		**Comiskey Park** *(p 164)*	**773-924-1000**
Professional Football	**Sept–Dec**		
Bears		**Soldier Field** *(p 112)*	**847-295-6600**
(CTA bus no. 128 express transport to games)			
Professional Basketball	**Oct–Apr**		
Bulls		**United Center**	**312-455-4000**
(CTA bus no. 19 express transport to games)			
Professional Hockey	**Oct–Apr**		
Blackhawks (NHL)		**United Center**	**312-455-7000**
(CTA bus no. 19 express transport to games)			
Wolves (IHL)		**Rosemont Horizon**	**847-390-0404**

Churchill & Klehr/Tony Stone Images

245

Index

MANUFACTURE FRANÇAISE DES PNEUMATIQUES MICHELIN
Société en commandite par actions au capital de 2000000000 de francs
Place des Carmes-Déchaux – 63 Clermont-Ferrand (France)
R.C.S. Clermont-Fd B 855 200 507
© Michelin et Cie, Propriétaires-Éditeurs 1996
Dépôt légal avril 96 — ISBN 2-06-159401-8 — ISSN 0763-1383

Printed in the United States of America 04.96 – Motheral Company, Fort Worth, Texas
Cover illustration by Robert V. Shuler